The Illustrated Virago Book of

WOMEN TRAVELLERS

The Illustrated Virago Book of

WOMEN TRAVELLERS

Edited and with an
introduction by Mary Morris
in collaboration with
Larry O'Connor

'One cannot divine nor forecast
the conditions that will make
happiness; one only stumbles upon
them by chance, in a lucky hour,
at the world's end somewhere,
and holds fast to the days...'

Willa Cather

To Kate, our Fellow Traveller

A Virago Book

First published in hardback by Virago Press in 1994
Published in paperback 1996
Reprinted 1996 (three times), 1998, 1999

This illustrated edition first published in Great Britain in 2000 by
Virago Press, a division of Little, Brown and Company UK

A CIP catalogue record for this book is available from the British Library.

ISBN 0 316 64797 7

Design by Andrew Barron & Collis Clements Associates

Printed and bound in Italy by Lego Spa

Virago
A Division of
Little, Brown and Company (UK)
Brettenham House
Lancaster Place
London WC2E 7EN

Contents

Introduction

The late John Gardner once said that there are only two plots in all of literature. You go on a journey or a stranger comes to town. Since women, for so many years, were denied the journey, they were left with only one plot in their lives – to await the stranger. Indeed, there is essentially no picaresque tradition among women novelists. While the latter part of the twentieth century has seen a change of tendency, women's literature from Austen to Woolf is by and large a literature about waiting, usually for love.

Denied the freedom to roam outside of themselves, women turned inward, into their emotions and their private, often amorous but chaste relations. Elaine Showalter comments on this phenomenon in her critical volume, *A Literature of Her Own*: 'Denied participation in public life, women were forced to cultivate their feelings and to over-value romance. . . . Emotions rushed in to fill the vacuum of experience.'

For centuries it was frowned upon for women to travel without escort, chaperon, or husband. To journey was to put oneself at risk, not only physically but morally as well. A little freedom could be a dangerous thing. Erica Jong chose well when she picked the metaphor of 'fear of flying' to represent the tremulous onset of a woman's sexual awakening. The language of sexual initiation is oddly similar to the language of travel. We speak of sexual 'exploits' or 'adventures'. Both the body and the globe are objects for exploration and the great 'explorers', whether Marco Polo or Don Juan, have been men.

BERYL MARKHAM

Gulliver begins his famous travels after the death of his 'good Master Bates' (much obvious discussion surrounds this phrase), with whom he has apprenticed. Facing a failing business as well, he consults his 'Wife' and determines 'to go again to Sea'. Flights and evasion, the need to escape domestic constraints and routine, to get away and at the same time to conquer – this form of flight from the home is more typical of the male experience.

Yet at the turn of the century Maud Parrish was not unlike Gulliver as she set off to the Yukon. 'So I ran away. I hurried more than if lions had chased me. Without telling him. Without telling my mother or father. There wasn't any liberty in San Francisco for ordinary women. But I found some. No jobs for girls in offices like there are now. You got married, were an old maid, or went to hell. Take your pick.' Similarly, Flora Tristan, at great social and financial risk, left her marriage and, as a 'pariah', travelled up and down Peru. And Margaret Fountaine journeyed the world ostensibly in search of butterflies, but really in pursuit of amorous adventures.

These women – and many of the women in this volume – are the exceptions. I find it revealing that the metal bindings in women's corsets were called 'stays'. Someone who wore 'stays' wouldn't be going far. Nor would a woman with bound feet. While cloaked under the guise of the aesthetics of their times and cultures, the corseting in stays in the West and the binding of feet in the Orient were essentially ways of restricting women's freedom of movement.

Lady Mary Wortley Montagu, a woman writer who went to Turkey with her husband in 1716 and is best known for her letters, offered an interesting anecdote about stays. Upon visiting a Turkish bath in Sophia in which the women implored her to undress, Lady Montagu writes: 'I was forced at last to open my shirt and shew them my stays; which satisfied them very well for, I saw, they believed I was so locked up in that machine that it was not in my power to open it, which contrivance they attributed to my husband.'

It has been said that women don't have what Baudelaire referred to as the 'gout du gouffre', the taste for the abyss. Even Louise Bogan has written that women have no wilderness in them. And Elizabeth Bishop in her poem 'Questions of Travel' addresses the ambivalence about travel when she speaks about going 'there', to another place, while yearning to be 'here', or home. Surely such musings don't indicate a serious impetus for travel or for serious travel writing by women.

Yet there have been many women who have travelled extensively and written seriously about their journeys. Their voices have not always been recognized and heard.

I began thinking about travel literature a number of years ago. In the mid-1980s the *New York Times Sunday Book Review* published a special summer issue on travel books. It reviewed some twenty-five or thirty recent volumes, virtually all written by men. It seemed strange to me that that issue had mentioned so few books by women.

I wondered why it was that the women who certainly travelled (I had travelled with many myself) weren't writing about their journeys. Perhaps they didn't travel as men did or perhaps they did not feel their experiences were comparable to those of men. Or perhaps they did write about them, but they were not finding their audience.

Women, I have come to feel, move through the world differently than men. The constraints and perils, the perceptions and complex emotions women journey with are different from those of men. The fear of rape, for example, whether crossing the Sahara or just crossing a city street at night, most dramatically affects the ways women move through the world. But there are other subtler forms of harassment. Christina Dodwell has to pretend she has fleas when a militiaman refuses to leave her campsite at night. In rural Japan a woman should hang her husband's washing on a separate clothesline from her own impure clothing, which we see in Leila Philip's account.

As I read through the literature of male travel writers in the 1980s, I found that their experiences did not correspond to or validate my own. Most explored a world that is essentially external and revealed only glimpses of who and what they are, whom they long for, whom they miss. The writers' own inner workings in most cases (with marvellous exceptions such as Peter Matthiessen in *The Snow Leopard*, Henry Miller in *The Colossus of Maroussi*, and Colin Thubron in his travel books on China and Russia) are obscured.

MARY WOLLSTONECRAFT

Lawrence Durrell, describing Freya Stark, wrote, 'A great traveller is a kind of introspective as she covers the ground outwardly, so she advances inwardly.' And indeed, for many women, the inner landscape is as important as the outer, the beholder as significant as the beheld. The landscape is shaped by the consciousness of the person who crosses it. There is a dialogue between what is happening within and without. The presence of a loved one such as Isabella Bird's 'Jim' in the excerpt from *A Lady's Life in the Rocky Mountains* or the ache of a painful absence in the case of Mary Wollstonecraft's poignant longing for her daughter as she journeys through Scandinavia are all part of a woman's experience. What is it like to fall in love or have to talk your way out of a difficult, sexually threatening situation. Often they bear witness to the experiences of women in different cultures; for instance, Mrs Bridges sympathizes with the plight of Mormon women, and Anna Leonowens recounts the abuse endured by the women of the harem in Siam.

'I am a connoisseur of roads,' the actor River Phoenix says in the film *My Own Private Idaho*. But for women perhaps the roads are different. The reality of a woman on the road is often a personal reality. This does not mean that the woman traveller is not politically aware, historically astute, or in touch with the customs and language of the place. But it does mean that a woman cannot travel and not be aware of her body and the limitations her sex presents. Isabelle Eberhardt, as well as

Sarah Hobson, travelled incognito, disguised as men. Eliza Farnham, crossing the American frontier in 1852, put her trunk and body against her door to keep a man out of the room in which she was bathing. And Kali (Gwendolyn MacEwen) in 'The Holyland Buffet' tells a contemporary story of being stoned by Arab boys who think she is a sabra and not 'a female tourist travelling alone'.

Gender often forms a bond between women travellers. Women confide in other women. They tell one another the secrets of their cycles, their children, their husbands, their lovers, the difficulties of their lives. They do this in bathrooms, on airplanes, and on the road, often with perfect strangers. In this, they are secret sharers. They may not hunt or fish together, but they can talk about a miscarriage and a miserable life as the Iranian woman does to Sarah Hobson when she realizes Hobson is a young woman, not a young man.

Our goal in making the selections gathered here was to find the best writing about travel by women. Perhaps there are women who have scaled greater heights, delved deeper into jungles, or were more renowned, but our main concerns were the quality of the writing and the vision behind that writing. At the same time, we wanted to assemble a significant body of work, representative of women and their journeys and providing examples of early and recent feminist travel literature.

ROSE MACAULAY

Some of these women are observers of the world in which they wander. Their writings are rich in description, remarkable in detail. Mary McCarthy conveys the vitality of Florence while Willa Cather's essay on Lavandou foreshadows her descriptions of the French countryside in later novels. Barbara Grizzuti Harrison's excerpt about the spiritual village of San Gimignano is a virtual love song. In M. F. K. Fisher's sensual portrayal of Dijon one can literally smell the mustard in the street. Others are more active as participants in the culture they are visiting, such as Leila Philip, as she harvests rice with chiding Japanese women, or Emily Carr, as she wins the respect and trust of the female chieftain of an Indian village in northern Canada where she has gone to do paintings of the unique totem poles of the region.

Often they are storytellers, weaving tales about the people they encounter. We find ourselves moved by the stories they told which we felt grew out of their sensibilities as women: Flora Tristan's story of the lovelorn ship's commander (a Marquezian character if there ever was one), separated from his beloved wife for years at a time as a result of a prenuptial promise exacted by his father-in-law; Mildred Cable and Francesca French's anecdote about the dissident Chinese fugitive in Mongolia who surreptitiously makes inquiries after his family; and Anna Leonowens's (best known as Anna from *The King and I*) tale of a child scorned and a mother flogged, despite the child's pleas, under the authoritarian rule of the King of Siam.

GERTRUDE BELL

In some cases gender is transcended, as in the remarkable story of Alexandra David-Neel, who saves herself and her adopted son from freezing to death on a wintry Tibetan plain by raising her body temperature through the *thumo reskiang* practice, in the acerbic wit of Freya Stark, and in the raw courage of Dervla Murphy or Christina Dodwell. In some cases these women assumed leadership roles traditionally attributed to men. In 1894 Isabella Bird became the first female member of the Royal Geographical Society. Mary Kingsley would follow. Gertrude Bell became the leading Middle East expert, with T. E. Lawrence, in Baghdad for the British Empire.

Perhaps they went as free spirits, as Maud Parrish went with banjo to Alaska. Or perhaps the goal was to gaze into Persian gardens as it was for Vita Sackville-West. But in each of these selections, a mosaic of the experiences of women on the road is revealed. In each case, the vision is personal and unique.

Each of these women had a reason for going. Some, such as the Lady Travellers, Mary Kingsley and Isabella Bird, went as Mabel Sharman Crawford says, because they were 'women of independent means and without domestic ties'. Some, such as Lady Montagu or Isak Dinesen, were accompanying their husbands; others, such as Maud Parrish, were running away from domestic entanglements. Mildred Cable and Francesca French went as missionaries.

Others seem to be fleeing: Isabella Bird was told that travel would help her back troubles and she never stopped moving after that, while Isabelle Eberhardt fled an unhappy aristocratic home even to the point of relinquishing her birthright. Both Mary Kingsley and Dervla Murphy set out upon their journeys after the death of their ailing parents whom they had nursed for years. After suffering extreme personal loss (the death of her husband and sons), Ethel Tweedie began to travel and write. Whether it is curiosity about the world or escape from personal tragedy, the women here approach their journeys with wit, intelligence, compassion, and empathy for the lives of others.

For some of these writers, the experience of writing from 'away' seems to have produced their greatest masterpieces. Lady Montagu was a prolific writer of prose and poetry (she is the only English-language woman poet of the eighteenth century who has a critical biography written about her), yet the book of hers that has remained in print since it was written is the collection of her letters from Turkey. When Mary Shelley (the daughter of Mary Wollstonecraft) and her husband, the Romantic poet, Percy Shelley, went to Italy, they took with them one book – Mary Wollstonecraft's travels in Scandinavia. Though Isak Dinesen and Rebecca West were famous writers of fiction in their own time, the books that are considered their masterworks are their writings on Africa and Yugoslavia, respectively. We have also chosen writers who wouldn't be considered travel writers per se – Annie Dillard and Joan Didion, for example – but whose sense of place serves as a catalyst to broader musings about the world.

Most of the women in this volume represent what as I have said above Crawford refers to as a 'woman of independent means and without domestic ties'. The early women travellers were women of the upper classes in European society, invariably white and privileged. This trend has not shifted greatly in the past two hundred years as we are left with the legacy of colonialism. Travel literature by both men and women awaits its full range of multicultural voices and perspectives. Yet as feminists the writers gathered here hold surprisingly progressive views considering the times in which they wrote and lived. It is hard not to be amazed by Lady Montagu's sense that the Turkish woman is the freest in the world because she can hide behind her veil and move about as she wishes, including anonymous rendezvous with her lover. Or Mrs Tweedie's plea for the elimination of the sidesaddle on the grounds that it is a preposterous invention, bad for women's health and ill-suited for serious riding. Or Mrs Bridges' indignation at polygamy in America.

We have tried to assemble a diverse body of work that charts feminism, over close to three hundred years, through women and their journeys. In some cases – Maud Parrish and Vivienne de Watteville, for example – the only traces of themselves these women left behind was their travel writing and it was difficult, therefore, to provide biographical information about them. For various reasons, we decided not to include involuntary travel. It would have seemed casual – disrespectful, even – to juxtapose slave narratives, pioneer literature, and war stories of flight and displacement with accounts of deserts crossed, swamps forded, and mountains climbed by choice.

Our criteria were very specific and in some cases we opted not to include writers who are well known for their travel writing because their views or experiences did not seem appropriate to the goal of this anthology. We regret the absence of more multicultural voices. It is our hope that in the future both the gender and racial gaps will be bridged, but for now the voices we present are those we found.

Since all travel is about return as well as departure, I go back to the beginning and John Gardner's premise that there are only two plots in literature. From Penelope to the present, women have waited – for a phone call, a proposal, or the return of the prodigal man from sea or war or a business trip. To wait like patients for a doctor, commuters for buses, prisoners for parole, is in a sense to be powerless. It is our hope that this volume will make it clear that both plots are available to women. If we grow weary of waiting, we can go on a journey. We can be the stranger who comes to town.

Mary Morris

ISAK DINESEN

Lady Mary Wortley Montagu

(1689–1762)

When Lady Mary Wortley Montagu, a poet and satirist with a respected reputation and friends who included writers Alexander Pope and Joseph Addison, left London in 1716 to follow her husband, the ambassador to Turkey, to Constantinople, she created a scandal. Women of her social class were not to travel without their husbands, particularly to the East. But Lady Montagu, the first woman to travel abroad for curiosity's sake, spurned societal expectations to the point of changing her dress for Turkish robes and inoculating her son and baby daughter with a vaccine presented to her by a local medicine woman (seventy years before the invention of the Jenner smallpox vaccination). At forty-nine, she again left London – and her husband – to pursue the man she loved to Italy, and although she failed in her romantic conquest, she lived the next twenty-two years on the Continent with an assortment of escorts. She did not return home to England until her husband died in 1762, and she died shortly thereafter. Her book of letters was published a year after her death.

from Embassy to Constantinople

To Lady Mar–

Adrianople April 1,1717

I wish to God (dear sister) that you was as regular in letting me have the pleasure of knowing what passes on your side of the globe as I am careful in endeavouring to amuse you by the account of all I see that I think you care to hear of. You content yourself with telling me over and over that the town is very dull. It may possibly be dull to you when every day does not present you with something new, but for me that am in arrear at least two months' news, all that seems very stale with you would be fresh and sweet here; pray let me into more particulars. I will try to awaken your gratitude by giving you a full and true relation of the novelties of this place, none of which would surprise you more than a sight of my person as I am now in my Turkish habit, though I believe you would be of my opinion that 'tis admirably becoming. I intend to send you my picture; in the meantime accept of it here.

The first piece of my dress is a pair of drawers, very full, that reach to my shoes and conceal the legs more modestly than your petticoats. They are of a thin, rose-colour damask brocaded with silver flowers, my shoes of white kid leather embroidered with gold. Over this hangs my smock of a fine white silk gauze edged with embroidery. This smock has wide sleeves hanging half-way down the arm and is closed at the neck with a diamond button, but the shape and colour of the bosom very well to be distinguished through it. The *antery* is a waistcoat made close to the shape, of white and gold damask, with very long sleeves falling back and fringed with deep gold fringe, and should have diamond or pearl buttons. My *caftan* of the same stuff with my drawers is a robe exactly fitted to my shape and reaching to my feet, with very long straight falling sleeves. Over this is the girdle of about four fingers broad, which all that can afford have entirely of diamonds or other precious stones. Those that will not be at the expense have it of exquisite embroidery on satin, but it must be fastened before with a clasp of diamonds. The *curdee* is a loose robe they throw off or put on according to the weather, being of a rich brocade (mine is green and gold) either lined with ermine or sables; the sleeves reach very little below the shoulders. The head-dress is composed of a cap called *talpack*, which is in winter of fine

'Upon the whole, I look upon the Turkish women as the only free people in the empire.'

velvet embroidered with pearls or diamonds and in summer of a light, shining silver stuff. This is fixed on one side of the head, hanging a little way down with a gold tassel and bound on either side with a circle of diamonds (as I have seen several) or a rich embroidered handkerchief. On the other side of the head the hair is laid flat, and here the ladies are at liberty to show their fancies, some putting flowers, others a plume of heron's feathers, and in short what they please, but the most general fashion is a large bouquet of jewels made like natural flowers, that is the buds of pearl, the roses of different coloured rubies, the jasmines of diamonds, jonquils of topazes, etc., so well set and enamelled 'tis hard to imagine anything of that kind so beautiful. The hair hangs at its full length behind, divided into tresses braided with pearl or riband, which is always in great quantity.

I never saw in my life so many fine heads of hair. I have counted one hundred and ten of these tresses of one lady's, all natural; but it must be owned that every beauty is more common here than with us. 'Tis surprising to see a young woman that is not very handsome. They have naturally the most beautiful complexions in the world and generally large black eyes. I can assure you with great truth that the Court of England (though I believe it the fairest in Christendom) cannot show so many beauties as are under our protection here. They generally shape their eyebrows, and the Greeks and Turks have a custom of putting round their eyes on the inside a black tincture that, at a distance or by candlelight, adds very much to the blackness of them. I fancy many of our ladies would be overjoyed to know this secret, but 'tis too visible by day. They dye their nails rose colour; I own I cannot enough accustom myself to this fashion to find any beauty in it.

As to their morality or good conduct, I can say like Harlequin, ''Tis just as 'tis with you'; and the Turkish ladies don't commit one sin the less for not being Christians. Now I am a little acquainted with their ways, I cannot forbear admiring either the exemplary discretion or extreme stupidity of all the writers that have given accounts of 'em. 'Tis very easy to see they have more liberty than we have, no woman of what rank soever being permitted to go in the streets without two muslins, one that covers her face all but her eyes and another that hides the whole dress of her head and hangs half-way down her back; and their shapes are wholly concealed by a thing they call a *ferigée*, which no woman of any sort appears without. This has strait sleeves that reach to their fingers' ends and it laps all round 'em, not unlike a riding hood. In winter 'tis of cloth, and in summer, plain stuff or silk. You may guess how effectually this disguises them, that there is no distinguishing the great lady from her slave, and 'tis impossible for the most jealous husband to know his wife when he meets her, and no man dare either touch or follow a woman in the street.

This perpetual masquerade gives them entire liberty of following their inclinations without danger of discovery. The most usual method of intrigue is to send an appointment to the lover to meet the lady at a Jew's shop, which are as notoriously convenient as our Indian houses, and yet even those that don't make that use of 'em do not scruple to go to buy penn'orths and tumble over rich goods, which are chiefly to be found amongst that sort of people. The great ladies seldom let their gallants know who they are, and 'tis so difficult to find it out that they can very seldom guess at her

name they have corresponded with above half a year together. You may easily imagine the number of faithful wives very small in a country where they have nothing to fear from their lovers' indiscretion, since we see so many that have the courage to expose themselves to that in this world and all the threatened punishment of the next, which is never preached to the Turkish damsels. Neither have they much to apprehend from the resentment of their husbands, those ladies that are rich having all their money in their own hands, which they take with 'em upon a divorce with an addition which he is obliged to give 'em. Upon the whole, I look upon the Turkish women as the only free people in the empire. The very Divan pays a respect to 'em, and the Grand Signior himself, when a Pasha is executed, never violates the privilege of the harem (or women's apartment) which remains unsearched entire to the widow. They are queens of their slaves, which the husband has no permission so much as to look upon, except it be an old woman or two that his lady chooses. 'Tis true their law permits them four wives, but there is no instance of a man of quality that makes use of this liberty, or of a woman of rank that would suffer it. When a husband happens to be inconstant (as those things will happen) he keeps his mistress in a house apart and visits her as privately as he can, just as 'tis with you. Amongst all the great men here I only know the *defterdar* (i.e., treasurer) that keeps a number of she slaves for his own use (that is, on his own side of the house, for a slave once given to serve a lady is entirely at her disposal), and he is spoke of as a libertine, or what we should call a rake, and his wife won't see him, though she continues to live in his house.

Thus you see, dear sister, the manners of mankind do not differ so widely as our voyage writers would make us believe. Perhaps it would be more entertaining to add a few surprising customs of my own invention, but nothing seems to me so agreeable as truth, and I believe nothing so acceptable to you. I conclude with repeating the great truth of my being, dear sister, etc.

Mary Wollstonecraft

(1759–1797)

A WRITER PASSIONATE ABOUT POLITICAL AND SOCIAL INJUSTICES, MARY WOLLSTONECRAFT, THE AUTHOR OF *A VINDICATION OF THE RIGHTS OF WOMAN*, FOUND THE IDEAL VEHICLE FOR HER SPONTANEOUS STYLE OF COMMENTARY IN HER *LETTERS WRITTEN DURING A SHORT RESIDENCE IN SWEDEN, NORWAY, AND DENMARK*. IN THIS WORK SHE OPPOSES THE DOMESTIC CUSTOM OF HIRING NURSES TO SUCKLE CHILDREN EVEN AS SHE CRITICIZES GOVERNMENT, CHURCH, AND THE PENAL SYSTEM. TRAVEL GAVE WOLLSTONECRAFT THE TIME TO REFLECT UPON THE WORLD AROUND HER, INCLUDING HER RELATIONSHIP WITH HER INFANT DAUGHTER, FANNY, WHO DID NOT ACCOMPANY HER ON THIS TRIP. SHE WOULD RETURN TO ENGLAND TO BE WITH HER DAUGHTER AND BE CLOSE TO THE FATHER, GILBERT IMLAY, WHO RECEIVED THE LETTERS THAT FORMED *A SHORT RESIDENCE*. IMLAY WAS UNFAITHFUL, AND EVENTUALLY SHE LEFT HIM. THE PERSONAL INFORMS HER VISION IN WAYS THAT ARE TRUE OF THE BEST MODERN TRAVEL WRITINGS OF REBECCA WEST, MARY LEE SETTLE, AND BARBARA GRIZZUTI HARRISON.

LATER, WOLLSTONECRAFT WOULD MARRY WILLIAM GODWIN, THE CELEBRATED AUTHOR, AND IN 1797 SHE WOULD DIE GIVING BIRTH TO A GIRL, MARY. (THIS SECOND DAUGHTER, MARY, WOULD WED PERCY BYSSHE SHELLEY IN 1816, THE SAME YEAR THAT HER HALF-SISTER FANNY KILLED HERSELF, AND IN 1818 PUBLISH *FRANKENSTEIN*.)

from Letters Written During a Short Residence in Sweden, Norway, and Denmark

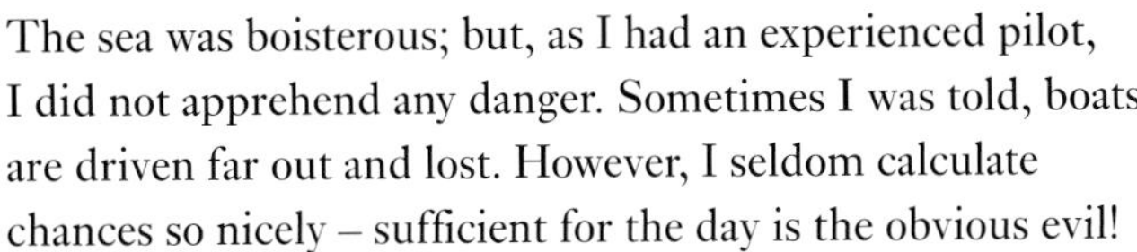

The sea was boisterous; but, as I had an experienced pilot, I did not apprehend any danger. Sometimes I was told, boats are driven far out and lost. However, I seldom calculate chances so nicely – sufficient for the day is the obvious evil!

We had to steer amongst islands and huge rocks, rarely losing sight of the shore, though it now and then appeared only a mist that bordered the water's edge. The pilot assured me that the numerous harbours on the Norway coast were very safe, and the pilot-boats were always on the watch. The Swedish side is very dangerous, I am also informed; and the help of experience is not often at hand, to enable strange vessels to steer clear of the rocks, which lurk below the water, close to the shore.

There are no tides here, nor in the Kattegat; and, what appeared to me a consequence, no sandy beach. Perhaps this observation has been made before, but it did not occur to me till I saw the waves continually beating against the bare rocks, without ever receding to leave a sediment to harden.

The wind was fair, till we had to tack about in order to enter Larvik, where we arrived towards three o'clock in the afternoon. It is a clean, pleasant town, with a considerable iron-work, which gives life to it.

As the Norwegians do not frequently see travellers, they are very curious to know their business, and who they are – so curious that I was half tempted to adopt Dr. Franklin's plan, when travelling in America, where they are equally prying, which was to write on a paper, for public inspection, my name, from whence I came, where I was going, and what was my business. But if I were importuned by their curiosity, their friendly gestures gratified me. A woman, coming alone, interested them. And I know not whether my weariness gave me a look of peculiar delicacy; but they approached to assist me, and enquire after my wants, as if they were afraid to hurt, and wished to protect me. The sympathy I inspired, thus dropping down from the clouds in a strange land, affected me more than it would have done, had not my spirits been

'Nature is the nurse of sentiment – the true source of taste – yet what misery, as well as rapture, is produced by a quick perception of the beautiful and sublime.'

harassed by various causes – by much thinking – musing almost to madness – and even by a sort of weak melancholy that hung about my heart at parting with my daughter for the first time.

You know that as a female I am particularly attached to her – I feel more than a mother's fondness and anxiety, when I reflect on the dependent and oppressed state of her sex. I dread lest she should be forced to sacrifice her heart to her principles, or principles to her heart. With trembling hand I shall cultivate sensibility, and cherish delicacy of sentiment, lest, whilst I lend fresh blushes to the rose, I sharpen the thorns that will wound the breast I would fain guard – I dread to unfold her mind, lest it should render her unfit for the world she is to inhabit – Hapless woman! what a fate is thine!

But whither am I wandering? I only meant to tell you that the impression the kindness of the simple people made visible on my countenance increased my sensibility to a painful degree. I wished to have had a room to myself; for their attention, and rather distressing observation, embarrassed me extremely. Yet, as they would bring me eggs, and make my coffee, I found I could not leave them without hurting their feelings of hospitality.

It is customary here for the host and hostess to welcome their guests as master and mistress of the house.

My clothes, in their turn, attracted the attention of the females; and I could not help thinking of the foolish vanity which makes many women so proud of the observation of strangers as to take wonder very gratuitously for admiration. This error they are very apt to fall into; when arrived in foreign country, the populace stare at them as they pass; yet the make of a cap, or the singularity of a gown, is often the cause of the flattering attention, which afterwards supports a fantastic superstructure of self-conceit.

Not having brought a carriage over with me, expecting to have met a person where I landed, who was immediately to have procured me one, I was detained whilst the good people of the inn sent round to all their acquaintance to search for a vehicle. A rude sort of *cabriole* was at last found, and a driver half drunk, who was no less eager to make a good bargain on that account. I had a Danish captain of a ship and his mate with me: the former was to ride on horseback, at which he was not very expert, and the latter to partake of my seat. The driver mounted behind to guide the horses, and flourish the whip over our shoulders; he would not suffer the reins out of his own hands. There was something so grotesque in our appearance, that I could not avoid shrinking into myself when I saw a gentleman-like man in the group which crowded round the door to observe us. I could have broken the driver's whip for cracking to call the women and children together; but seeing a significant smile on the face, I had before remarked,

I burst into a laugh, to allow him to do so too, – and away we flew. This is not a flourish of the pen; for we actually went on full gallop a long time, the horses being very good; indeed I have never met with better, if so good, post-horses, as in Norway; they are of a stouter make than the English horses, appear to be well fed, and are not easily tired.

I had to pass over, I was informed, the most fertile and best cultivated tract of country in Norway. The distance was three Norwegian miles, which are longer than the Swedish. The roads were very good; the farmers are obliged to repair them; and we scampered through a great extent of country in a more improved state than any I had viewed since I left England. Still there was sufficient of hills, dales, and rocks, to prevent the idea of a plain from entering the head, or even of such scenery as England and France afford. The prospects were also embellished by water, rivers, and lakes, before the sea proudly claimed my regard; and the road running frequently through lofty groves, rendered the landscapes beautiful, though they were not so romantic as those I had lately seen with such delight.

It was late when I reached Tønsberg; and I was glad to go to bed at a decent inn. The next morning, the 17th July, conversing with the gentlemen with whom I had business to transact, I found that I should be detained at Tønsberg three weeks; and I lamented that I had not brought my child with me.

The inn was quiet, and my room so pleasant, commanding a view of the sea, confined by an amphitheatre of hanging woods, that I wished to remain there, though no one in the house could speak English or French. The mayor, my friend, however, sent a young woman to me who spoke a little English, and she agreed to call on me twice a day, to receive my orders, and translate them to my hostess.

My not understanding the language was an excellent pretext for dining alone, which I prevailed on them to let me do at a late hour; for the early dinners in Sweden had entirely deranged my day. I could not alter it there, without disturbing the economy of a family where I was as a visitor; necessity having forced me to accept of an invitation from a private family, the lodgings were so incommodious.

Amongst the Norwegians I had the arrangement of my own time; and I determined to regulate it in such a manner, that I might enjoy as much of their sweet summer as I possibly could; – short, it is true, but 'passing sweet'.

I never endured a winter in this rude clime; consequently it was not the contrast, but the real beauty of the season which made the present summer appear to me the finest I had ever seen. Sheltered from the north and eastern winds, nothing can exceed the salubrity, the soft freshness of the western gales. In the evening they also die away; the aspen leaves tremble into stillness, and reposing nature seems to be warmed by the moon, which here assumes a genial aspect; and if a light shower has chanced to fall with the sun, the juniper, the underwood of the forest, exhales a wild perfume, mixed with a thousand nameless sweets, that, soothing the heart, leave images in the memory which the imagination will ever hold dear.

Nature is the nurse of sentiment – the true source of taste – yet what misery, as well as rapture, is produced by a quick perception of the beautiful and sublime, when it is exercised in observing animated nature, when every beauteous feeling and emotion excites responsive sympathy, and the harmonized soul sinks into melancholy, or rises to extasy, just as the chords are touched, like the aeolian harp agitated by the changing wind. But how dangerous is it to foster these sentiments in such an imperfect state of existence; and how difficult to eradicate them when an affection for mankind, a passion for an individual, is but the unfolding of that love which embraces all that is great and beautiful.

When a warm heart has received strong impressions, they are not to be effaced. Emotions become sentiments; and the imagination renders even transient sensations permanent, by fondly retracing them. I cannot, without a thrill of delight, recollect views I have seen, which are not to be forgotten, nor looks I have felt in every nerve which I shall never more meet. The grave has closed over a dear friend, the friend of my youth; still she is present with me, and I hear her soft voice warbling as I stray over the heath. Fate has separated me from another, the fire of whose eyes, tempered by infantine tenderness, still warms my breast; even when gazing on these tremendous cliffs, sublime emotions absorb my soul. And, smile not, if I add, that the rosy tint of morning reminds me of a suffusion, which will never more charm my senses, unless it reappears on the cheeks of my child. Her sweet blushes I may yet hide in my bosom, and she is still too young to ask why starts the tear, so near akin to pleasure and pain?

I cannot write any more at present. Tomorrow we will talk of Tønsberg.

Flora Tristan

(1803–1844)

The life of the reformer Flora Tristan was rescued from obscurity in 1925 when her unfinished journal, *Tour de France*, an account of her campaign for workers' rights in French industrial towns, was published. The woman who would be grandmother to artist Paul Gauguin was a charismatic leader whose early death from typhoid fever put an end to her work in France to create a universal workers' union that would facilitate equal rights for women. Tristan's trip alone to Peru in 1833 (to stake a claim to her family's fortune), which she wrote about in *Peregrinations of a Pariah*, marked the beginning of her political awakening. But her reformist zeal was most profoundly reflected in her outrage with laws pertaining to the sanctity of marriage: at a time when divorce was illegal in France, she left her husband, André Chazal, in 1825, resumed her maiden name, and then battled fiercely for more than a decade over custody of their two children. The landmark battle ended when the courts declared the couple legally separated after Chazal shot Tristan in the back; she recovered and Chazal served seventeen years in jail.

from **Peregrinations of a Pariah**

When you go from Arequipa to Islay you have the sun behind you and the wind in front, so you suffer far less from the heat than you do when going from Islay to Arequipa. I stood up to the journey very well; besides, my health had improved and I felt better able to endure its rigours this time. At midnight we arrived at the inn and I threw myself fully dressed upon my bed while supper was being prepared. Mr. Smith had a miraculous talent for making light of difficulties, and now he saw to everything – food, muleteers, animals – with remarkable speed and tact. Thanks to him we had a very good supper, after which we all stayed up talking, for none of us could sleep. At three in the morning we set out once more; the cold was so bitter that I wore three ponchos. When dawn appeared I was overcome with an irresistible desire for sleep and begged Mr. Smith to let me rest for just half an hour; I threw myself upon the ground and without giving the servant time to put down a mat for me I fell into so deep a sleep that nobody dared attempt to make me more comfortable. They let me sleep for an hour and I felt all the better for it; we were by then in the open pampa, so I mounted the horse and crossed the vast expanse at a gallop, in fact I managed the horse so well that Lieutenant Monsilla could not keep up with me, much less the two lancers. In the end Mr. Smith himself had to beg me to have mercy on his fine Chilean mare as he was afraid I would wear her out.

At midday we reached Guerrera, where we made a halt; we ate beneath the fresh shade of the trees, then arranged our beds on the ground and slept until five. We climbed the mountain at an easy pace and reached Islay at seven. Great was the surprise of Don Justo when he saw me. He is extremely kind and hospitable to all travellers and showed me particular attention. Islay was greatly changed since my previous stay. This time I was not invited to any balls. Nieto and his brave soldiers had laid the town waste in the twenty-four hours they had spent there; as well as requisitioning food they had practised every kind of extortion to obtain money from the unfortunate inhabitants. The good Don Justo never stopped repeating: 'Ah! mademoiselle, if I were younger I would leave with you; these endless wars have made it impossible to live here. I have already lost two of my sons, and I expect any day to hear of the death of the third, who is in Gamarra's army.'

I stayed three days in Islay waiting for our ship to leave, and I would have been very dull without the company of Mr. Smith, who also introduced me to the officers of an English frigate moored in the bay. I am happy to say that I have never met officers as distinguished for their manners and their intelligence as those of the *Challenger*; they all spoke French and had spent several years in Paris. They were in town clothes and their dress was remarkable for its immaculate cleanliness and elegant simplicity. The commander was a superb man, the ideal of masculine beauty. He was only thirty-two, yet a profound melancholy weighed upon him; all his words and deeds were tinged with a sadness which was painful to behold. I asked one of his officers the reason for this, and he said: 'Ah! yes, mademoiselle, he has good cause for sadness; for seven years he has been married to the loveliest woman in England; he loves her to distraction, just as she loves him, yet he must live apart from her.'

'What is the reason for this separation?'

'His profession; as he is one of our youngest captains he is always being sent on remote postings of three or four years' duration. We have been in these latitudes for three years, and we shall not be in England for another fifteen months. Judge for yourself what cruel suffering so long an absence causes him!'

'To say nothing of his wife! . . . But has he no fortune, then, to remain in a career which causes him and the woman he loves such torture?'

'No fortune! He has five thousand pounds a year of his own, and his wife, the richest heiress in England, brought him two hundred thousand; she is an only child and will have twice as much again on the death of her father.'

I was astonished. 'Then tell me, monsieur, what power is it that obliges your commander to live apart from his wife for four years, to languish on board his frigate and condemn so beautiful a woman to tears and grief?'

'It is necessary for him to attain a high position; our commander obtained this rich heiress from her father only on condition that he became an admiral. The young couple agreed, and to fulfil their promise he will have to stay at sea for at least another ten years, for with us, promotion depends on seniority.'

'So he accepts that he must live another ten years separated from his wife?'

'Yes, he must, in order to keep his promise; but when that time is up, he will be an admiral, he will enter the House of Lords, perhaps become a government Minister and end up one of the most powerful figures in the state. It seems to me, mademoiselle, that to attain such a position it is worth suffering for a few years!'

Ah! I thought, for the sake of such paltry tokens of grandeur men will trample underfoot everything that is most sacred! God himself was pleased to endow these two beings with every gift, beauty, brains and wealth; and the love they bear each other should have ensured for them a happiness as great as our nature is capable of enjoying; but the arrogance of a crazy old man has destroyed this prospect of earthly felicity: he insists that the best twenty years should be struck out of his children's lives. When they are reunited the wife will have lost her beauty, the husband his illusions; but he will be an admiral, a peer of the realm, a Minister, etc. What ridiculous vanity!

I cannot describe the bitter reflections this story caused me. Everywhere I encountered moral anguish; everywhere I saw that it proceeded from the evil prejudice that sets man against Providence, and I raged at the slow progress of human reason. I asked the handsome commander if he had any children. 'Yes,' he replied, 'a daughter as beautiful as her mother, and a son who is said to look very much like me; I have not seen him, he will be four years old when I do, if God permits it.' And the unhappy man repressed a sigh. He was still sensitive, because he was still young, but by the time he is fifty he will probably be as unfeeling as his father-in-law; and perhaps he will exact from his own son and daughter sacrifices as cruel as those imposed on him. This is how the prejudices which deprave our nature are transmitted; and the sequence will not be broken until there arise beings endowed by God with a firm will and resolute courage, who are prepared to suffer martyrdom rather than endure servitude.

On 30 April at eleven in the morning we sailed out of the Bay of Islay, and on 4 May at two in the afternoon we dropped anchor in the roads of Callao. This port did not seem to be as busy as Valparaiso. Recent political events had had a disastrous effect on trade and there were fewer ships than usual.

From the sea Lima is clearly visible on a hill surrounded by the mighty Andes. The size of the city, together with the imposing height of its many bell-towers, lend it an air of grandeur and enchantment.

We stayed at Callao until four o'clock waiting for the coach for Lima, which gave me ample time to examine the town. Like Valparaiso and Islay, Callao has grown so rapidly in the past ten years that after an absence of two or three years captains hardly recognise the place. The finest houses are owned by English or American merchants; they have large warehouses there, and their commercial activities give rise to continual movement between the port and the city some five miles away. Mr. Smith took me to the house of his correspondents, and here once more I found all the luxury and comfort characteristic of the English. The servants were English, and like their masters they were dressed just as they would have been in England. The house had a verandah, as do all the houses in Lima, and this is very convenient in hot countries, as it gives shelter from the sun and enables one to walk all round the house to take the air. This particular verandah was embellished with pretty English blinds. I stayed there for some time and could survey in comfort the only long wide street which constitutes the whole of Callao. It was a Sunday, and sailors in holiday attire were strolling about: I saw groups of Englishmen, Americans, Frenchmen, Dutchmen, Germans – in short, a mixture from nearly every nation – and I heard snatches of every tongue. As I listened to these sailors I began to understand the charm they find in their adventurous life and the enthusiasm it inspired in that *true sailor* Leborgne. When I tired of looking at the street I cast a glance into the large drawing-room whose windows overlooked the verandah, where five or six immaculately dressed Englishmen, their handsome faces calm and impassive, were drinking grog and smoking excellent Havana cigars as they swung gently to and fro in hammocks from Guayaquil suspended from the ceiling.

At last it was four o'clock and we climbed into the coach. The driver was French and all the people I found there spoke French or English. I met two Germans, great friends of Althaus, and immediately I felt at home. It was the first time I had been in a coach since I left Bordeaux, and the pleasure this gave me kept me happy all through the two-hour journey; I really thought I was back in civilisation.

The road out of Callao is bad, but after a mile or so it becomes tolerably good: very wide, smooth, and not too dusty. Just over a mile from Callao, on the right, lie the extensive ruins of some Indian city which had already ceased to exist when the Spaniards conquered the country. It would probably be possible to discover from Indian chronicles what this place was and how it came to be destroyed; but up to now the history of the Indians has not inspired sufficient interest in their conquerors for them to devote themselves to such research. A little further, on the left, is the village of Bella-Vista, where there is a hospital for sailors. Half-way to Lima, our driver stopped at an inn kept by a Frenchman, and after that, the city spread before us in all its magnificence, while the surrounding countryside provided a wealth of luxuriant vegetation in every shade of green: there were giant orange trees, clumps of bananas, lofty palms and many other species native to these regions, each with its distinctive foliage.

A mile or so before one enters the city the road is lined with great trees, and the effect of this avenue is truly majestic. There were quite a few people strolling on either side and several young men on horseback passed by our coach. I was told that this avenue is one of the principal promenades in Lima; among the women many were wearing the *saya*, and this costume struck me as so bizarre that it captured all my attention. Lima is a closed city, and at the end of the avenue we arrived at one of the gates. Its pillars are made of brick, and the façade, engraved with the arms of Spain, had been defaced. Officials searched the coach, just as they do at the gates of Paris. We went through much of the city; I thought the streets looked spacious and the houses quite different from the houses in Arequipa. Lima, so splendid from a distance, does not live up to its promise when you are inside; the houses are shabby, the windows are unglazed, and their iron grilles create an impression of suspicion and constraint; at the same time it is depressing to see so little sign of life in the streets. The coach stopped at a pleasant-looking house from which emerged a large stout lady whom I recognised immediately from the description the gentlemen of the *Mexicain* had given me as Madame Denuelle. This lady opened the door of the coach herself, helped me to alight, and said in the most affable manner: 'Mademoiselle Tristan, we have been impatiently awaiting your arrival for a long time. M Chabrié and M David have told us so much about you that we are very happy to have you with us.'

Frances Trollope

(1780–1863)

Like her son, Anthony, Frances Trollope was a prolific writer of novels. She wrote thirty-four of them. But unlike her son, Frances did not win acclaim and celebrity for her fiction. Rather it was the travel book *Domestic Manners of the Americans* that brought her notice. The book, a scathingly funny attack on the manners of the upstart Republicans, of 'eternal shaking hands' and of living in 'primaeval intimacy with our cow', has as its centre a concern for the role of women in America. Her novels were noted for their triumphant feminine spirit that heralded a new strong kind of heroine, and in *Domestic Manners* she bemoaned 'the lamentable insignificance of the American woman'. When her family suffered financial setbacks, Trollope, at the age of forty-eight, set off for the United States, and for four years she pursued many business and cultural enterprises for income. Most of the businesses failed, and it was in the face of these failures that she turned to writing. With subsequent travel books and novels, Trollope was never able to recapture the popularity of *Domestic Manners*. She died at eighty-three in Florence.

from **Domestic Manners of the Americans**

Removal to the Country – Walk in the Forest – Equality

At length my wish of obtaining a house in the country was gratified. A very pretty cottage, the residence of a gentleman who was removing into town, for the convenience of his business as a lawyer, was to let, and I immediately secured it. It was situated in a little village about a mile and a half from the town, close to the foot of the hills formerly mentioned as the northern boundary of it. We found ourselves much more comfortable here than in the city. The house was pretty and commodious, our sitting-rooms were cool and airy; we had got rid of the detestable mosquitoes, and we had an ice-house that never failed. Besides all this, we had the pleasure of gathering our tomatoes from our own garden, and receiving our milk from our own cow. Our manner of life was infinitely more to my taste than before; it gave us all the privileges of rusticity, which are fully as incompatible with a residence in a little town of Western America as with a residence in London. We lived on terms of primaeval intimacy with our cow, for if we lay down on our lawn she did not scruple to take a sniff at the book we were reading, but then she gave us her own sweet breath in return. The verge of the cool-looking forest that rose opposite our windows was so near, that we often used it as an extra drawing-room, and there was no one to wonder if we went out with no other preparation than our parasols, carrying books and work enough to while away a long summer day in the shade; the meadow that divided us from it was covered with a fine short grass, that continued for a little way under the trees, making a beautiful carpet, while sundry logs and stumps furnished our sofas and tables. But even this was not enough to satisfy us when we first escaped from the city, and we determined upon having a day's enjoyment of the wildest forest scenery we could find. So we packed up books, albums, pencils, and sandwiches, and, despite a burning sun, dragged up a hill so steep that we sometimes fancied we could rest ourselves against it by only leaning forward a little. In panting and in groaning we reached the top, hoping to be refreshed by the purest breath of heaven; but to have tasted the breath of heaven we must have climbed yet further, even to the tops of the trees themselves, for we soon found that the air beneath them stirred not, nor ever had stirred, as it seemed to us, since first it settled there, so heavily did it weigh upon our lungs.

Still we were determined to enjoy ourselves, and forward we went, crunching knee deep through aboriginal leaves, hoping to reach some spot less perfectly air-tight than our landing-place. Wearied with the fruitless search, we decided on reposing awhile on the trunk of a fallen tree; being all considerably exhausted, the idea of sitting down on this tempting log was conceived and executed simultaneously by the whole party, and the whole party sunk together through its treacherous surface into a mass of rotten rubbish that had formed part of the pith and marrow of the eternal forest a hundred years before.

We were by no means the only sufferers by the accident; frogs, lizards, locusts, katiedids, beetles, and hornets, had the whole of their various tenements disturbed, and testified their displeasure very naturally by annoying us as much as possible in return; we were bit, we were stung, we were scratched; and when, at last, we succeeded in raising ourselves from the venerable ruin, we presented as woeful a spectacle as can well be imagined. We shook our (not ambrosial) garments, and panting with heat, stings, and vexation, moved a few paces from the scene of our misfortune, and again sat down; but this time it was upon the solid earth.

We had no sooner begun to 'chew the cud' of the bitter fancy that had beguiled us to these mountain solitudes than a new annoyance assailed us. A cloud of mosquitoes gathered round, and while each sharp proboscis sucked our blood, they teased us with their humming chorus, till we lost all patience, and started again on our feet, pretty firmly resolved never to try the *al fresco* joys of an American forest again. The sun was now in its meridian splendour, but our homeward path was short, and down hill, so again packing up our preparations for felicity, we started homeward, or, more properly speaking, we started, for in looking for an agreeable spot in this dungeon forest we had advanced so far from the verge of the hill that we had lost all trace of the precise spot where we had entered it. Nothing was to be seen but multitudes of tall, slender, melancholy stems, as like as peas, and standing within a foot of each other. The ground, as far as the eye could reach (which certainly was not far), was covered with an unvaried bed of dried leaves; no trace, no track, no trail, as Mr Cooper would call it, gave us a hint which way to turn; and having paused for a moment to meditate, we remembered that chance must decide for us at last, so we set forward, in no very good mood, to encounter new misfortunes. We walked about a quarter of a mile, and coming to a steep descent, we thought ourselves extremely fortunate, and began to scramble down, nothing doubting that it was the same we had scrambled up. In truth, nothing could be more like, but, alas! things that are like are not the same; when we had slipped and stumbled down to the edge of the wood, and were able to look beyond it, we saw no pretty cottage with the shadow of its beautiful acacias coming forward to meet us; all was different; and, what was worse, all was distant from the spot where we had hoped to be. We had come down the opposite side of the ridge, and had now to win our weary way a distance of three miles round its base. I believe we shall none of us ever forget that walk. The bright, glowing, furnace-like heat of the atmosphere seems to scorch as I recall it. It was painful to tread, it was painful to breathe, it was painful to look round; every object glowed with the reflection of the fierce tyrant that glared upon us from above.

We got home alive, which agreeably surprised us; and when our parched tongues again found power of utterance, we promised each other faithfully never to propose any more parties of pleasure in the grim stove-like forests of Ohio.

We were now in daily expectation of the arrival of Mr T.; but day after day, and week after week passed by, till we began to fear some untoward circumstance might delay his coming till the Spring; at last, when we had almost ceased to look out for him, on the road which led from the town, he arrived, late at night, by that which leads across the country from Pittsburgh. The pleasure we felt at seeing him was greatly increased by his bringing with him our eldest son, which was a happiness we had not hoped for. Our walks and our drives now became doubly interesting. The young men, fresh from a public school, found America so totally unlike all the nations with which their reading had made them acquainted, that it was indeed a new world to them. Had they visited Greece or Rome they would have encountered objects with whose images their minds had been long acquainted, or had they travelled to France or Italy they would have seen only what daily conversation had already rendered familiar; but at our public schools America (except perhaps as to her geographical position) is hardly better known than Fairy Land; and the American character has not been much more deeply studied

'Nothing was to be seen but multitudes of tall, slender, melancholy stems, as like as peas, and standing within a foot of each other.'

than that of the Anthropophagi; all, therefore, was new, and every thing amusing.

The extraordinary familiarity of our poor neighbours startled us at first, and we hardly knew how to receive their uncouth advances, or what was expected of us in return; however, it sometimes produced very laughable scenes. Upon one occasion two of my children set off upon an exploring walk up the hills; they were absent rather longer than we expected, and the rest of our party determined upon going out to meet them; we knew the direction they had taken, but thought it would be as well to enquire at a little public-house at the bottom of the hill, if such a pair had been seen to pass. A woman, whose appearance more resembled a Covent Garden market-woman than any thing else I can remember, came out and answered my question with the most jovial good humour in the affirmative, and prepared to join us in our search. Her look, her voice, her manner, were so exceedingly coarse and vehement, that she almost frightened me; she passed her arm within mine, and to the inexpressible amusement of my young people, she dragged me on, talking and questioning me without ceasing. She lived but a short distance from us, and I am sure intended to be a very good neighbour; but her violent intimacy made me dread to pass her door; my children, including my sons, she always addressed by their Christian names, excepting when she substituted the word 'honey'; this familiarity of address, however, I afterwards found was universal throughout all ranks in the United States.

My general appellation amongst my neighbours was 'the English old woman', but in mentioning each other they constantly employed the term 'lady'; and they evidently had a pleasure in using it, for I repeatedly observed, that in speaking of a neighbour, instead of saying Mrs Such-a-one, they described her as 'the lady over the way what takes in washing', or as 'that there lady, out by the Gulley, what is making dip-candles'. Mr Trollope was as constantly called 'the old man', while draymen, butchers' boys, and the labourers on the canal were invariably denominated 'them gentlemen'; nay, we once saw one of the most gentlemanlike men in Cincinnati introduce a fellow in dirty shirt sleeves, and all sorts of detestable et cetera, to one of his friends, with this formula, 'D—— let me introduce this gentleman to you'.

Our respective titles certainly were not very important; but the eternal shaking hands with these ladies and gentlemen was really an annoyance, and the more so, as the near approach of the gentlemen was always redolent of whiskey and tobacco.

But the point where this republican equality was the most distressing was in the long and frequent visitations that it produced. No one dreams of fastening a door in Western America; I was told that it would be considered as an affront by the whole neighbourhood. I was thus exposed to perpetual, and most vexatious interruptions from people whom I had often never seen, and whose names still oftener were unknown to me.

Those who are native there, and to the manner born, seem to pass over these annoyances with more skill than I could ever acquire. More than once I have seen some of my acquaintance beset in the same way, without appearing at all distressed by it; they continued their employment or conversation with me, much as if no such interruption had taken place; when the visitor entered, they would say, 'How do you do?' and shake hands.

'Tolerable, I thank ye, how be you?' was the reply.

If it was a female, she took off her hat; if a male, he kept it on, then taking possession of the first chair in their way, they would retain it for an hour together, without uttering another

'I always remarked that the first silver line of the moon's crescent attracted the eye on the first day, in America, as strongly as it does here on the third.'

word; at length, rising abruptly, they would again shake hands, with, 'Well, now I must be going, I guess,' and so take themselves off, apparently well contented with their reception.

I could never attain this philosophical composure; I could neither write nor read, and I always fancied I must talk to them. I will give the minutes of a conversation which I once set down after one of their visits, as a specimen of their tone and manner of speaking and thinking. My visitor was a milkman.

'Well now, so you be from the old country? Ay – you'll see sights here, I guess.'

'I hope I shall see many.'

'That's a fact. I expect your little place of an island don't grow such dreadful fine corn as you sees here?'

'It grows no corn at all, sir.'

'Possible! no wonder, then, that we reads such awful stories in the papers of your poor people being starved to death.'

'We have wheat, however.'

'Ay, for your rich folks, but I calculate the poor seldom gets a belly full.'

'You have certainly much greater abundance here.'

'I expect so. Why they do say, that if a poor body contrives to be smart enough to scrape together a few dollars, that your King George always comes down upon 'em, and takes it all away. Don't he?'

'I do not remember hearing of such a transaction.'

'I guess they be pretty close about it. Your papers ben't like ourn, I reckon? Now we says and prints just what we likes.'

'You spend a good deal of time in reading the newspapers.'

'And I'd like you to tell me how we can spend it better. How should freemen spend their time, but looking after their government, and watching that them fellers as we gives offices to, doos their duty, and gives themselves no airs?'

'But I sometimes think, sir, that your fences might be in more thorough repair, and your roads in better order, if less time was spent in politics.'

'The Lord! to see how little you knows of a free country! Why, what's the smoothness of a road, put against the freedom of a free-born American? And what does a broken zig-zag signify, comparable to knowing that the men what we have been pleased to send up to Congress, speaks handsome and straight, as we chooses they should?'

'It is from a sense of duty, then, that you all go to the liquor store to read the papers?'

'To be sure it is, and he'd be no true born American as didn't. I don't say that the father of a family should always be after liquor, but I do say that I'd rather have my son drunk three times in a week, than not look after the affairs of his country.'

Our autumn walks were delightful; the sun ceased to scorch; the want of flowers was no longer peculiar to Ohio; and the trees took a colouring, which in richness, brilliance, and variety, exceeded all description. I think it is the maple, or sugar-tree, that first sprinkles the forest with rich crimson; the beech follows, with all its harmony of golden tints, from pale yellow up to brightest orange. The dog-wood gives almost the purple colour of the mulberry; the chestnut softens all with its frequent mass of delicate brown, and the sturdy oak carries its deep green into the very lap of winter. These tints are too bright for the landscape painter; the attempt to follow nature in an American autumn scene must be abortive. The colours are in reality extremely brilliant, but the medium through which they are seen increases the effect surprisingly. Of all the points in which America has the advantage of England, the one I felt most sensibly was the clearness and brightness of the atmosphere. By day and by night this exquisite purity of air gives tenfold beauty to every object. I could hardly believe the stars were the same; the Great Bear looked like a constellation of suns; and Jupiter justified all the fine things said of him in those beautiful lines, from I know not what spirited pen, beginning,

I looked on thee, Jove! till my gaze
Shrunk, smote by the pow'r of thy blaze.

I always remarked that the first silver line of the moon's crescent attracted the eye on the first day, in America, as strongly as it does here on the third. I observed another phenomenon in the crescent moon of that region, the cause of which I less understood. That appearance which Shakespeare describes as 'the new moon, with the old moon in her lap', and which I have heard ingeniously explained as the effect of *earth light*, was less visible there than here.

Cuyp's clearest landscapes have an atmosphere that approaches nearer to that of America than any I remember on canvas; but even Cuyp's *air* cannot reach the lungs, and, therefore, can only give an idea of half the enjoyment; for it makes itself felt as well as seen, and is indeed a constant source of pleasure.

Our walks were, however, curtailed in several directions by my old Cincinnati enemies, the pigs; immense droves of them were continually arriving from the country by the road that led to most of our favourite walks; they were often fed and lodged in the prettiest valleys, and worse still, were slaughtered beside the prettiest streams. Another evil threatened us from the same quarter, that was yet heavier. Our cottage had an ample piazza, (a luxury almost universal in the country houses of America), which, shaded by a group of acacias, made a delightful sitting-room; from this favourite spot we one day perceived symptoms of building in a field close to it; with much anxiety we hastened to the spot, and asked what building was to be erected there.

''Tis to be a slaughter-house for hogs,' was the dreadful reply. As then there were several gentlemen's houses in the neighbourhood, I asked if such an erection might not be indicted as a nuisance.

'A what?'

'A nuisance,' I repeated, and explained what I meant.

'No, no,' was the reply, 'that may do very well for your tyrannical country, where a rich man's nose is more thought of than a poor man's mouth; but hogs be profitable produce here, and we be too free for such a law as that, I guess.'

During my residence in America, little circumstances like the foregoing often recalled to my mind a conversation I once held in France with an old gentleman on the subject of their active police, and its omnipresent gens d'armerie; 'Croyez moi, Madame, il n'y a que ceux à qui ils ont à faire, qui les trouvent de trop.' Believe me, Madame, it is only those for whom they exist who find them to be excessive. And the old gentleman was right, not only in speaking of France, but of the whole human family, as philosophers call us. The well disposed, those whose own feeling of justice would prevent their annoying others, will never complain of the restraints of the law. All the freedom enjoyed in America, beyond what is enjoyed in England, is enjoyed solely by the disorderly at the expense of the orderly; and were I a stout knight, either of the sword or of the pen, I would fearlessly throw down my gauntlet, and challenge the whole Republic to prove the contrary; but being, as I am, a feeble looker on, with a needle for my spear, and 'I talk' for my device, I must be contented with the power of stating the fact, perfectly certain that I shall be contradicted by one loud shout from Maine to Georgia.

Eliza Farnham

(1815–1864)

THE LIFE OF ELIZA FARNHAM REBUTS TROLLOPE'S STEREOTYPE OF THE 'INSIGNIFICANT AMERICAN WOMAN'. BORN IN THE UPSTATE NEW YORK VILLAGE OF RENSSELAERVILLE, FARNHAM WAS SIX YEARS OLD WHEN HER MOTHER DIED AND SHE WAS ADOPTED BY A NEARBY AUNT. THE AUNT REFUSED TO SEND ELIZA TO SCHOOL AND INSTEAD KEPT THE YOUNG GIRL AS A DOMESTIC IN THE HOUSE UNTIL SHE TURNED FOURTEEN, WHEN FARNHAM, DETERMINED TO SUCCEED AND 'DECREASE THE MISERY IN THE WORLD', INSISTED UPON AN EDUCATION. AFTER SIX YEARS OF SCHOOLING, FARNHAM MOVED TO ILLINOIS WHERE SHE MET AND MARRIED THOMAS JEFFERSON FARNHAM, A LAWYER AND TRAVEL WRITER. IN ADDITION TO *LIFE IN PRAIRIE LAND*, AN ACCOUNT OF HER TRIP ALONE TO ILLINOIS, SHE WROTE TWO NOVELS AND A COLLECTION OF ESSAYS ENTITLED *WOMAN AND HER ERA*, IN WHICH SHE DISCUSSES VOCATIONS AND INTELLECTUAL INTERESTS FOR WOMEN. FARNHAM ALSO WORKED AS MATRON OF THE WOMEN'S DIVISION OF THE NEW YORK STATE PRISON AT SING SING AND DURING THE CALIFORNIA GOLD RUSH WENT WEST TO RALLY FOR BETTER CONDITIONS FOR NEEDY WOMEN.

from Life in Prairie Land

At four o'clock we reached the southern bank of Rock River, at a place called, indiscriminately, Dixon's Ferry, Dixon, and Dixonville. By the first of these names it has been known many years, as corresponding on Rock River, to Fort Clark, now Peoria, on the Illinois. There is much natural beauty about the upper part of the town. The bank of the river is broken, and a bold bluff of lime-rock rises abruptly to a considerable height above the lower level, the summit of which is wooded with open, beautiful barrens. The trees hang on the brow of the ledge, and wave their arms pleasantly to those below. A fine spring issues from the foot of the rock, but I did not visit it. Opposite this portion of the town is a beautiful plot of table-land, smooth as a summer lake, which its owner had converted into eastern capital and western promises, by consenting to divide it into town lots. He had paid liberally for an engraved map, on which the streets were adorned with trees, and the public grounds with churches and other lofty edifices. Neither the trees nor churches, however, seemed to have any very fair prospect of becoming distinguished elsewhere.

The old part of Dixonville, that around the ferry, is built upon a bed of cream-colored sand, abounding in fleas. The banks of the river are dotted with little copses and slightly broken. The northern one rises into a high bluff, which, just below the ferry, crowds up to the water's edge, and bears upon its face an occasional tree or shrub. On the southern side, the bluff bends away from the termination of the ledge, and sweeping inland, leaves a low track, the rear of which is broken by bushy gullies that come down from the height above, and terminate in the sand-bed before spoken of.

I was set down here, at another very filthy house. But that which so disgusted me on first entering, I soon found to be one of the least objectionable features of the establishment. The landlord was one of that class of people in whom all national and other distinctions are lost in the ineffaceable brand of villainy that is stamped upon them. One would never pause to inquire whether he were American, English, Irish, or Dutch. You felt conscious of the presence of a villain; one of those universal prowlers, whose business it is to prey upon society, and who, when it will be most advantageous, prosecute their schemes alone, and when otherwise, surround themselves with a gang of ruffians, whose less disguised vices form a barrier between their leader and public indignation.

He had a calm, imperturbable face, which, whenever he saw that his designs were detected, assumed an expression of the most profound meekness and resignation, as if its owner would say, I know your thoughts wrong me, but what then? I can bear even that!

I asked to be shown at once to a private room, and furnished with water and other things necessary to comfort, after a very warm and dusty ride. He escorted me to one adjoining the parlor. 'But sir,' said I, observing boots, hats, et cet., standing about, 'this appears to be a gentleman's room.'

'Yes, it is occupied by a gentleman, but he's out, and won't be here till night.'

'Have you no room unoccupied?' I inquired. 'Besides, there is no lock on the door!'

'You need not fear interruption,' he replied; 'I would give you the parlor, but we shall want to pass through there, and you can spend an hour here without any fear of being disturbed.'

'Very well, sir. Be so good as to send me the water and towels immediately.'

They were brought at the expiration of ten minutes, by a gross creature, who united the characters of mistress, housekeeper, and servant, to the miscreant landlord. Her whole person and manner were of the most disgusting description. She deposited her burthen, and then placing a hand on each side of her ungainly person, posted herself against the door, and commenced taking a deliberate survey of myself and my proceedings. I waited a moment, and finding that she intended to remain as long as her convenience or pleasure would permit, inquired if it formed any part of her orders to remain? 'No; but didn't I want some help?'

'Not at all; the most effectual way of serving me will be to remove yourself as quickly as possible from my sight.'

She disappeared, and I barricaded the door with trunks, chairs, and whatever else I could place against it. I had scarcely completed the task, when some person came rapidly up-stairs and through the hall, and seized the handle of the door with a violent push.

'Open this door,' exclaimed a harsh voice, accompanying the words with another push, that made the fortifications tremble. I now added my own strength to the other securities, and informed the person that a lady and stranger was occupying the room for a very short period only, and that she presumed he would, as a gentleman, only require to be informed of this to be induced to leave her in peaceable possession; or, if anything were wrong, to seek the landlord, who had placed her there. To this he replied, that any person who was in his room must leave it in a shorter space of time than it would be proper to describe; and that he would see the landlord where it was supposed to be much hotter than it was there, before he would go after him on any such business.

I now saw that I had done him great wrong, in supposing him accessible to any arguments that would touch a man or a gentleman, and, therefore, changed my ground.

'Sir,' said I, 'I shall not leave this room until I am ready, which will be a much longer time than you name. If you retire, and permit me, unmolested, to accomplish what I came here for, your room shall be vacated in fifteen minutes. If you remain there, I remain here; and I have, beside my personal strength, the aid of two very heavy trunks, and a rifle, placed against the door at about the height of a man's head. If you are not already acquainted with its contents, there is every chance that you will become so, if you open this door by violence.'

Muttering some terrific curses, he retreated down the stairs, and I proceeded to make my toilet, in a trepidation which shamefully belied my stout words. It was completed in a very short time, but even before it was done the door was again rudely assailed, and the inquiry made whether I 'was not yet ready'. I replied, that I should leave the room the first moment after I was ready, and that these visits, so far from facilitating my preparation, interrupted them entirely. Again the steps retreated, and, in a few moments, I removed the trunks and rifle, and walked into the parlor. At the same moment the wretch came up-stairs, and entered his room. He was a well-dressed, gentlemanly-looking person, and, strange to say, wore a wide crepe band on his hat! He peered sharply into the parlor as he passed, remained in his room about the fourth of a minute without closing the door, and then disappeared down the stairs, and lounged away the evening about the bar-room and door of the house.

Everything I now saw convinced me that I was in a den of the foulest iniquity; but imagination, stimulated as it was by fear, did not conceive the half of what I afterward learnt to be true of the vile people who consorted there. This place is the Vicksburg of Illinois, and the enterprising proprietors of the mail line had chosen the headquarters of the gamblers, counterfeiters, horse thieves, et cet., as the most fitting place of entertainment for their passengers. I afterward learned that there was an excellent house kept in the upper part of the town, remote from the pestiferous atmosphere of these wretches, but, being a stranger, I had no opportunity of profiting by it. The people who live here are persons whose daily business is the stealing of horses, the manufacture of counterfeit money, et cet.; and such was their strength at the period spoken of, that although the better population of the place, of which I was informed there was a highly respectable body, held them in the abhorrence which their acts merited, they could make no demonstration against them without endangering their own and the lives of their families. Sometimes, exasperated beyond all forbearance by their enormities, the citizens were driven to some feeble measure of self-defence; and, at this time, there was a set of counterfeiter's tools under execution. But these movements generally ended in some tacit compromise, by which the villains were left to pursue their iniquity as before.

One instance of the recklessness in crime, exhibited by the wretches referred to in the last chapter, was related to me. A settler, who had opened a prairie farm some miles below the town, became the owner of a very beautiful pair of horses. One morning they were both missing. He at once started in pursuit, went directly up to the town, and, a few miles on his way, discovered one of them lying dead by the road-side. It appeared that, for some reason, the robbers wanted but one, and, as the other followed his companion, they had shot him down to relieve themselves of his presence. These, and many more incidents, evincing the most shocking depravity, were related to me after I had escaped.

But meantime my desire to reach the residence of my friends that night, increased every moment. I therefore sent for the landlord, and inquired the distance to C—. By the way I should observe that he added to the various callings already specified, some pretensions to the practice of medicine, and that I had accidentally heard him speak to one of his comrades in the passage, of having but recently returned from a visit to one of his patients, about four miles above the place for which I inquired. The name, however, when I mentioned it, seemed entirely new to him. He mused a moment, and said that really he could not tell. It might be between twenty and thirty miles down the river. There had been a little place settled down there somewhere, about a year before, perhaps he could find some gentleman about the house who could inform me.

'Let the distance be what it may,' I said. 'I wish to go there to-night.'

'To-night! that is impossible. We could not send you there to-night on any terms. In the morning I may find it possible to take you, or procure an opportunity for you to go with some person that is travelling that way.'

'As you are ignorant of the distance,' I said, 'you cannot name your charge until you ascertain it.'

'No, though I think it would be reasonable to say five dollars.'

I had paid but six dollars for the previous one hundred miles. 'Do you know the distance to —,' naming the place which he had visited that day.

'Not exactly, but I think it is about—'

'You mean to say that you have never measured it with the chain, but having been there today, you could doubtless form a tolerably correct estimate.'

He said that he had spoken of visiting a patient somewhere in the neighbourhood of that place, it might be within half a dozen miles or so. I replied that it was useless to attempt deception in so small and obvious a matter; that I would willingly pay an exorbitant charge to get from his house that moment; but as it was impossible, I should make up my mind to endure a night in it. 'Let me hear from you,' I said, 'at the earliest hour in the morning, in reference to my departure; and now, if you will oblige me by showing me the room I am to occupy to-night, I shall require nothing more.'

'You are to sleep here,' he replied, 'there is no other room unoccupied.'

'But this door has no lock, and if I am to judge of my security, from that which you promised in the first instance, I shall sit up all night.'

Oh, there would not be the least necessity for anything of the kind. This was the parlor – it was never entered but by transient guests, and if any came, they could be shown to another room. He begged I would feel perfectly assured, and apologized in the humblest manner for the interruption I had experienced in the other room. The gentleman who occupied it had not seen him, and he did not know who might be in it or what they were doing. He regretted, et cet.

To this I replied, I should place no reliance on his promise, having found it worthy of none, but take good care to secure myself, and thus we parted.

It should be remarked here as evidence of a degree of

'"If you remain there, I remain here; and I have, beside my personal strength, the aid of two very heavy trunks, and a rifle, placed against the door at about the height of a man's head."'

civilized feeling among these ruffians, that they felt themselves wholly unworthy of the presence of a virtuous woman, and never expected one to appear at table with them. It was not the custom of the house, so the female before referred to informed me, for ladies to appear at the first table.

'And pray where do ladies take their meals,' I inquired, 'when they are so unfortunate as to be obliged to eat here?'

'If they are in a hurry to go, we *tote* it up *hyur* to 'em; if they ain't, they wait and go to the second table!'

'And who sits at the second table?'

'Mr. —, the landlord, and I, and the drivers and so on.'

A delightful circle, truly! I made no attempt to get a meal that day, though I had eaten nothing since early breakfast at P.

Making the best security I could, by placing the bedstead against the door, I prepared to retire.

The room was excessively warm, and had a stench which rendered it intolerable, except the window were thrown wide open. The bed itself would have been pronounced soiled by a jury of Irish landladies; I resolved, however, to make the best of the necessity which held me there, and addressed myself to rest with an earnestness which was well rewarded by seven hours of uninterrupted oblivion.

Amelia Edwards

(1831–1892)

Unlike most Victorian women who were enticed by the freedom of the road and then felt compelled to write of their insights and experiences, Amelia Edwards came to travel writing by the opposite route. By the 1860s, Edwards had published novels, poetry, stories, and history, and then she started travelling. Her guided journey through the Dolomites in the southeastern Tyrol, terrain impassable except on foot or by mule, stirred a sense of discovery, the feeling of being the 'first travellers who have come up this way', as a roadmakers' overseer tells Edwards and her companions in the following excerpt. The Italian 'ramble' proved a rugged test for her trip a year later up the Nile, recounted in *A Thousand Miles up the Nile*, the first general archaeological survey of Egypt's ruins. Later Edwards would help establish the first chair in Egyptology at University College, London.

from Untrodden Peaks and Unfrequented Valleys: A Midsummer Ramble in the Dolomites

So we go on, always in the green shade of the forest, till we come to a little group of cottages known collectively as the Casa di San Marco; a name recalling the old days of Venetian sovereignty, and still marking the frontier between Italy and Austria. Here, there being no officials anywhere about, we pass unquestioned under the black and yellow pole, and so arrive in a few moments at the opening point of the new government road which old Ghedina had given us directions to follow as far as it went.

This new government road, carried boldly up and through a steep hill-side of pine-forest, is considered – and no doubt with justice – to be an excellent piece of work; but old Holborn Hill with all the paving stones up would have been easy driving compared with it. As yet, indeed, it is not a road, but a rough clearing some twenty feet in width, full of stones and rubble and slags of knotted root, with the lately-felled pine-trunks lying prostrate at each side, like the ranks of slain upon a battlefield. No vehicle, it seems, has yet been brought this way, and though we all alight instantly, it seems doubtful whether the carriage can ever be got up. The horses, half maddened by clouds of gadflies, struggle up the rugged slope, stopping every now and then to plunge and kick furiously. The landau rocks and rolls like a ship at sea. Every moment the road becomes worse, and the blaze of noonday heat more intolerable. Presently we come upon a gang of road-makers some two hundred in number, women and children as well as men, swarming over the banks like ants, clearing, levelling, and stone-breaking. They pause in their work, and stare at us as if we were creatures from another world.

'You are the first travellers who have come up this way,' says the overseer, as we pass by. 'You must be Inglese!'

At length we reach a point where the road ceases altogether; its future course being marked off with stakes across a broad plateau of smooth turf. This plateau – a kind of natural arena in the midst of an upper world of pine-forest – is hemmed closely in by trees on three sides, but sinks away on the left into a wooded dell down which a clear stream leaps and sparkles. We look round, seeing no outlet, save by the way we have come, and wondering what next can be done with the carriage. To our amazement, the driver coolly takes the leader by the head and makes straight for the steep pitch dipping down to the torrent.

'You will not attempt to take the carriage down into that hole!' exclaims the writer.

'Con rispetta, Signora, there is no other way,' replies the driver, deferentially.

'But the horses will break their legs, and the carriage will be dashed to pieces!'

'Come lei piace, Signora,' says the driver, dimly recognising the truth of this statement.

We are standing now on the brink of the hollow, the broken bank shelving down to a depth of about thirty feet; the torrent tumbling and splashing at the bottom; and the opposite bank rising almost as abruptly beyond.

'Are we bound to get it across here?' I ask.

'Con rispetta, yes, Signora. That is to say, it can be sent back to Cortina all the way round by Auronzo and Pieve di Cadore. It is as the Signora pleases.'

Now it pleases neither of the Signoras to send the carriage back by a round of something like forty-five miles; so, after a hurried consultation, we decide to have the horses taken out, and the carriage hauled across by men. Giuseppe is thereupon despatched for a reinforcement of navvies; and thus, by the help of some three or four stalwart fellows, the landau is lifted bodily over; the horses are led across and reharnessed; and, after a little more pushing and pulling, a rough cart-track on the other side of this Rubicon is gained in safety.

Yet a few yards farther, and we emerge upon another space of grassy Alp – a green, smooth, sloping amphitheatre of perhaps some eighty acres in extent – to the East all woods; to the West all mountains; with one lonely little white house nestling against the verge of the forest about a quarter of a mile away. This amphitheatre is the Val Buona; that little white house is the cottage of Bastian the wood-ranger; yonder pale gigantic pinnacles towering in solitary splendour above the tree-tops to the rear of the cottage, are the crests of the Cristallo. But above all else, it is the view to the Westward that we have come here to see – the famous 'cirque' of the Croda Malcora. And in truth, although we have already beheld much that is wild and wonderful in the world of Dolomite, we have as yet seen nothing that may compare with this.

The green sward slopes away from before our feet and vanishes in a chasm of wooded valley of unknown depth and distance; while beyond and above this valley, reaching away far out of sight to right and left; piled up precipice above precipice, peak above peak; seamed with horizontal bars of snow-drift; upholding here a fold of glittering glacier; dropping there a thread of misty waterfall; cutting the sky-line with all unimaginable forms of jagged ridge and battlement, and reaching as it seems midway from earth to heaven, runs a vast unbroken chain of giant mountains. But what mountains? Familiar as we have become by this time with the Ampezzo Dolomites, there is not here one outline that either can recognise. Where, then, are we? And what should we see if we could climb yonder mighty barrier?

It takes some minutes' consideration and the help of the map, to solve these questions. Then, suddenly, all becomes clear. We are behind the Croda Malcora; directly behind Sorapis; and looking straight across in the direction of the Pelmo, which, however, is hidden by intervening mountains. The Antelao should be visible to the left, but is blocked out by the long and lofty range of the Marmarole. Somewhere away to the right, in the gap that separates this great panorama from the nearer masses of the Cristallo, lies the Tre Croce pass leading to Cortina. The main feature of the view, however, is the Croda Malcora; and we are looking at it from the back. Seen on this side, it shows as a sheer wall of impending precipice, too steep and straight to afford any resting places for the snow, save here and there upon a narrow ledge or shelf, scarce wide enough for a chamois. On the Ampezzo side, however, it flings out huge piers of rock, so that the Westward and Eastward faces of it are as unlike as though they belonged to two separate mountains. This form, as I by and by discover, is of frequent occurrence in Dolomite structure; the Civita affording, perhaps, the most remarkable case in point.

Having looked awhile at this wonderful view, we are glad once more to escape out of the blinding sunshine into the shade of the pine-woods. Here, by the help of rugs and cloaks, we make a tent in which to rest for a couple of hours during the great heat of the day; and so, taking luncheon, studying our books and maps, listening to the bees among the wild-flowers and to the thrushes in the rustling boughs overhead, we fancy ourselves in Arcadia, or the Forest of Arden. Meanwhile, the woodman's axe is busy among the firs on the hillside, and now and then we hear the crash of a falling tree.

The forester who lives in the white cottage yonder comes by and by to pay his respects to the Signore. His name is Bastian, and he turns out to be a brother of Santo Siorpaes. He also has been a soldier, and is glad now and then, when opportunity offers, to act as guide. He lives in this lost corner of the world the whole year round. It is 'molto tristo', he says; especially in winter. When autumn wanes, he provisions his little house as if for a long siege, laying in store of flour, cheese, sausage, coffee and the like. Then the snow comes, and for months no living soul ventures up from the valleys. All is white and silent, like death. The snow is as high as himself – sometimes higher;

'...reaching as it seems midway from earth to heaven, runs a vast unbroken chain of giant mountains.'

and he has to dig a trench about the house, that the light may not be blocked out of the lower windows. There was one winter, he says, not many years ago, when the falls were so sudden and so heavy, that he never went to bed at night without wondering whether he should be buried alive in his cottage before morning.

While he is yet speaking, a band of road-makers comes trooping by, whistling, and laughing, and humming scraps of songs. They are going back to work, having just eaten their mid-day mess of polenta; and their hearts are glad with wine – the rough red wine that Bastian sells at the cottage for about three kreutzers the litro, and which we at luncheon found quite undrinkable.

'The place is full of life now, at all events,' says L., consolingly.

He looks after them, and shakes his head.

'Yes, Signora,' he replies; 'but their work here will soon be done, and then it will seem more solitary than ever.'

The man is very like Santo, but has nothing of Santo's animation. The lonely life seems to have taken all that brightness out of him. His manner is sad and subdued; and when he is not speaking, he has just that sort of lost look that one sees in the faces of prisoners who have been a long time in confinement.

At two o'clock, we break up our camp, and prepare to start again. The polite driver, mindful of a possible buono-mano, comes to take leave, and is succeeded by the lad Giovanni, who has journeyed up from Cortina to meet us with the promised saddle-horses. And now our old friend the tall chestnut appears upon the scene with the Pezzé side-saddle on his back, followed by an equally big black horse with the Ghedina saddle; whereupon, having Giuseppe and Giovanni in attendance, we mount and ride away – not without certain shrewd suspicions that our gallant steeds are carrying ladies for the first time. Big as they are, they climb, however, like cats, clambering in a wonderful way up the steep and stony slope of fir-forest that rises behind Bastian's cottage and leads to the Misurina Alp beyond.

Mrs F. D. Bridges

(ca. 1840–?)

Frances Trollope didn't have the money to travel the world in the manner of F. D. Bridges and her husband, but if she had, the result would be something like Mrs Bridges' *Journal*. For the three years ending with 1880, the English couple visited such places as Greece, Egypt, India, China, Japan, and North America. Bridges resisted being carried in a palanquin, a covered litter used to transport honoured guests in India, and in all places stayed clear of 'English' food. The idea was to cast off all vestiges of home when away. 'The sooner one falls into the ways of a country the better,' she said. This being said, however, she, like Trollope, can be blunt and dismissive ('the American desert . . . is not interesting') and extremely nasty ('Mormonism has gathered together the low-class type of humanity and uneducated of all countries'). But in her critical observations of the Mormon practice of polygamy, Mrs Bridges is sympathetic to the desire of women to 'actually [have] a husband to themselves' and applauds the 'progress in civilisation' that would free the women of this exploitive practice.

from Journal of a Lady's Travels Round the World

Salt Lake City, August 15

We got on board the Atlantic mail (which does the 3,300 miles from ocean to ocean in about 160 hours) on Friday night, and found ourselves at noon on Sunday in the Mormon capital. Our two days of travel in a Pullman car were comfortable enough. During the day by taking a 'section' we had a space equal to about two seats each, which at night was made up into two large beds, one over the other, in the lofty carriage. Very different was this same journey a few years ago, when the emigrants bound westward toiled over the desolate plains, and took seven months to accomplish what is now done in five days. Crossing the Sierra Nevada range we passed through nearly thirty miles of snow-sheds – rough barns built over the line at high elevations – and saw at one station the gigantic snow-plough, which, with ten locomotives behind it, is used to cleave a way through the snow-drifts; for during what is called a 'wet winter' the snow falls to the depth of sixteen or twenty feet up here.

The American desert through which we travelled after leaving the mountains is not interesting. Sand and alkali plains as far as the eye can reach; as desolate as a great ocean bed from which 'the waters were gone'. Sometimes a patch of grey melancholy-looking sagebrush appears, but the sun's rays fall perpendicularly on this barren scene, burning and withering as though they would crush out any attempt which nature might make, to introduce vegetable life. Now and then we journeyed through a fertile valley where a little river made its way down from far-off mountains; people tell us there is more 'fancy than fact' about these rivers, for, except at certain seasons, they dwindle away into sad-looking pools, where the thirsty emigrant has to dig for sufficient water to supply his beasts. Sometimes a curious mirage makes one quite certain that a lovely lake and trees and gardens lie far away on the horizon; but very little of anything green did we see till, early yesterday morning, we caught sight of the silver streak of 'Great Salt Lake', and descended on the wide valley in which it lies, where the Mormons have turned the unprofitable plain into corn-fields and orchards. A sign-board, with 'ten miles of track in one day', marks the place where the Central Pacific Company, with four thousand workmen, accomplished the feat and laid the last sleeper (which has had to be twice renewed, clipped away by enthusiastic relic-hunting tourists) on their

'Sand and alkali plains as far as the eye can reach; as desolate as a great ocean bed from which "the waters were gone".'

eight hundred miles of railroad. Salt Lake City is about thirty miles off the main track, so we changed into the Saints' railway – built, however, by Gentiles – and wound our way through cultivated land, and by ugly little wooden farmhouses, stopping once to pick up a Mormon family on their way to Zion for a Sunday outing. We thought the husband looked bored at having to carry three bundles, three umbrellas and three shawls, evidently belonging to the domestic circle – his three wives, who accompanied him.

A four-horse omnibus deposited us at the door of this large and comfortable hotel, built by an ex-Mormon, who, finding it inconvenient, as his income increased, to pay a tenth of it to the Church, became a Gentile. After luncheon – during which a scientific lady informed us that the butter was 'oleomargarine', and the honey 'glucose' – we walked down the broad street, with young trees and a running stream of clear water at each side, where the Saints were enjoying Sabbath repose in rocking-chairs, chewing tobacco, with their heels elevated on the back of another chair. All was neat and orderly – and very, very ugly; the shops closed, and some of the thirty thousand Mormon Sunday-school children going about hymn-book in hand.

We entered the Tabernacle, a large oblong building, in the Mormon style of architecture – the ancient rule of thumb – over which these clever ignorant people have constructed one of the largest self-sustaining roots in the world, and were conducted to the strangers' seat, by a decorous German Elder. The building will hold eight thousand people; yesterday it was about half full. The large and really fine organ, also of native manufacture, was well played, and the choir of fashionably dressed young men and women sang nicely, out of the Mormon hymn-book, well-known Christian hymns. Church dignitaries and some of the twelve apostles sat on a high place round the velvet-covered desk, on which lay a large Bible and a small 'Book of Mormon' – the divine revelation which, in 1827, 'a holy Angel permitted the youth Joseph Smith of Manchester, New York, to take from the hill of Cumorrah, and translate through the aid of a sacred instrument, called the Urim and Thummim'. The metallic plates and sacred things were shown to three witnesses, by an angel from heaven, and five thousand copies of the inspired translation were printed in 1830.

Below the daïs stood rows of electro-plate bread-baskets and goblets of water; and, in the centre of the building, a fountain for Baptism. Men and women chiefly sat apart; looking round on the congregation, we thought ourselves back again in some remote part of Wales or Ireland; stupid good-natured, unintelligent faces – a curious contrast to the usual American crowd of keen-featured sharp-eyed citizens. And so indeed it is: Mormonism has gathered together the low-class type of humanity and uneducated of all countries, and formed them into an industrious community. One could not help feeling that many members of the congregation would have been in gaol, and living at the expense of the British taxpayer, had they not been sitting this pleasant Sunday afternoon drowsily listening – for they take their devotion easily – after a week's hard work, to one of their twelve apostles, preaching a practical but somewhat prosy sermon. I never saw so many ugly women, or so many sad-looking black bonnets; of course, if a woman has only a share in a husband, pin-money must also be shared – and not many new bonnets obtained. We discoursed with the friendly Elder. 'How many Mormons are there?' I impiously asked. 'Brother, how many saints are we?' he inquired of his neighbour. 'About one hundred and forty-four thousand,' was the reply. We were about to ask what proportion the womenkind bore to the population; but the preacher, Brother Orson Pratt, one of the original twelve apostles who led the Church into the wilderness – a venerable-looking old man (they say that through religious fervour and fasting his four wives were starved to death) – rose to preach.

The 50th anniversary of the Latter-day Saints has lately been held, and the Tabernacle was still hung with flowers and decorations, for, in 1830, 'Joseph Smith was ordained by John the Baptist, to preach the last Revelation to the world'; and it was also divinely revealed that his wife, Emma Smith, 'was to receive as many wives as he chose to take to himself, but that she was to abide and cleave to the prophet, and none else'. Persecution is proverbially good for a Church, and the Mormons had plenty of it, and throve accordingly. At last, in 1844, the Prophet Joseph Smith was murdered, 'lynched' by a mob in Illinois; and the Saints, under the leadership of their apostles, and President Brigham Young, a Yankee carpenter, determined to fly to the wilderness, and seek a Land of Promise in the Rocky Mountains. After terrible sufferings, they with their wives and children, in worn-out waggons, a really heroic company of fanatics, having crossed 1,000 miles of desert, began to take possession of a land, certainly not flowing with milk and honey – not an ear of corn could be grown without irrigation; and armies of grasshoppers, wild Indians, and Mexican brigands, constantly descended on their scanty crops.

Still the people grew and multiplied, and sent out missionaries to all parts of the world (there were twenty-five nationalities represented in the Tabernacle at the festival the other day) under Brigham Young's vigorous rule; and now out here, where thirty-three years ago the Mormon pioneers built their first mud fort, there is a flourishing town with 20,000 inhabitants, two lines of railway, school boards, daily papers, and co-operative societies.

Since the rich silver-mines of Utah and the transcontinental railway have brought in speculators and a wave of Gentile enterprise, the prosperity of Zion has increased rapidly; but Mormonism is losing its distinctive features – hard work, and plenty of wives to do it; – the younger women, who do not think 'that the half is as good as the whole', are declining co-operative matrimony, and actually want a husband all to themselves. No need for repressive measures and actions for bigamy; progress in civilisation and increased demand for the article, now that armies of silver-miners, digging up wealth, have come into the country, will soon make it impossible for a Saint to indulge in the luxury of more than one wife.

But all this time we were listening to Brother Orson Pratt's apostolic sermon, from the 20th Chapter of Revelation, supplemented by nonsense out of the 'Book of Mormon'. The latter is a silly mixture of the Koran and a modern romance, in which, however, it is allowed that 'not only the Bible and Book of Mormon, but all other good books, are inspired by God', and 'that men will be punished for their own sins, not for Adam's transgressions' – strangely liberal doctrines for the fiercely puritanical spirit of Mormonism to adopt. Like other would-be expounders of prophecy, the preacher turned the glorious visions of St. John into seemingly convincing proofs of his own theories – which none but the unconverted or sectarians could deny. Having triumphantly disposed of modern science, he proved that Adam had once resided in Jackson county, east of the Missouri River, but did not seem quite clear as to the location of the ultimate New Jerusalem, only it would certainly be on the American Continent, and include amongst its citizens the American Indians, who undoubtedly were the living descendants of the Lost Tribes (I devoutly hope the latter may remain on American soil – they have followed us all round the world).

Many admirable moral truths he preached, in the spirit of the last much-to-be-commended article of the Mormon Faith: 'We believe in being honest, true, chaste, temperate, benevolent, virtuous, and upright; and in doing good to all men'. Indeed, it is allowed that the Saints' treatment of the Indian tribes round them has been just and merciful. But of course there was much, to our minds, blasphemous rubbish in the sermon, like the hymn on 'Celestial marriage' in the hymn-book beside me, setting forth that the Mormons were 'to multiply wives, because, unlike other unprofitable servants, they made good use of their ten talents (ten wives), and that to him that hath shall be given.'

Our venerable-looking preacher, besides being an apostle, has done some fighting in his time. In 1857 he, at the head of the Mormon legion, completely routed the United States troops at Fort Bridger, carried off their stores, and left them in an almost destitute condition, to find their way back to civilisation across the desert.

We did not wait for the conclusion of the sermon, but took the excursion train to the Lake, where sundry Mormons of all ages were splashing about in quite elaborate bathing costumes. It is almost impossible to sink in the very clear salt water of this evaporating pan, which deposits salt and sulphur round its shores. The Great Salt Lake, more than 100 miles in length (like the Dead Sea on a large scale), has no outlet for the waters of the three rivers which flow into it; during the last twenty years it is said to have risen twelve feet, and to be rising steadily; yet, judging from the raised beaches, which can be distinctly traced high up on the sides of the surrounding hills, the lake must at one time have been an inland sea. No trees or vegetation, but picturesque islands, and distant mountain ranges, and wonderfully-coloured rocks in the foreground make a striking picture; but we certainly do not agree with Humboldt that 'here the beauty of Como and Killarney are combined'. A Gentile lady passenger gave us a very unfavourable account of Mormons and their ways: 'Guess they treat their women and children just like beasts; there's one of them – the old sinner!' she said, pointing to a farmer driving up a waggon, laden with his womankind, to the station. Two rather depressed-looking wives, ugly middle-aged women in poke bonnets, holding unlovely babies, sat in the back, while the new young wife, with her baby in smart hat and feathers, occupied the front seat with their lord and master; not a pleasant or poetical domestic picture; and they were all so ugly!

The sad conviction is growing upon us since leaving Japan, the land of loveliness, that the British lower classes, from which Mormonism largely draws its converts, though in the main a hardworking and religiously-minded people, are entirely devoid of all perception of the beautiful in Life, Art, or Religion. . . .

This morning, accompanied by a friendly literary lady from Boston, we drove through some miles of amazing fertility, rich crops of Indian corn and wheat (the practical Mormons do not grow many flowers) created by industry and irrigation, till we drew up at the convict prison. Capital punishment is rarely enforced in America; hence in flagrant cases of murder the mob take the law into their own hands, and 'lynch' the murderer on the spot. It seemed a misdirection of energy that about ten murderers should be taking unprofitable exercise round the prison yard, under the eye of an officer with loaded revolver, while the land beyond their gaol was lying barren for want of cultivation, waiting for human skill to turn it into the garden we had just passed through. Then we drove on to the Church farm – hundreds of acres of crops, representing the temporalities of the Mormon 'Establishment'; part of the proceeds will go to build the grand new temple, whose cutstone pillars and walls are slowly rising beside the old 'Tabernacle'. Some of the Saints are very rich. 'That ere old woman who lives in that ranche,' said our driver, pointing to a tiny wooden hut, 'owns the land my stables is on; I offered her most any money for it, and she declined; then I concluded to marry her right off' (he is a Gentile), 'and she declined. Can't come round them nohow,' he added with a sigh, and drove us off to Fort Douglas, where a garrison of United States troops overlook Zion, and keep the Saints in order. These are the first soldiers we have seen in America. It is remarkable how little show of force is required to keep the peace in this country. The few policemen in San Francisco looked more like Methodist preachers in long frock-coats and wide-brimmed hats than officers of justice.

Hard by was the grave of a Gentile who, rumour says, was finally put out of the way by Brigham Young. Beyond, a lovely view over the fertile country dotted with villages, and far away the mountains and shining lake. A little later we passed Brigham Young's private residence, surrounded by the hencoop-like houses in which we were told his various wives were lodged, and, further on, the grand 'villa residence' built for his last wife. Not far off was his grave, under the hill where he sat and had visions and revelations, and where he now lies buried in a commodious coffin, which, according to his will, was 'not to be scrimped in length, but leave comfortable room to turn in, where I can rest and have a good sleep until the morning of the first resurrection'. No doubt Brigham Young was a man of much talent and strength of character, and governed his subjects on the whole wisely; but like other and wiser rulers, he embarked too largely in matrimony. The United States Government prosecuted him latterly for bigamy and murder, but he died a few years ago before the case was decided. . . .

Seeing 'Woman's Exponent Office' over a door, we drew up, and went in (sending H. first of all to explore). A pretty, nicely-dressed young lady, niece of the lady editor, received us in the 'Editor's parlour'. She seemed pleased to give us information concerning her faith, and presented us with copies of the 'Woman's Exponent', a neat little monthly magazine – written, published, and printed entirely by 'the women of Zion'. 'Yes, we all vote in Utah,' she said, and seemed to think there was no need to agitate for women's suffrage; but when Utah becomes a state (at present it is only a territory and cannot vote in Congress) the Federal Government may object that women are not 'persons' – nowhere in the States have women the political suffrage.

Evidently polygamy is rather a sore subject; but our young lady informed us that her father had seven wives and twenty-six children. 'I call them aunts, you know, and I like most of my brothers and sisters.' Some of the wives live together, but the majority have separate establishments. We remarked that last year we were in a country where it was the fashion to have many husbands, and had the pleasure of knowing a lady who had made sixteen lawful marriages; that it appeared to us that both customs (having many wives or many husbands) had their inconveniences – to which our young friend assented, and said that her sisters had married with the understanding that no additional ladies were to be 'sealed' to their husbands; adding, 'The young folks like marrying single, and feel bad when there is another wife now-a-days.' She was really a lady-like girl – a niece of the late Brigham Young – and seemed sensible and well-informed, more so than most of her sisterhood, we imagine, if they are to be judged of by the 'Address of the Women of Utah' at the festival the other day, in which, after much very 'tall talk', they ask, 'What would the Pilgrim Fathers have done without the Pilgrim Mothers?' and pronounce that the year of Jubilee, which is now being celebrated, 'historically resurrects the past, and prophetically opens up the future'.

Our Mormon friend seemed to regard matrimony as an almost sacred duty imposed on women; but I felt, in spite of many explanations, that Mormon marriages were difficult to understand. 'Till death us do part', is easy of comprehension; but here you may marry for 'Time and Eternity', or you may enter into a matrimonial engagement for 'Time', or 'Eternity', or you may unite yourself in Celestial marriage to some defunct Saint; or a widow may, with the consent of the Church, arrange a marriage for her deceased husband with some eligible deceased friend; and at last I got puzzled and came away with the impression that in Utah a man may marry his own widow.

After luncheon we visited the funny little museum, and the very funny little old Mormon professor who had collected most of the curiosities in it: minerals from the rich mines of Utah, prehistoric implements, Indian scalps, stuffed birds, and Mormon relics; the trumpet and compass which led the Saints through the wilderness; and amongst these various odds and ends a richly embroidered apron, once belonging to Queen Elizabeth, inherited by some New England family, which has finally found its way to this strange place. The poor old self-taught professor, who appeared to be a really sincere believer in the martyr-prophet Joseph Smith, was glad to talk to an English Gentile, and tell of the long and eventful years that had passed since he lived as caretaker or something of the sort of Warwick Castle. Afterwards we were taken to a large building with 'Holiness to the Lord', 'Zion's Co-operative Institution', over the door – quite the Army and Navy stores on a rather smaller scale. 'Brother, what may this be worth?' asked an intelligent Mormon shopman to another Saint, when I inquired the price of Crosse and Blackwell's marmalade. Piles of goods of every description lay around this large and exclusively Mormon establishment, and I believe a velvet gown would have been forthcoming had we asked for it.

Mary Kingsley

(1862–1900)

With her delightful sense of humour, Mary Kingsley experiences a range of hair-raising situations: crocodiles pawing the gunnels of her riverboats, leopards face to face ('I can confidently say I am not afraid of any wild animal – until I see it – and then – well I will yield to nobody in terror'), and remnants of cannibalism ('the hand was fresh, the others only so so'). Once she fell into an animal trap with twelve-inch spikes ('It is at these moments you realize the blessings of a good thick skirt').

The following excerpt tells of two separate experiences; the first as she began to work her way above the tide line of the Ogowé River and the second en route to another river, the Rembwé. Kingsley spent her early life caring for her ailing family like a good, dutiful Victorian daughter. In 1892, when she was thirty, her parents died within six weeks of one another. The next year she went to West Africa for six months. She returned in 1894 and stayed a year, working as a trader and gathering fish and fetishes. Kingsley volunteered as a nurse during the Boer War but died shortly after arriving in South Africa.

from Travels in West Africa

I should like here to speak of West Coast dangers because I fear you may think that I am careless of, or do not believe in them, neither of which is the case. The more you know of the West Coast of Africa, the more you realise its dangers. For example, on your first voyage out you hardly believe the stories of fever told by the old Coasters. That is because you do not then understand the type of man who is telling them, a man who goes to his death with a joke in his teeth. But a short experience of your own, particularly if you happen on a place having one of its periodic epidemics, soon demonstrates that the underlying horror of the thing is there, a rotting corpse which the old Coaster has dusted over with jokes to cover it so that it hardly shows at a distance, but which, when you come yourself to live alongside, you soon become cognisant of. Many men, when they have got ashore and settled, realise this, and let the horror get a grip on them; a state briefly and locally described as funk, and a state that usually ends fatally; and you can hardly blame them. Why, I know of a case myself. A young man who had never been outside an English country town before in his life, from family reverses had to take a situation as book-keeper down in the Bights. The factory he was going to was in an isolated out-of-the-way place and not in a settlement, and when the ship called off it, he was put ashore in one of the ship's boats with his belongings, and a case or so of goods. There were only the firm's beach-boys down at the surf, and as the steamer was in a hurry the officer from the ship did not go up to the factory with him, but said good-bye and left him alone with a set of naked savages as he thought, but really of good kindly Kru boys on the beach. He could not understand what they said, nor they what he said, and so he walked up to the house and on to the verandah and tried to find the Agent he had come out to serve under. He looked into the open-ended dining-room and shyly round the verandah, and then sat down and waited for some one to turn up. Sundry natives turned up, and said a good deal, but no one white or comprehensible, so in desperation he made another and a bolder tour completely round the verandah and noticed a most peculiar noise in one of the rooms and an infinity of flies going into the venetian shuttered window. Plucking up courage he went in and found what was left of the white Agent, a considerable quantity of rats, and most of the flies in West Africa. He then presumably had fever, and he was taken off, a fortnight afterwards, by a French boat, to whom the natives signalled, and he is not coming down the Coast again. Some men would have died right out from a shock like this.

But most of the new-comers do not get a shock of this order. They either die themselves or get more gradually accustomed to this sort of thing, when they come to regard death and fever as soldiers, who on a battle-field sit down, and laugh and talk round a camp fire after a day's hard battle, in which they have seen their friends and companions falling round them; all the time knowing that to-morrow the battle comes again and that to-morrow night they themselves may never see. It is not hard-hearted callousness, it is only their way. Michael Scott put this well in *Tom Cringle's Log*, in his account of the yellow fever during the war in the West Indies. Fever, though the chief danger, particularly to people who go out to settlements, is not the only one; but as the other dangers, except perhaps domestic poisoning, are incidental to pottering about in the forests, or on the rivers, among the unsophisticated tribes, I will not dwell on them. They can all be avoided by any one with common sense, by keeping well out of the districts in which they occur; and so I warn the general reader that if he goes out to West Africa, it is not because I said the place was safe, or its dangers overrated. The cemeteries of the West Coast are full of the victims of those people who have said that Coast fever is 'Cork fever', and a man's own fault, which it is not; and that natives will never attack you unless you attack them: which they will – on occasions.

My main aim in going to Congo Français was to get up above the tide line of the Ogowé River and there collect fishes; for my object on this voyage was to collect fish from a river north of the Congo. I had hoped this river would have been the Niger, for Sir George Goldie had placed at my disposal great facilities for carrying on work there in comfort; but for certain private reasons I was disinclined to go from the Royal Niger Protectorate into the Royal Niger Company's territory; and the Calabar, where Sir Claude MacDonald did everything he possibly could to assist me, I did not find a good river for me to collect fishes in. These two rivers failing me, from no fault of either of their own presiding genii, my only hope of doing anything now lay on the South West Coast river, the Ogowé, and everything there depended on Mr. Hudson's attitude towards scientific research in the domain of ichthyology. Fortunately for me that gentleman elected to take a favourable view of this affair, and in every way in his power assisted me during my entire stay in Congo Français. But before I enter into a detailed description of this wonderful bit of West Africa, I must give you a brief notice of the manners, habits and customs of West Coast rivers in general, to make the thing more intelligible.

There is an uniformity in the habits of West Coast rivers, from the Volta to the Coanza, which is, when you get used to it, very taking. Excepting the Congo, the really great river comes out to sea with as much mystery as possible; lounging lazily along among its mangrove swamps in a what's-it-matter-when-one-comes-out and where's-the-hurry style, through quantities of channels inter-communicating with each other. Each channel, at first sight as like the other as peas in a pod, is bordered on either side by green-black walls of mangroves, which Captain Lugard graphically described as seeming 'as if they had lost all count of the vegetable proprieties, and were standing on stilts with their branches tucked up out of the wet, leaving their gaunt roots exposed in mid-air'. High-tide or low-tide, there is little difference in the water; the river, be it broad or narrow, deep or shallow, looks like a pathway of polished metal; for it is as heavy weighted with stinking mud as water e'er can be, ebb or flow, year out and year in. But the difference in the banks, though an unending alternation between two appearances, is weird.

At high-water you do not see the mangroves displaying their ankles in the way that shocked Captain Lugard. They look most respectable, their foliage rising densely in a wall irregularly striped here and there by the white line of an aërial root, coming straight down into the water from some upper branch as straight as a plummet, in the strange, knowing way an aërial root of a mangrove does, keeping the hard straight line until it gets some two feet above water-level, and then spreading out into blunt fingers with which to dip into the water and grasp the mud. Banks indeed at high water can hardly be said to exist, the water stretching away into the mangrove swamps for miles and miles, and you can then go, in a suitable small canoe, away among these swamps as far as you please.

This is a fascinating pursuit. For people who like that sort of thing it is just the sort of thing they like, as the art critic of a provincial town wisely observed anent an impressionist picture recently acquired for the municipal gallery. But it is a pleasure to be indulged in with caution; for one thing, you are certain to come across crocodiles. Now a crocodile drifting down in deep water, or lying asleep with its jaws open on a sand-bank in the sun, is a picturesque adornment to the landscape when you are on the deck of a steamer, and you can write home about it and frighten your relations on your behalf; but when you are away among the swamps in a small dug-out canoe, and that crocodile and his relations are awake – a thing he makes a point of being at flood tide because of fish coming along – and when he has got his foot upon his native heath – that is to say, his tail within holding reach of his native mud – he is highly interesting, and you may not be able to write home about him – and you get frightened on your own behalf. For crocodiles can, and often do, in such places, grab at people in small canoes. I have known of several natives losing their lives in this way; some native villages are approachable from the main river by a short cut, as it were, through the mangrove swamps, and the inhabitants of such villages will now and then go across this way with small canoes instead of by the constant channel to the village, which is almost always winding. In addition to this unpleasantness you are liable – until you realise the danger from experience, or have native advice on the point – to get tide-trapped away in the swamps, the water falling round you when you are away in some deep pool or lagoon, and you find you cannot get back to the main river. For you cannot get out and drag your canoe across the stretches of mud that separate you from it, because the mud is of too unstable a nature and too deep, and sinking into it means staying in it, at any rate until some geologist of the remote future may come across you, in a fossilised state, when that mangrove swamp shall have become dry land. Of course if you really want a truly safe investment in Fame, and really care about Posterity, and Posterity's Science, you will jump over into the black batter-like, stinking slime, cheered by the thought of the terrific sensation you will produce 20,000 years hence, and the care you will be taken of then by your fellow-creatures, in a museum. But if you are a mere ordinary person of a retiring nature, like me, you stop in your lagoon until the tide rises again; most of your attention is directed to dealing with an 'at home' to crocodiles and mangrove flies, and with the fearful stench of the slime round you. What little time you have over you will employ in wondering why you came to West Africa, and why, after having reached this point of absurdity, you need have gone and painted the lily and adorned the rose, by being such a colossal ass as to come fooling about in mangrove swamps. Twice this chatty little incident, as Lady MacDonald would call it, has happened to me, but never again if I can help it. On one occasion, the last, a mighty Silurian, as *The Daily Telegraph* would call him, chose to get his front paws over the stern of my canoe, and endeavoured to improve our acquaintance. I had to retire to the bows, to keep the balance right,* and fetch him a clip on the snout with a paddle, when he withdrew, and I paddled into the very middle of the lagoon, hoping the water there was too deep for him or any of his friends to repeat the performance. Presumably it was, for no one did it again. I should think that crocodile was eight feet long; but don't go and say I measured him, or that this is my outside measurement for crocodiles. I have measured them when they have been killed by other people, fifteen, eighteen, and twenty-one feet odd. This was only a pushing young creature who had not learnt manners.

Still, even if your own peculiar tastes and avocations do not take you in small dug-out canoes into the heart of the swamps, you can observe the difference in the local scenery made by the flowing of the tide when you are on a vessel stuck on a sand-bank, in the Rio del Rey for example. Moreover, as you will have little else to attend to, save mosquitoes and mangrove flies, when in such a situation, you may as well pursue the study. At the ebb gradually the foliage of the lower branches of the mangroves grows wet and muddy, until there is a great black band about three feet deep above the surface of the water in all directions; gradually a network of gray-white roots rises up, and below this again, gradually, a slope of smooth and lead-brown slime. The effect is not in the least as if the water had fallen, but as if the mangroves had, with one accord, risen up out of it, and into it again they seem silently to sink when the flood comes. But by this more safe, if still unpleasant, method of observing mangrove swamps, you miss seeing in full the make of them, for away in their fastnesses the mangroves raise their branches far above the reach of tide line, and the great gray roots of the older trees are always sticking up in mid-air. But, fringing the rivers, there is always a hedge of younger mangroves whose lower branches get immersed.

* It is no use saying because I was frightened, for this miserably understates the case.

At corners here and there from the river face you can see the land being made from the waters. A mud-bank forms off it, a mangrove seed lights on it, and the thing's done. Well! not done, perhaps, but begun; for if the bank is high enough to get exposed at low water, this pioneer mangrove grows. He has a wretched existence though. You have only got to look at his dwarfed attenuated form to see this. He gets joined by a few more bold spirits and they struggle on together, their network of roots stopping abundance of mud, and by good chance now and then a consignment of miscellaneous *débris* of palm leaves, or a floating tree-trunk, but they always die before they attain any considerable height. Still even in death they collect. Their bare white sticks remaining like a net gripped in the mud, so that these pioneer mangrove heroes may be said to have laid down their lives to make that mud-bank fit for colonisation, for the time gradually comes when other mangroves can and do colonise on it, and flourish, extending their territory steadily; and the mud-bank joins up with, and becomes a part of, Africa.

Anyhow I was glad to see the mangrove belt; all the gladder because I did not then know how far it was inland from the sea, and also because I was fool enough to think that a long line I could see, running E. and W. to the north of where I stood, was the line of the Rembwé river; which it was not, as we soon found out. Cheered by this pleasing prospect, we marched on forgetful of our scratches, down the side of the hill, and down the foot slope of it, until we struck the edge of the swamp. We skirted this for some mile or so, going N.E. Then we struck into the swamp, to reach what we had regarded as the Rembwé river. 'Nature was at its ghastliest,' as *Chambers's Magazine* said, and hurt the feelings of the locality by saying, of the Oil Rivers scenery. We found ourselves at the edge of that open line we had seen from the mountain. Not standing, because you don't so much as try to stand on mangrove roots unless you are a born fool, and then you don't stand long, but clinging, like so many monkeys, to the net of aërial roots which surrounded us, looking blankly at a lake of ink-black slime. It was half a mile across, and some miles long. We could not see either the west or east termination of it, for it lay like a rotten serpent twisted between the mangroves. It never entered into our heads to try to cross it, for when a swamp is too deep for mangroves to grow in it, 'No bottom lib for them dam ting,' as a Kruboy once said to me, anent a small specimen of this sort of ornament to a landscape. But we just looked round to see which direction we had better take. Then I observed that the roots, aërial and otherwise, were coated in mud, and had no leaves on them, for a foot above our heads. Next I noticed that the surface of the mud before us had a sort of quiver running through it, and here and there it exhibited swellings on its surface, which rose in one place and fell in another. No need for an old coaster like me to look at that sort of thing twice to know what it meant, and feeling it was a situation more suited to Mr. Stanley than myself, I attempted to emulate his methods and addressed my men. 'Boys,' said I, 'this beastly hole is tidal, and the tide is coming in. As it took us two hours to get to this sainted swamp, it's time we started out, one time, and the nearest way. It's to be hoped the practice we have acquired in mangrove roots in coming, will enable us to get up sufficient pace to get out on to dry land before we are all drowned.' The boys took the hint. Fortunately one of the Ajumbas had been down in Ogowé, it was Gray Shirt, who 'sabed them tide palaver'. The rest of them, and the Fans, did not know what tide meant, but Gray Shirt hustled them along and I followed, deeply regretting that my ancestors had parted prematurely with prehensile tails for four limbs, particularly when two of them are done up in boots and are not sufficient to enable one to get through a mangrove swamp network of slimy roots rising out of the water, and swinging lines of aërial ones coming down to the water *à la* mangrove, with anything approaching safety. Added to these joys were any quantity of mangrove flies, a broiling hot sun, and an atmosphere three quarters solid stench from the putrifying ooze all round us. For an hour and a half thought I, Why did I come to Africa, or why, having come, did I not know when I was well off and stay in Glass? Before these problems were settled in my mind we were close to the true land again, with the water under us licking lazily among the roots and over our feet.

We did not make any fuss about it, but we meant to stick to dry land for some time, and so now took to the side of a hill that seemed like a great bubble coming out of the swamp, and bore steadily E. until we found a path. This path, according to the nature of paths in this country, promptly took us into another swamp, but of a different kind to our last – a knee-deep affair, full of beautiful palms and strange water plants, the names whereof I know not. There was just one part where that abomination, *pandanus*, had to be got through, but, as

'...great banks of screw pine, and coppices of wine palm, with their lovely fronds reflected back by the still, mirror-like water, so that the reflection was as vivid as the reality...'

swamps go, it was not at all bad. I ought to mention that there were leeches in it, lest I may be thought too enthusiastic over its charms. But the great point was that the mountains we got to on the other side of it, were a good solid ridge, running, it is true, E. and W., while we wanted to go N.; still on we went waiting for developments, and watching the great line of mangrove swamp spreading along below us to the left hand, seeing many of the lines in its dark face, which betokened more of those awesome slime lagoons that we had seen enough of at close quarters.

About four o'clock we struck some more plantations, and passing through these, came to a path running north-east, down which we went. I must say the forest scenery here was superbly lovely. Along this mountain side cliff to the mangrove swamp the sun could reach the soil, owing to the steepness and abruptness and the changes of curves of the ground; while the soft steamy air which came up off the swamp swathed everything, and although unpleasantly strong in smell to us, was yet evidently highly agreeable to the vegetation. Lovely wine palms and raffia palms, looking as if they had been grown under glass, so deliciously green and profuse was their feather-like foliage, intermingled with giant red woods, and lovely dark glossy green lianes, blooming in wreaths and festoons of white and mauve flowers, which gave a glorious wealth of beauty and colour to the scene. Even the monotony of the mangrove-belt alongside gave an additional charm to it, like the frame round a picture.

As we passed on, the ridge turned N. and the mangrove line narrowed between the hills. Our path now ran east and more in the middle of the forest, and the cool shade was charming after the heat we had had earlier in the day. We crossed a lovely little stream coming down the hillside in a cascade; and then our path plunged into a beautiful valley. We had glimpses through the trees of an amphitheatre of blue mist-veiled mountains coming down in a crescent before us, and on all sides, save due west where the mangrove-swamp came in. Never shall I forget the exceeding beauty of that valley, the foliage of the trees round us, the delicate wreaths and festoons of climbing plants, the graceful delicate plumes of the palm trees, interlacing among each other, and showing through all a background of soft, pale, purple-blue mountains and forest, not really far away, as the practised eye knew, but only made to look so by the mist, which has this trick of giving suggestion of immense space without destroying the beauty of detail. Those African misty forests have the same marvellous distinctive quality that Turner gives one in his greatest pictures. I am no artist, so I do not know exactly what it is, but I see it is there. I luxuriated in the exquisite beauty of that valley, little thinking or knowing what there was in it besides beauty, as Allah 'in mercy hid the book of fate'. On we went among the ferns and flowers until we met a swamp, a different kind of swamp to those we had heretofore met, save the little one last mentioned. This one was much larger, and a gem of beauty; but we had to cross it. It was completely furnished with characteristic flora. Fortunately when we got to its edge we saw a woman crossing before us, but unfortunately she did not take a fancy to our appearance, and instead of staying and having a chat about the state of the roads, and the shortest way to N'dorko, she bolted away across the swamp. I noticed she carefully took a course, not the shortest, although that course immersed her to her arm-pits. In we went after her, and when things were getting unpleasantly deep, and feeling highly uncertain under foot, we found there was a great log of a tree under the water which, as we had seen the lady's care at this point, we deemed it advisable to walk on. All of us save one, need I say that one was myself, effected this with safety. As for me, when I was at the beginning of the submerged bridge, and busily laying about in my mind for a definite opinion as to whether it was better to walk on a slippy tree trunk bridge you could see, or on one you could not, I was hurled off by that inexorable fate that demands of me a personal acquaintance with fluvial and paludial ground deposits; whereupon I took a header, and am thereby able to inform the world, that there is between fifteen and twenty feet of water each side of that log. I conscientiously went in on one side, and came up on the other. The log, I conjecture, is dum or ebony, and it is some fifty feet long; anyhow it is some sort of wood that won't float. I really cannot be expected, by the most exigent of scientific friends, to go botanising under water without a proper outfit. Gray Shirt says it is a bridge across an under-swamp river. Having survived this and reached the opposite bank, we shortly fell in with a party of men and women, who were taking, they said, a parcel of rubber to Holty's. They told us N'dorko was quite close, and that the plantations we saw before us were its outermost ones, but spoke of a swamp, a bad swamp. We knew it, we said, in the foolishness of our hearts thinking they meant the one we had just forded, and leaving them resting, passed on our way; half-a-mile further on we were wiser and sadder, for then we stood on the rim of one of the biggest swamps I have ever seen south of the Rivers. It stretched away in all directions, a great sheet of filthy water, out of which sprang gorgeous marsh plants, in islands, great banks of screw pine, and coppices of wine palm, with their lovely fronds reflected back by the still, mirror-like water, so that the reflection was as vivid as the reality, and above all remarkable was a plant,* new and strange to me, whose pale-green stem came up out of the water and then spread out in a flattened surface, thin, and in a peculiarly graceful curve. This flattened surface had growing out from it leaves, the size, shape and colour of lily of the valley leaves; until I saw this thing I had held the wine palm to be the queen of grace in the vegetable kingdom, but this new beauty quite surpassed her.

Our path went straight into this swamp over the black rocks forming its rim, in an imperative, no alternative, 'Come-along-this-way' style. Singlet, who was leading, carrying a good load of bottled fish and a gorilla specimen, went at it like a man, and disappeared before the eyes of us close following him, then and there down through the water. He came up, thanks be, but his load is down there now, worse luck. Then I said we must get the rubber carriers who were coming this way to show us the ford; and so we sat down on the bank a tired, disconsolate, dilapidated-looking row, until they arrived. When they came up they did not plunge in forthwith; but leisurely set about making a most nerve-shaking set of preparations, taking off their clothes, and forming them into bundles, which, to my horror, they put on the tops of their heads. The women carried the rubber on their backs still, but rubber is none the worse for being under water. The men went in first, each holding his gun high above his head. They skirted the bank before they struck out into the swamp, and were followed by the women and by our party, and soon we were all up to our chins.

We were two hours and a quarter passing that swamp. I was one hour and three-quarters; but I made good weather of it, closely following the rubber-carriers, and only going in right over head and all twice. Other members of my band were less fortunate. One finding himself getting out of his depth, got hold of a palm frond and pulled himself into deeper water still, and had to roost among the palms until a special expedition of the tallest men went and gathered him like a flower. Another got himself much mixed up and scratched because he thought to make a short cut through screw pines. He did not know the screw pine's little ways,** and he had to have a special relief expedition. One and all, we got horribly infested with leeches, having a frill of them round our necks like astrachan collars, and our hands covered with them, when we came out. The depth of the swamp is very uniform, at its ford we went in up to our necks, and climbed up on the rocks on the hither side out of water equally deep.

Knowing you do not like my going into details on such matters, I will confine my statement regarding our leeches, to the fact that it was for the best that we had some trade salt with us. It was most comic to see us salting each other; but in spite of the salt's efficacious action I was quite faint from loss of blood, and we all presented a ghastly sight as we made our way on into N'dorko. Of course the bleeding did not stop at once, and it attracted flies and – but I am going into details, so I forbear.

* Specimen placed in Herbarium at Kew.

** *Pandanus candelabrum* – a marsh tree from 20 to 30 feet high growing in dense thickets, the stout aërial roots coming down into the water and forming with the true stems a network even more dense than that of mangroves. Their leaves, which grow in clusters, are sword-shaped, and from 4 to 6 feet in length with sharp spiny margins, and the whole affair is exceedingly tough and scratchy.

Isabella Bird

(1831–1904)

The year Mary Kingsley booked passage to West Africa, Isabella Bird accepted an invitation to be the first woman to address a meeting of the prestigious Royal Geographical Society. The work and travels of this one woman had broken the barriers of gender that had so nettled Mabel Crawford and proved that feminine as well as masculine 'eccentricity or originality of character' can be admired. Until she was forty, Bird stayed at home to care for family members, and she probably would have remained there indefinitely had not doctors prescribed travel to cure her bad back and insomnia. For the next more than thirty years until she died in Edinburgh, Bird was scarcely without her luggage corded. Books recount travels from Tibet to Japan to the Rocky Mountains. Her early volumes, particularly *A Lady's Life in the Rocky Mountains* – a collection of letters she wrote to her beloved sister Henrietta – display an exuberance and freshness absent in the later ones and offer rare insight into the vulnerability of the single woman on the road.

from A Lady's Life in the Rocky Mountains

Slipping, faltering, gasping from the exhausting toil in the rarefied air, with throbbing hearts and panting lungs, we reached the top of the gorge and squeezed ourselves between two gigantic fragments of rock by a passage called the 'Dog's Lift', when I climbed on the shoulders of one man and then was hauled up. This introduced us by an abrupt turn round the south-west angle of the Peak to a narrow shelf of considerable length, rugged, uneven, and so overhung by the cliff in some places that it is necessary to crouch to pass at all. Above, the Peak looks nearly vertical for 400 feet; and below, the most tremendous precipice I have ever seen descends in one unbroken fall. This is usually considered the most dangerous part of the ascent, but it does not seem so to me, for such foothold as there is is secure, and one fancies that it is possible to hold on with the hands. But there, and on the final, and, to my thinking, the worst part of the climb, one slip, and a breathing, thinking, human being would lie 3000 feet below, a shapeless, bloody heap! 'Ring' refused to traverse the lodge, and remained at the 'Lift' howling piteously.

From thence the view is more magnificent even than that from the 'Notch'. At the foot of the precipice below us lay a lovely lake, wood embosomed, from or near which the bright St. Vrain and other streams take their rise. I thought how their clear cold waters, growing turbid in the affluent flats, would heat under the tropic sun, and eventually form part of that great ocean river which renders our far-off islands habitable by impinging on their shores. Snowy ranges, one behind the other, extended to the distant horizon, folding in their wintry embrace the beauties of Middle Park. Pike's Peak, more than one hundred miles off, lifted that vast but shapeless summit which is the landmark of Southern Colorado. There were snow patches, snow slashes, snow abysses, snow forlorn and soiled-looking, snow pure and dazzling, snow glistening above the purple robe of pine worn by all the mountains; while away to the east, in limitless breadth, stretched the green-grey of the endless Plains. Giants everywhere reared their splintered crests. From thence, with a single sweep, the eye takes in a distance of 300 miles – that distance to the west, north, and south being made up of mountains ten, eleven, twelve, and thirteen thousand feet in height, dominated by Long's Peak, Gray's Peak, and Pike's Peak, all nearly the height of Mont Blanc! On the Plains we traced the rivers by their fringe of cotton-woods to the distant Platte, and between us and them lay glories of mountain, canyon, and lake, sleeping in depths of blue and purple most ravishing to the eye.

As we crept from the Ledge round a horn of rock, I beheld what made me perfectly sick and dizzy to look at – the terminal Peak itself – a smooth, cracked face or wall of pink granite, as nearly perpendicular as anything could well be up which it was possible to climb, well deserving the name of the 'American Matterhorn'.*

Scaling, not climbing, is the correct term for this last ascent. It took one hour to accomplish 500 feet, pausing for breath every minute or two. The only foothold was in narrow cracks or on minute projections on the granite. To get a toe in these cracks, or here and there on a scarcely obvious projection, while crawling on hands and knees, all the while tortured with thirst and gasping and struggling for breath, this was the climb; but at last the Peak was won. A grand, well-defined mountain-top it is, a nearly level acre of boulders, with precipitous sides all round, the one we came up being the only accessible one.

It was not possible to remain long. One of the young men was seriously alarmed by bleeding from the lungs, and the intense dryness of the day and the rarefaction of the air, at a height of nearly 15,000 feet, made respiration very painful. There is always water on the Peak, but it was frozen as hard as a rock, and the sucking of ice and snow increases thirst. We all suffered severely from the want of water, and the gasping for breath made our mouths and tongues so dry that articulation was difficult, and the speech of all unnatural.

From the summit were seen in unrivalled combination all the views which had rejoiced our eyes during the ascent. It was something at last to stand upon the storm-rent crown of this lonely sentinel of the Rocky Range, on one of the mightiest of the vertebrae of the backbone of the North American continent, and to see the waters start for both oceans. Uplifted above love and hate and storms of passion, calm amidst the eternal silences, fanned by zephyrs and bathed in living blue, peace rested for that one bright day on the Peak, as if it were some region

Where falls not rain, or hail, or any snow,
Or ever wind blows loudly.

We placed our names, with the date of ascent, in a tin within a crevice, and descended to the Ledge, sitting on the smooth granite, getting our feet into cracks and against projections, and letting ourselves down by our hands, 'Jim' going before me, so that I might steady my feet against his powerful shoulders. I was no longer giddy, and faced the precipice of 3500 feet without a shiver. Repassing the Ledge and Lift, we accomplished the descent through 1500 feet of ice and snow, with many falls and bruises, but no worse mishap, and there separated, the young men taking the steepest but most direct way to the Notch, with the intention of getting ready for the march home, and 'Jim' and I taking what he thought the safer route for me – a descent over boulders for 2000 feet, and then a tremendous ascent to the 'Notch'. I had various falls, and once hung by my frock, which caught on a rock, and 'Jim' severed it with his hunting-knife, upon which I fell into a crevice full of soft snow. We were driven lower down the mountains than he had intended by impassable tracts of ice, and the ascent was tremendous. For the last 200 feet the boulders were of enormous size, and the steepness fearful. Sometimes I drew myself up on hands and knees, sometimes crawled; sometimes 'Jim' pulled me up by my arms or a lariat, and sometimes I stood on his shoulders, or he made steps for me of his feet and hands, but at six we stood on the Notch in the splendour of the sinking sun, all colour deepening, all peaks glorifying, all shadows purpling, all peril past.

'Jim' had parted with his *brusquerie* when we parted from the students, and was gentle and considerate beyond anything, though I knew that he must be grievously disappointed, both in my courage and strength. Water was an object of earnest desire. My tongue rattled in my mouth, and I could hardly articulate. It is good for one's sympathies to have for once a severe experience of thirst. Truly, there was

Water, water, everywhere,
But not a drop to drink.

Three times its apparent gleam deceived even the mountaineer's practised eye, but we found only a foot of 'glare ice'. At last, in a deep hole, he succeeded in breaking the ice, and by putting one's arm far down one could scoop up a little

* Let no practical mountaineer be allured by my description into the ascent of Long's Peak. Truly terrible as it was to me, to a member of the Alpine Club it would not be a feat worth performing.

'...I would not now exchange my memories of its perfect beauty and extraordinary sublimity for any other experience of mountaineering in any part of the world.'

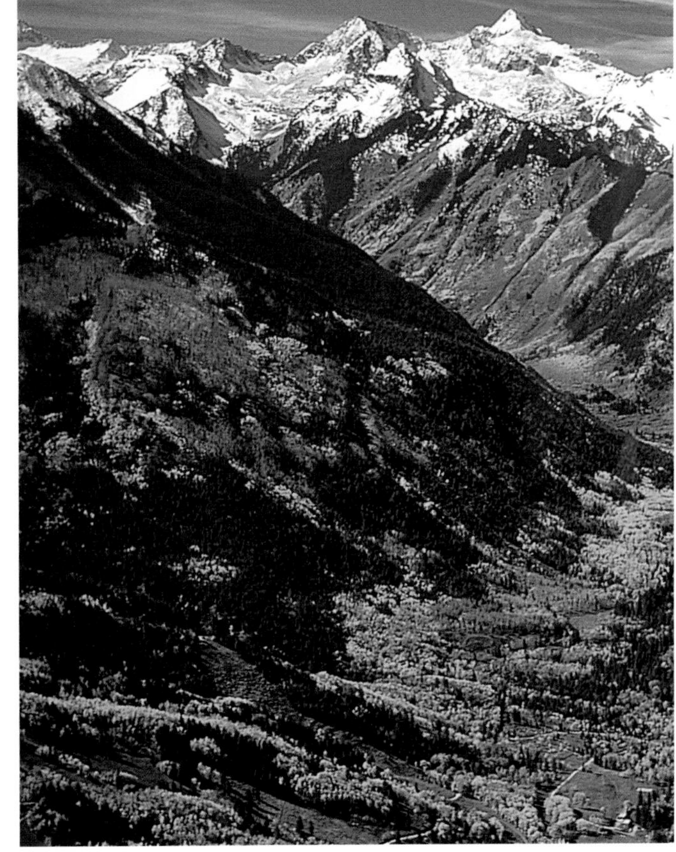

water in one's hand, but it was tormentingly insufficient. With great difficulty and much assistance I recrossed the 'Lava Beds', was carried to the horse and lifted upon him, and when we reached the camping ground I was lifted off him, and laid on the ground wrapped up in blankets, a humiliating termination of a great exploit. The horses were saddled, and the young men were all ready to start, but 'Jim' quietly said, 'Now, gentlemen, I want a good night's rest, and we shan't stir from here to-night.' I believe they were really glad to have it so, as one of them was quite 'finished'. I retired to my arbour, wrapped myself in a roll of blankets, and was soon asleep. When I woke, the moon was high shining through the silvery branches, whitening the bald Peak above, and glittering on the great abyss of snow behind, and pine logs were blazing like a bonfire in the cold still air. My feet were so icy cold that I could not sleep again, and getting some blankets to sit in, and making a roll of them for my back, I sat for two hours by the camp fire. It was weird and gloriously beautiful. The students were asleep not far off in their blankets with their feet towards the fire. 'Ring' lay on one side of me with his fine head on my arm, and his master sat smoking, with the fire lighting up the handsome side of his face, and except for the tones of our voices, and an occasional crackle and splutter as a pine knot blazed up, there was no sound on the mountain side. The beloved stars of my far-off home were overhead, the Plough and Pole Star, with their steady light; the glittering Pleiades, looking larger than I ever saw them, and 'Orion's studded belt' shining gloriously. Once only some wild animals prowled near the camp, when 'Ring', with one bound, disappeared from my side; and the horses, which were picketed by the stream, broke their lariats, stampeded, and came rushing wildly towards the fire, and it was fully half an hour before they were caught and quiet was restored. 'Jim', or Mr. Nugent, as I always scrupulously called him, told stories of his early youth, and of a great sorrow which had led him to embark on a lawless and desperate life. His voice trembled, and tears rolled down his cheek. Was it semi-conscious acting, I wondered, or was his dark soul really stirred to its depths by the silence, the beauty, and the memories of youth?

We reached Estes Park at noon of the following day. A more successful ascent of the Peak was never made, and I would not now exchange my memories of its perfect beauty and extraordinary sublimity for any other experience of mountaineering in any part of the world. Yesterday snow fell on the summit, and it will be inaccessible for eight months to come.

Isabelle Eberhardt

(1877–1904)

When Isabelle Eberhardt travelled through North Africa, as a Muslim convert and dressed as a man, she moved within an Arab world that was shifting from its colonial attachments to national consciousness and independence. But Eberhardt (who called herself Si Mahmoud) took no interest in these events. Written at the turn of the century, Eberhardt's diary is a journey into the self, a meditation that explores the psyche rather than the countryside. A daughter of an aristocratic family from Geneva, Eberhardt made two trips to North Africa. In the first she became enchanted with the exotic life-styles, the freedom from the strictures of home and family obligations. Home again in Geneva, she spurned her responsibilities, even left to return to North Africa without waiting a few weeks for a substantial inheritance. A nervous, conflicted woman, she spent her meagre resources on drugs and became a homeless addict who begged food. The diary is written during her final months alive and reflects her life as an outcast from two very different worlds: the expatriate European society in the Arab states which would not accept her after her conversion to Islam and the Arab society where posing as a man barred her from formal contact with women. Eberhardt died at twenty-eight in a flash flood at Ain Sefra.

from The Passionate Nomad

Batna, 26 April 11 P.M.

I am feeling depressed tonight in a way I cannot define. I feel lonely without Ouïha, and cannot stand the boredom. Yesterday's storm has left Batna inundated, dark and freezing, and it is full of mud and filthy gutters. My poor Souf is very ill, so that I cannot even go for my strolls along the open road, or up to that desolate graveyard where damaged tombs, terrifying windows upon the spectacle of human dust, lie scattered among the fragrant tufts of grey chih near a green meadow full of purple flax, white anemones and scarlet poppies in full bloom.

The other day I wandered around among a crowd of Muslims brandishing the flags of ancient religious ceremonial occasions; to the accompaniment of tambours and flutes they prayed for rain, for an extension of their fleeting Algerian spring which already, in its haste to move on, is blending summer flowers with those of spring.

After six long days of only seeing Rouh for brief and furtive moments by the gate of the hated barracks where he is quartered, he came to see me yesterday. . . . I held him in my arms and after the first wild, almost savage embrace, tears ran down our cheeks, and each of us felt a very mysterious fear, even though neither of us had said a word or knew why.

I realised yesterday once again how honest and beautiful is my Slimène's soul, because of his joy that Augustin was making up with me and was doing justice to us both. In spite of my past, present and future misfortunes I bless God and my destiny for having brought me to this desert and given me to this man, who is my *only solace*, my only reason for happiness in this whole world.

I have often been hard on him and unfair, I have been impatient for no good reason, so insane as to hit him, although secretly ashamed because he did not strike back but merely smiled at my blind rage. Afterwards I always feel truly miserable and disgusted with myself for the injustice I might have committed.

This afternoon I went to see the police official who is without a doubt an enemy spy in charge of keeping an eye on me. *He* was the first to come out with the theory that P was the one who had wanted me killed, and that the murderer was bound to go scotfree. If so, that means I am doomed to die anywhere I go in the South, which is the only place where we can live.

If the crime committed at Behima is only slightly punished or not at all, that will amount to a clear signal to the Tidjanyas: 'Go ahead and kill Si Mahmoud, you have nothing to fear.'

Yet God did stay the assassin's hand once, and Abdallah's sabre was deflected. If God wants me to die a martyr, God's will is bound to find me wherever I am. If not, the plots of all those who conspire against me will be their undoing.

I am not afraid of death, but would not want to die in some obscure or pointless way. Having seen death close up, and having felt the brush of its black and icy wings, I know that its proximity means instant renunciation of the things of this world. I also know that my nerves and willpower will hold out in times of great personal ordeals, and that I will never give my enemies the satisfaction of seeing me run in cowardice or fear.

Yet, as I think of the future, there is one thing that does frighten me: misfortunes that might befall Slimène or Augustin. Faced with those, I would have no strength whatsoever. It would be hard to imagine worse poverty than the kind I am up against right now: yet the only reason it worries me is that our debts stand to spell disaster for Slimène.

Fortunately, my enemies think I am rich. I was right to spend money the way I did two years ago, here and in Biskra, for a reputation of wealth is just as useful for our defence as actual wealth would have been. Oh, if those rascals were to know that I am utterly destitute and that the slightest humiliation could be my undoing, they would not hesitate for a moment!

It is obvious that they are afraid. Otherwise they would arrest me as a spy, or expel me.

I was right to account for the wretched way I live down here as mere eccentricity: that way, it is not too obvious that I am in fact destitute.

I have begun to make a point of going to people's houses to *eat*, for the sole purpose of keeping fit, something that would have been *anathema* in the old days, like the other thing I have been doing lately, namely going to see marabouts, just to beg them for money.

I must have an iron constitution, for my health is holding up contrary to all expectation: those frightening last days in El Oued, the injury, the shock to the nervous system and the haemorrhage in Behima, the hospital, the journey, half of which I made on foot, my poverty here, the cold and the poor diet, which mostly consists of bread, none of that has got me down. How long will I be able to hold out?

How can one explain the fact that at home, where I had warm clothes, an outstandingly healthy diet, and Mummy's idolatrous care, the slightest chill I caught would degenerate into bronchitis; whereas here, having suffered freezing temperatures at El Oued, and at the hospital as well, having travelled in all kinds of weather, while literally always getting wet feet, going around in thin clothes and torn shoes, I don't even catch a cold?

The human body is nothing, the human soul is all.

Why do I adore Rouh's eyes so? Not for their shape or colour, but for the sweet and guileless radiance in their expression, which is what makes them beautiful.

The way I see it, there is no greater spiritual beauty than fanaticism, of a sort so sincere it can only end in martyrdom.

'I was right to account for the wretched way I live down here as mere eccentricity: that way, it is not too obvious that I am in fact destitute.'

Lady Mary Anne Barker
(1831–1911)

'It really was like walking down the side of a house,' Mary Barker writes about descending a steep cliff in *Station Life in New Zealand*. In part thanks to her wry wit, Lady Mary Anne Barker managed to stake out territory few other women could claim: experiences toe-to-toe with men in distant colonial outposts. In 1865, when Barker's husband sailed to New Zealand to establish a sheep farm near Christchurch, she began writing about her activities – sheepshearing and bush trekking – and earned popularity among women readers at home in England. After leaving New Zealand in 1868, her husband was appointed colonial secretary in Natal and then Mauritius, governor of Western Australia and finally of Trinidad. Barker, a hardy, jolly example of the Spirit of the Empire, wrote three additional travel books and a memoir.

from Station Life in New Zealand

We had finished breakfast by seven o'clock the following morning, and were ready to start. Of course the gentlemen were very fussy about their equipments, and hung themselves all over with cartridges and bags of bullets and powder-flasks; then they had to take care that their tobacco-pouches and match-boxes were filled; and lastly, each carried a little flask of brandy or sherry, in case of being lost and having to camp out. I felt quite unconcerned, having only *my* flask with cold tea in it to see about, and a good walking-stick was easily chosen. My costume may be described as uncompromising, for it had been explained to me that there were no paths but real rough bush walking; so I dispensed with all little feminine adornments even to the dearly-loved chignon, tucked my hair away as if I was going to put on a bathing-cap, and covered it with a Scotch bonnet. The rest of my toilette must have been equally shocking to the eyes of taste, and I have reason to believe the general effect most hideous; but one great comfort was, no one looked at me, they were all too much absorbed in preparations for a great slaughter, and I only came at all upon sufferance; the unexpressed but prevailing dread, I could plainly see, was that I should knock up and become a bore, necessitating an early return home; but I knew better!

An American waggon and some ponies were waiting to take the whole party to the entrance of the bush, about four miles off, and, in spite of having to cross a rough river-bed, which is always a slow process, it did not take us very long to reach our first point. Here we dismounted, just at the edge of the great dense forest, and, with as little delay as possible in fine arrangements, struck into a path or bullock-track, made for about three miles into the bush for the convenience of dragging out the felled trees by ropes or chains attached to bullocks; they are not placed upon a waggon, so you may easily imagine the state the track was in, ploughed up by huge logs of timber dragged *on* the ground, and by the bullocks' hoofs besides. It was a mere slough with deep holes of mud in it, and we scrambled along its extreme edge, chiefly trusting to the trees on each side, which still lay as they had been felled, the men not considering them good enough to remove. At last we came to a clearing, and I quite despair of making you understand how romantic and lovely this open space in the midst of the tall trees looked that beautiful spring morning. I involuntarily thought of the descriptions in 'Paul and Virginia', for the luxuriance of the growth was quite tropical. For about two acres the trees had been nearly all felled, only one or two giants remaining; their stumps were already hidden by clematis and wild creepers of other kinds, or by a sort of fern very like the hart's-tongue, which will only grow on the bark of trees, and its glossy leaves made an exquisite contrast to the rough old root. The 'bushmen' – as the men who have bought twenty-acre sections and settled in the bush are called – had scattered English grass-seed all over the rich leafy mould, and the ground was covered with bright green grass, kept short and thick by a few tame goats browsing about. Before us was the steep bank of the river Waimakiriri, and a few yards from its edge stood a picturesque gable-ended little cottage surrounded by a rustic fence, which enclosed a strip of garden gay with common English spring flowers, besides more useful things, potatoes, &c. The river was about two hundred yards broad just here, and though it foamed below us, we could also see it stretching away in the distance almost like a lake, till a great bluff hid it from our eyes. Overhead the trees were alive with flocks of wild pigeons, ka-kas, parroquets, and other birds, chattering and twittering incessantly; and as we stood on the steep bank and looked down, I don't think a minute passed without a brace of wild ducks flying past – grey, blue, and Paradise. These latter are the most beautiful plumaged birds I ever saw belonging to the duck tribe, and, when young, are very good eating, quite as delicate as the famous canvas-back. This sight so excited our younger sportsmen that they scrambled down the high precipice, followed by a water-spaniel, and in five minutes had bagged as many brace. We could not give them any more time, for it was past nine o'clock, and we were all eager to start on the serious business of the day; but before we left, the mistress of this charming 'bush-hut' insisted on our having some hot coffee and scones and wild honey, a most delicious second breakfast. There was a pretty little girl growing up, and a younger child, both the picture of health; the only drawback seemed to be the mosquitoes; it was not very lonely, for one or two other huts stood in clearings adjoining, and furnished us with three bushmen as guides and assistants. I must say, they were the most picturesque of the party, being all handsome men, dressed in red flannel shirts and leathern knickerbockers and gaiters; they had fine beards, and wore 'diggers' hats,' a head-dress of American origin – a sort of wide-awake made of plush, capable of being crushed into any shape, and very becoming. All were armed with either rifle or gun, and one carried an axe and a coil of rope; another had a gun such as is seldom seen out of an arsenal; it was an old flint lock, but had been altered to a percussion; its owner was very proud of it, not so much for its intrinsic beauty, though it once had been a costly and splendid weapon and was elaborately inlaid with mother-of-pearl, but because it had belonged to a former Duke of Devonshire. In spite of its claims to consideration on this head as well as its own beauty, we all eyed it with extreme disfavour on account of a peculiarity it possessed of not going off when it was intended to do so, but about five minutes afterwards.

It was suggested to me very politely that I might possibly prefer to remain behind and spend the day in this picturesque spot, but this offer I declined steadily; I think the bushmen objected to my presence more than any one else, as they really meant work, and dreaded having to turn back for a tired 'female' (they never spoke of me by any other term). At last all the information was collected about the probable whereabouts of the wild cattle – it was so contradictory, that it must have been difficult to arrange any plan by it – and we started. A few hundred yards took us past the clearings and into the very heart of the forest. We had left the sun shining brightly overhead; here it was all a 'great green gloom'. I must describe to you the order in which we marched. First came two of the most experienced 'bush-hands', who carried a tomahawk or light axe with which to clear the most cruel of the brambles away, and to notch the trees as a guide to us on our return; and also a compass, for we had to steer for a certain point, the bearings of which we knew – of course the procession was in Indian file: next to these pioneers walked, very cautiously, almost on tiptoe, four of our sportsmen; then I came; and four or five others, less keen or less well armed, brought up the rear. I may here confess that I endured in silence agonies of apprehension for my personal safety all day. It was so dreadful to see a bramble or wild creeper catch in the lock of the rifle before me, and to reflect that, unless its owner was very careful, it might 'go off of its own accord', and to know that I was exposed to a similar danger from those behind.

We soon got on the fresh tracks of some cows, and proceeded most cautiously and silently; but it could hardly be called walking, it was alternately pushing through dense undergrowth, crawling beneath, or climbing over, high barricades made by fallen trees. These latter obstacles I found the most difficult, for the bark was so slippery; and once, when with much difficulty I had scrambled up a pile of *débris* at least ten feet high, I incautiously stepped on some rotten wood at the top, and went through it into a sort of deep pit, out of which it was very hard to climb. On comparing notes afterwards, we found, that although we had walked without a moment's cessation for eleven hours during the day, a pedometer only gave twenty-two miles as the distance accomplished. Before we had been in the bush half an hour our faces were terribly scratched and bleeding, and so were the gentlemen's hands; my wrists also suffered, as my gauntlets would not do their duty and lie flat. There were myriads of birds around us, all perfectly tame; many flew from twig to twig, accompanying us with their little pert heads on one side full of curiosity; the only animals we saw were some wild sheep looking very disreputable with their long tails and torn, trailing fleeces of six or seven years' growth. There are supposed to be some hundreds of these in the bush who have strayed into it years ago, when they were lambs, from neighbouring runs. The last man in the silent procession put a match into a dead tree every here and there, to serve as a torch to guide us back in the dark; but this required great judgment for fear of setting the whole forest on fire: the tree required to be full of damp decay, which would only smoulder and not blaze. We intended to steer for a station on the other side of a narrow neck of the Great Bush, ten miles off, as nearly as we could guess, but we made many *détours* after fresh tracks. Once these hoof-marks led us to the brink of such a pretty creek, exactly like a Scotch burn, wide and noisy, tumbling down from rock to rock, but not very deep. After a whispered consultation, it was determined to follow up this creek to a well-known favourite drinking-place of the cattle, but it was easier walking in the water than on the densely-grown banks, so all the gentlemen stepped in one after another. I hesitated a moment with one's usual cat-like antipathy to wet feet, when a stalwart bushman approached, with rather a victimised air and the remark: 'Ye're heavy, nae doot, to carry'. I was partly affronted at this prejudgment of the case, and partly determined to show that I was equal to the emergency, for I immediately jumped into the water, frightening myself a good deal by the tremendous splash I made, and meeting reproving glances; and nine heads were shaken violently at me.

Nothing could be more beautiful than the winding banks of this creek, fringed with large ferns in endless variety; it was delightful to see the sun and sky once more overhead, but I cannot say that it was the easiest possible walking, and I soon found out that the cleverest thing to do was to wade a little way behind the shortest gentleman of the party, for when *he* disappeared in a hole I knew it in time to avoid a similar fate; whereas, as long as I persisted in stalking solemnly after my own tall natural protector, I found that I was always getting into difficulties in unexpectedly deep places. I saw the bushmen whispering together, and examining the rocks in some places, but I found on inquiry that their thoughts were occupied at the moment by other ideas than sport; one of them had been a digger, and was pronouncing an opinion that this creek was very likely to prove a 'home of the gold' some day. There is a strong feeling prevalent that gold will be found in great quantities all over the island. At this time of the year the water is very shallow, but the stream evidently comes down with tremendous force in the winter; and they talk of having 'found *the* colour' (of gold) in some places. We proceeded in this way for about three miles, till we reached a beautiful, clear, deep pool, into which the water fell from a height in a little cascade; the banks here were well trodden, and the hoof-prints quite recent; great excitement was caused by hearing a distant lowing, but after much listening, in true Indian fashion, with the ear to the ground, everybody was of a different opinion as to the side from whence the sound proceeded, so we determined to keep on our original course; the compass was once more produced, and we struck into a dense wood of black birch.

Ever since we left the clearing from which the start was made, we had turned our backs on the river, but about three o'clock in the afternoon we came suddenly on it again, and stood on the most beautiful spot I ever saw in my life. We were on the top of a high precipice, densely wooded to the water's edge. Some explorers in bygone days must have camped here, for half-a-dozen trees were felled, and the thick brush-wood had been burnt for a few yards, just enough to let us take in the magnificent view before and around us. Below roared and foamed, among great boulders washed down from the cliff, the Waimakiriri; in the middle of it lay a long narrow strip of white shingle, covered with water in the winter floods, but now shining like snow in the bright sunlight. Beyond this the river flowed as placidly as a lake, in cool green depths, reflecting every leaf of the forest on the high bank or cliff opposite. To our right it stretched away, with round headlands covered with timber running down in soft curves to the water. But on our left was the most perfect composition for a picture: in the foreground a great reach of smooth water, except just under the bank we stood on, where the current was strong and rapid; a little sparkling beach, and a vast forest rising up from its narrow border, extending over chain after chain of hills, till they rose to the glacial region, and then the splendid peaks of the snowy range broke the deep blue sky line with their grand outlines.

All this beauty would have been almost too oppressive, it was on such a large scale and the solitude was so intense, if it had not been for the pretty little touch of life and movement afforded by the hut belonging to the station we were bound for. It was only a rough building, made of slabs of wood with cob between; but there was a bit of fence and the corner of a garden and an English grass paddock, which looked about as big as a pocket-handkerchief from where we stood. A horse or two and a couple of cows were tethered near, and we could hear the bark of a dog. A more complete hermitage could not have been desired by Diogenes himself, and for the first time we felt ashamed of invading the recluse in such a formidable body, but ungrudging, open-handed hospitality is so universal in New Zealand that we took courage and began our descent. It really was like walking down the side of a house. And no one could stir a step without at least one arm round a tree. I had no gun to carry, so I clung frantically with both arms to each stem in succession. The steepness of the cliff was the reason we could take in all the beauty of the scene before us, for the forest was as thick as ever; but we could see over the tops of the trees, as the ground dropped sheer down, almost in a straight line from the plateau we had been travelling on all day. As soon as we reached the shingle, on which we had to walk for a few hundred yards, we bethought ourselves of our toilettes; the needle and thread I had brought did good service in making us more presentable. We discovered, however, that our faces were a perfect network of fine scratches, some of which *would* go on bleeding, in spite of cold-water applications. Our boots were nearly dry; and my petticoat, short as it was, proved to be the only damp garment: this was the fault of my first jump into the water. We put the least scratched and most respectable-looking member of the party in the van, and followed him, amid much barking of dogs, to the low porch; and after hearing a cheery 'Come in', answering our modest tap at the door, we trooped in one after the other till the little room was quite full. I never saw such astonishment on any human face as on that of the poor master of the house, who could not stir from his chair by the fire, on account of a bad wound in his leg from an axe. There he sat quite helpless, a moment ago so solitary, and now finding himself the centre of a large, odd-looking crowd of strangers. He was a middle-aged Scotchman, probably of not a very elevated position in life, and had passed many years in this lonely spot, and yet he showed himself quite equal to the occasion.

After that first uncontrollable look of amazement he did the honours of his poor hut with the utmost courtesy and true good-breeding. His only apology was for being unable to rise from his arm-chair (made out of half a barrel and an old flour-sack by the way); he made us perfectly welcome, took it for granted we were hungry – hunger is a very mild word to express *my* appetite, for one – called by a loud coo-ée to his man Sandy, to whom he gave orders that the best in the house should be put before us, and then began to inquire by what road we had come, what sport we had, &c., all in the nicest way possible. I never felt more awkward in my life than when I stooped to enter that low doorway, and yet in a minute I was quite at my ease again; but of the whole party I was naturally the one who puzzled him the most. In the first place, I strongly suspect that he had doubts as to my being anything but a boy in a rather long kilt; and when this point was explained, he could not understand what a 'female', as he also called me, was doing on a rough hunting expedition. He particularly inquired more than once if I had come of my own free will, and could not understand what pleasure I found in walking so far. Indeed he took it so completely for granted that I must be exhausted, that he immediately began to make plans for F— and me to stop there all night, offering to give up his 'bunk' (some slabs of wood made into a shelf, with a tussock mattress and a blanket), and to sleep himself in his arm-chair.

In the meantime, Sandy was preparing our meal. There was an open hearth with a fine fire, and a big black kettle hanging over it by a hook fastened somewhere up the chimney. As soon as this boiled he went to a chest, or rather locker, and brought a double-handful of tea, which he threw into the kettle; then he took from a cupboard the biggest loaf of bread I ever saw – a huge thing, which had been baked in a camp oven – and flapped it down on the table with a bang; next he produced a tin milk-pan, and returned to the cupboard to fetch out by the shank-bone a mutton-ham, which he placed in the milk-dish: a bottle of capital whisky was forthcoming from the same place; a little salt on one newspaper, and brown, or rather *black*, sugar on another, completed the arrangements, and we were politely told by Sandy to 'wire in' – digger's phraseology for an invitation to commence – which we did immediately, as soon as we could make an arrangement about the four tin plates and three pannikins. I had one all to myself, but the others managed by twos and threes to each plate. I never had a better luncheon in my life; everything was excellent in its way, and we all possessed what we are told is the best sauce. Large as the supplies were, we left hardly anything, and the more we devoured the more pleased our host seemed. There were no chairs; we sat on logs of trees rudely chopped into something like horse-blocks, but to tired limbs which had known no rest from six hours' walking they seemed delightful. After we had finished our meal, the gentlemen went outside to have half a pipe before setting off again; they dared not smoke whilst we were after the cattle, for fear of their perceiving some unusual smell; and I remained for ten minutes with Mr. — I found that he was very fond of reading; his few books were all of a good stamp, but he was terribly hard-up for anything which he had not read a hundred times over. I hastily ran over the names of some books of my own, which I offered to lend him for as long a time as he liked: and we made elaborate plans for sending them, of my share in which I took a memorandum. He seemed very grateful at the prospect of having anything new, especially now that he was likely to be laid up for some weeks, and I intend to make every effort to give him this great pleasure as soon as possible.

We exchanged the most hearty farewells when the time of parting came, and our host was most earnest in his entreaties to us to remain; but it was a question of getting out of the bush before dusk, so we could not delay. He sent Sandy to guide us by a rather longer but easier way than climbing up the steep cliff to the place where the little clearing at its edge which I have mentioned had been made; and we dismissed our guide quite happy with contributions from all the tobacco-pouches, for no one had any money with him. We found our way back again by the notches on the trees as long as the light lasted, and when it got too dark to see them easily, the smouldering trunks guided us, and we reached the clearing from which we started in perfect safety. Good Mrs. D—had a bountiful tea ready; she was much concerned at our having yet some three miles of bad walking before we could reach the hut on the outskirts of the bush, where we had left the trap and the ponies. When we got to this point there was actually another and still more sumptuous meal set out for us, to which, alas! we were unable to do any justice; and then we found our way to the station across the flat, down a steep cutting, and through the river-bed, all in the dark and cold. We had supper as soon as we reached home, tumbling into bed as early as might be afterwards for such a sleep as you Londoners don't know anything about.

'...I strongly suspect that he had doubts as to my being anything but a boy in a rather long kilt; and when this point was explained, he could not understand what a "female", as he also called me, was doing on a rough hunting expedition.'

I have only described one expedition to you, and that the most unsuccessful, as far as killing anything goes; but my hunting instincts only lead me to the point of *reaching* the game; when it comes to that, I always try to save its life, and if this can't be done, I retire to a distance and stop my ears; indeed, if very much over-excited, I can't help crying. Consequently, I enjoy myself much more when we don't kill anything; and, on the other occasions, I never could stop and see even the shot fired which was to bring a fine cow or a dear little calf down, but crept away as far as ever I could, and muffled my head in my jacket. The bushmen liked this part of the performance the best, I believe, and acted as butchers very readily, taking home a large joint each to their huts, a welcome change after the eternal pigeons, ka-kas, and wild ducks on which they live.

Ethel Brilliana Tweedie

(ca. 1860–1940)

FEW WOMEN WRITERS IN EDWARDIAN ENGLAND TRAVELLED IN THE WAY ETHEL TWEEDIE DID. AFTER HER FATHER, HUSBAND, AND BOTH SONS WERE KILLED, SHE THREW HERSELF INTO FAR-FLUNG TOURS OF THE WORLD. AMONG THE TITLES OF HER TEN TRAVEL BOOKS ARE *THROUGH FINLAND IN CARTS* AND *MEXICO AS I SAW IT*. SHE WROTE ABOUT EVERYTHING FROM ETIQUETTE TO ANTI-COMMUNISM. LATER IN LIFE SHE PUBLISHED THE BOOK *MY TABLE-CLOTHS: A FEW REMINISCENCES*. BUT TWEEDIE'S INGENUOUS, RIGHTEOUS MANNER FORESTALLED PARODY; SHE PERSONIFIED THE AXIOM THAT THERE ARE NO DULL SUBJECTS, ONLY DULL WRITERS. IN HER FIRST TRAVEL BOOK, *A GIRL'S RIDE IN ICELAND*, TWEEDIE CHALLENGED THE HABIT OF WOMEN RIDING SIDE-SADDLE AND BECAME AN INFLUENTIAL ADVOCATE FOR MAKING RIDING ASTRIDE SOCIALLY ACCEPTABLE FOR WOMEN.

from **A Girl's Ride in Iceland**

When this little volume (my maiden effort) was published five years ago, it unwittingly originated an angry controversy by raising the question 'Should women ride astride?'

It is astonishing what a great fire a mere spark may kindle, and accordingly the war, on what proved to be a very vexed subject, waged fast and furious. The picture papers inserted cleverly-illustrated articles *pro* and *con*; the peace of families was temporarily wrecked – for people were of course divided in their opinions – and bitter things were said by both sides concerning a very simple and harmless matter. For a time it seemed as though the 'Ayes' would win; but eventually appearances carried the day, and women still use side-saddles when on horseback, though the knickerbockers and short skirts (only far shorter) I advocated for rough country riding are now constantly worn by the many female equestrians who within the last couple of years have mounted bicycles.

It is nearly four years since, from an hotel window in Copenhagen, I saw, to my great surprise, for the first time a woman astride a bicycle! How strange it seemed! Paris quickly followed suit, and now there is a perfect army of women bicyclists in that fair capital; after a decent show of hesitation England dropped her prejudices, and at the present minute, almost without a murmur, allows her daughters, clad in unnecessarily masculine costume, to scour the country in quest of fresh air astride a bicycle.

If women may ride an iron steed thus attired, surely they might be permitted to bestride a horse in like manner clothed in like fashion.

My own experience as to comfort will be found in the following pages, and I can only add that greater knowledge has strengthened that opinion. When discussing the subject with Sir John Williams – one of the greatest authorities on the diseases of women – he said, 'I do not see that any harm could arise from women riding like men. Far from it. I cannot, indeed, conceive why the side-saddle was ever invented at all.' What more could be urged in favour of cross riding?

Saudárkrók was to witness a new experiment in our mounting arrangements. On arrival, intending riding into the interior as usual, we applied at the only inn in the place for ponies, when to our discomfiture we learnt no such thing as a lady's side-saddle was to be obtained. The innkeeper and our party held a long consultation as to what was to be done, during which the inhabitants of the place gathered round us in full force, apparently much interested in our proceedings.

At last one of the lookers-on disappeared, and presently returned in triumph with a chair-saddle, which he had unearthed from some remote corner where it had probably lain, judging by its appearance, since the Middle Ages. This was assigned to Miss T. No second one, however, was obtainable, and I had to choose between remaining behind or overcoming the difficulty of riding lady-fashion on a man's saddle. My determination was quickly taken, and much to the amusement of our party, up I mounted, the whole village stolidly watching the proceeding, whilst the absence of a pommel contributed considerably to the difficulty I had in keeping my seat.

Off we started, headed by our guide, and as long as the pony walked I felt very comfortable without a pommel, so much so that I ventured to try a trot, when round went the saddle and off I slipped. Vaughan came to my rescue, and after readjusting the saddle, and tightening the girths, I remounted, but only with the same result. How was I to get along at this rate?

I had often read that it was the custom for women in South America, Albania, &c., who have to accomplish long distances on horseback, to ride man fashion. Indeed, women rode so in England, until side-saddles were introduced by Anne of Bohemia, wife of Richard II, and many continued to ride across the saddle until even a later date. In Iceland I had seen women ride as men, and felt more convinced than ever that this mode was safer and less fatiguing. Although I had ridden all my life, the roughness of the Icelandic roads and ponies made ladywise on a man's saddle impossible, and the sharpness of the pony's back, riding with no saddle, equally so. There was no alternative: I must either turn back, or mount as a man. Necessity gives courage in emergencies. I determined therefore to throw aside conventionality, and do in 'Iceland as the Icelanders do'. Keeping my brother at my side, and bidding the rest to ride forward, I made him shorten the stirrups, and hold the saddle, and after sundry attempts, succeeded in landing myself man fashion on the animal's back. The position felt very odd at first, and I was also somewhat uncomfortable at my attitude, but on Vaughan's assuring me there was no cause for my uneasiness, and arranging my dress so that it fell in folds on either side, I decided to give the experiment a fair trial, and in a very short time got quite accustomed to the position, and trotted along merrily. Cantering was at first a little more difficult, but I persevered, and in a couple of hours was quite at home in my new position, and could trot, pace, or canter alike, without any fear of an upset. The amusement of our party when I overtook them, and boldly trotted past, was intense; but I felt so comfortable in my altered seat that their derisive and chaffing remarks failed to disturb me. Perhaps my boldness may rather surprise my readers; but after full experience, under most unfavourable circumstances, I venture to put on paper the result of my experiment.

Riding man-fashion is less tiring than on a side-saddle, and I soon found it far more agreeable, especially when traversing rough ground. My success soon inspired Miss T. to summon up courage and follow my lead. She had been nearly shaken to pieces in her chair pannier, besides having only obtained a one-sided view of the country through which she rode; and we both returned from a twenty-five mile ride without feeling tired, whilst from that day till we left the island we adopted no other mode of travelling, I am quite sure had we allowed conventional scruples to interfere, we should never have accomplished in three days and a half the 160 miles' ride to the Geysers, which was our ultimate achievement.

I may here mention our riding costume. We had procured very simply made thick blue serge dresses before leaving home, anticipating rough travelling. The skirts being full and loose, hung well down on each side when riding, like a habit on the off and near sides, and we flattered ourselves that, on the whole, we looked both picturesque and practical. Our very long waterproof boots (reaching above the knee) proved a great comfort when fording rivers, which in an Iceland ride must be crossed every few miles, sometimes oftener. For the rest we wore ordinary riding attire.

The crooked position on a side-saddle – for one must sit crooked to look straight – is very fatiguing to a weak back, and many women to whom the exercise would otherwise prove of the greatest benefit cannot stand the strain: so this healthy mode of exercise is debarred them, because Society says they must not ride like men. Society is a hard taskmaster. Nothing is easier than to stick on a side-saddle, of course, and nothing more difficult than to ride on one gracefully.

For comfort and safety, I say, ride like a man. If you have not courage to do this, when visiting Iceland take your own side-saddle and bridle (for a pony), as, except in Reykjavik, horse furniture is of the most miserable description, and the constant breakages cause many delays, while there are actually no side-saddles, except in the capital, and a chair is an instrument of torture not to be recommended even to your worst enemy.

In past times women have ridden in every possible position, and in every conceivable costume. They have ridden sideways on both the near and off sides, they have ridden astride (as the Mexicans, Indians, Tartars, Roumanians, Icelanders, &c., do to-day), and they have also ridden pillion. Queen Elizabeth rode thus behind the Earl of Leicester on public occasions, in a full hoop skirt, low-necked bodice, and large ruff. Nevertheless, she dispensed with a cavalier when out hawking at the ripe age of seventy-six.

When hunting, hawking, or at tournaments, women during the Middle Ages always rode astride in this country, reserving their side-saddles merely for State functions. Judging from old pictures, they then mounted, arrayed in full ball dresses, in long-veiled headdresses (time of Edward II), and in flowing skirts, while their heads were often ornamented with huge plumed hats.

Formerly, every church door, every roadside inn, had its horse block or 'jumping-on stone' – called in Kent and some other southern counties the 'joust stone', and in Scotland the 'louping-on stane'. These were necessary in the olden days of heavy armour, and at a time when women rode astride. Men can now mount alone, although the struggles of a small man to climb to the top of a big horse are sometimes mightily entertaining; but women have to trust to any capable or incapable man who can assist them into their saddles.

Fashion is ephemeral. Taste and public opinion, having no corporal identity, are nothing but the passing fancy of a given generation.

Dress to a woman should always be an important matter, and to be well dressed it is necessary to be suitably clothed. Of course breeches, high boots or leggings are essential in riding; but a neatly arranged divided skirt, reaching well below the knee, can be worn over these articles, and the effect produced is anything but inelegant. Of one thing we may be certain – namely, that whenever English women summon up enough courage to ride their horses man fashion again, every London tailor will immediately set himself to design becoming and useful divided skirts for the purpose.

I strongly advocate the abolition of the side-saddle for the country, hunting, or rough journeys, for three reasons – 1st, safety; 2nd, comfort; 3rd, health.

I. Of course nothing is easier under ordinary circumstances than to 'stick on' a side-saddle, because the pommels almost hold one there: wherein lies much danger. In the case of a horse falling, for instance, a woman (although doubtless helped by the tight skirts of the day) cannot extricate herself. She is caught in the pommels or entangled by the stirrup, both of which calamities mean dragging, and often result in a horrible death.

II. Miss Bird, in her famous book of travels, tells us how terribly her back suffered from hard riding on a side-saddle, and how easily she accomplished the same distances when, disregarding conventionalities, she adopted a man's seat.

The wife of a well-known Consul-General, who, in company with her husband, rode in a similar fashion from Shanghai to St. Petersburg through Siberia, always declared such a feat would have been impossible for her to have achieved on a side-saddle. Further, the native women of almost all countries ride astride to this day, as they did in England in the fourteenth century.

III. Cross-riding doubtless has been considered injurious to health by a few members of the medical profession, but the majority, and notably the highest authorities, hold a different opinion.

Are we not all aware that many girls become crooked when learning to ride, and have to mount on the off side in order to counteract the mischief. Is this not proof in itself of how unnatural the position must be?

As women ride at the present moment, horses with sore backs are unfortunately no rarity. It is true that these galls are caused by bad riding; still, such things would be avoided with a man's saddle, which is far lighter than a woman's, and easier to carry, because the rider's weight is not on one side, but equally distributed – a great comfort to a horse's loins and withers.

We know that a woman's horse is far sooner knocked up with a hard day than one ridden by a man, although the man is probably the heavier weight of the two, and this merely because he is properly balanced.

Therefore, ye women travellers, before starting on long and fatiguing expeditions, lay these facts to heart, and remember cross-riding is no novelty; our female ancestors all mounted that way, and all native women who ride for business and not for pleasure sit astride. My own personal experience only endorses its advisability and practicability.

Anna Leonowens

(1834–1914)

In 1945 Margaret Landon won immediate acclaim when her book, *Anna and the King of Siam*, based on Anna Leonowens's memoirs, became an overnight best-seller. The musical, starring Gertrude Lawrence, and film, starring Deborah Kerr as Anna and Yul Brynner reprising his stage role Rama IV of Siam, followed. But few know the book that began it all. As the following excerpt demonstrates, Leonowens was a marvellous storyteller, conveying emotional truths of the royal children, wives, and slaves of the King's harem with a rare compassion. Unlike many other writers of her time, Leonowens was personally involved in the lives of the people around her. In poor health, Leonowens left the king and his court in 1867 and, after publishing two accounts of her life there, failed to encourage theatrical interest in her story, despite her confidence in its dramatic appeal. She spent her final years in Montreal but continued to correspond regularly with many of her former students.

from The English Governess at the Siamese Court

Shadows and Whispers of the Harem

As, month after month, I continued to teach in the palace – especially as the language of my pupils, its idioms and characteristic forms of expression, began to be familiar to me – all the dim life of the place 'came out' to my ken, like a faint picture, which at first displays to the eye only a formless confusion, a chaos of colours, but by force of much looking and tracing and joining and separating, first objects and then groups are discovered in their proper identity and relation, until the whole stands out, clear, true, and informing in its coherent significance of light and shade. Thus, by slow processes, as one whose sight has been imperceptibly restored, I awoke to a clearer and truer sense of the life within 'the city of the beautiful and invincible angel'.

Sitting at one end of the table in my school-room, with Boy at the other, and all those far-off faces between, I felt as though we were twenty thousand miles away from the world that lay but a twenty minutes' walk from the door; the distance was but a speck in space, but the separation was tremendous. It always seemed to me that here was a sudden, harsh suspension of nature's fundamental law – the human heart arrested in its functions, ceasing to throb, and yet alive.

The fields beyond are fresh and green, and bright with flowers. The sun of summer, rising exultant, greets them with rejoicing; and evening shadows, falling soft among the dewy petals, linger to kiss them good-night. There the children of the poor – naked, rude, neglected though they be – are rich in the freedom of the bounteous earth, rich in the freedom of the fair blue sky, rich in the freedom of the limpid ocean of air above and around them. But within the close and gloomy lanes of this city within a city, through which many lovely women are wont to come and go, many little feet to patter, and many baby citizens to be borne in the arms of their dodging slaves, there is but cloud and chill, and famishing and stinting, and beating of wings against golden bars. In the order of nature, evening melts softly into night, and darkness retreats with dignity and grace before the advancing triumphs of the morning; but here light and darkness are monstrously mixed, and the result is a glaring gloom that is neither of the day nor of the night, nor of life nor of death, nor of earth nor of – yes, hell!

In the long galleries and corridors, bewildering with their everlasting twilight of the eye and of the mind, one is forever coming upon shocks of sudden sunshine or shocks of sudden

'How I have pitied those ill-fated sisters of mine, imprisoned without a crime! If they could but have rejoiced once more in the freedom of the fields and woods, what new births of gladness might have been theirs…'

shadow – the smile yet dimpling in a baby's face, a sister bearing a brother's scourging; a mother singing to her 'sacred infant,' a slave sobbing before a deaf idol. And O, the forlornness of it all! You who have never beheld these things know not the utterness of loneliness. Compared with the predicament of some who were my daily companions, the sea were a home and an iceberg a hearth.

How I have pitied those ill-fated sisters of mine, imprisoned without a crime! If they could but have rejoiced once more in the freedom of the fields and woods, what new births of gladness might have been theirs – they who with a gasp of despair and moral death first entered those royal dungeons, never again to come forth alive! And yet have I known more than one among them who accepted her fate with a repose of manner and a sweetness of smile that told how dead must be the heart under that still exterior. And I wondered at the sight. Only twenty minutes between bondage and freedom – such freedom as may be found in Siam! only twenty minutes between those gloomy, hateful cells and the fair fields and the radiant skies! only twenty minutes between the cramping and the suffocation and the fear, and the full, deep, glorious inspirations of freedom and safety!

I had never beheld misery till I found it here; I had never looked upon the sickening hideousness of slavery till I encountered its features here; nor, above all, had I comprehended the perfection of the life, light, blessedness and beauty, the all-sufficing fulness of the love of God as it is in Jesus, until I felt the contrast here – pain, deformity, darkness, death, and eternal emptiness, a darkness to which there is neither beginning nor end, a living which is neither of this world nor of the next. The misery which checks the pulse and thrills the heart with pity in one's common walks about the great cities of Europe is hardly so saddening as the nameless, mocking wretchedness of these women, to whom poverty were a luxury, and houselessness as a draught of pure, free air.

And yet their lot is light indeed compared with that of their children. The single aim of such a hapless mother, howsoever tender and devoted she may by nature be, is to form her child after the one strict pattern her fate has set her – her master's will; since, otherwise, she dare not contemplate the perils which might overtake her treasure. Pitiful indeed, therefore, is the pitiless inflexibility of purpose with which she wings from her child's heart all the dangerous endearments of childhood – its merry laughter, its sparkling tears, its trustfulness, its artlessness, its engaging waywardness; and in their place instils silence, submission, self-constraint, suspicion, cunning, carefulness, and an ever-vigilant fear. And the result is a spectacle of unnatural discipline simply appalling. The life of such a child is an egg-shell on an ocean; to its helpless speck of experience all horrors are possible. Its passing moment is its eternity; and that overwhelmed with terrors, real or imaginary, what is left but that poor little floating wreck, a child's despair?

I was often alone in the school-room, long after my other charges had departed, with a pale, dejected woman, whose name translated was 'Hidden-Perfume'. As a pupil she was remarkably diligent and attentive, and in reading and translating English her progress was extraordinary. Only in her eager, inquisitive glances was she childlike; otherwise, her expression and demeanour were anxious and aged. She had long been out of favour with her 'lord'; and now, without hope from him, surrendered herself wholly to her fondness for a son she had borne him in her more youthful and attractive days. In this young prince, who was about ten years old, the same air of timidity and restraint was apparent as in his mother, whom he strikingly resembled, only lacking that cast of pensive sadness which rendered her so attractive, and her pride, which closed her lips upon the past, though the story of her wrongs was a moving one.

It was my habit to visit her twice a week at her residence,* for I was indebted to her for much intelligent assistance in my study of the Siamese language. On going to her abode one afternoon, I found her absent; only the young prince was there, sitting sadly by the window.

'Where is your mother, dear?' I inquired.

'With his Majesty upstairs, I think,' he replied, still looking anxiously in one direction, as though watching for her.

This was an unusual circumstance for my sad, lonely friend, and I returned home without my lesson for that day.

Next morning, passing the house again, I saw the lad sitting in the same attitude at the window, his eyes bent in the same direction, only more wistful and weary than before. On questioning him, I found his mother had not yet returned. At the pavilion I was met by the Lady Tâlâp, who, seizing my hand, said, 'Hidden-Perfume is in trouble.'

'What is the matter?' I inquired.

'She is in prison,' she whispered, drawing me closely to her. 'She is not prudent, you know – like you and me,' in a tone which expressed both triumph and fear.

'Can I see her?' I asked.

'Yes, yes! if you bribe the jailers. But don't give them more than a tical each. They'll demand two; give them only one.'

In the pavilion, which served as a private chapel for the ladies of the harem, priests were reading prayers and reciting homilies from the sacred book of Buddha called *Sâsânâh Thai*, 'The Religion of the Free'; while the ladies sat on velvet cushions with their hands folded, a vase of flowers in front of each, and a pair of odoriferous candles, lighted. Prayers are held daily in this place, and three times a day during the Buddhist Lent. The priests are escorted to the pavilion by Amazons, and two warriors, armed with swords and clubs, remain on guard till the service is ended. The latter, who are eunuchs, also attend the priests when they enter the palace, in the afternoon, to sprinkle the inmates with consecrated water.

Leaving the priests reciting and chanting, and the rapt worshippers bowing, I passed a young mother with a sleeping babe, some slave-girls playing at *sabâh*** on the stone pavement, and two princesses borne in the arms of their slaves, though almost women grown, on my way to the palace prison.

If it ever should be the reader's fortune, good or ill, to visit a Siamese dungeon, whether allotted to prince or peasant, his attention will be first attracted to the rude designs on the rough stone walls (otherwise decorated only with moss and fungi and loathsome reptiles) of some nightmared painter, who has exhausted his dyspeptic fancy in portraying hideous personifications of Hunger, Terror, Old Age, Despair, Disease, and Death, tormented by furies and avengers, with hair of snakes and whips of scorpions – all beyond expression devilish. Floor it has none, nor ceiling, for, with the Meinam so near, neither boards nor plaster can keep out the ooze. Underfoot, a few planks, loosely laid, are already as soft as the mud they are meant to cover; the damp has rotted them through and through. Overhead, the roof is black, but not with smoke; for here, where the close steam of the soggy earth and the reeking walls is almost intolerable, no fire is needed in the coldest season. The cell is lighted by one small window, so heavily grated on the outer side as effectually to bar the ingress of fresh air. A pair of wooden trestles, supporting rough boards, form a makeshift for a bedstead, and a mat (which may be clean or dirty, the ticals of the prisoner must settle that) is all the bed.

In such a cell, on such a couch, lay the concubine of a supreme king and the mother of a royal prince of Siam, her feet covered with a silk mantle, her head supported by a pillow of glazed leather, her face turned to the clammy wall.

There was no door to grate upon her quivering nerves; a trap-door in the street overhead had opened to the magic of silver, and I had descended a flight of broken steps of stone. At her head, a little higher than the pillow, were a vase of flowers, half faded, a pair of candles burning in gold candlesticks, and a small image of the Buddha. She had brought her god with her. Well, she needed his presence.

I could hardly keep my feet, for the footing was slippery and my brain swam. Touching the silent, motionless form, in a

* Each of the ladies of the harem has her own exclusive domicile, within the inner walls of the palace.

** Marbles, played with the knee instead of the fingers.

voice scarcely audible I pronounced her name. She turned with difficulty, and a slight sound of clanking explained the covering on her feet. She was chained to one of the trestles.

Sitting up, she made room for me beside her. No tears were in her eyes; only the habitual sadness of her face was deepened. Here, truly, was a perfect work of misery, meekness, and patience.

Astonished at seeing me, she imagined me capable of yet greater things, and folding her hands in an attitude of supplication, implored me to help her. The offence for which she was imprisoned was briefly this:

She had been led to petition, through her son,* that an appointment held by her late uncle, Phya Khien, might be bestowed on her elder brother, not knowing that another noble had already been preferred to the post by his Majesty.

Had she been guilty of the gravest crime, her punishment could not have been more severe. It was plain that a stupid grudge was at the bottom of this cruel business. The king, on reading the petition, presented by the trembling lad on his knees, became furious, and, dashing it back into the child's face, accused the mother of plotting to undermine his power, saying he knew her to be at heart a rebel, who hated him and his dynasty with all the rancour of her Peguan ancestors, the natural enemies of Siam. Thus lashing himself into a rage of hypocritical patriotism, and seeking to justify himself by condemning her, he sent one of his judges to bring her to him. But before the myrmidon could go and come, concluding to dispense with forms, he anticipated the result of that mandate with another – to chain and imprison her. No sooner was she dragged to this deadly cell, than a third order was issued to flog her till she confessed her treacherous plot; but the stripes were administered so tenderly,** that the only confession they extorted was a meek protestation that she was 'his meanest slave, and ready to give her life for his pleasure'.

'Beat her on the mouth with a slipper for lying!' roared the royal tiger; and they did, in the letter, if not in the spirit, of the brutal sentence. She bore it meekly, hanging down her head. 'I am degraded forever!' she said to me.

When once the king was enraged, there was nothing to be done but to wait in patience until the storm should exhaust itself by its own fury. But it was horrible to witness such an abuse of power at the hands of one who was the only source of justice in the land. It was a crime against all humanity, the outrage of the strong upon the helpless. His madness sometimes lasted a week; but weeks have their endings. Besides, he really had a conscience, tough and shrunken as it was; and she had, what was more to the purpose, a whole tribe of powerful connections.

As for myself, there was but one thing I could do; and that was to intercede privately with the Kralahome. The same evening, immediately on returning from my visit to the dungeon, I called on him; but when I explained the object of my visit he rebuked me sharply for interfering between his Majesty and his wives.

'She is my pupil,' I replied. 'But I have not interfered; I have only come to you for justice. She did not know of the appointment until she had sent in her petition; and to punish one woman for that which is permitted and encouraged in another is gross injustice.' Thereupon he sent for his secretary, and having satisfied himself that the appointment had not been published, was good enough to promise that he would explain to his Majesty that 'there had been delay in making known to the Court the royal pleasure in this matter'; but he spoke with indifference, as if thinking of something else.

I felt chilled and hurt as I left the premier's palace, and more anxious than ever when I thought of the weary eyes of the lonely lad watching for his mother's return; for no one dared tell him the truth. But, to do the premier justice, he was more troubled than he would permit me to discover at the mistake the poor woman had made; for there was good stuff in the moral fabric of the man – stern rectitude, and a judgment unlike the king's, not warped by passion. That very night† he repaired to the Grand Palace, and explained the delay to the king, without appearing to be aware of the concubine's punishment.

On Monday morning, when I came to school in the pavilion, I found, to my great joy, that Hidden-Perfume had been liberated, and was at home again with her child. The poor creature embraced me ardently, glorifying me with grateful epithets from the extravagant vocabulary of her people; and,

* A privilege granted to all the concubines.

** In these cases the executioners are women, who generally spare each other if they dare.

† All consultations on matters of state and of court discipline are held in the royal palace at night.

taking an emerald ring from her finger, she put it upon mine, saying, 'By this you will remember your thankful friend.'

On the following day she also sent me a small purse of gold thread netted, in which were a few Siamese coins, and a scrap of paper inscribed with cabalistic characters – an infallible charm to preserve the wearer from poverty and distress.

Among my pupils was a little girl about eight or nine years old, of delicate frame, and with the low voice and subdued manner of one who had already had experience of sorrow. She was not among those presented to me at the opening of the school. Wanne Ratâna Kania was her name ('Sweet Promise of my Hopes'), and very engaging and persuasive was she in her patient, timid loveliness. Her mother, the Lady Khoon Chom Kioa, who had once found favour with the king, had, at the time of my coming to the palace, fallen into disgrace by reason of her gambling, in which she had squandered all the patrimony of the little princess. This fact, instead of inspiring the royal father with pity for his child, seemed to attract to her all that was most cruel in his insane temper. The offence of the mother had made the daughter offensive in his sight; and it was not until long after the term of imprisonment of the degraded favourite had expired that Wanne ventured to appear at a royal *levée*. The moment the king caught sight of the little form, so piteously prostrated there, he drove her rudely from his presence, taunting her with the delinquencies of her mother with a coarseness that would have been cruel enough if she had been responsible for them and a gainer by them, but against one of her tender years, innocent toward both, and injured by both, it was inconceivably atrocious.

On her first appearance at school she was so timid and wistful that I felt constrained to notice and encourage her more than those whom I had already with me. But I found this no easy part to play; for very soon one of the court ladies in the confidence of the king took me quietly aside and warned me to be less demonstrative in favour of the little princess, saying, 'Surely you would not bring trouble upon that wounded lamb.'

It was a sore trial to me to witness the oppression of one so unoffending and so helpless. Yet our Wanne was neither thin nor pale. There was a freshness in her childish beauty, and a bloom in the transparent olive of her cheek, that were at times bewitching. She loved her father, and in her visions of baby faith beheld him almost as a god. It was true joy to her to fold her hands and bow before the chamber where he slept. With that steadfast hopefulness of childhood which can be deceived without being discouraged, she would say, 'How glad he will be when I can read!' and yet she had known nothing but despair.

Her memory was extraordinary; she delighted in all that was remarkable, and with careful wisdom gathered up facts and precepts and saved them for future use. She seemed to have built around her an invisible temple of her own design, and to have illuminated it with the rushlight of her childish love. Among the books she read to me, rendering it from English into Siamese, was one called *Spring-time*. On translating the line, 'Whom He loveth he chasteneth', she looked up in my face, and asked anxiously: 'Does thy God do that? Ah! lady, are *all* the gods angry and cruel? Has he no pity, even for those who love him? He must be like my father; *he* loves us, so he has to be *rye* (cruel), that we may fear evil and avoid it.'

Meanwhile little Wanne learned to spell, read, and translate almost intuitively; for there were novelty and hope to help the Buddhist child, and love to help the English woman. The sad look left her face, her life had found an interest; and very often, on *fête* days, she was my only pupil; when suddenly an ominous cloud obscured the sky of her transient gladness.

Wanne was poor; and her gifts to me were of the riches of poverty – fruits and flowers. But she owned some female slaves; and one among them, a woman of twenty-five perhaps (who had already made a place for herself in my regard), seemed devotedly attached to her youthful mistress, and not only attended her to the school day after day, but shared her scholarly enthusiasm, even studied with her, sitting at her feet by the table. Steadily the slave kept pace with the princess. All that Wanne learned at school in the day was lovingly taught to Mai Noie in the nursery at night; and it was not long before I found, to my astonishment, that the slave read and translated as correctly as her mistress.

Very delightful were the demonstrations of attachment interchanged between these two. Mai Noie bore the child in her arms to and from the school, fed her, humoured her every whim, fanned her naps, bathed and perfumed her every night, and then rocked her to sleep on her careful bosom, as tenderly as she would have done for her own baby. And then it was charming to watch the child's face kindle with love and comfort as the sound of her friend's step approached.

‘She seemed to have built around her an invisible temple of her own design, and to have illuminated it with the rushlight of her childish love.’

Suddenly a change; the little princess came to school as usual, but a strange woman attended her, and I saw no more of Mai Noie there. The child grew so listless and wretched that I was forced to ask the cause of her darling's absence; she burst into a passion of tears, but replied not a word. Then I inquired of the stranger, and she answered in two syllables – *My ru* (‘I know not’).

Shortly afterward, as I entered the school-room one day, I perceived that something unusual was happening. I turned toward the princes' door, and stood still, fairly holding my breath. There was the king, furious, striding up and down. All the female judges of the palace were present, and a crowd of mothers and royal children. On all the steps around, innumerable slave-women, old and young, crouched and hid their faces.

But the object most conspicuous was little Wanne's mother manacled, and prostrate on the polished marble pavement. There, too, was my poor little princess, her hands clasped helplessly, her eyes tearless but downcast, palpitating, trembling, shivering. Sorrow and horror had transformed the child.

As well as I could understand, where no one dared explain, the wretched woman had been gambling again, and had even staked and lost her daughter's slaves. At last I understood Wanne's silence when I asked her where Mai Noie was. By some means – spies probably – the whole matter had come to the king's ears, and his rage was wild, not because he loved the child, but that he hated the mother.

Promptly the order was given to lash the woman; and two Amazons advanced to execute it. The first stripe was delivered with savage skill; but before the thing could descend again, the child sprang forward and flung herself across the bare and quivering back of her mother.

Ti chan, Tha Moom! Poot-thoo ti chan, Tha Mom!* (‘Strike *me*, my father! Pray, strike me, O my father!’)

The pause of fear that followed was only broken by my boy, who, with a convulsive cry, buried his face desperately in the folds of my skirt.

There indeed was a case for prayer, *any* prayer! – the prostrate woman, the hesitating lash, the tearless anguish of the Siamese child, the heart-rending cry of the English child, all those mothers with grovelling brows, but hearts uplifted among the stars, on the wings of the Angel of Prayer. Who could behold so many women crouching, shuddering, stupefied, dismayed, in silence and darkness, animated, enlightened only by the deep whispering heart of maternity, and not be moved with mournful yearning?

The child's prayer was vain. As demons tremble in the presence of a god, so the king comprehended that he had now to deal with a power of weakness, pity, beauty, courage, and eloquence. ‘Strike *me*, O my father!’ His quick, clear sagacity measured instantly all the danger in that challenge; and though his voice was thick and agitated (for, monster as he was at that moment, he could not but shrink from striking at every mother's heart at his feet), he nervously gave the word to remove the child, and bind her. The united strength of several women was not more than enough to loose the clasp of those loving arms from the neck of an unworthy mother. The tender hands and feet were bound, and the tender heart was broken. The lash descended then, unforbidden by any cry.

* *Tha Mom* or *Moom*, used by children in addressing a royal father.

Margaret Fountaine

(1862–1940)

'Signorina, I would so much like to see your butterflies,' the ardent suitor says. Fountaine ranks as a resounding favourite among people who admire the lady travellers. In the lives of most women travellers, husbands and fathers played minor roles if they weren't obstacles to overcome: Mary Kingsley never married and waited until her father died before she began travelling; Isabella Bird married late in life and (luckily for her wandering self) her husband died soon after; Anna Leonowens was widowed eight years after her marriage. But Margaret Fountaine was inspired by a love of men. In diaries that she began in 1878, her seventeenth year, Fountaine told of her travels to Europe, North and South America, Africa, Asia, Australia, and New Zealand in search of butterflies. And of the men she met along the way. For twenty-three years Fountaine wrote of her travels in this way, and then she met Khalil Neimy in Damascus. The two of them travelled together until he died in 1929. When Fountaine died she left instructions that her diaries not be opened until April 15, 1978, a hundred years after they were begun.

from Love Among the Butterflies

When I arrived at Palermo, though it was scarcely more than 4 A.M. the sun was up, and had already left the mountains golden. Oh, that I were there now! I never spent one dull moment when I was at Palermo. I will not endure the loneliness I have known in the past ever again, and I was determined wherever I was to make friends with all who I met. My first step was to hunt up Signor Ragusa, a well-known Sicilian entomologist; he was the proprietor of the Grand Hotel des Palmes, so I lost no time in repairing thither. The information he gave me was most valuable, for *M. Pherusa*, the butterfly I most wished to find, was, I knew, like all butterflies of that genus, most local in its habits; it was therefore a grand point for me to hear the precise locality for it, at the foot of Monte Cuccio, about five miles from Palermo.

I would drive to Bocco di Falco, a straggling dirty village, full of hens and goats, and spend the long hours of those sweet summer days hunting the *Pherusa*, a wild, wind-blown creature who would often lead me a long and arduous chase over the loose stones and tangled herbage, to escape in the end, but they were so common in this one spot that to lose sight of one was soon to see another, so I always returned home with a crowded pocket box. Then I would spend my time setting them in my bedroom at the Hotel de France, till it was nearly dinner time, when I would go down, always trying to make myself agreeable to anyone I happened to be sitting next, probably to find myself the only woman at the table with some fifteen to twenty men.

So the long, happy, sunny days went by and I loved each one as it passed, though I will not say I altogether cared for the attention I attracted when I walked along the Corso in butterfly attire – net, knap-sack and all complete. But all the same, every empty 'carrozza' seemed to think I was sufficiently respectable, the sponge man never failed to solicit my custom, and the beggars seemed to consider me a person of means. Another time when I would be dressed to my best advantage, going along the same Corso for shopping or what not, I would wonder however I dared to make my appearance in butterfly attire among so many smartly dressed people.

'...I went up to my room not without some misgivings but knowing that I had a head on my shoulders and ought, at my age, to be able to take care of myself.'

A new epoch was beginning in my life which I attributed almost entirely to my having discovered a new and very becoming way of doing my hair! (A foolish reason, but Uncle Edward always used to say, the difference between a pretty woman and an ugly one was the way she did her hair.) The very first day I walked out (not, however, in butterfly attire) with this new fashion adopted, I was followed and finally joined by three Palermo youths, who afterwards on their own evidence I found belonged to the fastest set in the town. I spent the morning with them, and pleasantly enough too; we all went together to see the view from Santa Maria di Jesu, a walk some way out into the country, along dusty white roads, hot enough for anything. Then I and these boys (for they really were only boys, compared with the weight of years *I* carried on my shoulders!) sat down in a lemon garden, and drank lemon water, and ate the white skins of the lemons, a fourth having joined the party, an indescribably comical youth who evidently considered that he was my champion, and as I had no objection to having the flowers etc. carried for me, I graciously accepted his attentions.

He did not come the whole way back to Palermo, but with much importance explained that he was obliged to return to look after his peasants who, he said, would be lazy without his supervision. But before he went, he had persuaded me to say (rather against my better judgement) that I would go to the theatre that evening with him and his companions.

Now, there was staying in the hotel a tall Italian with a dark beard, who had shown me some little civilities, such as lending me his Baedeker. This man spoke English extremely well, and as I had rather suspected him of taking a slight interest in me, I resolved to relate to him at dinner my adventures of the morning and ask his opinion about the discretion of my going to the theatre. He listened with some interest, and only said: 'Very kind of them.'

'So you advise me to go?' I asked.

'If you think you would care to go to the theatre this evening, yes, by all means, but will you not come out with me?'

'How can I, if I am going with them?' I innocently enquired. So it was left so, and I went up to my room not without some misgivings but knowing that I had a head on my shoulders and ought, at my age, to be able to take care of myself. I had not been there long when a knock came at the door. 'Avanti!' I said at once, thinking it was the waiter come to announce the arrival of my knights below, but only another knock came, so I opened the door.

Two figures were standing outside in the dim light in the passage. They neither of them spoke, so I stepped out, and having moved into a better light, soon recognised the comical youth, and one of his friends. They seemed slightly embarrassed at their own boldness, and I didn't wonder at it. However, they recovered their composure and said they had come to inform me that tonight it was a 'Riposo' at the theatre, but if I would like a walk they were at my disposition. It was a hot, dark summer's night, and we walked along the Marina, down by the sea, and talked gaily enough. The comical youth said he did not wish me to think of him as 'comico' but rather as 'simpatico'. Of course, I soon saw the bent of his inclinations, and was wondering how I should parry the blow, when it came in this wise: 'Signorina, a che ora va a' letto?' (What time do you go to bed?) I replied early, adding, and up early in the morning. This voluntary, additional information put him off his stroke for a moment, but only for a moment. I knew an improper proposition was coming, and soon enough out it came. 'Signorina, when you go to bed, do you go to sleep quickly?' I replied that I always did go to sleep very quickly and pretended not to understand his meaning.

Nothing daunted, the comical youth returned to the charge; 'Signorina,' he began somewhat plaintively, 'I would so much like to see your butterflies.'

I gave my consent and said he might see them tomorrow, as they looked prettier in the day time. This was a poser, for a moment, and then he persisted in saying that to *him* they would look prettier at night. And then I followed the idea, he evidently conjectured that to see my butterflies would entail a visit to my bedroom, but as I did not intend to have my virgin room invaded by him or anybody else, I said, 'Very well, so you shall see them, and if you and your friend like to go and wait in the Salon, I will bring them down and show them to you.' This was one too many for him; he was quite disconcerted at last. I wished them both goodnight just inside the hotel, and never again did I set eyes on the comical youth and his companions.

The tall Italian, with the dark beard, was more attentive than ever the next day, begging hard that I would not decide to leave for Syracuse, so soon as the following Saturday. But I was obdurate. The more he wished me to stay, the more for that very reason alone, if for no other, did I intend to go. However, when he took it almost as a matter of course that I should go out with him that evening, I raised no objections, and the next day we spent the long afternoon in the Villa Belmonte, a wild, rambling garden, half cultivated, half left to run to ruin. It came on to rain, a soft, warm saturating rain, which made me feel I was in England, as I heard the rain-drops dripping on the leaves, and smelt the sweet scent. But he never forced himself upon me as others might have done, through those long hours we spent alone together, for he was a high-bred gentleman, though I did not then know that he was a baron.

[Next morning, despite the Baron's pleas, Miss Fountaine left Palermo for Girgenti ('the ruined temples are very famous but I do not care for antiquities'), Syracuse ('a flat uninteresting place') and Taormina ('I was half wishing myself back in Palermo – ah, where would the men be if it wasn't for the vanity of women?'). There she set out, with Pancrazio, the son of the hotel keeper, as a guide.]

We had not gone very far on our way before he began to tell me how, from the first moment he had seen me, he had thought that I was 'si jolie, si blanche'. He had never seen anyone 'si blanche' before, and so on. I must do him the justice to say that his eloquence, especially in a language that was not his own, quite astonished me. He told me how each time he had seen me, he had found that I was 'encore plus jolie qu'il avait pensé', and how he had become more and more 'amoureux' in consequence. I said I was sure that in a few days he would begin to feel much better, and though he insisted his feelings would be unchanged 'always, always', I laughed, refusing to believe he meant what he was saying.

All this time we were slowly wending our way up Monte Venere. No wonder these southern natures are quick and passionate when every scene around them is such sensuous loveliness! A world of blue and tideless seas, and gleaming, sunny shores – blue the atmosphere, blue the glittering sea far below, blue the distant mountains on the shores of Italy, and I laughed from sheer delight at the scene beneath my feet. Not so my companion; miserable and dejected, he saw not the loveliness around us, his dark eyes fixed their gaze upon *me*! We had now nearly reached the summit of the mountain, I had a fall, and cut my knee – a punishment, my companion said it was, for having been so unkind to him. So I sat down to rest on some rocks, while he sat at my feet, and we sighed in unison, for in truth I now pitied him – he was still telling me the same story that man has told to woman since creation, pleading in accents that were almost irresistible, but what was I to do? I could not so lower myself as to allow the son of an hotel proprietor to kiss me!

I was glad enough when this conversation was interrupted by two men approaching, and one of them, apparently a German tourist, raising his hat, began speaking to me in English (he probably recognized me by my butterfly net), saying he was the bearer of a message to me from an Italian gentleman with a dark beard at Palermo, evidently the Baron, and even at that moment, I felt gratified to find that he had not yet forgotten me.

In the meantime the morning had clouded over, and soon heavy rain began to fall; my red sunshade was utterly useless against such a torrent and we both soon became drenched to the skin. At last we reached a cottage, and I was given into the charge of a peasant woman, who lighted a stove of hot ashes, and having taken off some of my things to dry them, lent me one of her own dresses to wear in the meantime. Then Pancrazio came in, and I sat warming and drying myself over the stove, chatting with the peasants, and rather enjoying the novelty of the situation. My companion had no thought except for me, and that his own jacket had never been dried at all he didn't even seem to notice. Before leaving we each wrote something in a sort of visitors' book (for this cottage was evidently a constant refuge for strangers), and Pancrazio said that by and by when I should have gone away from Taormina, he would come up here alone and read over and over again what we had written together. But I need hardly say that I made no more expeditions with Pancrazio as my companion.

At Messina the Crinacria was a large commercial hotel, full of nothing but men as usual, and though I had really tried to be as unnoticeable as the circumstances would admit of, I soon knew well enough that I *was* noticed, very appreciably too, by more than one of them. I found myself at dinner sitting next a newcomer, who was certainly possessed of a person to advantage, and who was not troubled with bashfulness or reserve. He spoke French with great fluency, so we talked and laughed together all dinner time (much to the apparent chagrin of a gentleman opposite who himself had cast admiring glances at me but had never yet spoken), so that I forgot all my resolutions of being more reserved, and when he suggested that we should go out for a stroll after dinner, I readily assented. As it was Sunday the band was playing in the Piazza Municipale, and I felt proud of the man on whose arm I leant, for he was tall and well-favoured, with an audacity which in a man never fails to inveigle itself into the good graces of a woman. I readily received his compliments and pretty speeches, yet I felt an inward misgiving, for I knew well enough what this was leading up to, nor was it long in coming.

When I returned to the hotel, what was I going to do, he asked, looking hard into my face. I pretended not to notice. 'I believe I am going to bed right away,' I replied – an answer he seemed well satisfied with. After a moment's pause, however, he went on to say: 'And I – what am I going to do?' To which I promptly answered, laughing, that he must do as he pleased. This put him off his stroke for a minute, but he soon began again, this time going straight to the point. He hoped that we could complete our relationship, and that I would permit him to come to my room. I felt subdued and rather unhappy as I answered that I didn't do that sort of thing. Had I never tried it, he asked, apparently with some surprise. 'Then you'll have to try tonight with me!' But I only repeated as before 'Je ne fais pas ça' and hoped that this would end the matter.

We now left the brilliantly lighted Piazza, walking up a street, and then down on to the Marina. What a night it was, the vast infinite heavens above us studded with myriads of worlds. What more was he asking than what was justly due to the nature God had given him?

My hand trembled in his grasp, and yet I would not have had him loosen it for one moment. But he never knew as I gazed out over the gleaming waters, towards the dark Calabrian mountains, so cold and impassive as I stood beside him, so decidedly had I declined to go out with him in a boat, or drive in a carriage – he never knew how nearly he had conquered.

We shook hands, and wished each other goodnight just inside the Hotel, I purposely wishing the porters etc. to see that our relation ended there. But had it ended there?

I thought so, but evidently he thought differently. I had been upstairs in my room about half an hour, and was in my nightgown, almost ready to get into bed, when I distinctly heard a knock at the door. I took no notice, but soon another knock came, and then someone spoke in a loud whisper, his

'Perhaps if I had not known that this man was not really the least in love with me I might have yielded to him; as it was, a certain pride made me still determined to snub him all I could.'

voice trembling, I suppose with excitement. I thought of the prayer I had said with my Mother far away in England on the eve of my departure. What would her feelings be if she could see me now? At last he said, 'Mlle, is your door closed?'

'Yes,' I said in a stern voice. He tried it, and the lock was none so secure either. When he asked again, 'Mlle are you going to open the door?' I replied shortly that I wasn't, and that when he was tired he could go. Soon afterwards I heard his retreating footsteps.

The day after this I was sitting in a small public garden near the Crinacria when I saw my companion of last night coming towards me. He addressed me just as though nothing had happened. I vouchsafed no reply whatever. He asked if I were angry with him, and began all sorts of explanations. My momentary anger had quite melted away and had he but known it I was smiling in spite of myself under my sunshade. Having received a reply in the affirmative to his question if I found his society but little agreeable, he walked off. The moment he was gone I could not help feeling sorry I had sent him so abruptly away.

However, there was the dinner that evening at the hotel, when I supposed I should again sit next him – rather embarrassing too that would be, after what had just passed. It's an ill wind that blows nobody any good, and the gentleman opposite looked relieved, as well as somewhat surprised, when he saw me come in and take my place without a single sign of recognition passing between me and the man with whom only the previous evening I had been so intimate. But his joy was of short duration: in a large mirror opposite I and my friend on the left could see each other quite plainly all the time, and though I managed successfully to withstand the close scrutiny he would occasionally turn round and bestow upon me, the effect of us peeping at each other through the mirror upset my gravity at last, I relaxed into a smile, and he saw his advantage in a moment. He had not gained quite so much as he chose to fancy, for I declined to go out with him again that evening, but peace was proclaimed, and our poor vis-à-vis discomforted.

When I retired, on the landing at the foot of the last flight of stairs leading up to my room I saw in the dim light a tall figure waiting. I would have passed him by, but he detained me to entreat me again to come out with him, if only for five minutes.

I was quite infatuated by this man, and I might never have such a lover as he was again, but I was obdurate. 'Well, you are a woman of spirit. Come with me again this evening, only for a little while,' he said. He asked if I was annoyed because he had come to my room last night, and I said I was. 'But you said yourself that I could come,' he replied and he repeated my very words: 'You can come if you like but you will find the door locked,' which alas was true enough, so he had me there, but I still persisted, saying I was really too tired.

And so I left him, angry enough, I dare say. Perhaps if I had not known that this man was not really the least in love with me I might have yielded to him; as it was, a certain pride made me still determined to snub him all I could. So when I passed him by, just inside the hotel the next morning, I only just acknowledged his salutation, hurrying past with a shrug of the shoulders, pretending not to see that he advanced to speak with me. I doubt if being snubbed like this before the porters added to the charm of it, and I never saw him again, though sometimes I found myself wishing he would come back. . . .

Before I came to Sicily, I had through the kindness of Uncle Lawes received letters of introduction from an Italian in London, through which I had already made the acquaintance of Signor Vitale (a co-leopterist), who one day brought to see me a young Italian, who it seemed was prepared to be my knight in attendance on all occasions. Many, many happy hours we spent together, roving over the hills round Messina, beneath a glorious sky, with the same pursuit in view, for he, like me, had 'una vera passione per le farfalle,' and indeed the very butterflies themselves were not more light-hearted than we. Almost like two children together, I and this dark-eyed youth would chase the glorious *Charaxes Iasius*, which occurred quite commonly on the arbutus-covered slopes of Gravitelli, quarrelling and disputing sometimes in hot discussions, while the music of the beautiful language in which we always conversed would add power and grace to our words. Then we would sit down and eat our luncheon beneath the shade of an olive tree, and it would seem as though the whole of nature's world, the flowers, the sunshine and the butterflies, were only made and created for us two, as we sat or lounged. And though it is a very pleasant thing to have a lover, and consequently a somewhat unpleasant thing to have lost one, I soon began to find that a good long day out butterflying with Signor Amenta, making several good catches, went a good way towards healing the wound. A regular 'butterfly companion', ready to comply with my every whim and to give me all he caught, was not an advantage to be met with every day. True, if I went back to Palermo I should spend my time mooning about with the Baron, but Amenta was young and rather good-looking, while the Baron, in my opinion, was neither though I knew many people (especially mammas) would consider him to be both. Then again Amenta shared my passion for butterflies, against which the Baron talked English really remarkably well; and last, but by no means least, the Baron was in love with me, while I had not the smallest reason to suppose otherwise than that if I and Amenta were the only two people left in the world the race of mankind would die out. And yet we were as happy together as the day was long.

During these years of travel, there are amongst the rest places I love to dream of, and surely Monte Ciccia will rank with these. The way was long, the broad, dry river-bed with its burning hot sands often made me foot-sore, and the ascent up the rocky side of the mountain was steep and arduous, but a breeze fresh from the ocean would fan our heated brows the moment we gained the summit. And then, too, such a world of flowers and butterflies into which we presently descended on the other side! Tall orange marigolds grew in rank profusion beneath the slender shades of the umbrella pines, while the hot winds would murmur through their branches, and far, far below lay the blue straits of Messina, and in a mist of heat the Calabrian mountains shimmered and glowed. And *Pandora*, the *Argynnis* of southern shores, thronged the flowers of the marigolds, or swept in their regal grace over the ferns and rich vegetation. And by and by we would descend by another way to which we had come up, hot and thirsty with our day's chase, and longing to reach the spot where we would stop and drink from a mountain spring.

There was another *Argynnis* too on Monte Ciccia besides *Pandora*, which neither of us seemed to know for certain, Amenta stating that it was *A. Addipe*, var. *Cleodoxa* (which I *knew* it was not), while he declared it could not be *A. Niobe*, var. *Eris*, as that did not occur in Sicily. So it remained a disputed point between us, and in fact it was the capture of this insect that made me resolve I would go back to Palermo for a few days at least, and show it to Ragusa.

So I left Messina, and said goodbye to Amenta. The day before we had not gone out butterflying, but he came in during the afternoon for music, for which he had quite a genius, and more than once on our 'off' butterfly days, he had come to play to me and accompany me in some of my songs. That day he said he was not well, and complained of a pain in his head, which I was not altogether surprised at, as he always persisted in wearing a black, felt hat out butterflying, in spite of all I could say in favour of a broad brimmed straw. And now he was telling me that perhaps he would die, and no one would care if he did! I suggested his parents were likely to feel some regrets at his demise, for really I was perfectly unaware of the sentiments which were prompting him to speak like this.

Next day I found myself back at Palermo. The Baron met me on the stairs as I came in, and I could not feel otherwise than flattered by the warm welcome he gave me, but my business here was with Ragusa, and I lost no time in taking him a specimen of 'our butterfly'. He looked at it with great interest, said in any case it was new for Sicily, and finally decided to send off the example I had brought with me to a German entomologist of his acquaintance. I even feebly hoped that my dream would be realised of discovering a new kind of butterfly, which should be called the 'Hurleyensis' (after Hurley); but that this discovery should be one of the larger members of the genus *Argynnis* seemed too good to be true.

Gertrude Bell

(1868–1926)

When Vita Sackville-West dropped in on the leading English scholar and expert on Middle East affairs in Baghdad, Gertrude Bell was asked if she would like to have tea with King Faisal. With a saluki at her feet, Bell talked to Sackville-West of world affairs, gardening, and the heat. Few women – or men – of the time had explored so thoroughly the diverse landscapes of Syria (from which the following excerpt is drawn), Iraq along the Euphrates River, Turkey, and Assyria. In 1914, she travelled into the heart of the Arabian desert. An intrepid observer of cultures, Bell became an inspiration to travellers interested in desert peoples. She was named political adviser to King Faisal of Iraq, a job she told Sackville-West about with zest that afternoon in Baghdad before they strolled to the palace for more tea and cake with the King.

from The Desert and the Sown

There could scarcely have been a better example of the freedom with which the Druzes control their own affairs than was offered by an incident that took place on the very evening of my arrival. It has already been intimated on the authority of Fendi that the relations between the Mountain and the Desert were fraught with the usual possibilities of martial incident, and we had not spent an afternoon in Salkhad without discovering that the great raid that had occurred some months previously was the topic that chiefly interested Nasīb and his brother. Not that they spoke of it in their conversations with me, but they listened eagerly when we told of the raid on the Hassaniyyeh and the part the Sukhūr had played in it, and they drew from us all we knew or conjectured as to the present camping grounds of the latter tribe, how far the raiders had come, and in which direction retreated. The muleteers overheard men whispering at the street corners, and their whispers were of warlike preparations; the groups round Mikhāīl's fire, ever a centre of social activity, spoke of injuries that could not be allowed to pass unnoticed, and one of the many sons of Muhammad's uncle had provided that famished Beyrouti with a lunch flavoured with dark hints of a league between the Wādi Sirhan and the Beni Sakhr which must be nipped in the bud ere it had assumed alarming proportions. The wave of the ghazu can hardly reach as far as Salkhad itself, but the harm is done long before it touches that point, especially in the winter when every four-footed creature, except the mare necessary for riding, is far away in the southern plain.

My camp was pitched in a field outside the town at the eastern foot of the castle hill. The slopes to the north were deep in snow up to the ruined walls of the fortress, and even where we lay there were a few detached snowdrifts glittering under the full moon. I had just finished dinner, and was debating whether it were too cold to write my diary, when a sound of savage singing broke upon the night, and from the topmost walls of the castle a great flame leapt up into the sky. It was a beacon kindled to tell the news of the coming raid to the many Druze villages scattered over the plain below, and the song was a call to arms. There was a Druze zaptieh sitting by my camp fire; he jumped up and gazed first at me and then at the red blaze above us. I said: 'Is there permission to my going up?'

He answered: 'There is no refusal. Honour us.'

We climbed together over the half frozen mud, and by the snowy northern side of the volcano, edged our way in the darkness round the castle walls where the lava ashes gave beneath our feet, and came out into the full moonlight upon the wildest scene that eyes could see. A crowd of Druzes,

> '...a sound of savage singing broke upon the night, and from the topmost walls of the castle a great flame leapt up into the sky.'

young men and boys, stood at the edge of the moat on a narrow shoulder of the hill. They were all armed with swords and knives and they were shouting phrase by phrase a terrible song. Each line of it was repeated twenty times or more until it seemed to the listener that it had been bitten, as an acid bites the brass, onto the intimate recesses of the mind.

Upon them, upon them! oh Lord our God! that the foe may
  fall in swathes before our swords!
Upon them, upon them! that our spears may drink at their
  hearts!
Let the babe leave his mother's breast!
Let the young man arise and be gone!
Upon them, upon them! oh Lord our God! that our swords
  may drink at their hearts. . . .

So they sang, and it was as though the fury of their anger would never end, as though the castle walls would never cease from echoing their interminable rage and the night never again know silence, when suddenly the chant stopped and the singers drew apart and formed themselves into a circle, every man holding his neighbours by the hand. Into the circle stepped three young Druzes with bare swords, and strode round the ring of eager boys that enclosed them. Before each in turn they stopped and shook their swords and cried:

'Are you a good man? Are you a true man?'

And each one answered with a shout:

'Ha! ha!'

The moonlight fell on the dark faces and glittered on the quivering blades, the thrill of martial ardour passed from hand to clasped hand, and earth cried to heaven: War! red war!

And then one of the three saw me standing in the circle, and strode up and raised his sword above his head, as though nation saluted nation.

'Lady!' he said, 'the English and the Druze are one.'

I said: 'Thank God! we, too, are a fighting race.'

Indeed, at that moment there seemed no finer thing than to go out and kill your enemy.

And when this swearing in of warriors was over, we ran down the hill under the moon, still holding hands, and I, seeing that some were only children not yet full grown, said to the companion whose hand chance had put in mine:

'Do all these go out with you?'

He answered: 'By God! not all. The ungrown boys must stay at home and pray to God that their day may soon come.'

When they reached the entrance of the town, the Druzes leapt on to a flat house roof, and took up their devilish song. The fire had burnt out on the castle walls, the night struck suddenly cold, and I began to doubt whether if Milhēm and the Vāli of Damascus could see me taking part in a demonstration against the Sukhur they would believe in the innocence of my journey; so I turned away into the shadow and ran down to my tents and became a European again, bent on peaceful pursuits and unacquainted with the naked primitive passions of mankind.

Edith Wharton

(1862–1937)

Until quite recently, Edith Wharton has too often been dismissed as an aristocratic grand dame who divided her time between the glittering high societies of New York and the Continent, and an author whose work didn't measure up to that of her friend and literary companion, Henry James. Quite to the contrary, though, her fiction – *The House of Mirth*, the Pulitzer Prize-winning *The Age of Innocence*, and the acclaimed novella *Ethan Frome* – are masterworks of psychological insight and social nuance. But Wharton also had an exacting eye as a traveller and wrote some of her most luminous descriptive prose while abroad. A prose classic – almost an extended poem – *In Morocco* is a haunting mix: the exotic, infinite beauty of Marrakech and the restrained prose of Wharton. Her selection of detail ('sunlight through the thatch flames on round flanks of beaten copper') catches the spirit of the place.

from **In Morocco**

The Bahia

Whoever would understand Marrakech must begin by mounting at sunset to the roof of the Bahia.

Outspread below lies the oasis-city of the south, flat and vast as the great nomad camp it really is, its low roof extending on all sides to a belt of blue palms ringed with desert. Only two or three minarets and a few noblemen's houses among gardens break the general flatness; but they are hardly noticeable, so irresistibly is the eye drawn toward two dominant objects – the white wall of the Atlas and the red tower of the Koutoubya.

Foursquare, untapering, the great tower lifts its flanks of ruddy stone. Its large spaces of unornamented wall, its triple tier of clustered openings, lightening as they rise from the severe rectangular lights of the first stage to the graceful arcade below the parapet, have the stern harmony of the noblest architecture. The Koutoubya would be magnificent anywhere; in this flat desert it is grand enough to face the Atlas.

The Almohad conquerors who built the Koutoubya and embellished Marrakech dreamed a dream of beauty that extended from the Guadalquivir to the Sahara; and at its two extremes they placed their watch-towers. The Giralda watched over civilized enemies in a land of ancient Roman culture; the Koutoubya stood at the edge of the world, facing the hordes of the desert.

The Almoravid princes who founded Marrakech came from the black desert of Senegal; themselves were leaders of wild hordes. In the history of North Africa the same cycle has perpetually repeated itself. Generation after generation of chiefs have flowed in from the desert or the mountains, overthrown their predecessors, massacred, plundered, grown rich, built sudden places, encouraged their great servants to do the same; then fallen on them, and taken their wealth and their palaces. Usually some religious fury, some ascetic wrath against the self-indulgence of the cities, has been the motive of these attacks; but invariably the same results followed, as they followed when the Germanic barbarians descended on Italy. The conquerors, infected with luxury and mad with power, built vaster palaces, planned grander cities; but Sultans and Viziers camped in their golden houses as if on the march, and the mud huts of the tribesmen within their walls were but one degree removed from the mud-walled tents of the *bled*.

This was more especially the case with Marrakech, a city of Berbers and blacks, and the last outpost against the fierce black world beyond the Atlas from which its founders came. When one looks at its site, and considers its history, one can only marvel at the height of civilization it attained.

The Bahia itself, now the palace of the Resident-General, though built less than a hundred years ago, is typical of the architectural megalomania of the great southern chiefs. It was built by Ba-Ahmed, the all-powerful black Vizier of the Sultan Moulay-el-Hassan (reigned from 1873–1894). Ba-Ahmed was evidently an artist and an archaeologist. His ambition was to re-create a Palace of Beauty such as the Moors had built in the prime of Arab art, and he brought to Marrakech skilled artificers of Fez, the last surviving masters of the mystery of chiselled plaster and ceramic mosaics and honeycombing of gilded cedar. They came, they built the Bahia, and it remains the loveliest and most fantastic of Moroccan palaces.

Court within court, garden beyond garden, reception halls, private apartments, slaves' quarters, sunny prophets' chambers on the roofs and baths in vaulted crypts, the labyrinth of passages and rooms stretches away over several acres of ground. A long court enclosed in pale-green trellis-work, where pigeons plume themselves about a great tank and the dripping tiles glitter with refracted sunlight, leads to the fresh gloom of a cypress garden, or under jasmine tunnels bordered with running water; and these again open on arcaded apartments faced with tiles and stucco-work, where, in languid twilight, the hours drift by to the ceaseless music of the fountains.

The beauty of Moroccan palaces is made up of details of ornament and refinements of sensuous delight too numerous to record; but to get an idea of their general character it is worthwhile to cross the Court of Cypresses at the Bahia and follow a series of low-studded passages that turn on themselves till they reach the center of the labyrinth. Here, passing by a low padlocked door leading to a crypt, and known as the 'Door of the Vizier's Treasure-House', one comes on a painted portal that opens into a still more secret sanctuary: the apartment of the Grand Vizier's Favorite.

This lovely prison, from which all sight and sound of the outer world are excluded, is built about an atrium paved with disks of turquoise and black and white. Water trickles from a central *vasca* of alabaster into a hexagonal mosaic channel in the pavement. The walls, which are at least 25 feet high, are roofed with painted beams resting on panels of traceried stucco in which is set a clerestory of jewelled glass. On each side of the atrium are long recessed rooms closed by vermilion doors painted with gold arabesques and vases of spring flowers; and into these shadowy inner rooms, spread with rugs and divans and soft pillows, no light comes except when their doors are opened into the atrium. In this fabulous place it was my good luck to be lodged while I was in Marrakech.

In a climate where, after the winter snow has melted from the Atlas, every breath of air for long months is a flame of fire, these enclosed rooms in the middle of the palaces are the only places of refuge from the heat. Even in October the temperature of the Favorite's apartment was deliciously reviving after a morning in the bazaars or the dusty streets, and I never came back to its wet tiles and perpetual twilight without the sense of plunging into a deep sea-pool.

From far off, through circuitous corridors, came the scent of citron-blossom and jasmine, with sometimes a bird's song before dawn, sometimes a flute's wail at sunset, and always the call of the muezzin in the night; but no sunlight reached the apartment except in remote rays through the clerestory, and no air except through one or two broken panes.

Sometimes, lying on my divan, and looking out through the vermilion doors, I used to surprise a pair of swallows dropped down from their nest in the cedar-beams to preen themselves on the fountain's edge or in the channels of the pavement; for the roof was full of birds who came and went through the broken panes of the clerestory. Usually they were my only visitors; but one morning just at daylight I was waked by a soft tramp of bare feet, and saw, silhouetted against the cream-colored walls a procession of eight tall negroes in linen tunics, who filed noiselessly across the atrium like a moving frieze of bronze. In that fantastic setting, and the hush of that twilight hour, the vision was so like the picture of a 'Seraglio Tragedy', some fragment of a Delacroix or Decamps floating up into the drowsy brain, that I almost fancied I had seen ghosts of Ba-Ahmed's executioners revisiting with dagger and bowstring the scene of an unavenged crime.

A cock crew, and they vanished . . . and when I made the mistake of asking what they had been doing in my room at that hour I was told (as though it were the most natural thing in the world) that they were the municipal lamp-lighters of Marrakech, whose duty it is to refill every morning the two hundred acetylene lamps lighting the Palace of the Resident-General. Such unforeseen aspects, in this mysterious city, do the most ordinary domestic functions wear.

The Bazaars

Marrakech is the great market of the south; and the south means not only the Atlas with its feudal chiefs and their wild clansmen, but all that lies beyond of heat and savagery: the Sahara of the veiled Touaregs, Dakka, Timbuctoo, Senegal and the Soudan. Here come the camel caravans from Demnat and Tameslout, from the Moulouya and the Souss, and those from the Atlantic ports and the confines of Algeria. The population of this old city of the southern march has always been even more mixed than that of the northerly Moroccan towns. It is made up of the descendants of all the people conquered by a long line of Sultans who brought their trains of captives across the sea from Moorish Spain and across the Sahara from Timbuctoo. Even in the highly cultivated region of the lower slope of the Atlas there are groups of varied ethnic origin, the descendants of tribes transplanted by long-gone rulers and still preserving many of their original characteristics.

In the bazaars all these peoples meet and mingle: cattle-dealers, olive growers, peasants from the Atlas, the Souss and the Draa. Blue Men of the Sahara, blacks from Senegal and the Soudan, coming in to trade with the wool-merchants, tanners, leather-merchants, silk-weavers, armourers, and makers of agricultural implements.

Dark, fierce and fanatical are these narrow *souks* of Marrakech. They are mere mud lanes roofed with rushes, as in South Tunisia and Timbuctoo, and the crowds swarming in them are so dense that it is hardly possible, at certain hours, to approach the tiny raised kennels where the merchants sit like idols among their wares. One feels at once that something more than the thought of bargaining – dear as this is to the African heart – animates these incessantly moving throngs. The *souks* of Marrakech seem, more than any others, the central organ of a native life that extends far beyond the city walls into secret clefts of the mountains and far-off oases where plots are hatched and holy wars fomented – farther still, to yellow deserts whence negroes are secretly brought across the Atlas to that inmost recess of the bazaar where the ancient traffic in flesh and blood still surreptitiously goes on.

All these many threads of the native life, woven of greed and lust, of fetishism and fear and blind hate of the stranger, form, in the *souks*, a thick network in which at times one's feet seem literally to stumble. Fanatics in sheep skins glowering from the guarded thresholds of the mosques, fierce tribesmen with inlaid arms in their belts and the fighters' tufts of wiry hair escaping from camel's-hair turbans, mad negroes standing stark naked in niches of the walls pouring down Soudanese incantations upon the fascinated crowd, consumptive Jews with pathos and cunning in their large eyes and smiling lips, lusty slave-girls with earthen oil-jars resting against swaying hips, almond-eyed boys leading fat merchants by the hand, and bare-legged Berber women, tattooed and insolently gay, trading their striped blankets, or bags of dried roses and irises, for sugar, tea or Manchester cottons – from all these hundreds of unknown and unknowable people, bound together by secret affinities, or intriguing against each other with secret hate, there emanated an atmosphere of mystery and menace more stifling than the smell of camels and spices and black bodies and smoking fry which hangs like a fog under the close roofing of the *souks*.

And suddenly one leaves the crowd and the turbid air for one of those quiet corners that are like the back-waters of the bazaar: a small square where a vine stretches across a shop-front and hangs ripe clusters of grapes through the reeds. In the patterning of grape-shadows a very old donkey, tethered to a stone-post, dozes under a pack-saddle that is never taken off; and near by, in a matted niche, sits a very old man in white. This is the chief of the Guild of 'Morocco' Workers of Marrakech, the most accomplished craftsmen in Morocco in the preparing and using of the skins to which the city gives its name. Of these sleek moroccos, cream-white or dyed with cochineal or pomegranate skins, are made the rich bags of the Chleuh dancing-boys, the embroidered slippers for the harem, the belts and harnesses that figure so largely in Moroccan trade – and of the finest, in old days, were made the pomegranate-red morocco bindings of European bibliophiles.

From this peaceful corner one passes into the barbaric splendor of a *souk* hung with innumerable plumy bunches of floss silk – skeins of citron yellow, crimson, grasshopper green and pure purple. This is the silk-spinners' quarter, and next to it comes that of the dyers, with great seething vats into which the raw silk is plunged, and ropes overhead where the rainbow masses are hung out to dry.

Another turn leads into the street of the metal workers and armourers, where the sunlight through the thatch flames on round flanks of beaten copper or picks out the silver bosses of ornate powder-flasks and pistols; and nearby is the *souk* of the ploughshares, crowded with peasants in rough Chleuh cloaks who are waiting to have their archaic ploughs repaired, and that of the smiths, in an outer lane of mud huts where negroes squat in the dust and sinewy naked figures in tattered loin cloths bend over blazing coals. And here ends the maze of the bazaar.

Willa Cather

(1876–1947)

MORE THAN TEN YEARS BEFORE THE PUBLICATION OF WILLA CATHER'S FIRST NOVEL, *O PIONEERS!*, THE WRITER TOURED ENGLAND AND FRANCE AND SENT FOURTEEN TRAVEL ARTICLES BACK HOME FOR PUBLICATION IN THE *NEBRASKA STATE JOURNAL*. IT WAS THE FIRST TRIP TO EUROPE FOR CATHER, A HIGH-SCHOOL TEACHER OF ENGLISH AND LATIN IN PITTSBURGH ON SUMMER LEAVE. WITH HER FRIEND ISABELLE MCCLUNG, SHE VISITED WITH GENUINE WONDER SUCH SIGHTS AS LONDON'S EAST END AND PARIS'S NOTRE DAME. THE EXCERPT THAT FOLLOWS HINTS AT WORKS TO COME, *SHADOWS ON THE ROCK* AND *DEATH COMES FOR THE ARCHBISHOP*, WHICH BOTH DRAW ON THE FRENCH LANDSCAPE FOR INSPIRATION ('THERE IS NOTHING BUT A LITTLE CARDBOARD HOUSE OF STUCCO, AND A PLATEAU OF BROWN PINE NEEDLES, AND GREEN FIR TREES, THE SCENT OF DRIED LAVENDER ALWAYS IN THE AIR, AND THE SEA REACHING LIKE A WIDE BLUE ROAD INTO THE SKY'). CATHER WON THE PULITZER PRIZE IN FICTION FOR *ONE OF OURS* IN 1922. SHE WAS BORN IN VIRGINIA AND DIED IN NEW YORK CITY.

from Willa Cather in Europe

Le Lavandou, September 10, 1902

We came to Lavandou chiefly because we could not find anyone who had ever been here, and because in Paris people seemed never to have heard of the place. It does not exist on the ordinary map of France, and Baedeker, in his *Southern France*, merely mentions it. Lavandou is a fishing village of less than a hundred souls, that lies in a beautiful little bay of the Mediterranean. Its score or so of houses are built on the narrow strip of beach between the steep hillside and the sea. They are scarcely more than huts, built of mud and stone on either side of one narrow street. There is one café, and before it is a little square of sycamore trees, where the sailors, always barefoot, with their corduroy trousers and tam-o'-shanter caps, play some primitive game of ball in the afternoon. There is one very fairly good hotel, built on the sea, and from the windows of our rooms we have the whole sweep of ocean before us. There is a long veranda running the full length of the house on the side facing the sea, straw-thatched and overgrown by gourd vines, where all our meals are served to us. The fare is very good for a semi-desert country, though the wine here is thin and sour and brackish, as though the sea-wash had got into the soil that grew it. The wine of the country just here is all red, for the white grapes which flourish about Avignon grow poorly here. We have good fish, however, excellent sauces, plenty of fresh figs and peaches, and the fine little French lobster called *langouste*. Every morning the one little train that rattles in over the narrow-gauge tracks from Hyères brings us our piece of ice, done up in a bit of sailcloth, and we watch for it eagerly enough. This little train constitutes our railroad service, and it comprises a toy engine, a coal car, a mail and baggage car, and two coaches, one for first and one for second class.

The coast for a hundred miles on either side of us is quite as wild as it was when the Saracens held it. It is one endless succession of pine hills that terminate in cliffs jutting over the sea. There are no cattle or pigs raised here, and the people drink only goat's milk besides their own wines. The gardens are for the most part pitiful little hillside patches of failure. Potatoes, figs, olives, and grapes are almost the only things that will grow at all in this dry, sandy soil. The sea is an even more uncertain harvest, as, with the exception of the lobsters, the fish of the Mediterranean are not particularly good, and bring

'One cannot divine nor forecast the conditions that will make happiness; one only stumbles upon them by chance, in a lucky hour, at the world's end somewhere, and holds fast to the days, as to fortune or fame.'

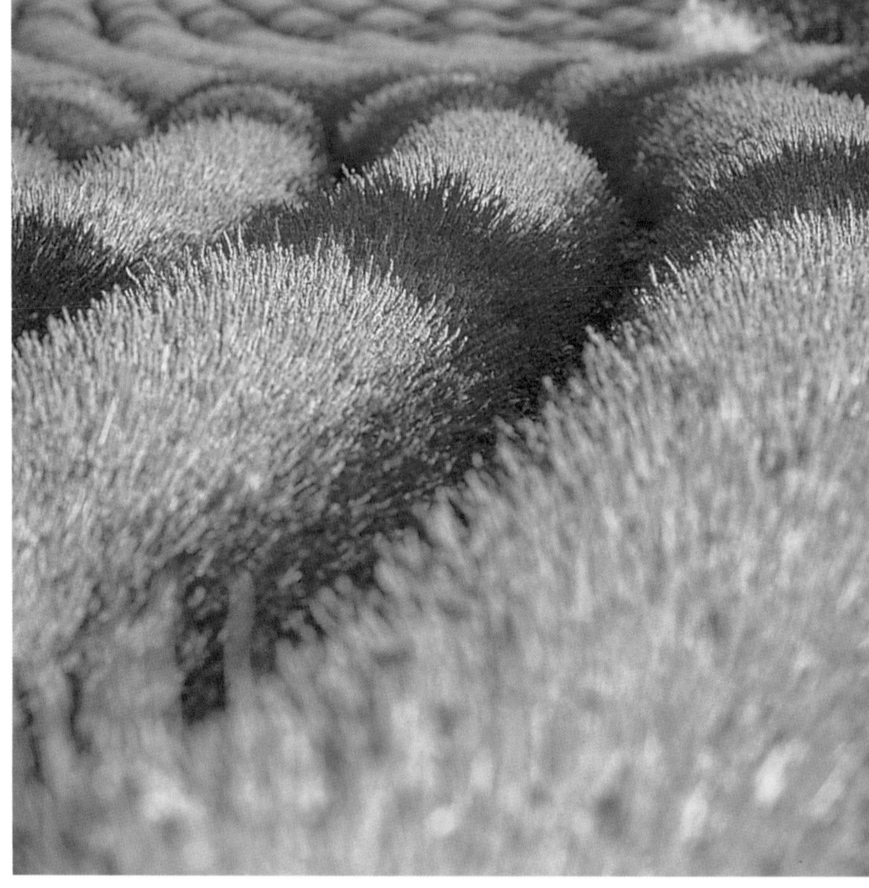

a low price in the market. The water, indeed, is not cold enough to produce good fish. How the people live at all I am not able to discover. They burn pine knots and cones for fuel – the thermometer never goes down to freezing-point – and they are able to make a savoury dish of almost anything that grows. They are very fond of a salad they make of little sea-grass, dressed with the oil they get from their olives. But never imagine they are not happy, these poor fishermen of this smiling, niggardly sea. Every day we see them along the road as we walk back to the village; before every cottage the table set under an arbour or under an olive tree, with the family seated about, eating their figs and sea-grass salad, and drinking their sour wine, and singing – always singing.

Out of every wandering in which people and places come and go in long successions, there is always one place remembered above the rest because the external or internal conditions were such that they most nearly produced happiness. I am sure that for me that one place will always be Lavandou. Nothing else in England or France has given anything like this sense of immeasurable possession and immeasurable content. I am sure I do not know why a wretched little fishing village, with nothing but green pines and blue sea and a sky of porcelain, should mean more than a dozen places that I have wanted to see all my life. No books have ever been written about Lavandou, no music or pictures ever came from here, but I know well enough that I shall yearn for it long after I have forgotten London and Paris. One cannot divine nor forecast the conditions that will make happiness; one only stumbles upon them by chance, in a lucky hour, at the world's end somewhere, and holds fast to the days, as to fortune or fame.

About a mile down the shore from the village there is a little villa of white stucco, with a red-tiled roof and a little stone porch, built in the pines. It is the winter studio of a painter who is in Paris now. He has managed to keep away from it all the disfiguring and wearisome accompaniments of houses made with hands. There is no well, no stable, no yard, no driveway. It is a mere lodge, set on a little table of land between two cliffs that run out into the sea. All about it are the pines, and the little porch and plateau are covered with pine needles. You approach it by a winding path that runs down through the underbrush from the high-road. There, for the last week, we have taken up our abode. Nominally we stopped at the Hôtel de la Méditerrané, but we only slept and ate there. For twelve hours out of the twenty-four we were the possessors of a villa on the Mediterranean, and the potentates of a principality of pines. There is before the villa a little plateau on the flat top of a cliff extending out into the sea, brown with pine needles, and shaded by one tall, straight pine tree that grows on the very tip of the little promontory. It is good for one's soul to sit there all the day through, wrapped in a steamer rug if the sea breeze blows strong, and to do nothing for hours together but stare at this great water that seems to trail its delft-blue mantle across the world. Then, as Daudet said, one becomes a part of the foam that drifts, of the wind that blows, and of the pines that answer.

Besides having a manor, we have a demesne as well, a fair demesne of lavender tufts that grow thick over the hills; and their odourous blossoms, drying in the sun, mingle their fresh, salt perfume with the heavier odour of the pines. Our only labour is to gather these blossoms; but so regal is our idleness that we have much ado to accomplish it.

Going to and fro, we have made the acquaintance of certain neighbouring princes and princesses whose kingdoms lie round about. There are, in the first place, two little girls, whom we meet every day seeking pasture for their goat. As the goat supplies the milk and butter for the family, it is most necessary that she should have good grass; and that, on this arid coast, is not easy to find in September. When they have found a green spot, they carefully tether her, and with many parting injunctions to her not to run away, and to eat all she can, and be a good little goat, they leave her. Then there is the old man who lives in a thatch on the hillside, from whom we buy figs; and the woman who goes about with scales and basket, selling lobsters. At the hotel there is an old Parisian who has exiled himself from the gaieties of the capital, and is living out the remainder of a misspent life in the solitudes of his native south. His eyes fairly devour anyone who comes from Paris, and he beams when a bicyclist or two pump into Lavandou to solace his loneliness. For several days he has been the only guest at the hotel besides ourselves, and he eats his lobster and sips his benedictine in sadness.

The other day we left our manor long enough to make a royal progress to Cavalaire, a village six miles down the coast. The road is a wild one: on one side the steep hillside, on the other the sea. If we had not tested the kindliness of these southerners before, we might have been rather intimidated by the loneliness of the road. We met nothing more terrible than a sailor boy sitting on the stone coping of a bridge, trying to tie up a badly bruised foot in a piece of cloth torn from the sash about his waist. He had been put ashore that morning off a freight boat because his foot disabled him, and was limping along to St. Praid, twenty-five miles down the coast, where his people lived. He did not ask for charity, nor vouchsafe his story until he was questioned. We gave him some money, and a pin to keep the cloth on his foot, and as we were returning late in the afternoon, we met him limping on his way. We met also a few fishermen, and several women walking beside little carts drawn by a donkey no bigger than a sheep, and every woman was knitting busily as she walked, stopping only long enough to greet us. The village of Cavalaire consists of a station house and a little tavern by the roadside. The station agent lay asleep on a bench beside his door, and his old mother and wife were knitting beside him. The place is not a little like certain lonely way stations in Wyoming and Colorado. Before we reached our own village that night the moon was already throwing her tracks of troubled light across the sea.

But always we come back to the principality of pines and decide there is nothing else quite so good. As I said before, there is nothing but a little cardboard house of stucco, and a plateau of brown pine needles, and green fir trees, the scent of dried lavender always in the air, and the sea reaching like a wide blue road into the sky. But what a thing it is to lie there all day in the fine breeze, with the pine needles dropping on one, only to return to the hotel at night so hungry that the dinner, however homely, is a fête, and the menu finer reading than the best poetry in the world! Yet we are to leave all this for the glare and blaze of Nice and Monte Carlo; which is proof enough that one cannot become really acclimated to happiness.

Vita Sackville-West

(1892–1962)

Virginia Woolf wrote of the best work of her lifelong friend Vita Sackville-West that one gets 'the sense of all the fine things you have dropped in to it, so that it is full of beauty in itself when nothing is happening'. Few among her contemporaries extolled the virtues and beauty of the little things in life as Sackville-West did. Sackville-West eschewed traversing deserts, climbing mountaintops, and fording dangerous rivers for her material. Her work is meditative, consistently brushing up against poetry. In her travels, recorded in *Passenger to Teheran*, she visited in 1925 the countries of the Middle East and went home to England by way of Russia. While on the journey she attended the coronation of the reigning Shah of Persia.

from Passenger to Teheran

Ever since I have been in Persia I have been looking for a garden and have not yet found one. Yet Persian gardens enjoy a great reputation. Hafiz and Sa-adi sang frequently, even wearisomely, of roses. Yet there is no word for rose in the Persian language; the best they can manage is 'red flower'. It looks as though a misconception had arisen somewhere. Indeed I think the misconception is ours, sprung from that national characteristic by which the English exact that everything should be the same, even in Central Asia, as it is in England, and grumble when it is not. 'Garden?' we say; and think of lawns and herbaceous borders, which is manifestly absurd. There is no turf in this parched country; and as for herbaceous borders, they postulate a lush shapeliness unimaginable to the Persian mind. Here, everything is dry and untidy, crumbling and decayed; a dusty poverty, exposed for eight months of the year to a cruel sun. For all that, there are gardens in Persia.

But they are gardens of trees, not of flowers; green wildernesses. Imagine that you have ridden in summer for four days across a plain; that you have then come to a barrier of snow-mountains and ridden up the pass; that from the top of the pass you have seen a second plain, with a second barrier of mountains in the distance, a hundred miles away; that you know that beyond these mountains lies yet another plain, and another, and another; and that for days, even weeks, you must ride, with no shade, and the sun overhead, and nothing but the bleached bones of dead animals strewing the track. Then when you come to trees and running water, you will call it a garden. It will not be flowers and their garishness that your eyes crave for, but a green cavern full of shadow, and pools where goldfish dart, and the sound of little streams. That is the meaning of a garden in Persia, a country where the long slow caravan is an everyday fact, and not a romantic name.

Such gardens there are; many of them abandoned, and these one may share with the cricket and the tortoise undisturbed through the hours of the long afternoon. In such a one I write. It lies on a southward slope, at the foot of the snowy Elburz, looking over the plain. It is a tangle of briars and grey sage, and here and there a judas tree in full flower stains the whiteness of the tall planes with its incredible magenta. A cloud of pink, down in a dip, betrays the peach trees in blossom. Water flows everywhere, either in little wild runnels, or guided into a straight channel paved with blue tiles, which pours down the slope into a broken fountain between four cypresses. There, too, is the little pavilion, ruined, like everything else; the tiles of the façade have fallen out and lie smashed upon the terrace; people have built, but, seemingly, never repaired; they have built, and gone away, leaving nature to turn their handiwork into this melancholy beauty. Nor is it so sad as it might be, for in this spacious, ancient country it is not of man that one thinks; he has made no impression on the soil, even his villages of brown mud remain invisible until one comes close up to them, and, once ruined, might have been ruined for five or five hundred years, indifferently; no, one thinks only of the haven that this tangled enclosure affords, after the great spaces. One is no longer that small insect creeping across the pitiless distances.

There is something satisfying in this contrast between the garden and the enormous geographical simplicity that lies beyond. The mud walls that surround the garden are crumbling, and through the breaches appears the great brown plain, crossed by the three pale roads: to the east, the road to Meshed and Samarcand; to the west, the road to Bagdad; to the south, the road to Isfahan. The eye may travel, or, alternately, return to dwell upon the little grape-hyacinth growing close at hand. These Asian plains are of exceeding beauty, but their company is severe, and the mind turns gratefully for a change to something of more manageable size. The garden is a place of spiritual reprieve, as well as a place of shadows. The plains are lonely, the garden is inhabited; not by men, but by birds and beasts and lowly flowers; by hoopoes, crying 'Who? Who?' among the branches; by lizards rustling like dry leaves; by the tiny sea-green iris. A garden in England seems an unnecessary luxury, where the whole countryside is so circumscribed, easy and secure; but here, one begins to understand why the garden drew such notes from Sa-adi and from Hafiz. As a breeze at evening after a hot day, as a well in the desert, so is the garden to the Persian.

The sense of property, too, is blessedly absent; I suppose that this garden has an owner somewhere, but I do not know who he is, nor can any one tell me. No one will come up and say that I am trespassing; I may have the garden to myself; I may share it with a beggar; I may see a shepherd drive in his brown and black flock, and, sitting down to watch them browse, sing a snatch of the song that all Persians sing at the turn of the year, for the first three weeks of spring. All are equally free to come and enjoy. Indeed there is nothing to steal, except the blossom from the peach trees, and no damage to do that has not already been done by time and nature. The same is true of the whole country. There are no evidences of law anywhere, no sign-posts or milestones to show the way; the caravanserais stand open for any one to go in and rest his beasts; you may travel along any of those three roads for hundreds of miles in any direction, without meeting any one or anything to control you; even the rule of the road is nominal, and you pass by as best you can. If you prefer to leave the track and take to the open, then you are free to do so. One remembers – sometimes with irritation, sometimes with longing, according to the fortunes of the journey – the close organisation of European countries.

'...a green cavern full of shadow, and pools where goldfish dart, and the sound of little streams. That is the meaning of a garden in Persia...'

The shadows lengthen, and the intense light of sunset begins to spread over the plain. The brown earth darkens to the rich velvet of burnt umber. The light creeps like a tide up the foothills, staining the red rock to the colour of porphyry. High up, above the range of the Elburz, towers the white cone of Demavend, white no longer now, but glowing like a coal; that white loneliness, for ten minutes of every day, suddenly comes to life. It is time to leave the garden, where the little owls are beginning to hoot, answering one another, and to go down into the plain, where the blue smoke of the evening fires is already rising, and a single star hangs prophetic in the west.

Alexandra David-Neel

(1868–1969)

No writer in this volume prepared herself for as long or in the way Alexandra David-Neel did for a single journey. In 1923 David-Neel was the first Western woman to pass through the gates of Lhasa. Twelve years earlier, she had met the Dalai Lama in India and had become enchanted with Tibetan religion. Then she met Yongden, a young priest whom she would later adopt and with whom she shared all her travels. Together they went to Burma, Bhutan, Japan, and Korea, before returning to a monastery on the Sino-Tibetan frontier. It was there that for three years she perfected the ancient practice of *thumo reskiang*, the ability to raise body temperature through meditation. David-Neel's purpose in travelling and studying was to prepare herself for a pilgrimage through treacherous mountain passes to Lhasa, the place she called her spiritual home but a place at the time closed to women. The Frenchwoman wrote scholarly books on Tibetan mysticism and in 1937 went to live in China for eight years. She died in Provence at the age of one hundred.

from **My Journey to Lhasa**

We ought to have left the *dokpas*' camp in the middle of the night to cross the pass at noon. But we were tired, and the warmth that we felt, lying next to a big fire, kept us sleeping longer than we had planned. I shrank also from the idea of starting without eating and drinking hot tea, for on the higher level we would find no fuel. What would happen? What would the road be like? We could not guess. Was the pass even practicable? People had only told us that it might be. Yongden, of course, felt reluctant to go so far to fetch water, inasmuch as the few places where the stream flowed freely in daytime might be covered with ice after dark. Anyhow, he went, and we drank our tea. But the day broke before we had left the place.

Later in the morning we reached a *latza*, which, from a distance, we had taken as marking the top of the pass. Behind it extended a completely barren valley enclosed between a high ridge of crumbling reddish stones on one side, and perpendicular cliffs of various pretty greyish and mauve shades on the other. In the middle of this valley we again saw the river, the water of which we had drunk at our breakfast. It fell nearly straight down in a narrow gorge from the upper valley to the lower one. I looked for traces of *dokpas*' summer encampments – those low stone walls forming enclosures in which cattle are penned, but there were none. I could understand from the barrenness of the landscape that cattle were probably never brought so high.

A nearly straight reddish line – the sharp summit of a ridge it seemed – blocked the horizon at the end of that desolate valley. The distance without being considerable, appeared great enough to people ascending with loads on their backs, in the rarefied air of these high altitudes. Still, the hope of seeing the end of the climb gave us courage, and we endeavoured to accelerate our pace. One thing, however, made me uneasy – I did not discover any *latza* on that ridge, and Thibetans never fail to erect at least one, at the top of a pass. The explanation came when we had reached the point from which we had supposed that we would descend the opposite side of the mountain.

How could I express what we felt at that moment? It was a mixture of admiration and grief. We were at the same time wonderstricken and terrified. Quite suddenly an awe-inspiring landscape, which had previously been shut from our sight by the walls of the valley, burst upon us.

Think of an immensity of snow, an undulating tableland limited far away at our left by a straight wall of blue-green glaciers and peaks wrapped in everlasting, immaculate whiteness. At our right extended a wide valley which ascended in a gentle slope until we reached the neighbouring summits on the sky line. In front, a similar but wider stretch of gradually sloping ground vanished in the distance, without our being able to discern whether it led to the pass or to another tableland.

Words cannot give an idea of such winter scenery as we saw on these heights. It was one of those overpowering spectacles that make believers bend their knees, as before the veil that hides the Supreme Face.

But Yongden and I, after our first admiration had subsided, only looked at each other in silence. No talk was needed; we clearly understood the situation.

Which was the way, we did not know! It could just as well be to our right, as ahead of us. The snow did not allow one to see any trace of a trail. It was already late in the afternoon, and to miss the road meant to remain wandering all night on these frozen summits. We had a sufficient experience in mountaineering in Thibet to know what it would mean – the exploration would be ended at its first step, and the explorers would never live to tell their tale.

I looked at my watch; it was three in the afternoon. We had still several hours of daylight before us, and, happily, the moon would shine brightly at night. We had not yet cause to be really alarmed – the important thing was to avoid missing the road and to make haste.

I looked once more at the valley on our right, then decided: 'Let us proceed straight forward.' And so we went.

I grew excited and, although the snow became deeper and deeper, I walked rather quickly. We had not been able to follow the advice of the Tashi Tse villagers and carry much food with us. Our host could only sell us a small quantity of *tsampa*. His neighbours had hardly enough for themselves. They informed us that we could buy some from the servants of the *pönpo*. To avoid giving them cause to talk we had said that we would go to the *zong* early the next morning, which, of course, we didn't! My bag was, therefore, rather light, whereas Yongden, carrying the tent, its iron pegs, and sundries, was much more heavily loaded.

I forged quickly ahead. Dominated by the idea of reaching the top of the pass, or of discovering if we were going in a wrong direction, I tramped with the utmost energy through the snow that reached my knees.

Was the lama far behind? I turned to look at him. Never shall I forget the sight! Far, far below, amidst the white silent immensity, a small black spot, like a tiny Lilliputian insect, seemed to be crawling slowly up. The disproportion between the giant glacier range, that wild and endless slope, and the two puny travellers who had ventured alone in that extraordinarily phantasmagoric land of the heights, impressed me as it had never done before. An inexpressible feeling of compassion moved me to the bottom of my heart. It could not be possible that my young friend, the companion of so many of my adventurous travels, should meet his end in a few hours on that hill. I would find the pass; it was my duty. I knew that I would!

There was no time for useless emotion. Evening was already beginning to dim the shining whiteness of the landscape. We ought by then to have been far beyond and below the pass. I strode on, now through the snow field, jumping sometimes with the help of my long staff, proceeding I could not say how, but progressing quickly. At last I discerned a white mound and emerging from it, branches on which hung flags covered with snow and fringed with ice. It was the *latza*, the top of the pass! I signalled to Yongden, who appeared still more distant and tiny. He did not see me at once, but after a while he too waved his staff. He had understood that I had arrived.

There the scenery was grand beyond all description. Behind extended the waste I had crossed. In front of me was a precipitous fall of the mountain. Stretching far below, black undulating crests vanished into the darkness. The moon rose as I looked around in a trance of admiration. Its rays touched the glaciers and the high snow-robed peaks, the whole white plain, and some silvery unknown valleys toward which I was to proceed. The impassive landscape of the day seemed to awaken under the blue light which metamorphosed it, sparks glittered to and fro, and faint sounds were wafted by the wind. . . . Maybe elves of the frozen waterfalls, fairies of the snow, and djin-keepers of mysterious caves were to assemble and play and feast on the illuminated white tableland; or perhaps some grave council was to take place between the giants whose heads wore helmets of cold radiance. What mysteries could not have been discovered by the inquisitive pilgrim who, hidden, dared remain there motionless till dawn. Not that he could ever have related the wonder of the bewitching night, for his tongue would soon have been stiffened by the frost!

Thibetans do not shout '*lha gyalo*' after dark. I complied with the custom and threw only in six directions the old Sanskrit mantra, '*Subham astu sarvajagatam* [May all beings be happy].'

Yongden, who, after having understood that he neared the *latza*, had taken courage and quickened his pace, caught up with me. We began to descend. Traces of a track were visible now and then, for on that side of the mountain the snow was not deep and the ground, a yellowish gravel, was often visible.

What might have been the exact level of the pass we had crossed I would not venture to tell, as I could not make any observation. Still, from the comparison of the plants and various other particulars, one who has tramped for years through many mountain ranges, in the same country, may make a rough guess. I had carefully looked at the lichens, and observed a few other things; and I felt nearly certain that the pass was about 19,000 feet high, even higher perhaps than the Dokar *la* I had crossed about two months before, higher than the Nago *la* and others that reached from 18,299 to 18,500.

Although we knew that we should have to walk a part of the night before we should reach a spot where fuel would be available, we rejoiced at having found the pass open and at having crossed it safely. In this agreeable mood we reached a valley whose bottom was almost entirely covered by a frozen stream. There, on the ice, no trace of a track was of course visible, and we began again to roam to and fro in search of some sign to show us our direction. To follow the course of the frozen river was the safest way, if we did not find any better one. It would take us to a lower level, no doubt, but it could also happen that the stream would disappear into a narrow gorge or fall over a cliff. Still, I had decided to continue on the ice – at least as long as the valley was open. But then I found the track again, near the foot of the hill, and we had only to follow it down, proceeding slowly.

The walk was rather agreeable beneath a beautiful moon. Here and there we began to see a few bushes scattered in pasture grounds. Otherwise the country was quite barren. We could not think of stopping without lighting a fire, for motion alone kept us warm. No shelter whatsoever was in sight, and the cold wind from the snow rushed through the valley, which had now become rather wide.

We tramped until two o'clock in the morning. For nineteen hours we had been walking, without having stopped or refreshed ourselves in any way. Strangely enough, I did not feel tired, but only sleepy!

Yongden had gone in the direction of the hills in search of fuel, and I found some near the river, in a flat place, which must have been a camping-place in the summer, where travellers from the Po country go to the Dainshin province, either to trade or on robbery expeditions.

I called the young man back, gathered as much fuel as I could, and, certain that nobody was wandering in that wilderness, we decided to pitch our tent in a low place among a few bushes. The flint and steel which, according to Thibetan custom, Yongden carried attached to his belt in a pouch, had become wet during our passage across the snow fields, and now it did not work at all. This was a serious matter. Of course we were no longer on the top of the range and we had only a few hours to wait before the sun would rise; but even if we escaped being frozen, we were not at all certain that we should not catch pneumonia or some other serious disease.

'Jetsunma,'* said Yongden, 'you are, I know, initiated in the *thumo reskiang* practice. Warm yourself and do not bother about me. I shall jump and move to keep my blood moving.'

True, I had studied under two Thibetan *gompchens* the strange art of increasing the internal heat. For long I had been puzzled by the stories I had heard and read on the subject and as I am of a somewhat scientific turn of mind I wanted to make the experiment myself. With great difficulties, showing an extreme perseverance in my desire to be initiated into the secret, and after a number of ordeals, I succeeded in reaching my aim. I saw some hermits seated night after night, motionless on the snow, entirely naked, sunk in meditation, while the terrible winter blizzard whirled and hissed around them! I saw under the bright full moon the test given to their disciples who, on the shore of a lake or a river in the heart of the winter, dried on their bodies, as on a stove, a number of sheets dipped in the icy water! And I learned the means of performing these feats. I had inured myself, during five months of the cold season, to wearing the single thin cotton

* 'Jetsunma' or 'Jetsun Kusho': 'Reverend lady' or 'your reverend ladyship', is the highest honourific title of address for a woman belonging to the religious order.

'Soon I saw flames arising around me; they grew higher and higher; they enveloped me, curling their tongues above my head. I felt deliciously comfortable.'

garment of the students at a 13,000-foot level. But the experience once over, I felt that a further training would have been a waste of time for me, who, as a rule, could choose my dwelling in less severe climates or provide myself with heating apparatus. I had, therefore, returned to fires and warm clothes, and thus could not be taken for an adept in the *thumo reskiang*, as my companion believed! Nevertheless, I liked at times to remember the lesson I had learned and to sit on some snowy summit in my thin dress of *reskiang*. But the present was not the time to look selfishly after my own comfort. I wanted to try to kindle a fire that had nothing miraculous about it, but which could warm my adopted son as well as myself.

'Go!' said I to Yongden, 'collect as much dry cow dung and dry twigs as you can; the exertion will prevent you from getting cold. I will see after the fire business.'

He went, convinced that the fuel was useless; but I had got an idea. After all, the flint and steel were wet and cold. What if I warmed them on me, as I had dried dripping sheets when a student of *thumo reskiang*? *Thumo reskiang* is but a way devised by the Thibetan hermits of enabling themselves to live without endangering their health on the high hills. It has nothing to do with religion, and so it can be used for ordinary purposes without lack of reverence.

I put the flint and steel and a pinch of the moss under my clothes, sat down, and began the ritualistic practice. I mentioned that I felt sleepy on the road; the exertion while collecting fuel and pitching the tent, the effort to kindle the fire, had shaken my torpor, but now, being seated, I began to doze. Yet my mind continued to be concentrated on the object of the *thumo* rite. Soon I saw flames arising around me; they grew higher and higher; they enveloped me, curling their tongues above my head. I felt deliciously comfortable.

A loud report awakened me. The ice on the river was rending. The flames suddenly died down as if entering the ground. I opened my eyes. The wind was blowing hard and my body burned. I made haste. The flint and steel and moss would work this time; I was convinced of it. I was still half dreaming, although I had got up and walked toward the tent. I felt fire bursting out of my head, of my fingers.

I placed on the ground a little dry grass, a small piece of very dry cow dung, and I knocked the stone. A spark sprang out of it. I knocked again; another sprang out . . . another . . . another . . . a miniature fireworks. . . . The fire was lighted; it was a little baby flame which wanted to grow, to eat, to live. I fed it and it leaped higher and higher. When Yongden arrived with a quantity of dry cow dung in the lap of his dress and some branches between his arms, he was joyfully astonished.

'How have you done it?' he asked.

'Well, it is the fire of *thumo*,' I answered, smiling.

The lama looked at me.

'True,' he said. 'Your face is quite red and your eyes are so bright . . .'

'Yes,' I replied, 'that is all right. Let me alone now, and make a good buttered tea quickly. I need a very hot drink.'

I feared a little for the morrow, but I awakened in perfect health when the sun touched the thin cloth of our tent.

Isak Dinesen

(1885–1962)

Isak Dinesen told close friends that she could do two things – cook and possibly write. Karen Blixen used the pen name Isak, Hebrew for 'one who laughs', and Dinesen, her maiden name, for books published in English and did not claim authorship until her first book, *Seven Gothic Tales*, published in 1934, became a success. *Out of Africa* is often called the best travel book ever written and perhaps the best pastoral of our time. A storyteller who compresses images into small powerful sentences, Dinesen works to rout 'the brute realities of the twentieth century from her prose', as one reviewer wrote. Blixen operated a coffee farm, first with her husband, Bror Blixen-Finecke, and then, after they divorced, for ten years alone. Falling commodity prices forced her to abandon the farm in 1931 and to return to Denmark. Denys of the following excerpt was Denys Finch-Hatton, a longtime companion who joined her on many of her African adventures.

from Out of Africa

One day Denys and I flew to Lake Natron, ninety miles South-East of the farm, and more than four thousand feet lower, two thousand feet above Sea level. Lake Natron is the place from where they take soda. The bottom of the lake and the shores are like some sort of whitish concrete, with a strong, sour and salt smell.

The sky was blue, but as we flew from the plains in over the stony and bare lower country, all colour seemed to be scorched out of it. The whole landscape below us looked like delicately marked tortoise-shell. Suddenly, in the midst of it was the lake. The white bottom, shining through the water, gives it, when seen from the air, a striking, an unbelievable azure-colour, so clear that for a moment you shut your eyes at it; the expanse of water lies in the bleak tawny land like a big bright aquamarine. We had been flying high, now we went down, and as we sank our own shade, dark-blue, floated under us upon the light-blue lake. Here live thousands of Flamingoes, although I do not know how they exist in the brackish water – surely there are no fish here. At our approach they spread out in large circles and fans, like the rays of a setting sun, like an artful Chinese pattern on silk or porcelain, forming itself and changing, as we looked at it.

We landed on the white shore, that was white-hot as an oven, and lunched there, taking shelter against the sun under the wing of the aeroplane. If you stretched out your hand from the shade, the sun was so hot that it hurt you. Our bottles of beer when they first arrived with us, straight out of the ether, were pleasantly cold, but before we had finished them, in a quarter of an hour, they became as hot as a cup of tea.

While we were lunching, a party of Masai warriors appeared on the horizon, and approached quickly. They must have spied the aeroplane landing from a distance, and resolved to have a close look at it, and a walk of any length, even in a country like this, means nothing to a Masai. They came along, the one in front of the other, naked, tall and narrow, their weapons glinting; dark like peat on the yellow grey sand. At the feet of each of them lay and marched a small pool of shadow; these were, besides our own, the only shadows in the country as far as the eye reached. When they came up to us they fell in line, there were five of them. They stuck their heads together and began to talk to one another about the aeroplane and us. A generation ago they would have been fatal to us to meet. After a time one of them advanced and spoke to us. As they could only speak Masai and we understood but little of the language, the conversation soon slackened, he stepped back to his fellows and a few minutes later they all turned their back upon us, and walked away, in single file, with the wide white burning salt-plain before them.

'Would you care,' said Denys, 'to fly to Naivasha? But the country lying between is very rough, we could not possibly land anywhere on the way. So we shall have to go up high and keep up at twelve thousand feet.'

The flight from Lake Natron to Naivasha was *Das Ding an sich*. We took a bee-line, and kept at twelve thousand feet all the way, which is so high that there is nothing to look down for. At Lake Natron I had taken off my lambskin-lined cap, now up here the air squeezed my forehead, as cold as iced water; all my hair flew backwards as if my head was being pulled off. This path, in fact, was the same as was, in the opposite direction, every evening taken by the Roc, when, with an Elephant for her young in each talon, she swished from Uganda home to Arabia. Where you are sitting in front of your pilot, with nothing but space before you, you feel that he is carrying you upon the out-stretched palms of his hands, as the Djinn carried Prince Ali through the air, and that the wings that bear you onward are his. We landed at the farm of our friends at Naivasha; the mad diminutive houses, and the very small trees surrounding them, all threw themselves flat upon their backs as they saw us descending.

When Denys and I had not time for long journeys we went out for a short flight over the Ngong Hills, generally about sunset. These hills, which are amongst the most beautiful in the world, are perhaps at their loveliest seen from the air, when the ridges, bare towards the four peaks, mount, and run side by side with the aeroplane, or suddenly sink down and flatten out into a small lawn.

Here in the hills there were Buffaloes. I had even, in my very young days – when I could not live till I had killed a specimen of each kind of African game – shot a bull out here. Later on, when I was not so keen to shoot as to watch the wild animals, I had been out to see them again. I had camped in the hills by a spring halfway to the top, bringing my servants, tents, and provisions with me, and Farah and I had been up in the dark, ice cold mornings to creep and crawl through bush and long grass, in the hope of catching a glimpse of the herd; but twice I had had to go back without success. That the herd lived there, neighbours of mine to the West, was still a value in the life on the farm, but they were serious-minded, self-sufficient neighbours, the old nobility of the hills, now somehow reduced; they did not receive much.

But one afternoon as I was having tea with some friends of mine from up-country, outside the house, Denys came flying from Nairobi and went over our heads out Westwards; a little while after he turned and came back and landed on the farm. Lady Delamere and I drove down to the plain to fetch him up, but he would not get out of his aeroplane.

'The Buffalo are out feeding in the hills,' he said, 'come out and have a look at them.'

'I cannot come,' I said, 'I have got a tea-party up at the house.'

'But we will go and see them and be back in a quarter of an hour,' said he.

This sounded to me like the propositions which people make to you in a dream. Lady Delamere would not fly, so I went up with him. We flew in the sun, but the hillside lay in a transparent brown shade, which soon we got into. It did not take us long to spy the Buffalo from the air. Upon one of the long rounded green ridges which run, like folds of a cloth gathered together at each peak, down the side of the Ngong mountain, a herd of twenty-seven Buffalo were grazing. First we saw them a long way below us, like mice moving gently on a floor, but we dived down, circling over and along their ridge, a hundred and fifty feet above them and well within shooting distance; we counted them as they peacefully blended and separated. There was one very old big black bull in the herd, one or two younger bulls, and a number of calves. The open stretch of sward upon which they walked was closed in by bush; had a stranger approached on the ground they would have heard or scented him at once, but they were not prepared for advance from the air. We had to keep moving above them all the time. They heard the noise of our machine and stopped grazing, but they did not seem to have it in them to look up. In the end they realized that something very strange was about; the old bull first walked out in front of the herd, raising his hundredweight horns, braving the unseen enemy, his four feet planted on the ground – suddenly he began to trot down the ridge and after a moment he broke into a canter. The whole clan now followed him, stampeding headlong down, and as they switched and plunged into the bush, dust and loose stones rose in their wake. In the thicket they stopped and kept close together, it looked as if a small glade in the hill had been paved with dark grey stones. Here they believed themselves to be covered to the view, and so they were to anything moving along the ground, but they could not hide themselves from the

'These hills, which are amongst the most beautiful in the world, are perhaps at their loveliest seen from the air…'

eyes of the bird of the air. We flew up and away. It was like having been taken into the heart of the Ngong Hills by a secret unknown road.

When I came back to my tea-party, the teapot on the stone table was still so hot that I burned my fingers on it. The Prophet had the same experience when he upset a jug of water, and the Archangel Gabriel took him, and flew with him through the seven heavens, and when he returned, the water had not yet run out of the jug.

In the Ngong Hills there also lived a pair of eagles. Denys in the afternoons used to say: 'Let us go and visit the eagles'. I have once seen one of them sitting on a stone near the top of the mountain, and getting up from it, but otherwise they spent their life up in the air. Many times we have chased one of these eagles, careening and throwing ourselves on to one wing and then to the other, and I believe that the sharp-sighted bird played with us. Once, when we were running side by side, Denys stopped his engine in mid air, and as he did so I heard the eagle screech.

The Natives like the aeroplane, and for a time it was the fashion on the farm to portray her, so that I would find sheets of paper in the kitchen, or the kitchen wall itself, covered with drawings of her, with the letters ABAK carefully copied out. But they did not really take any interest in her or in our flying.

Natives dislike speed, as we dislike noise, it is to them, at the best, hard to bear. They are also on friendly terms with time, and the plan of beguiling or killing it does not come into their heads. In fact the more time you can give them, the happier they are, and if you commission a Kikuyu to hold your horse while you make a visit, you can see by his face that he hopes you will be a long, long time about it. He does not try to pass the time then, but sits down and lives.

Neither do the Natives have much sympathy with any kind of machinery or mechanics. A group of the young generation have been carried away by the enthusiasm of the European for the motor-car, but an old Kikuyu said to me of them that they would die young, and it is likely that he was right, for renegades come of a weak line of the nation. Amongst the inventions of civilization which the Natives admire and appreciate are matches, a bicycle and a rifle, still they will drop these the moment there is any talk of a cow.

Frank Greswolde-Williams, of the Kedong Valley, took a Masai with him to England as a Sice, and told me that a week after his arrival he rode his horses in Hyde Park as if he had been born in London. I asked this man when he came back to Africa what he found very good in England. He thought my question over with a grave face and after a long time courteously said that the white men had got very fine bridges.

I have never seen an old Native who, for things which moved by themselves without apparent interference by man or by the forces of Nature, expressed anything but distrust and a certain feeling of shame. The human mind turns away its eye from witchcraft as from something unseemly. It may be forced to take an interest in the effects of it, but it will have nothing to do with the inside working, and no one has ever tried to squeeze out of a witch the exact recipe for her brew.

Once, when Denys and I had been up, and were landing on the plain of the farm, a very old Kikuyu came up and talked to us:

'You were up very high to-day,' he said, 'we could not see you, only hear the aeroplane sing like a bee.'

I agreed that we had been up high.

'Did you see God?' he asked.

'No, Ndwetti,' I said, 'we did not see God.'

'Aha, then you were not up high enough,' he said, 'but now tell me: do you think that you will be able to get up high enough to see him?'

'I do not know, Ndwetti,' I said.

'And you, Bedâr,' he said, turning to Denys, 'what do you think? Will you get up high enough in your aeroplane to see God?'

'Really I do not know,' said Denys.

'Then,' said Ndwetti, 'I do not know at all why you two go on flying.'

Kate O'Brien

(1897–1974)

Kate O'Brien was 'once and for all infatuated' with Spain, the setting for her most admired novel, *For One Sweet Grape*, a study of personalities and intrigue in the Spanish court of Phillip II that was later adapted for the stage and for a motion picture that starred Olivia de Havilland. *Farewell Spain*, her only travel book, seeks to capture the spirit of a lost place yet does not forsake wit and irony. At one point, O'Brien, chafing at not having had for two hours any kind of reviving drink, wonders, 'Is it odd if I decided to hate Salamanca?' An author of nine novels, she was one of the few Irish writers to consider as subjects members of the middle class, not the working or peasant classes. O'Brien was born in Limerick, Ireland, and died in Faversham, England.

from Farewell Spain

In retrospect I admire Salamanca and desire to return there, but while I was in the place for a variety of capricious reasons I did not truly appreciate it.

The journey there from Santiago had been a desperate business – occupying from four in the afternoon until seven the next morning. In broiling weather, and with a change of trains and two hours' delay at Astorga at 2 A.M. However, Spain can't help being a large place, and complicated cross-country journeys between its provincial towns must be taken philosophically. But on arrival there and at an attractive hotel on the Plaza Mayor, to be coldly assured that there could be no question of coffee or of hot water until after nine o'clock, for some mystic reason for ever withheld – that did not help my never very philosophic temperament towards sympathy with Salamanca. Withal, dejected and dirty, to have to say a sudden good-bye to a conception which had held my imagination strongly since childhood, I really got off on the wrong foot in Salamanca.

When I was ten and read the *Lay of the Last Minstrel* I took a tenacious liking to the name of the place where Michael Scott got his magic – *Salamanca's Cave*. This liking stayed with me and brought a specific idea with it, or rather two ideas, a picture and an intention. A picture of a dark, small rainy place of grey stone, where it was practically always night, and where everything was done by stealth and almost as if by sleep-walkers. And an intention to see it. It is the only place which I remember when I was young being absolutely determined to see sometime. God knows why, because the above description of my fantasy, which is as near as I can get to it, strikes me as revolting now, and I wasn't, I think, overweeningly interested in magicians and their goings-on. But I liked the words 'Salamanca's Cave', and they made me curious. 'Curious' is the *mot juste*, I think – nothing else. The curiosity stayed with me in adult life. So that honestly – I'm not trying to be whimsy-whamsy now – when I at last saw Salamanca I was quite considerably set back, superior though the bright reality is to my dank and silly notion. It was all the more childish of me to be surprised, as, although this town was new to me then, Castile was not, and I ought to have realised that there would be no chance of finding darkness, rain and sleep-walkers in any corner of that alive and vivid region. Still – my brain was not functioning well that morning. It was battered – practically in shreds. For I had travelled for fifteen hours in the company of the Barber of Salamanca and his silent wife and brother-in-law. They were returning from their summer holiday on the coast, and were very kind to us when we boarded the train. Gave us good advice about this and that, and, incidentally, told us to go to our unwelcoming but, as it afterwards proved, very pleasant hotel. (I had been going to go to the 'Bull's Head' where Borrow stayed, and which was listed in my 1932 Spanish Hotel book as good and inexpensive. But this nearly killed the Barber! How did I possibly not know that that hotel had been pulled down last May, and was being rebuilt? But how did I not know? He laughed till the tears flowed.) Anyway the Barber talked all night, and fidgeted and chuckled and talked and talked. All through the long pause in the canteen at Astorga too – where we leant in strange green lamplight against a wall and waited for very bad coffee; where I remember Mary muttered to me – in a surprising pause of the Barber's – that the Barber's brother-in-law was a Picasso harlequin. He had a masked and weary face. The Barber was physically a Sancho Panza but with none of Sancho's wit and less of his steadiness. I shall remember him for ever. I am tired already now through letting the memory of him become too definite.

Salamanca was his mania. He was just that proud of it he couldn't say! Not as an ancient university town of fame and beauty – though of course he wouldn't have a word said against a single stone of it, however old and out of date – No, Sir! But he admired Salamanca as their citizens might admire, say, Omaha, or Carthage, Ill.

Boredom is of two kinds, passive and active. The passive kind tells on one in the end, but the active is immediate agony, and leaves a cicatrice that is liable to throb again if touched in later life. I am rather subject to active boredom – but the scar inflicted by the Barber of Salamanca is one of my worst, and will never be completely insensitive. (It is certainly as bad as that inflicted by two women whom I knew in America fifteen years ago, and which still responds uneasily to my memory of them.) I have sometimes believed that I could see shadows spread under people's eyes when they were being frantically bored. I have seen faces age and sag under the onslaught of amiable extrovertism – and then I've known exactly what was happening in the victims' agonised heads. Well, the Barber turned night into day that night. He told me – the others were feigning sleep, but I couldn't because I can't keep still when I'm in pain – he told me the seating capacity of every restaurant and cinema in Salamanca. He told me the names of all the films which had come to those cinemas since their inception – and his own opinions on them. He told me the names of all the cafés and hotels, of all the doctors, dentists, lawyers, chemists and shoeblacks. He told me everyone's income, and the make of everyone's car. He corrected himself, he recanted, he woke his wife to get her ruling on certain statistics, he did sums, he remembered, he recalled, he agreed with himself. He was right – that was so, yes, of course he was right! Ha, ha! And he began again. In sheer delight he began again. He boasted frightfully without a pause.

That was the night we put down. So that as dark lifted outside from the scene which, with certain parts of Ireland, I believe to be without peer for beauty, as light returned to the golden plain that I had not seen for twelve months and exposed its morning innocence, the stillness of its villages, the peace of its scattered shepherds standing like Gothic saints among their gentle goats – I didn't care, I couldn't look.

And when the frantic business was over, when there had been about five sweet minutes of the silence and absence of the Barber, to be told – in the minimum of quiet words, I admit – that for two hours there could be no kind of reviving drink! Is it odd if I decided to hate Salamanca?

Eventually of course there was coffee. A bath, aspirin and sleep. In a lovely bed in a room with a marble floor. So that by afternoon one was able to light a cigarette, stroll on the balcony and look at Salamanca. Unfortunately some facts of the Barber's about the recent removal of the trees from the Plaza Mayor, and the why and the wherefore of it all, came over one in a muddled rush – you know how nightmares can create a hang-over. But I had myself in hand a bit at last. I refused to bother about the trees. The Plaza is lovely without them, anyhow. It is very wide, and quite square, I think. It is all of a piece, pure seventeenth century, colonnaded on its four sides, and with light, narrow balconies running along the first and second floors. All the houses are of the same height, four storeys – rather low and ample of face. The Town Hall, in the centre of the eastern side, and some other public office exactly facing it on the west, are more decorated than the other façades, but Baroque had laid its young, light hand symmetrically and thoughtfully over the whole square, which is full of Castilian sunlight. It is a most satisfactory example of civic building. A bright and inviting Plaza.

I remembered Borrow's sneers at the sinister clerics mumbling and plotting together under the colonnades. Those were the dark Carlist days, of course. And these are darker days for Spain, but the clerics seem to be well and truly muzzled now. Not much plotting left for them to do even here in their centuries-old preserve on which their tradition has impressed so much nobility. Curiously tough and engaging, that bigoted, honest fellow, Borrow. Catholic in all my blood, for years I could not bring myself to read *The Bible in Spain.* The idea of a member of the English Bible Society setting out to sell Bibles to Spain might suggest courage, but there was also too much obtuseness in it to make the record seem worth reading. However, in the end I read and re-read it. It is a shrewd and entertaining book – and yet, as the writer records with a faintly smug simplicity his conversations and friendly negotiations with this bookseller, that professor and the other priest, one has an embarrassing suspicion that, for all his shrewdness and working knowledge of human nature, his sturdy leg was sometimes gravely and unostentatiously pulled. Maybe I'm wrong. Anyway, when he was in Salamanca he had dealings with the Irish priests at the Irish Seminary – and his generous tribute to them, which sweeps him on exuberantly to toast the Irish scene and Irishwomen, comes very sweetly and disarmingly from the self-confident Bible-seller.

And that reminds me of my duty in regard to his book. I don't often borrow books, but I borrowed Borrow's *Bible in Spain*, and left it, where it might well feel at home, in a bedroom in Burgos. I borrowed it again – merely to look up something – in London. And it has disappeared again – vanished out of my flat. It really looks as if one of these days I shall have to buy three copies of *The Bible in Spain.*

In spite of the Barber, or perhaps because of him, I did not find the Salamanca cinemas up to much, or the cafés either. Though I suppose the latter were all right. Any café would serve under those colonnades with that sunny square to look out upon. And Salamancans, like all Spaniards, live out of doors, taking incessant leisurely *paseitos*, little strolls. So that except at the siesta hour, there is ample entertainment without going into cinemas. It is a widespread town, built harmoniously outward from the Plaza over the sides of a hardly perceptible hillock. The river Tormes washes past it, flowing west to join the Douro at the Portuguese frontier. All about is the open, austere plain, broken around the city's skirts and, in some of the squares, by acacia trees and lines of poplars. Almost every façade in Salamanca is beautiful, and the general tone is of buff, or of granite that is almost white. The famous Gothic House of the Shells seems at first a pretty novelty, but after a day or two one is weary of it. The Cathedral, romanesque-renascence and sandstone, like Santiago, falls very far indeed below the standard set for it by Galicia, for though from far off, from across the river, it can look noble enough with baroque tower and dome, close up its details irritate, and the bright splendours of the interior are quite shocking. There is more than a touch of the Barber's civic swagger about the inside of his Cathedral. But the big Dominican church of San Estéban is beautiful and beautifully cloistered. And they have a confessional box there – as in many other churches of Castile – where Saint Teresa confessed her sins. And the little church of San Martin is lovely romanesque.

In the University they show you, preserved now, not used, the lecture-room of Luis de León, and the guide tells the good story, that you already know, but that bears repeating – that the great poet-theologian, editor of Saint Teresa, was arrested by the Inquisition in 1572, and kept a prisoner for four and a half years while the Holy Office tried to trap him into heresy; he was released in 1576 and restored to his chair in Salamanca, and that on the day of his first lecture after his return, when the hall was packed and everyone expected some dramatic piece of self-justification – he took his chair and began: 'Gentlemen, as I said in my last lecture . . .' His lecture-room is very pleasant, whitewashed and luminous, with the narrow worn benches and ledges for note-taking heavily scarred with initials of forgotten theologians. The whole University is attractive, with renascence staircases, sunny courts and whitewashed lecture-halls. And the Irish Residencia, still full of Irish seminarists, is a place of quiet grassy courts and sixteenth-century cloisters.

When I read now in the books of journalists who have come back from the Spanish war of the brave new idea of some of the anti-clericals to save the more beautiful churches and convents from the anarchists – save the structures, that is, letting them have the furniture to burn – and to use them for garages and markets and so on, I am, I confess, very much bewildered. Of course, if there is to be no more praying, if that is done with for ever – then the number of empty museum churches, too beautiful to destroy, which Spain will have on her hands, will be a very ludicrous burden. But garages, markets! Oh, Heaven, how humourless people can be, how smugly blind to the strong reality behind life's great expressions! Will they make a dance-hall of Santiago de Compostela? No, no. The thing is not so easy as all that. Young men born yesterday can't be so ridiculously right when apparently all the centuries have been so wrong. They must think again about what to do with their priceless, emptied structures. Give me an anarchist every time rather than these bright, utilitarian dullards.

'Almost every façade in Salamanca is beautiful, and the general tone is of buff, or of granite that is almost white.'

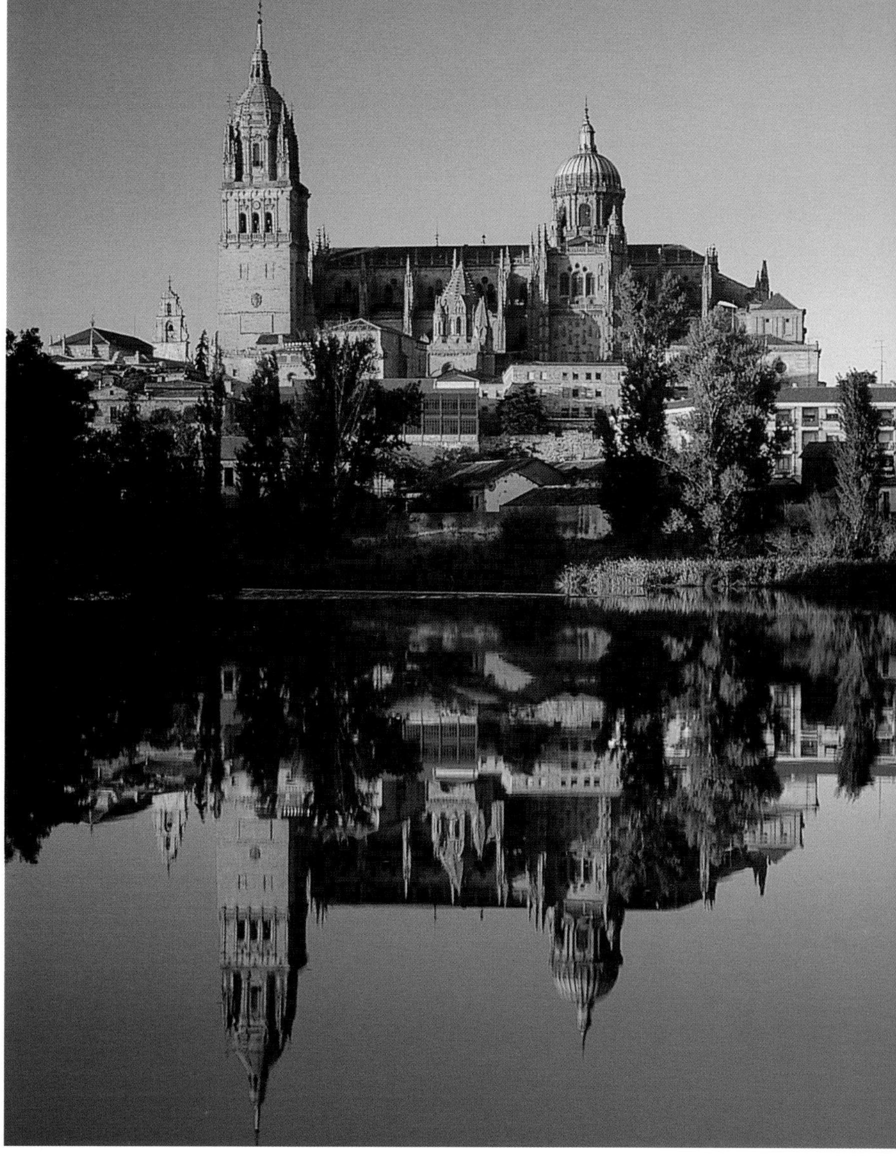

But let us leave Salamanca – by the same long and many-arched bridge over which a very famous son of the region departed about four hundred years ago on the first of his cynical adventures – as a blind man's guide. Lazarillo de Tormes, better known to modern Spaniards, who really know the comic characters of their literature, than the great Luis de León. Lazarillo's story, written anonymously, appeared in 1554 and was the first picaresque novel. It is very short, and in its manner of matter-of-fact, laconic cynicism had probably never been bettered. It shows the Spanish genius in one of its most successful and characteristic moods, realistic and cruel humour. I have not read it in Castilian, though I believe it must be limpid and easy reading for a foreigner, but in its contemporary English version by David Rowland, so strongly recommended by Fitzmaurice Kelly. Lazarillo is a young devil who lives on his wits, and tells his own past adventures when, as town-crier of Toledo, with a wife who is under the benevolent protection of the Archdeacon of San Salvador, he has reached his peak of bland prosperity. It is an admirably neat and amusing story and, as the authoritative Fitzmaurice Kelly says, 'may be read with as much edification and amusement as on the day of its first appearance'. So over the bridge with us, seeking less tricky fortune than Lazarillo, and only looking back to reflect that Salamanca is at its best in this perspective – seen as a whole, as a shapely assemblage, a successful municipal achievement. Which it would please the Barber to hear. God be with him. And now two hours to Avila by bus. Two hours of summer evening on a Castilian road.

Maud Parrish

(1878–1976)

In her memoir, Maud Parrish relates her life of madcap adventure with the breathless, excitable energy of one who cannot stand still. Parrish worked as a dance-hall girl in Dawson City, Yukon, and Nome, Alaska (after she had fled from an ill-fated marriage), and operated a gambling house in Peking at the turn of the century. With her 'nine pounds of luggage' and a banjo, she claimed to have gone around the world sixteen times, up and down continents, and around and about exotic islands. Parrish died at the age of ninety-eight. *Nine Pounds of Luggage* was her only book.

from Nine Pounds of Luggage

So I ran away. I hurried more than if lions had chased me. Without telling him. Without telling my mother or father. There wasn't any liberty in San Francisco for ordinary women. But I found some. No jobs for girls in offices like there are now. You got married, were an old maid, or went to hell. Take your pick.

That didn't help much – just made worry for everybody. My parents finally found me and took me home. My husband's family came out, some all the way from their dear 'old New England' home, and begged me to come back to their only son. I just couldn't do it. There was nothing the matter with him for somebody else. He might have made a good husband for another. So I tried to get a divorce.

But the poor old judge said I was too young. There must be a reconciliation. Something about the fine old East and the fresh young West getting along together. But those pretty words were a short-lived prophecy. As I rose to leave the courtroom, the fine old East delegation sneered a bit too much for my little five-foot-two mother who was born and raised in California. She knocked a couple of teeth down my still husband's throat, flattening out one Maine grin. Pa tossed him down a flight of stairs. The opposing lawyers calmly put down their brief cases and went to work on each other.

Soon the whole courtroom was in an uproar. I've seen some real battles in dance halls all over the world, but few to beat that one. Some of the proper, if pinched, Maine aunts fainted, others got out smelling salts, and the fight surged into the corridors. Everybody from everywhere else in the City Hall came to see, and soon all the grudges in the place were being ironed out in the mêlée. Like when two dogs bark and fight and other dogs – from Gawd knows where – come and stop, look and listen, and then pile in just for the fun of it.

By this time, I, 'the bone' the fight was over, had crawled under the bench. The judge had left to join the fight. I saw ink bottles comet across space. I heard a skull crack with a noise like a batted baseball. Even a heavy chair slid off a bald head in a way that made me wince as I held my hand over my eyes.

It was a mess by the time the ambulances and patrol wagons came. The lawyers were in rags, hats were crushed, shirt-tails (those left whole) hung out. Both victors and vanquished were carted off.

That couldn't happen since the 'passing of the old West', but I never hear the expression 'rugged individualism' that I don't think of that courtroom fight.

My father took me to some of his land in Trinity County, to get away from the scandal that nearly sunk the *Maine*. I had time to think it out up there, walking or riding horseback, in the woods. I knew I couldn't go back to the husband the judge had left me tied to legally. And to me that meant I couldn't live in San Francisco. Some see life in black and white; others – and they're the lucky ones – in old-gold hues. But the life I knew then made me see red. Wanderlust can be the most glorious thing in the world sometimes, but when it gnaws and pricks at your innards, especially in spring, with your hands and feet tied, it's awful. So I left. Without telling a soul.

I had a little money, and my banjo. I didn't know what I'd do when the money ran out, but I went anyway, to Seattle, and quick as a wink I got passage on a boat for Alaska. The air was full of the Klondyke. The lure of adventure pulled me aboard and the tied-down feeling stayed ashore.

Here I saw people I could understand. Here were those in the flesh who had filled my imagination, who had lived and traveled in my mental map of Old Mother Earth. Imagination is a grand, stimulating thing like a cocktail, but to find reality is the full course dinner with champagne. Those miners, prospectors, contractors, adventurers, gamblers; those other mysterious characters whose business it would be difficult to figure, suited my dream. There were a few women on the boat, planning to start hotels or restaurants, or do their mining in dance halls, and one or two like myself who just wanted to see what the Klondyke had in store for them. There were no prospectors' wives, because prospectors didn't have wives – not to mention. But no matter who they were or where they were from, both old and young had the spirit I admired.

From Skagway I went over the Pass to White Horse, part of the way hiking and part by dog team. I really felt free then in that country! From there by dog team five hundred miles to Dawson. Dogs and people were bursting to get into that capital of the frozen northland. I arrived with but ten dollars, but Mr. Rockefeller himself never felt richer. In that exhilarating atmosphere, I'd have bet I could clear the mountains with a hop, skip, and jump. The very air was electric, and the people were electric too, one hundred per cent alive, whatever else ailed them. What if they had run away from wives or husbands, conventions and restrictions? The call of adventure, the call of the wild, was in most of them, no matter what they were doing.

I can still hear the voice of the driver of that dog team yelling 'Mush on!' (from the French Canadian 'marchons') in the cold crisp air. I was glad I went by dog team. Many who went by boat later in the summer were lost in the rapids. There's a graveyard outside White Horse of bodies recovered.

Dawson was a small place, sprawled along the bank of the Yukon, at the foot of a hill with a big scar across it, most likely from mining activities. The Canadian Mounties and un-mounties kept it very well under control compared to the conditions I found later in Nome, which was in United States territory. For awhile I shared a log cabin with a very sweet, beautiful and fair-minded girl – a visionary dreamer, honest as the day is long. I have thought of her through the years as the girl in Robert W. Service's poem, *My Madonna*, for she had just such an expression – and eyes are the windows of the soul no matter what life we outwardly live. 'My madonna – I hailed me a woman from the streets – shameless but, oh, so fair!' Years later I learned of her death in a prison to which she had been sentenced for the crime of theft of thousands. I am sure she never committed it. She loved a bartender, and many bartenders became rich through stealing from miners, drunkards, and others, when weighing out gold dust for drinks. She must have been used as a decoy. She was too good to ever be crooked. Regardless of what the people who live by somebody's rules (God didn't make them) may think about adventurers, they often have deeper feelings and loyalties than those who go in for show or behave because it's supposed to be correct. The out-of-the-way places have their tragedies too – without any tear-jerking hokum thrown in.

At first I played my banjo in a variety hall, but the dance hall across the street, one of fifty or more ranged along the river front, was more exciting. So over I went. It was a popular place. Everybody gravitated there. Inside was a long bar, tables and chairs, a place to dance and a few rooms for the amorous ones. A big warm stove stood in the corner (it was cherry-red when forty below outside). The husky, happy-go-lucky men with their gold dust gathered there, and the beautiful girls from all over the world, flitted around like exotic butterflies. Even now, I feel the zip boom hurrah bang of that dance hall and the 'what do we care' spirit in the air. No wonder Rex Beach glorified those girls in his novels. I've no doubt many have glorified themselves since and are now sitting on top of the world, for there's nothing like a combination of liveliness and loveliness for landing a place in the sun.

There were, for instance, the three jolly Lamar sisters who married, one at a time, the happy-go-lucky prospector and miner, Swift Water Bill. 'Twas a family affair. All three threw their dice on the one man, and each in turn annexed a large chunk of his fortune along with a divorce. One day when we were eating together, the wittiest of the Lamars confided a story that illuminated the inner workings of Swift Water's mind. It seems she liked bacon and eggs for breakfast, but eggs were eggs in Dawson and Bill had bought them all, cornered the market, so that his lady love, who had been drifting in her affections, would either eat her eggs out of his hand or no eggs at all. No prolonged animal-trainer tactics for Swift Water Bill.

One girl I knew stayed for two winters with a miner on a Klondyke claim, for twenty thousand dollars. Another, a married girl, had come up to get some money because her husband was hurt and they weren't doing well at home. She made several thousand, went back home, and bought a hotel in a mid-western city, and took care of her husband. They've done well since.

During my first night in the dance hall, the owner of a little restaurant clearing one hundred dollars a day (mostly from beans), an Austrian, came up and invited me to waltz.

'If you don't promise these men you will go with them later, they won't dance with you,' he coached me. 'But you can always kid them along and fool them at the end.'

I was so young he thought I was green. I thanked him and said I would follow his advice. But he gave me no chance to dance with anyone else. He danced with me again and again, and became very confidential.

'Yes,' I agreed to everything he proposed, and then, finally, simply, 'Good night.'

He seemed hurt and reproached me angrily, 'But you promised!'

'Didn't you tell me to?' I asked.

How that story traveled!

Oh, it was grand to be free and think up your own line. And up there I wasn't thought wild and headstrong and naughty.

It was two dollars a dance for a dance of a minute, dancing all night, and we got half, plus fifty cents on every drink we drank with patrons – weighed over the bar in gold dust. What a bonanza! But my mind was on how soon I could earn enough to go the two thousand miles down the Yukon to St. Michaels and Nome. I've always tired of places quickly.

Toward the wee small hours, as the liquor began to take its toll of brains, usually a fight would start and likewise finish. Disputes over mining claims and the jumping of claims were often settled in bars and dance halls where most of the people spent most of their time while in Dawson. I saw two men killed over a mining dispute the first week I was there. One was at the bar, with murder in his heart, by the expression on his face. The other came in to kill him, and both shot each other. One died instantly, the other a few hours later. Shortly before this happened, I had met an elderly woman on the trail whom I admired very much because she had come alone to such a place at her age. She was an artist and was doing very well, painting signs for people. We became good friends and she wished to see the place where I worked. So I had brought her with me on this evening. It was probably the first time in her life she was ever in a bar and to see two men killed ten minutes after she entered was something of a shock.

As soon as the ice broke in June, I went out.

The Yukon River was 'new' then. The channel had not been charted and often, during the months of the year that the river was navigable, the boats were stuck on the sandbars until rescued.

In the cabin on one side of me was a very sedate U.S. Marshal from Washington, D.C., bringing a prisoner to Nome. The cabin on my other side was occupied by French 'Elise', a lady from Lousetown.

Lousetown, across the river from Dawson, was given over entirely to a district glowingly lit up in red, and in the hour before the boat started down the river, I watched the jolly French girls coming aboard, making a racket like a brood of cackling hens. This was the first boat out that year.

One passenger had visions of building a toll bridge near Nome. Another, a rich man from New York, had received no news of money he had invested through partners and so was on his way to investigate the mine in person. Whenever we were high and dry on a sandbar, he insisted on panning for gold. One day, a comedian dropped a tiny nugget into his pan while his back was turned. After that, he'd have remained, like Crusoe, on that sandbar if he hadn't been told it was under water most of the time.

We played ball on one sandbar near Circle City (Arctic Circle) until another river boat came alongside and slid us off by churning the water with its sidewheel for hours until we were free.

At Circle City, the cook threw the garbage into the river near the bank. Indian malamutes swam in after it and you could see those dogs, chewing mouths' full of bones, while still under the water. Safety first. They were beautiful and the last word in intelligence. Many a tale went around about malamutes stealing food cached in trees miles from nowhere.

One young prospector, named Thiers, told me of having been awakened from sleep one night by a malamute's jumping down from a tree, so full of purloined bacon that when he landed it knocked a sort of bark out of him. (Malamutes don't bark.) Later he had to kill the dog. After hunting all day, Thiers only was able to bring back one Arctic ptarmigan, a big bird good to eat. While he was pulling out the feathers, the dog came by on the dead run, snatched the bird from his hands and ran off with it. Loss of supplies could easily mean loss of life, and so the thief had to be killed as a measure of self-defense.

Years afterward, two maiden ladies named Thiers moved into my house in San Francisco. 'Did you ever have a brother in the Arctic?' I asked.

'Yes,' they answered, and it turned out that my prospector friend was he. I learned then that he, his half-breed Eskimo wife and their two sons had come to the States to live. Later I spent a very happy week with them on their cattle ranch in Arizona.

At the mouth of the Koyukuk River, above the Circle, two prospectors and a small boatload of supplies were lowered over the side. They were to be in the Arctic, alone, away from every settlement, for a year. A lump rose in my throat as I watched them drift off fearlessly and with such hope into the great unknown, and contrasted them with all the people living at home who, despite their comforts, are full of grouches and aspirin.

At an old Russian settlement near St. Michaels four blighted and withered but undiscouraged men came on board. Having missed the last boat out the season before, by one day, they had been compelled to remain, marooned, in that dark little village for eight months.

It was grand to reach Nome, at long last, but the town couldn't hold a candle to Dawson. It was like coming into a calm pool after shooting the rapids. The most fascinating places, of course, were the dance halls, and, as in Dawson, I made the round of them. It was very curious to see the Eskimos standing all night like cigar store Indians inside the entrances of the dance halls, drinking in the passing show while motionlessly offering for sale beautiful carved cribbage boards of walrus tusks. What must the music, the people, the bars and the dancing have seemed to those poor hypnotized fellas, who had never seen the like before and who should have been out gathering supplies of fish and game for the long night? No doubt many of them starved that winter.

Nome was a bad town, wild and crooked, full of thieves and murderers and real lawlessness; while in Dawson people could leave their gold dust in bags outside a door and it would be safe. You couldn't do anything like that in Nome. Dawson was under Canadian control and Nome under the United States, but the real reason for the better conditions in Dawson wasn't that – or the Mounties. It was so hard to get to Dawson that you had to have something in you to desire to go there, while Nome was on the direct route from San Francisco and Seattle. Everybody – every kind – that had the price of a ticket, dumped themselves in Nome to live off the hardier ones. But the opportunities were less.

'The air was full of the Klondyke. The lure of adventure pulled me aboard…'

One night in a tough little 'theater' (Gawd save the mark for calling it that, but nothing else describes it so well), I got fed up, and homesick. At seventeen, no matter how anxious you are to get away, you long for Ma and Pa and the familiar things. I was playing 'Swanee River', with variations, and 'Old Black Joe', and such. Lots of us got right homesick. We were talking about it to four fine chaps, prospectors off for another gold rush in Patagonia. When they said I could stop off in San Francisco and show my mother and father I was alive and well, I agreed to go along as their mascot. Just like that, on the spur of the moment, I was off from one end of the Americas right down to the other. It was the only way I could have gotten passage. One captain, when asked, said, 'Damn the passengers. I'm filling up with freight.' Freight paid profits and didn't have to eat and sleep. But the four men had made arrangements.

Vivienne de Watteville

(1900–1957)

Vivienne de Watteville was no stranger to Africa when she arrived in Nairobi during the 1930s with dreams of going into 'the wilds unarmed and in some unforeseen way win friendship with the beasts', and of scaling Mount Kilimanjaro. She had been there before with her father, a zoologist and big-game hunter, and had written about it in *Out in the Blue*, an account filled with the adventure of the safari – lions, elephants, rhinos, and crocodiles – but with a tragic end. When her father was mauled and killed by a lion, she took command of the expedition. Later de Watteville returned alone on a film-making expedition which had to be modified when Kenyan officials wouldn't let her go into the jungle without armed guides. Eventually she would decide to forbear from serious film-making because (as the *Times* of London wrote in its review of *Speak to the Earth*, her account of this journey), 'any material trophy of the hunter, whether a skin or strip of film, falls short of whatever is in the hunter's heart to possess or in his sense to memorize'. She did manage to get as close as possible to the most dangerous of animals (as the following excerpt shows). While de Watteville never made it to the top of Kilimanjaro, she did live for a time alone in a hut on neighbouring Mount Kenya.

from **Speak to the Earth: Wanderings and Reflections Among Elephants and Mountains**

Then, suddenly, toiling upwards through trees and creepers, I came out onto an open crest, and there before me, lifting its head above the forest, was the bare, grey summit. It might have been three hours away and it might have been thirty: all depended upon what lay between those intervening ridges suffocating under the tangled green barriers of forest. But to the eye it looked attainable, and the more I looked, the more it lured me on. It was no use discussing the possibilities with the men, and I took a high hand.

'The mountain is near enough,' I said, 'we'll follow the crest,' but I dared not meet Mohamed's eye, nor did I glance at him.

Sometimes one guide led, sometimes the other, and when they flagged, or cast about, I struck ahead. But all at once it was borne in upon me that their resistance and also that of the jungle itself had both given out at the same time. Finding that I was not to be put off they had now cheerfully accepted the position, and put their interest in what lay ahead. As for the jungle, we had left the worst of it behind, and the ridge brought us out into the daylight clear above it. Following one ridge to the next, with occasional drops into the forest, we climbed a straight and broad path which was hemmed in on either side by dense hedges of greenery.

It was paved all the way with the droppings of rhino, buffalo and elephant. I was ahead and walking along with my eyes bent on the spoor, when I came to a grey boulder lying across the path. I was in the act of walking round it when it suddenly heaved itself up beside me with the terrifying snort of a rhino. I recoiled and leapt backwards, while the rhino (who was presumably facing the other way) tore off in the opposite direction. This is only conjecture; for the instant the boulder sprang to life, I did not wait for a second glance but turned and bolted, colliding with the man behind me, who also turned and ran for his life shouting 'Faru! faru!' (rhino) and in the twinkling of an eye we had scattered like chaff.

The rhino had disappeared, and the forest gradually settled back into silence. One by one, with hearts still beating with fright, we stole out of our several retreats and back to the path.

I suppose that the boys were now worked up to the adventure, or that they had hopes of finding more ivory, for none of them thought of using this as a pretext for going home before worse befell. Still out of breath, they laughed over the scare as each contributed some detail to our comically expeditious flight. But as I started off again, now a trifle daunted and very much on the alert, I began to think that losing the way was a minor evil compared with nearly falling over a sleeping rhino. I was trespassing in a sanctuary where no human being (according to the natives) had ever set foot before, and I could not tell but what there might be plenty more rhino ahead. The forest was ominously silent, and everything pointed to its being unusually full of big and possibly dangerous game. If any of them took it into their heads to charge, and casualties resulted, the blame would be mine for exposing my men to undue risk. It was an unpleasant thought and responsibility began to sit so heavily upon my shoulders that I almost wished that I had given in to the boys an hour back, and left the forest alone.

The rhino, very naturally, had been annoyed at having his sleep so rudely disturbed; and since the path was the only place where a rhino could bask in the sun, the path was obviously a dangerous one to walk, and other sleeping rhino, (or buffalo) might be less good-natured.

I was debating within myself whether I was at all justified in going on, when sure enough I detected another grey cumbersome shape above the grass-stalks ahead. It was only a few yards off, but I trained the glasses on it to make certain, and they showed up clearly the grey corrugations of a rhino's hide. I retreated on tiptoe and held a consultation with the boys. A détour was made impossible by the thickness of the jungle on either hand, but Lembogi, always the resourceful one of the party, said that if we retired to safety down-wind, he would climb a tree, wake the rhino by throwing sticks at him, and try to drive him away.

The reader may well wonder why I did not seize this golden opportunity myself, and (with the wind blowing so true) nothing would have been easier than to have crept up to the sleeping rhino and scratched him behind his ears. He might have loved it (and introduced me to the whole forest as a reward) but on the other hand if he hadn't, my chances for experiment would have been for ever curtailed. This would always be the difficulty, for when chances came I did not dare.

So Lembogi threw sticks and bits of caked mud at him till he awoke, and with many surprised and indignant snorts he took himself off, and we continued on our way.

Each time I hoped that we were on the final crest I would come to another disheartening drop. Mohamed urged me afresh to turn back, saying we should be benighted. I minded very little if we were, for it would hurt none of us; we had matches and could make a fire. The more work I put into that climb, the less I could relinquish it. It is one thing to come home dead-beat but successful, and quite another to be defeated after all; not only that, but I could never get the boys to face it again, and even I was not over-keen on a third venture.

Finally, it was the boys themselves who pointed to the summit and said that it was not very far.

Enviously I admired the way they could climb. As for me, I had put all my energies into the lead when it had been necessary, and now, under the burning midday sun beating fiercely down between thunderclouds, I was badly spent; my knees trembled as I panted up through the reeling boulders. We rested a little, and Asani pointed (as I thought) into a treetop at 'a bird that makes a noise like a motor-car'. I scanned the tree vainly for some strange kind of hooting vulture, when I heard the unmistakable throb of an engine, and picked up a black speck in the sky. I looked at it with profound disgust. Artistically, dramatically, from every point of view, its appearance was ill-timed, not to say tactless. Just as I was blazing the unknown trail, to find I was being actually looked down upon was sheer anticlimax. The fact that the aeroplane was ten miles off was only very mildly consoling. 'But at least,' I thought, 'he can't land on the summit'; and I pushed on.

At last I climbed above the forest zone, passing beneath the last outposts – stunted trees ragged with beard-moss in whose chequered shade lay a carpet of tiny peas (a kind of vetch with a leaf like wood sorrel, probably the *Parechetus communis*) whose blossoms were a lovely transparent blue. Above them flitted miniature blue butterflies, as though the petals themselves had taken wing.

Heath and boulders rose up against the flying clouds and deep blue sky. I waded through billowing masses of white

'I drew to within forty yards of the rhino, yet they still looked like a couple of grey boulders as they browsed off an isolated patch of sere grass.'

flowering shrubs, and beyond, all the ground was decked gold and blue and purple with flowers. There must have been fifty different kinds (possibly far more) and one I have never seen anywhere before or since clung to the rock in profusion like a blue mist. It had velvet purplish leaves and clusters of little powdery blue flowers like down, with a sprinkling of golden stamens.

This part of the mountain was a paradise of wild flowers. The Alps in the full glory of springtide could not have unfolded anything more tender or more vivid; indeed, the intensity of those burning blues and golds nodding in the hot scented air against the almost sapphire sky and the shimmering pillars of cloud produced an effect that was peculiarly Alpine. I lingered there, willy-nilly, promising myself that I would return another day when I should have plenty of time. How often one bribes oneself with these false promises to return to something specially entrancing glimpsed on the road to something else!

The top, when at last I reached it was, after all, not really the top, and beyond a dipping saddle another granite head still frowned down upon me.

But meanwhile, below me the south side disclosed a grassy depression girt about by the two summits and bare granite screes; and amid that desolation the grass stretched so green and rural that you had looked there for shepherds with their flocks. Instead of which, on the far side of a quaking bog, I saw – grey among the grey slabs – two rhino.

Leaving Lembogi, Kabechi and the old guide behind, I took Asani with the cameras and ran down the slope, crossed the bog and climbed up the far side. Mohamed was to follow at a short distance, on account of the clatter of his boots on the rocks. I drew to within forty yards of the rhino, yet they still looked like a couple of grey boulders as they browsed off an isolated patch of sere grass. The bleached stalks bowing before the wind alone gave a flicker of life to that adamantine expanse of stone.

The wind had risen to a tearing gale, and nosing straight into it I approached the rhino somewhat downhill. There was no chance of this steady blow jumping round to betray me, and it was strong enough to carry away any sound of my footsteps. Precaution was therefore unnecessary, and I walked boldly up to them. Just how close I was, it is hard to say; but I felt that I could have flipped a pebble at them, and I noted subconsciously that the eye of the one nearest me was not dark brown as I had imagined it, but the colour of sherry.

And the experience has left me in some doubt whether a

rhino has such poor sight as is commonly believed. Perhaps they heard the clicking of the cinema camera. This may have given the nearer one my direction, and then my coat or the brim of my hat flapping in the wind possibly caught his eye. At any rate, his ears pricked up, his champing jaws were held in suspense, and that little pale eye was very definitely focused straight upon me.

He lifted his head, trying to catch the wind. It told him nothing, but he now came deliberately towards me, nose to the ground and horn foremost, full of suspicion. I pressed the button and tried to keep a steady hand. This was not easy; for a rhino seen through the finder of a small cinema camera looks remote, and it is only when you take the camera down to make sure, that you are horribly startled to see how near he really is. In the finder I saw his tail go up, and knew that he was on the point of charging. Though it was the impression of a fraction of a second, it was unforgettable. He was standing squarely upon a flat boulder that raised him like a pedestal, and he seemed to tower up rugged and clear-cut as a monument against the flying clouds.

Such a chance could never possibly occur again, and the magnificence of that picture for the moment blinded me to all else. I had done better to bolt then, while he was still hesitating. I read the danger signal, yet in a kind of trance of excitement I still held the camera against my forehead. Then Mohamed fired a shot over the rhino's head to scare him, and I turned and fled for my very life.

The rhino was only momentarily taken aback. Before I had time to skip out of his sight he had made up his mind to charge me. The angry thunder of his snort, mingled with a screech like an engine blowing off steam, lent me wings. When I dared throw a glance over my shoulder I saw that both rhino were bearing down upon me with frightening speed. The boys had had a start of me, and as I raced after them across the vistas of stone bare as asphalt without a blade of cover anywhere, conviction swept over me that this time the game was up.

Though I ran and ran as I had never run in my life before, and my heart pounded in my ears and my lungs stiffened with the pain of drawing breath, time went suddenly into slow motion. Each step was weighted with lead; I wanted to fly over the ground and, as in some horrid nightmare, I felt as though I were scarcely moving.

The rhino were swiftly gaining upon me; their furious snorts overtook me on the wings of the gale. The boys, on the other hand, had disappeared as though the earth had swallowed them. I made one more desperate spurt and then, as I realised the utter futility of it, a fold in the hillside opened to receive me also. I tumbled headlong down a little cliff and landed on a ledge of heather.

The rhino would never face this drop even if they looked over and saw me. I glanced up apprehensively, but there was no sign of them.

In this sheltered place there was not a sound, and even the wind had dropped. With a thankful heart I stretched myself face downward on the heather, and panted as though I could never get a complete lungful of air again, while waves of crimson and orange rushed and throbbed before my eyes.

The boys climbed up to me (they had landed farther down) and seeing Mohamed's lugubrious expression of disapproval I quickly put my word in first.

'That,' said I, 'is the best picture I have ever taken!' And though unable at once to control my trembling fingers, I turned my attention to the intricate business of changing the film. Asani, taking his cue from me, stoutly declared he had never seen anything like the way the rhino had stood out on that rock; and the three Masai, who had witnessed the whole thing from the other side of the bog, now joined us and gave their version. Even at the time, I had been dimly aware that they were yelling with excitement as though they were cheering the winner of the Grand National. It must have been worth watching, and the pity was that there had not been a second photographer.

During their graphic recounting of what had happened, even Mohamed began to unbend and smile. Congratulations rained down upon his modest head, as well they ought, for his well-timed shot had undoubtedly saved my life.

As I was busy with the camera and listened to their talk, I too began quietly to enjoy myself. There is nothing like an escape to give you the feeling of exhilaration. The pleasant glow of it was stealing over me when I made a crushing discovery. In changing the film I found that I had overshot the end by fully six feet. This meant that the rhino's mad rush and the dramatic moment when he had stood silhouetted against the sky, were recorded on nothing but blind, red paper. The disappointment was bitter, so bitter that there were no words for it. The boys still talked of the marvellous picture, and I had not the heart to undeceive them.

Freya Stark

(1893–1993)

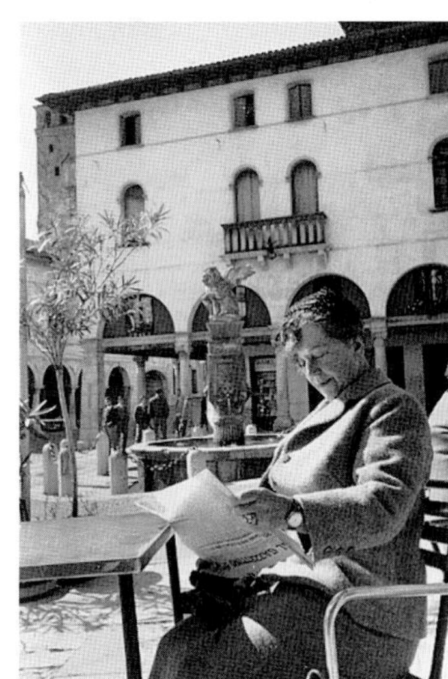

With Freya Stark one doesn't know where the traveller stops and the writer begins. Few can match Stark's ability to seize upon the *mot juste*, her luminous descriptive style, or the breadth of her sensitivity, whether she is writing about archaeological history, the personality of Robin (her donkey), or a baby in a leather cradle. The book *Winter in Arabia* was published when Stark was employed as southern Arabia expert for the Ministry of Information in London. A loyalist to the British Crown, she was highly valued as an expert in Arabic dialects, particularly during the war years. She has travelled extensively in every decade (except the 1990s) since World War II, visiting Turkey, China, Afghanistan, and Nepal. Freya Stark was named Dame of the British Empire in 1972; she died in England in 1993.

from Winter in Arabia

Robin

My donkey had no name, his master Ahmed told me, so I called him Robin. I had been charmed to see that Ahmed fed him on dates, sharing his own lunch in equal portions. Now, as I began to know the pair more intimately, Ahmed's attachment to this soulless animal began to show itself for what it was – an obstacle to the whole progress of our caravan.

Everyone knows that a donkey should go faster than a camel; the seven days from Mukalla to Du'an are five days only to an active ass. But this unspeakable Robin knew that he had but to droop his ears and look pathetic, to pause knock-kneed before a boulder perfectly easy to circumvent – his master's heart went out to him, thoughts even of gain were forgotten – if the hillside happened to be moderately steep, I would be asked to walk.

This happened at the very beginning of the 'aqaba of Khurje, by which we climbed from Radhhain in the morning. I had already fallen off once beside the ancient dam, and been held by Ahmed in his agitation firmly pinned among the donkey's hoofs. I had been roused in the earliest dawn by braying when the millet stalks which Robin looked upon as breakfast were accidently rustled by a passing foot. And his lethargy was mere pretence: the sight of a female donkey, even on the far horizon, would set him off with cries, Ahmed hanging to the halter for his life, nearly pulling me off under the obviously inaccurate impression that a donkey and its rider are inseparable.

So I refused to dismount, and we crawled slower and more slowly up the hill with a feeling of coldness between us. Ahmed was a tall angular peasant with high cheek-bones and narrow eyes, and a mild expression due largely to the fact that he had none of those small wrinkles produced by thought. He walked with his head down, asleep to the landscape about him, considering small financial problems in his soul. The peasant and the beduin are two different species. But when I had spent a day wearying of his dullness, I would see him go with his ungainly walk to say his prayers apart, or watch him spreading the millet stalks with an air of tenderness before the indolent Robin, and would feel ashamed when I considered how these endless small sums of his were devoted to the support of three orphan relatives besides his wife and daughters and two sisters – burdens accepted without murmur or repining. I would feel ashamed but I would also observe how the accumulated efforts of Christianity have failed to make us enjoy the sight of mere virtue unadorned, for the fact is that Ahmed was quite unattractive.

Far different was Awwad of the Deyyin who was leading us to his castle on the jōl.* Black-bearded with a large, lascivious

* Jōl: barren plateau in the Arabian peninsula.

'It is strange to feel that one is a monster. The children looked at me with solemn interest, then turned their heads, weeping, to their mother.'

mouth and always cheerful, he had come as far as 'Amd partly to meet us, partly to arrange for a third wife, since the second one says the work is too hard and wants to leave him. Apart from the difficulty of providing funds for this transition, which was still rather problematical, Awwad's head was not troubled by finance: freer than a millionaire from its problems, he was able to concentrate on pleasant things when they came – the cooking of a sheep for dinner, or the brewing of tea in the shade. Now, at 6:40 A.M., with the sun pouring in to the Wadi Sobale as if it were a cup, he led the way up a zigzag track where smooth milky stones laid neatly still show an antique causeway to the pass.

They have remained intact in a protected place, sheltered from winds and landslides by the cliff: and where the cliff breaks away in a perpendicular tower, the causeway creeps behind it, through a tunnel in whose semi-darkness lies a smooth block of limestone, with pre-Islamic letters scratched upon it, sign of an ancient roadway to the sea. It was the first *certain* pre-Islamic object since Hureidha. The cleft was made, said 'Ali, by the sword of a saint of Islam.

'Do you imagine he wrote the Himyaritic letters?' I asked.

'Ali looked at me nonplussed for a moment. Then he laughed with his usual generosity, admitting defeat. 'Nothing escapes the English,' said he.

Our camels lumbered by, their quarters gigantic in the shadows: a few hundred yards on, an hour from the bottom, we broke by a chasm into the white sunlight of the jōl.

Into the thin and clean reviving air. Over the edge, far down, Wadi Sobale pursued uninhabited windings between gnarled cliffs. But over the plain a silver mistiness made every distance gentle in the sun: our journey lay flat and far and visible before us, flanked, like an avenue, by brown truncated mounds. Flints of palaeolithic man lay strewn here, glistening on the ground; and I thought of the Archaeologist with a gleam of warmth; grateful for the pleasure of now recognizing these small and intimate vestiges of time.

Awwad the bedu rejoiced at being out of the lowlands and encouraged us with fallacious distances. Three hours, he said, would bring us home. We therefore rode gently through the morning, leaving on our left hand the track to Du'an. I had decided to push on for the south.

The jōl was dry as a bone: the water-holes we passed were waterless; two years had gone by without rain. At eleven-twenty-five we dipped into a valley, the head of Wadi Zerub.

The charm of all the western jōl lies in these shallow valley heads where, just below the upper rocky rim, rain-water collects and trees are sheltered from the wind. A few solitary towers, or small fortified villages stand there, surrounded by thinly scratched fields. In the distance, on our left, we could see several of them as we rode – Berawere and Berire, fair-sized clusters, belonging to sayyids. Through them ran the Van der Meulen's track to Dhula'a, a tiny market town. That was the main way for caravans to Hajr; but we, led by Awwad, kept to the west among the Deyyin beduin, and rested till three-thirty at Zarub, under the shadow of their 'ilb trees. Three little forts stood up and down the pastoral low valley, and the few inhabitants, friendly and wild and shy, stood in a fringe around. The men talked and accepted us as guests of the Deyyin – but a young woman, advancing carelessly and seeing me of a sudden, stood petrified with fear. The whole party, hers and our own, urged her on, saying that I would not bite, or words to that effect, and she finally came gingerly, touched my hand with frightened fingers, and fled to safety. She had five wild little children about her, and a brass-bound girdle at her waist. It is strange to feel that one is a monster. The children looked at me with solemn interest, then turned their heads, weeping, to their mother. Only the smallest accepted me, not having reached the age of understanding; it lay in a leather cradle, with leather fringes and a leather top to cover it, head and all: its mother carries it, slung like a basket on her arm; and when she has to labour in the fields, erects a tripod of three sticks from which it swings. These women are unveiled, small and sturdy like their men; they look as if their families went back to the beginnings of time. Their tiny, solitary villages must be very old, with careful pebble-lined half-empty ponds.

At three-thirty, rested and happy, I noticed that Awwad's perpetual optimism seemed ruffled: he was chafing to be off.

'But,' said I, 'we must be quite near. You said three hours this morning and here we have been riding for three and a half already on the jōl.'

'Ah, well,' said Awwad, 'it is not very far.'

'Shall we get there by sunset?' I asked. When it is impossible to get exactitude even for the present, it is simply a waste of time to wrangle for it in the past.

'If we hurry, we may,' said Awwad doubtfully.

We still had, I found, two valley ravines to dip into – Mlah, and Sobale, our wadi of the morning. They were delightful places, with the charm of things which live for their own pleasure, serving no utilitarian end of man, like the loveliness of childhood, free of conscious purpose. These cradles of valleys had the same innocent happiness about them. The waters had scooped them with a rush and left visible traces as one scrambled from ledge to ledge, undercut by the violence of the past. Little tufts of wild palm grow there and a great variety of shrubby trees, that keep their branches low, not to emerge into the wild currents that sweep the jōl above. You go steeply down and steeply up the other side, and the slow-footed camels take their time; and, in a blank space of the map, the existence of these ravines makes it impossible to guess even roughly how long a journey will take across the jōl. I was finding it just double what I had been told.

Awwad was anxious now, and tried to urge Robin and the unresponsive Ahmed with unavailing words: lengthening blue shadows began to lie to the east of every mound. In the emptiness a curly-headed lad from 'Azzan had appeared, flapping in sandals made of a ragbag of leathers stitched anyhow. I have read somewhere that the people of 'Azzan wear these to brush away scorpions from their path. However this may be, the young lad adopted us and took matters in hand. He trotted singing behind Robin, with a sharp stick in his hand: Robin understood. Awwad and a black cousin of his, with guns upon their shoulders, joined the chorus. Robin trotted, while his master sloped behind us begging the company in vain 'to have a heart'. I laughed; even Robin enjoyed it; the jōl now was flat as a landing-ground with limestone snouts pushed here and there along it. The sun dipped and blackish clouds sailed from the east with spots of rain. At this moment we came to an edge and saw Romance in the varied light of evening – a little castle, walled and towered, in an island of 'ilb trees gilded by slanting shafts of sun. The long barrow of Awwad's Himyaritic ruins was there beside it; two more towers among trees on the left; and on the southern horizon, improbable as some medieval background, a cluster of five towers, the fortress of Hajlein.

As we climbed down the blocks of limestone Awwad's baby son toddled in the path to meet us: his father picked him up on to the shoulder that had no gun. The little family of the castle were at the gate. The place looked poor and bare when we drew near, but strong, built of small jōl stones laid flat and stuck with mud, the central keep with battlements crowned with brush wood, and brushwood also round the outer wall: inside it were pens built with low roofs for cattle.

The only two women of the place, the precarious bride and a sister, took me by the hand up shallow slabs of steps to the guest room in the keep – a good room, old and black and low. Its door was carved, its small windows one foot by eight inches shuttered with thick blocks, the ceiling sustained by a tree-trunk column. The men hung their guns and cartridge belts on pegs about the walls. Two palm mats and two black strips of goatwool were all the furnishing, except a hearth for coffee dug in the earthen floor. Here a bedu soon sat down with husks in a mortar, and beat with an alabaster pestle picked from the ruins nearby. His hair, with a fillet bound around his brow, flared out above his shoulders, his big nose and thin mouth made him look like some medieval page. The smoke from the fire curled through a hole in the ceiling. The restless wind, pushing against the tower, as the darkness fell showed the wisdom of small windows. When the camels were tethered and my bed made in one corner, our party gathered here – 'All and Qasim, three camel-men, Ahmed and the lad from 'Azzan with the men and women of the fort in a circle. They talked, and spat at intervals on to the middle of the floor. On the outer edge Awwad's small son rolled about playing with a toy – a tin bucket with Charlie Chaplin stamped in gaudy colours. Awwad did not know where it came from. 'Is it a man or a woman?' he asked, 'or *what* is it?' Apart from my bed, it was the only touch of Europe in our sight.

Rebecca West

(1892–1983)

When Rebecca West (Cicily Isabel Fairfield) travelled with her husband, H. M. Andrews, through the provinces of Yugoslavia between the two World Wars, she encountered and wrote about ethnic fears and prejudices among the people she met. 'There was immanent the Balkan feeling of a shiftless yet just doom,' she wrote in *Black Lamb and Grey Falcon*, a meditation on the destiny of modern man, with a haunting relevance to events today. An insightful, sensitive observer of the Balkan people ('their choice of destiny might be made on grounds so private as to mean nothing to any other human being'), West was especially equipped to write of the dark, inscrutable side of these peoples, who are now engaged in brutal civil war.

The following excerpt is about Mostar, a Muslim town bombed extensively during the current war. West was a writer of novels, histories and criticism, but she received her greatest praise for *Black Lamb*. She was educated in Edinburgh and died in England.

from Black Lamb and Grey Falcon

Mostar

I was so wearied by the rushing rain that I slept, and woke again in a different country. Our road ran on a ledge between the bare mountains and one of these strange valleys that are wide lakes in winter and dry land by summer. This, in spite of the rain, was draining itself, and trees and hedges floated in a mirror patterned with their own reflections and the rich earth that was starting to thrust itself up through the thinning waters. We came past a great tobacco factory to Metkovitch, a river port like any other, with sea-going ships lying up by the quay, looking too big for their quarters. There we stopped in the hotel for some coffee, and for the first time recognized the fly-blown, dusty, waking dream atmosphere that lingers in Balkan districts where the Turk has been. In this hotel I found the most westward Turkish lavatory I have ever encountered: a hole in the floor with a depression for a foot on each side of it, and a tap that sends water flowing along a groove laid with some relevance to the business in hand. It is efficient enough in a cleanly kept household, but it is disconcerting in its proof that there is more than one way of doing absolutely anything.

Later we travelled in a rough Scottish country, where people walked under crashing rain, unbowed by it. They wore raincoats of black fleeces or thickly woven grasses, a kind of thatch; and some had great hoods of stiffened white linen, that made a narrow alcove for the head and a broad alcove for the shoulders and hung nearly to the waist. These last looked like inquisitors robed for solemn mischief, but none of them were dour. The women and girls were full of laughter, and ran from the mud our wheels threw at them as if it were a game. Moslem graveyards began to preach their lesson of indifference to the dead. The stone stumps, carved with a turban if the commemorated corpse were male and left plain if it were female, stood crooked among the long grasses and the wild irises, which the rain was beating flat. Under a broken Roman arch crouched an old shepherd, shielding his turban, which, being yellow, showed that he had made the pilgrimage to Mecca.

The rain lifted, we were following a broad upland valley and looked over pastures and a broad river at the elegance of a small Moslem town, with its lovely minarets. It was exquisitely planned, its towers refined by the influence of the minarets, its red-roofed houses lying among the plumy foliage of their walled gardens; it was in no way remarkable, there are thousands of Moslem towns like it. We left it unvisited, and went on past an aerodrome with its hangars, past the barracks and the tobacco factory that stand in the outskirts of any considerable Herzegovinian town, and were in Mostar, '*Stari most*', old bridge. Presently we were looking at that bridge, which is falsely said to have been built by the Emperor Trajan, but is of medieval Turkish workmanship. It is one of the most beautiful bridges in the world. A slender arch lies between two round towers, its parapet bent in a shallow angle in the centre.

To look at it is good; to stand on it is as good. Over the grey-green river swoop hundreds of swallows, and on the banks mosques and white houses stand among glades of trees and bushes. The swallows and the glades know nothing of the mosques and houses. The river might be running through unvisited hills instead of a town of twenty thousand inhabitants. There was not an old tin, not a rag of paper to be seen. This was certainly not due to any scavenging service. In the Balkans people are more apt to sit down and look at disorder and discuss its essence than clear it away. It was more likely to be due to the Moslem's love of nature, especially of running water, which would prevent him from desecrating the scene with litter in the first place. I marvelled, as I had done on my previous visit to Yugoslavia, at the contradictory attitudes of the Moslem to such matters.

They build beautiful towns and villages. I know of no country, not even Italy or Spain, where each house in a group will be placed with such invariable taste and such pleasing results for those who look at it and out of it alike. The architectural formula of a Turkish house, with its reticent defensive lower story and its projecting upper story, full of windows, is simple and sensible; and I know nothing neater than its interior. Western housewifery is sluttish compared to that aseptic order. Yet Mostar, till the Austrians came, had no hotels except bug-ridden shacks, and it was hard to get the Moslems to abandon their habit of casually slaughtering animals in the streets. Even now the average Moslem shop is the antithesis of the Moslem house. It is a shabby little hole, often with a glassless front, which must be cold in winter and stifling in summer, and its goods are arranged in fantastic disorder. In a stationer's shop the picture-postcards will have been left in the sun till they are faded, and the exercise-books will be foxed. In a textile shop the bolts of stuff will be stacked in untidy tottering heaps. The only exceptions are the bakeries, where the flat loaves and buns are arranged in charming geometric patterns, and the greengroceries, where there is manifest pleasure in the colour and shape of the vegetables. There are, indeed, evident in all Moslem life co-equal strains of extreme fastidiousness and extreme slovenliness, and it is impossible to predict where or why the one or the other is going to take control. A mosque is the most spick-and-span place of worship in the world; but any attempt to postulate a connexion in the Moslem mind between holiness and cleanliness will break down at the first sight of a mosque which for some reason, perhaps a shifting of the population, is no longer used. It will have been allowed to fall into a squalor that recalls the worst Western slums.

The huge café of our hotel covered the whole ground floor, and had two billiard-tables in the centre. For dinner we ate the trout of the place, which is famous and, we thought, horrible, like fish crossed with slug. But we ate also a superb cheese soufflé. The meal was served with incredible delay, and between the courses we read the newspapers and looked about us. Moslems came in from the streets, exotic in fezes. They hung them up and went to their seats and played draughts and drank black coffee, no longer Moslems, merely men. Young officers moved rhythmically through the beams of white light that poured down upon the acid green of the billiard-tables, and the billiard balls gave out their sound of stoical shock. There was immanent the Balkan feeling of a shiftless yet just doom. It seemed possible that someone might come into the room, perhaps a man who would hang up his fez, and explain, in terms just comprehensible enough to make it certain they were not nonsensical, that all the people at the tables must stay there until the two officers who were playing billiards at that moment had played a million games, and that by the result their eternal fates would be decided; and that this would be accepted, and people would sit there quietly waiting and reading the newspapers.

Here in Mostar the really adventurous part of our journey began. Something that had been present in every breath we drew in Dalmatia and Croatia was absent when we woke the next morning, and dressed and breakfasted with our eyes on the market square beneath our windows. It might be identified as conformity in custom as well as creed. The people we were watching adhered with intensity to certain faiths. They were Moslem, they were Catholic, they were Orthodox. About marriage, about birth, about death, they practised immutable rites, determined by these faiths and the older faiths that lie behind them. But in all other ways they were highly individualistic. Their goings and comings, their eating and drinking, were timed by no communal programme, their choice of destiny might be made on grounds so private as to mean nothing to any other human being. Such an attitude showed itself in the crowds below us in a free motion that is the very antithesis in spirit to what we see when we watch people walking to their work over London Bridge in the morning. It showed too in their faces, which always spoke of thought that was never fully shared, of scepticism and satire and lyricism that felt no deed to have been yet finally judged.

It showed itself also in their dress. Neither here nor anywhere else do single individuals dare while sane to dress entirely according to their whim; and the Moslems keep to their veils and fezes with a special punctilio, because these mark them out as participants in the former grandeur of the Ottoman Empire. But here the smallest village or, in a town, a suburb or even a street, can have its own fantasy of costume. The men go in less for variations than the women, for in the classic costume of these parts the male has found as becoming a dress as has ever been devised for him. The stiff braided jacket has a look of ceremony, of mastership about it, and the trousers give the outer line of the leg from the hip to the ankle and make it seem longer by bagging between the thighs. But the women presented us with uncountable variations. We liked two women, grey-haired and harsh-featured, who looked like Margate landladies discussing the ingenious austerities of the day's menus, until a boy wheeled away a barrow and we could see their long full serge bloomers. Other women wore tight bodices and jackets and baggy trousers, each garment made of a different sort of printed material, such as we use for country curtains; but though these wore the Moslem trousers they were Christians, for their faces were unveiled, and they covered their heads loosely with what we know as Paisley shawls. The Moslems slid about black-muzzled, wearing their cotton wrappers, which were usually striped in coldish colours, greys and slate-blues and substanceless reds, except for those who wore that costume one sees in Mostar and not again when one leaves it, unless one's journey takes one very far: to Turkestan, I have heard it said.

The costume is as stirring to the imagination and as idiotically unpractical as any I have ever seen. The great point in favour of Moslem dress in its Yugoslavian form is a convenience in hot weather, which in these parts is a serious consideration, for even in Mostar the summer is an affliction. The cotton overall keeps the hair and the clothes clean, and the veil protects the face from dust and insects and sunburn. This is not true of the heavy horse-hair veil worn in the real East, where the accumulation of dust is turned by the breath of the mouth and nostrils to actual mud, but the light black veil of voile or cotton does no harm and a great deal of good. There is, however, no such justification for the traditional Mostar costume. It consists of a man's coat, made in black or blue cloth, immensely too large for the woman who is going to wear it. It is cut with a stiff military collar, very high, perhaps as much as eight or ten inches, which is embroidered inside, not outside, with gold thread. It is never worn as a coat. The woman slips it over her, drawing the shoulders above her head, so that the stiff collar falls forward and projects in front of her like a visor, and she can hide her face if she clutches the edges together, so that she need not wear a veil. The sleeves are allowed to hang loose or are stitched together at the back, but nothing can be done with the skirts, which drag on the ground.

We asked the people in the hotel and several tradesmen in Mostar, and a number of Moslems in other places, whether there was any local legend which accounted for this extraordinary garment, for it seemed it must commemorate some occasion when a woman had disguised herself in her husband's coat in order to perform an act of valour. But if there was ever such a legend it has been forgotten. The costume may have some value as a badge of class, for it could be worn with comfort and cleanliness only by a woman of the leisured classes, who need not go out save when she chooses. It would be most inconvenient in wet weather or on rough ground, and a woman could not carry or lead a child while she was wearing it. But perhaps it survives chiefly by its poetic value, by its symbolic references to the sex it clothes.

It has the power of a dream or a work of art that has several interpretations, that explains several aspects of reality at one and the same time. First and most obviously the little woman in the tall man's coat presents the contrast between man and woman at its most simple and playful, as the contrast between heaviness and lightness, between coarseness and fragility, between that which breaks and that which might be broken but is instead preserved and cherished, for the sake of tenderness and joy. It makes man and woman seem as father and daughter. The little girl is wearing her father's coat and laughs at him from the depths of it, she pretends that it is a magic garment and that she is invisible and can hide from him. Its dimensions favour this fantasy. The Herzegovinian is tall, but not such a

giant as this coat was made to fit. I am barely five-foot-four and my husband is close on six-foot-two, but when I tried on his overcoat in this fashion the hem was well above my ankles; yet the Mostar garment trails about its wearer's feet.

But it presents the female also in a more sinister light: as the male sees her when he fears her. The dark visor gives her the beak of a bird of prey, and the flash of gold thread within the collar suggests private and ensnaring delights. A torch is put to those fires of the imagination which need for fuel dreams of pain, annihilation, and pleasure. The austere yet lubricious beauty of the coat gives a special and terrifying emphasis to the meaning inherent in all these Eastern styles of costume which hide women's faces. That meaning does not relate directly to sexual matters; it springs from a state of mind more impersonal, even metaphysical, though primitive enough to be sickening. The veil perpetuates and renews a moment when man, being in league with death, like all creatures that must die, hated his kind for living and transmitting life, and hated woman more than himself, because she is the instrument of birth, and put his hand to the floor to find filth and plastered it on her face, to affront the breath of life in her nostrils. There is about all veiled women a sense of melancholy quite incommensurate with the inconveniences they themselves may be suffering. Even when, like the women of Mostar, they seem to be hastening towards secret and luxurious and humorous love-making, they hint of a general surrender to mortality, a futile attempt of the living to renounce life.

Emily Carr

(1871–1945)

One of the best known and loved of Canadian artists, Emily Carr came to writing late in life – as did her recognition as an artist. Her first major exhibition of art did not occur until she was fifty-six; her first book was not published until she turned seventy. Carr's creative life was distinguished by an extraordinary sensibility for the mountainous, wooded landscape of the West Coast of Canada and the native people who lived there. She is best known for her impressionistic paintings of sacred and decorative totem poles, which were deteriorating and being removed throughout the British Columbian coastal region. Carr lived a solitary life in Victoria (her parents died when she was a teenager) and was an eccentric figure known to push a perambulator full of dogs, cats, and a monkey along the street. Her book of anecdotes, *Klee Wyck* (or Laughing One), from which the following excerpt is drawn, won the Governor General's Award for nonfiction in 1941.

from **Klee Wyck**

Kitwancool

When the Indians told me about the Kitwancool totem poles, I said:

'How can I get to Kitwancool?'

'Dunno,' the Indians replied.

White men told me about the Kitwancool poles too, but when I told them I wanted to go there, they advised me – 'Keep out.' But the thought of those old Kitwancool poles pulled at me. I was at Kitwangak, twenty or so miles from Kitwancool.

Then a halfbreed at Kitwangak said to me, 'The young son of the Kitwancool Chief is going in tomorrow with a load of lumber. I asked if he would take you; he will.'

'How can I get out again?'

'The boy is coming back to Kitwangak after two days.'

The Chief's son Aleck was shy, but he spoke good English. He said I was to be at the Hudson's Bay store at eight the next morning.

I bought enough food and mosquito oil to last me two days; then I sat in front of the Hudson's Bay store from eight to eleven o'clock, waiting. I saw Aleck drive past to load his lumber. The wagon had four wheels and a long pole. He tied the lumber to the pole and a sack of oats to the lumber; I was to sit on the oats. Rigged up in front somehow was a place for the driver – no real seat, just a couple of coal-oil boxes bound to some boards. Three men sat on the two boxes. The road was terrible. When we bumped, the man on the down side of the boxes fell off.

A sturdy old man trudged behind the wagon. Sometimes he rode a bit on the end of the long pole, which tossed him up and down like a see-saw. The old man carried a gun and walked most of the way.

The noon sun burnt fiercely on our heads. The oat-sack gave no support to my back, and my feet dangled. I had to clutch the corner of the oat-sack with one hand to keep from falling off – with the other I held my small griffon dog. Every minute I thought we would be pitched off the pole. You could seldom see the old man because of clouds of yellow dust rolling behind the wagon. The scrub growth at the road-side smelt red hot.

The scraggy ponies dragged their feet heavily; sweat cut rivers through the dust that was caked on their sides.

One of the three men on the front seat of the wagon seemed to be a hero. The other men questioned him all the way, though generally Indians do not talk as they travel. When one of the men fell off the seat he ran round the wagon to the high side and lumped up again and all the while he did not stop asking the hero questions. There were so many holes in the road and the men fell off so often that they were always changing places, like birds on a roost in cold weather.

Suddenly we gave such an enormous bump that we all fell off together, and the horses stopped. When the wheels were not rattling any more we could hear water running. Then the old man came out of the clouds of dust behind us and said there was a stream close by.

We threw ourselves on to our stomachs, put our lips to the water and drank like horses. The Indians took the bits out of their horses' mouths and gave them food. Then the men crawled under the wagon to eat their lunch in its shade; I sat by the shadiest wheel. It was splendid to put my legs straight out and have the earth support them and the wheel support my back. The old man went to sleep.

After he woke and after the horses had pulled the wagon out of the big hole, we rumbled on again.

When the sun began to go down we were in woods, and the clouds of mosquitoes were as thick as the clouds of dust, but more painful. We let them eat us because, after bumping for seven hours, we were too tired to fight.

At last we came to a great dip where the road wound around the edge of a ravine shaped like an oblong bowl. There were trees growing in this earth bowl. It seemed to be bottomless. We were level with the tree-tops as we looked down. The road was narrow – its edges broken.

I was afraid and said, 'I want to walk.'

Aleck waved his hand across the ravine. 'Kitwancool,' he said and I saw some grey roofs on the far side of the hollow. After we had circled the ravine and climbed the road on the other side we would be there, unless we were lying dead in that deep bowl.

I said again, 'I want to walk.'

'Village dogs will kill you and the little dog,' said Aleck. But I did walk around the bend and up the hill until the village was near. Then I rode into Kitwancool on the oat-sack.

The dogs rushed out in a pack. The village people came out too. They made a fuss over the hero-man, clustering about him and jabbering. They paid no more attention to me than to the oat-sack. All of them went into the nearest house taking Aleck, the hero, the old man and the other man with them, and shut the door.

I wanted to cry, sticking alone up there on top of the oats and lumber, the sagging horses in front and the yapping dogs all round, nobody to ask about anything and very tired. Aleck had told me I could sleep on the verandah of his father's house, because I only had a cot and a tent-fly with me, and bears came into the village often at night. But how did I know which was his father's house? The dogs would tear me if I got down and there was no one to ask, anyway.

Suddenly something at the other end of the village attracted the dogs. The pack tore off and the dust hid me from them.

Aleck came out of the house and said, 'We are going to have dinner in this house now.' Then he went in again and shut the door.

The wagon was standing in the new part of the village. Below us, on the right, I could see a row of old houses. They were dim, for the light was going, but above them, black and clear against the sky stood the old totem poles of Kitwancool. I jumped down from the wagon and came to them. That part of the village was quite dead. Between the river and the poles was a flat of green grass. Above, stood the houses, grey and broken. They were in a long, wavering row, with wide, windowless fronts. The totem poles stood before them there on the top of a little bank above the green flat. There were a few poles down on the flat too, and some graves that had fences round them and roofs over the tops.

When it was almost dark I went back to the wagon.

The house of Aleck's father was the last one at the other end of the new village. It was one great room like a hall and was built of new logs. It had seven windows and two doors; all the windows were propped open with blue castor-oil bottles.

I was surprised to find that the old man who had trudged behind our wagon was Chief Douse – Aleck's father.

Mrs. Douse was more important than Mr. Douse; she was a chieftainess in her own right, and had great dignity. Neither of them spoke to me that night. Aleck showed me where to put my bed on the verandah and I hung the fly over it. I ate a dry scrap of food and turned into my blankets. I had no netting, and the mosquitoes tormented me.

My heart said into the thick dark, 'Why did I come?'

And the dark answered, 'You know.'

In the morning the hero-man came to me and said, 'My mother-in-law wishes to speak with you. She does not know

'"I want to make pictures of them, so that your young people as well as the white people will see how fine your totem poles used to be."'

English words so she will talk through my tongue.'

I stood before the tall, cold woman. She folded her arms across her body and her eyes searched my face. They were as expressive as if she were saying the words herself instead of using the hero's tongue.

'My mother-in-law wishes to know why you have come to our village.'

'I want to make some pictures of the totem poles.'

'What do you want our totem poles for?'

'Because they are beautiful. They are getting old now, and your people make very few new ones. The young people do not value the poles as the old ones did. By and by there will be no more poles. I want to make pictures of them, so that your young people as well as the white people will see how fine your totem poles used to be.'

Mrs. Douse listened when the young man told her this. Her eyes raked my face to see if I was talking 'straight'. Then she waved her hand towards the village.

'Go along,' she said through the interpreter, 'and I shall see.' She was neither friendly nor angry. Perhaps I was going to be turned out of this place that had been so difficult to get into.

The air was hot and heavy. I turned towards the old village with the pup Ginger Pop at my heels. Suddenly there was a roar of yelpings, and I saw my little dog putting half a dozen big ones to rout down the village street. Their tails were flat, their tongues lolled and they yelped. The Douses all rushed out of their house to see what the noise was about, and we laughed together so hard that the strain, which before had been between us, broke.

The sun enriched the old poles grandly. They were carved elaborately and with great sincerity. Several times the figure of a woman that held a child was represented. The babies had faces like wise little old men. The mothers expressed all womanhood – the big wooden hands holding the child were so full of tenderness they had to be distorted enormously in order to contain it all. Womanhood was strong in Kitwancool. Perhaps, after all, Mrs. Douse might let me stay.

I sat in front of a totem mother and began to draw – so full of her strange, wild beauty that I did not notice the storm that was coming, till the totem poles went black, flashed vividly white and then went black again. Bang upon bang, came the claps of thunder. The hills on one side tossed it to the hills on the other; sheets of rain washed over me. I was beside a grave down on the green flat; some of the pickets of its fence were gone, so I crawled through on to the grave with Ginger Pop in my arms to shelter under its roof. Stinging nettles grew on top of the grave with mosquitoes hiding under their leaves. While I was beating down the nettles with my easel, it struck the head of a big wooden bear squatted on the grave. He startled me. He was painted red. As I sat down upon him my foot hit something that made a hollow rattling noise. It was a shaman's rattle. This then must be a shaman's, a medicine-man's grave, and this the rattle he had used to scare away evil spirits. Shamen worked black magic. His body lay here just a few feet below me in the earth. At the thought I made a dash for the broken community house on the bank above. All the Indian horses had got there first and taken for their shelter the only corner of the house that had any roof over it.

I put my stool near the wall and sat upon it. The water ran down the wall in rivers. The dog shivered under my coat – both of us were wet to the skin. My sketch sack was so full of water that when I emptied it on to the ground it made the pool we sat in bigger.

After two hours the rain stopped suddenly. The horses held their bones stiff and quivered their skins. It made the rain fly out of their coats and splash me. One by one they trooped out through the hole in the wall. When their hooves struck the baseboard there was a sodden thud. Ginger Pop shook himself too, but I could only drip. Water poured from the eyes of the totems and from the tips of their carved noses. New little rivers trickled across the green flat. The big river was whipped to froth. A blur like boiling mist hung over it.

When I got back to the new village I found my bed and things in a corner of the Douses' great room. The hero told me, 'My mother-in-law says you may live in her house. Here is a rocking-chair for you.'

Mrs. Douse acknowledged my gratitude stolidly. I gave Mr. Douse a dollar and asked if I might have a big fire to dry my things and make tea. There were two stoves – the one at their end of the room was alight. Soon, mine too was roaring and it was cosy. When the Indians accepted me as one of themselves, I was very grateful.

The people who lived in that big room of the Douses were two married daughters, their husbands and children, the son Aleck and an orphan girl called Lizzie. The old couple came and went continually, but they ate and slept in a shanty at the back of the new house. This little place had been made round them. The floor was of earth and the walls were of cedar. The fire on the ground sent its smoke through a smoke-hole in the roof. Dried salmon hung on racks. The old people's mattress was on the floor. The place was full of themselves – they had breathed themselves into it as a bird, with its head under its wing, breathes itself into its own cosiness. The Douses were glad for their children to have the big fine house and be modern but this was the right sort of place for themselves.

Life in the big house was most interesting. A baby swung in its cradle from the rafters; everyone tossed the cradle as he passed and the baby cooed and gurgled. There was a crippled child of six – pinched and white under her brown skin; she sat in a chair all day. And there was Orphan Lizzie who would slip out into the wet bushes and come back with a wild strawberry or a flower in her grubby little hand, and, kneeling by the sick child's chair, would open her fingers suddenly on the surprise.

There was no rush, no scolding, no roughness in this household. When anyone was sleepy he slept; when they were hungry they ate; if they were sorry they cried; and if they were glad they sang. They enjoyed Ginger Pop's fiery temper, the tilt of his nose and particularly the way he kept the house free of Indian dogs. It was Ginger who bridged the gap between their language and mine with laughter. Ginger's snore was the only sound in that great room at night. Indians sleep quietly.

Orphan Lizzie was shy as a rabbit but completely unselfconscious. It was she who set the food on the big table and cleared away the dishes. There did not seem to be any particular meal-times. Lizzie always took a long lick at the top of the jam-tin as she passed it.

The first morning I woke at the Douses', I went very early to wash myself in the creek below the house. I was kneeling on the stones brushing my teeth. It was very cold. Suddenly I looked up – Lizzie was close by me watching. When I looked up, she darted away like a fawn, leaving her water pails behind. Later, Mrs. Douse came to my corner of the house, carrying a tin basin; behind her was Lizzie with a tiny glass cream pitcher full of water, and behind Lizzie was the hero.

'My mother-in-law says the river is too cold for you to wash in. Here is water and a basin for you.'

Everyone watched my washing next morning. The washing of my ears interested them most.

One day after work I found the Douse family all sitting round on the floor. In the centre of the group was Lizzie. She was beating something in a pail, beating it with her hands; her arms were blobbed with pink froth to the elbows. Everyone stuck his hand into Lizzie's pail and hooked out some of the froth in the crook of his fingers, then took long delicious licks. They invited me to lick too. It was 'soperlallie', or soap berry. It grows in the woods; when you beat the berry it froths up and has a queer bitter taste. The Indians love it.

For two days from dawn till dark I worked down in the old part of the village. On the third day Aleck was to take me back to Kitwangak. But that night it started to rain. It rained for three days and three nights without stopping; the road was impossible. I had only provisioned for two days, and had been here five and had given all of the best bits from my box to the sick child. All the food I had left for the last three days was hard tack and raisins. I drank hot water, and rocked my hunger to the tune of the rain beating on the window. Ginger Pop munched hard tack unconcerned – amusing everybody.

The Indians would have shared the loaf and jam-tin with me, but I did not tell them that I had no food. The thought of Lizzie's tongue licking the jam-tin stopped me.

When it rained, the Indians drowsed like flies, heavy as the day itself.

On the sixth day of my stay in Kitwancool the sun shone again, but we had to wait a bit for the puddles to drain.

I straightened out my obligations and said goodbye to Mr. and Mrs. Douse. The light wagon that was taking me out seemed luxurious after the thing I had come in on. I climbed up beside Aleck. He gathered his reins and 'giddapped'.

Mrs. Douse, followed by her husband, came out of the house and waved a halt. She spoke to Aleck.

'My mother wants to see your pictures.'

'But I showed her every one before they were packed.'

At the time I had thought her stolidly indifferent.

'My mother wishes to see the pictures again.'

I clambered over the back of the wagon, unpacked the wet canvases and opened the sketchbooks. She went through them all. The two best poles in the village belonged to Mrs. Douse. She argued and discussed with her husband. I told Aleck to ask if his mother would like to have me give her pictures of her poles. If so, I would send them through the Hudson's Bay store at Kitwangak. Mrs. Douse's neck loosened. Her head nodded violently and I saw her smile for the first time.

Repacking, I climbed over the back of the seat to Aleck.

'Giddap!'

The reins flapped: we were off. The dust was laid; everything was keen and fresh; indeed the appetites of the mosquitoes were very keen.

When I got back to Kitwangak the Mounted Police came to see me.

'You have been in to Kitwancool?'

'Yes.'

'How did the Indians treat you?'

'Splendidly.'

'Learned their lesson, eh?' said the man. 'We have had no end of trouble with those people – chased missionaries out and drove surveyors off with axes – simply won't have whites in their village. I would never have advised anyone going in – particularly a woman. No, I would certainly have said, "Keep out."'

'Then I am glad I did not ask for your advice,' I said. 'Perhaps it is because I am a woman that they were so good to me.'

'One of the men who went in on the wagon with you was straight from jail, a fierce, troublesome customer.'

Now I knew who the hero was.

Mildred Cable

(1878–1952)

Francesca French

(1871–1960)

No two Western women travellers and writers in modern times knew the desert in the way Mildred Cable and Francesca French did. With French's sister, Evangeline, the three missionaries, known simply as 'The Trio,' crossed and recrossed the Gobi Desert five times in the fifteen years between 1926 and 1941. Yet their writings do not have the ring of melodrama of much of the writing of their time, nor do they sound the shrill note of the overly pious. Instead, Cable and French weave stories against a quiet, forceful desert backdrop, showing controlled respect for the spirit of the places they encounter. Upon leaving China, the trio visited missions in New Zealand, Australia, and India. Their last venture together was their journey to South America in 1950, when Mildred was seventy-two, Francesca, seventy-nine, and Evangeline, eighty-one.

from The Gobi Desert

There is one caravan route which occasionally brings a merchant from Paotow or the Temple of the Larks to the banks of the Etzingol River. It is called the Winding Road, and most of those who use it are straight-forward business men, dealers in pelts, camel's hair or liquorice, but now and again it brings a man whose object it is to disappear from his native land and never be heard of again. Such men often have a strange background, and they travel under an assumed name and on fictitious business. Sometimes there is even a price on their heads. The Etzingol camping-grounds are an attractive place to the mock nomad, for there is good profit to be made in handling barter and exchange among people who are so elementary in methods of commerce as these Mongols. Such enigmatic guests generally join the caravan at a small halting-place, and hope for a free passage by acting as cook's helper or junior puller. The *bash** is not deceived, nor is he surprised if, before the journey's end, they fail to report when the camp moves on, and are never seen again. If any comment is made he will merely remark, 'To every man his own business,' and dismiss the subject.

A strange chain of circumstances brought us in contact with such an exile. We were drinking camel's milk and eating *zamba*** in a Mongol tent one day when a man lifted the door-curtain, stepped inside, and, according to Mongol custom, exchanged snuff-bottles with the host. After this correct greeting the stranger sat down and was given a bowl of milk, while the interrupted talk was resumed. Our host was eager to know something of our country, and asked many questions regarding its King, its customs, its people, and regarding certain strange inventions the wonders of which had been reported to him. 'Was it really true,' he asked, 'that there were carts which flew in the air?' He knew that one horseless cart sometimes crossed Mongolia, but he had heard that it often refused to move, and that camel-caravans, though they travelled more slowly, might overtake the huge monster where it lay stuck in a rut. He had heard of the 'iron road' at Paotow, but had never himself seen it, nor had he any wish to do so, for, as he said, 'In this country camels are best.' He spoke fairly good colloquial Chinese and expressed admiration of our

* Caravan leader.

**Barley meal dish; also Tibetan tsanysa.

easy use of that language, to which we replied that before we came to these parts we had already lived for many years in Central Shansi. At these words the new arrival looked sharply in our direction, then turned away and continued his conversation in Mongolian about the business which had brought him there. It was quite clear that his interest had been arrested, but we were used to being the centre of notice in such a group and thought little of it. Presently he turned and spoke to us in Chinese, and it was evident that, though dressed as a Mongol, this was his native tongue and his intonation was that of Shansi. 'From which part of the province did you come?' he asked. I mentioned the name of a city where we had lived for many years, but he said little more and soon took his departure. Later in the day we met him in other tents, and he always asked us a few questions in Chinese and always left us hurriedly.

Next day we were watching baby camels at their frolics in an enclosure near one of the encampments when a rider broke through the tamarisk thicket, tied his horse to a branch of the growth, and strode toward us. It was the same man again, and he was evidently well known here too, for he joined the family group like an *habitué*. Once again he spoke: 'You said that you came from Shansi. Do you know many of the towns?' he asked. 'We know most of them,' I answered. We then talked of that province, of its various localities, its progressive Governor and of its prosperity, but again he broke off abruptly and chatted in Mongolian with the family, drank another bowl of salted tea, saluted, leapt on his horse and rode off.

Two days later we stood in the *yurt* which housed the head lama of the Etzingol. It was a handsome tent and richly furnished with all the goods which indicate nomadic wealth. The brass and copper kettles were of the largest and heaviest description, the bowls were made of polished wood rimmed with silver, and the *zamba* boxes were lacquered in golden-bronze tints. The raised portion of the tent floor was larger than usual, and on it was placed a long, low table spread with the complete paraphernalia of ecclesiastical usage. There was a filigree jug of holy water, a bunch of peacock's feathers with which to sprinkle the worshippers, rosaries to mark the recitation of mantras, a bell to sound at rhythmic intervals, a little hand-gong and a small prayer-wheel, an effigy of the thunderbolt, a wooden crab, a hammer with which to strike it, a conch which is blown to assemble the lamas, and most important of all, a vase which held bamboo slips inscribed with answers to the prayers of those who wished to fix a lucky day for some undertaking. There were also many brass bowls filled with butter, and a brazier in which to offer it as a burnt-offering. Behind the lama was placed the great cockscomb head-dress, kept in readiness for ritual occasions.

Facing the temple furnishings sat a man of such an evil countenance that he might well be accustomed to hold intercourse with dark forces. He was draped like an idol, in yellow and deep red brocade, and never ceased from muttering the one sentence: '*O mane padhme hum*' (O thou precious jewel in the lotus). He had been saying it so perpetually and for so long that his chin was moulded by the words into a strange shape. He never took his hand from the beads, and the muttered prayer persisted during every break in the conversation.

Several times the door-curtain was lifted to admit a Tibetan or a Mongol who knelt to receive the lama's blessing, and among them was the same sham nomad whom we had already seen so often. He made an obeisance to the lama, who sprinkled him with holy water, then sat down on the ground near me, and while my companions continued talking with the lama he began to question me again about the district of Central Shansi, its towns and its villages.

'Do you know Peach Bloom Farms in the Eastern Hills?' he asked. 'The village is not far from the town where you lived.'

'I know it well,' I said.

'Do you know the Li family who live there?' he asked again, his face tense with interest.

'I do,' I replied, 'and I have often stayed in their home.'

When he asked that question I immediately realised to whom I was speaking, but I think that I succeeded in so controlling the expression of my face that he suspected nothing. Now that I held the key to his identity, the striking likeness of this Mongol to my old Shansi friends, the Li family, was unmistakable. He listened intently, and I spoke as naturally as possible of the young daughter-in-law and her child, and of the death of the old parents. Though I sat in the Mongolian tent and talked with this mysterious stranger, actually I was more vividly conscious of standing in a Shansi courtyard at Peach Bloom Farms, where a young woman was pouring out a strange story which concerned her dead husband. I knew her well, for she had been first a pupil, then a student, under my care, and it was natural that she should speak to me in her perplexity. The boy to whom she was betrothed had been a firebrand of revolutionary activity from schooldays, and after the marriage, while the young bride cared for his parents, he went off to a distant town, where he became involved in a political plot. It was discovered and he was arrested, condemned to death and executed. Later on, the rough coffin holding his body was brought home and buried at Peach Bloom Farms among the family graves.

'A week after his funeral,' the young widow was saying to me, 'I came to the grave to mourn for my husband, and there I found a girl dressed, like me, in coarse white mourning. She crouched at my husband's grave, wailing for the dead. I had never seen her before, and I asked her who she was and where she came from. She only said, "I have come to wail for my brother." "You are mistaken," I replied, "this is our family grave and my husband was buried here not long ago." She only shook her head and rocked to her wailing. I was frightened and ran home. There I found a stranger talking to my parents. He said that when my child's father was condemned to death many tried to help him to escape, and a few hours before the execution a man was found who sold his own life for a large sum of money and let himself be shot in his place. That stranger said: "The coffin which is buried in your field does not hold the body of your son, but of the man who took his place, and his sister has come here to wail so that his spirit shall not be among the neglected dead. As to your son, he is alive, but he has fled to a distant country, from which he must never return to China."'

Sitting in the lama's *yurt* I thought of the old parents, of the girl who was neither wife nor widow, and of the grave which held the body of the man who had parted so carelessly with his life. I looked into the face of this mock Mongol and he gave me one searching glance. We both understood, but even at this distance from his home it was better not to say more, though I knew that I was speaking to the fugitive son, and he knew that I knew. He rose, gave the lama a final *kowtow*, turned to us with a Chinese salutation, and left the tent. He did not cross our path again, but his persistent inquisitiveness had not escaped the notice of our vigilant Chinese servants. They knew nothing of our side of the story, but took an opportunity to tell us that this man was no Mongol, but a Chinese fugitive, disguised and hiding in the forests of the Etzingol.

Desert dwellers have keener sight than other men, for looking out over wide spaces has adjusted their eyes to vastness, and I also learnt to turn my eyes from the too constant study of the minute to the observation of the immense. I had read about planets, stars and constellations, but now, as I considered them, I realised how little the books had profited me. My caravan guide taught me how to set a course by looking at one constellation, to check the progress of the night by observing the shifting position of others, to recognize the succession of morning and evening stars, and to observe the seasons by the phase of Orion in the heavens. The quiet, forceful, regular progress of these mighty spheres indicated control, order and discipline. To me they spoke of the control of an ordered life and the obedience of a rectified mind which enables man, even in a world of chaos, to follow a God-appointed path with a precision and dignity which nothing can destroy.

My guide also taught me another lesson, and that was how to walk by starlight. At first I stumbled and hurt my feet among the stones, but I saw that he walked as quickly, as securely and as freely by night as by day. Then I realised that he had used his daylight powers of sense to train the more subtle instinct which served him in the dark, and gradually I too learnt the art of training and then trusting my instincts until I also felt secure in the clear darkness, which is the only darkness that the desert knows. I remembered a wise word spoken by an old prophet concerning a man who was faithful and obedient yet who walked in darkness and had no light. Surely, like the desert wayfarer who walks securely by starlight, that man had learnt obedience and quick response in days of normal experience, and when dark hours came he walked confidently, his heart stayed upon God and relying on the certainties which he had proved in the hour of clear vision.

I recalled my early fears when the uncanny loneliness of the night made me shudder as I realised the utter isolation of our solitary way. We had embarked on an enterprise of which our most experienced Chinese friends spoke only in terms of warning; the natural shrinking from such loneliness, however, soon became a thing of the past, and those particular fears ceased for ever directly I realised that they were but the mock armaments of a foe with no power really to hurt, but who, a master in the region of fear, tries to dominate through frightening suggestions.

If, as those soldier-boys at Kiayükwan had so confidently declared, the Gobi is the haunt of demons, then the night should have been the time when their presence was most real, yet in fact it was more by day than by night that the word *kwei* (demon) was on the driver's lips, and most often it was the desert dust-spout which provoked it. However breezeless the day, somewhere on the horizon a slender spiral of sand would rise, move, circle, walk across the plain, leave the earth and vanish in the sky. Sometimes the whole desert floor was alive with them. At a distance they seemed insignificant, but close at hand they were fearful in their cyclonic force. Travellers call them dust-spouts from their likeness to an ocean water-spout, but the desert dweller, certain that these waterless places are peopled by *kwei*, calls them dust-demons. The pillar of sand gives the impression of an invisible being daintily folding a garment of dust round its unseen form. Some whirl from left to right, and some from right to left. 'This one is the male and that one the female *kwei*,' said the men; 'you can distinguish them by the way they fold the dust cloak around them, right to left or left to right; see how they come in pairs.'

The couple came gliding across the plain in our direction, then suddenly turned aside, passing quite close, yet enveloped in such a narrow whirlwind that the curtains of the cart scarcely moved, though we saw sand and stones lifted high from the ground. A laden camel can scarcely resist the full force of a dust-spout, and when I was caught in the fringe of one, it nearly swept me off my feet.

The scientific mind of the Westerner studies the phenomenon with a view to understanding the atmospheric conditions which cause it, but the oasis man who lives and dies among desert scenes believes that waterless places are peopled by spirits who desire to be reclothed with flesh. 'The best for the demon,' they say, 'is when a living human will let himself be possessed, but, failing this, the *kwei* uses the dust from which flesh is made as cover for its nakedness.'

The spirit which agitates the long night hours uses fear as its weapon, but the demon of noon is the demon of discouragement. When the chill of night is dispelled by the sun's rays the heat quickly grows in intensity until the midday hour brings unutterable weariness to every member of the caravan. The landscape itself seems to take on a metallic and inimical aspect, and every hill and boulder is rimmed with a yellow aura which gives a hard and repellent outline to the unfriendly scene. The expectant joyousness of the morning start has faded away, pleasant anticipation of the journey's end is still too far ahead to be any consolation, and although half the stage is accomplished yet there is as much still to cover as lies behind, so the half-way line brings no sense of exhilaration. This is the moment when the noonday demon has power to transmute physical exhaustion into such weariness of spirit as drains all joy from service, leaving only stern duty to issue orders. Inertia invades beasts as well as men, and it is useless to urge flagging powers to greater effort. This, however, is no new difficulty to the caravan *bash*, and experience has taught him how to meet it. A halt must be called and a pause allowed in which to release tension and recover poise. In the desert there can be no rest without escape from the direct rays of the sun, the glare and the scorching heat, therefore some shade must be secured. The shadow of a rock is best, but where there is no rock there may be a man-built landmark made of desert clay, which throws reliable shade. Sometimes there was only the plain and its uncompromising nakedness, then the desert guide taught me how to use the shadow of my own cart and seek refuge between its high wheels. A brief period of rest for man and beast sent the caravan on its way renewed in strength and courage. The noonday demon had been overcome by recognising the noontide right to relax.

The still days when dust-demons walk abroad are good for caravans on the march, but sooner or later the time comes when the camels, alert as a barometer to atmospheric changes, show signs of uneasiness and become restive. The driver knows the indications and scans the horizon for signs of the coming storm, then moves among his animals, tightening ropes and securing packs. Before long there is a distant roar, and a cloud like rolling smoke with a livid edge advances and invades the sky, blotting out sun and daylight; then suddenly the sand-storm breaks on the caravan. No progress is possible and human beings shelter behind a barrage of kneeling camels from the flying stones and choking sand. When such a blinding storm is in progress there is no indication by which to find the way, and the only safe course is to stay still until it has exhausted itself by the surcharge of its own violence. It is a stirring of earth's surface which blots out the light of day, robs the atmosphere of its purity, blurs the outline of tracks and landmarks and takes all sense of direction from men, making them helpless to use even their natural powers of orientation. It cannot be overcome by resistance, and those who dissipate energy in fighting it will inevitably be exhausted by its fury. The camel-driver is too wise to waste strength in fight and, following the instinct of the camel that kneels in order to offer less resistance, he learns to shelter till the terrible blast passes over. Such a storm will not last many hours, and as soon as it has spent itself the sun reappears in a serene sky, the violently disturbed sand and stones sink to their own place, and the caravan can continue its journey.

Had I been without an experienced guide I should certainly have been deceived when I first heard that strange illusory voice calling for help, of which so many travellers have spoken.

'Halt,' I said, 'there is someone calling!'

'There is no one calling,' said the *bash*, 'and there is no reason to halt.'

'Cannot you hear?' I persisted. 'Someone is calling from among the dunes.'

'Never listen to those voices,' he replied. 'It is not a man's cry, and those who follow it may never come back to the caravan. We must push on.' He urged the beasts forward and refused to listen. As he trudged ahead he spoke again: 'Those voices are heard all over Gobi, but are worse in the Desert of Lob. One night when I was travelling there I got separated from my caravan. I heard a shout and the sound of camel-bells which I tried to overtake for hours. Then the moon rose and I saw there were no recent tracks of camels, so I halted, and turned back, but something held me and the voice still called. At last, with a great effort I retraced my steps to where I could see the tracks of our camels leading off in another direction. It was a strange experience, but as soon as I was on the right road those devilish voices ceased, and by midday I caught up with the caravan once more. They nearly had me that time, as they have had many others.'

'What then,' I asked, 'are those strange voices which I heard?'

'The people of Lob call them *Azghun*,' he replied, 'and say that it is a *kwei* which lives among the sand-hillocks and sometimes takes the form of a black eagle. If travellers listen, it leads them away to waterless places where they perish.'

Dust-demons, phantom voices with their insistence, always trying to turn travellers out of the way – it sounded so fantastic that at first I was inclined to dismiss it all with an incredulous smile, but something in the subconscious arrested me, and I repeated aloud those words: 'When an evil spirit has left a man it roams about in the desert, seeking rest.' I had to acknowledge that they were spoken by the only One Who really knows, so I thought on those words and kept silence.

It seemed as though the pastime of those demons was to make sport of the few lonely human beings who ventured into

'Mirage is the desert traveller's constant companion and his perpetual torment. As soon as the sun is high above the horizon, the sand begins to glitter like water and appears to move like wavelets…'

the desert, by encircling them with every manner of deception.

By night, lights which were like flames from a camp-fire played on the horizon, but no one has ever located them or come any nearer by following them. Watching my two companions walking ahead of the caravan one day, I was amazed to see four people where I had believed there were only two. My eyes saw something which my reason refused to accept. I overtook them and there were but two: I dropped back, and again there were four. Thus do the refractions of desert light shake confidence in the powers of discernment and call for a new standard of discrimination in which things seen with mortal eye are not to be relied upon, whereas the things which are relied on may be contrary to the evidence of the senses.

Mirage is the desert traveller's constant companion and his perpetual torment. As soon as the sun is high above the horizon, the sand begins to glitter like water and appears to move like wavelets, while the clumps of camel-thorn look like tall bushes or stunted trees, and seem to be set by the edge of a lake. All through the day this illusion persists, and not until near sunset does the mirage vanish, the sand cease to glitter, and the landscape show itself for what it really is, a dull grey surface. Even the old traveller must never reckon himself free from the snare of illusion. On one occasion we were to spend a night in a Qazaq tent, but it was autumn, and the coarse desert-grass grew rank and hid the encampment. In the late afternoon the carter gave the cry: '*Dao-liao!*' (We have arrived), and, sure enough, there were the tents, the herds and the pasturing flocks. A man hurried on to prospect, and we urged our tired beasts to further effort. In an hour's time the tents, herds and pastures, though still there, were no nearer, and when darkness fell the voice of our man was heard shouting: 'We are lost! I cannot find any *yurts*. We must stay here till morning.' In the straight clear light of dawn we saw the plain in its true aspect; there were no tents, no cattle and no water in sight. Not till the following sunset did we reach the encampment.

How terrible if in this realm of illusion where that which seemed real was not true, and where true things appeared false, I were left to find my way without a guide. Never could I hope to disentangle the web of deception, and free both mind and sense from its impalpable net. In the desert I learnt to detect some of the illusions which constantly surround me on the greater journey of life, and to depend for direction on the wisdom of Him Who is my unerring guide.

Without water the desert is nothing but a grave, and is useless either as a dwelling-place or even as a high-road for the living. If the traveller's food is poor he will go hungry, if his road is long he will be weary, if his lot is hard he will be lonely, but to all these things he can become inured. No one, however, can be inured to thirst. When the craving for water assails a man he will forget all else in his frantic search for it, knowing that life itself depends on finding it, and that failing it he will soon be the victim of delirium, madness and death.

When a traveller first starts out to cross the desert he is inclined to take water for granted, and though the old innkeepers warn everyone to carry it, he may refuse to listen and prefer taking a risk to being burdened with a water-bottle, but once that man has experienced the torture of thirst his outlook is changed, and nothing will induce him to start upon any stage without a supply.

As the long hours pass, the burning sun seems to sap the moisture through every pore of the skin, until thirst is not only felt in the dry throat and cracked lips, but throughout the body, and as the days of rationed water go by, the whole system, tormented by a craving which becomes more and more urgent, calls out for the sight, the smell and the feeling of moisture. Sometimes the sunset hour brings a caravan to a lonely spot where a water-hole should be found but is hard to detect. All members of the caravan dismount and hunt for the small depression, perhaps marked only by a stone. It is so easy to miss, and once darkness has fallen it would be impossible to locate it. Then a shout is heard, 'Water, water!' and all run to the spot to quench their desperate thirst.

The mirage has been a decoy to many thirsty men. I myself, when I first saw a lovely lake with trees standing on its farther bank in mid-Gobi, urged the drivers to push on and reach it quickly, but the *bash* only smiled and spoke indulgently, as one might speak to an ignorant child: 'That's not water,' he said, 'that's glitter sand – dry water.' That lake was but a mirage, and the farther we went the farther it receded, tantalising our thirst with its falsity.

I was caught by another deception to which weary wayfarers are subject, and this time it was not 'glitter sand' but the brackish water of the salt desert. The sparkle of the limpid spring was irresistible, but when I ran toward it, certain this time of the water's reality, the same gruff voice cautioned me: 'Drink as little of that water as you can,' it said. This time I cared for none of his warnings, for I had found real water and would enjoy it to the full. I soon learnt that the *bash* knew better than I, for the more I took of this water, the more parched I became. It was brackish – neither salt nor sweet. Not salt as seawater which drives to madness, nor sweet like spring-water which heals and refreshes, but brackish, leaving thirst for ever unquenched. I drank my fill, and came again, but I was thirsty still.

This experience made me wary of all desert waters, and when I came to the oasis of Ever-Flowing-Stream, though the water looked so tempting and so cool in the little grotto under the shady trees, I was shy of it, for other water had looked cool and tempting too. I tasted it cautiously, but here there was no deception and it was a stream of sweet, satisfying quality. This was *karez* water and came direct from the eternal snows of the distant mountains. Through a deep underground channel it had crossed the torrid plain, and when it emerged at the place where I stood it was as sweet, as cool and as pure as when it left the foot of the glacier, nor would the stream run dry so long as the snow-clad hills remained and the channel was kept unchoked.

Occasionally I heard a desert spring spoken of as 'living

water', and when I saw one I understood the expression. Its vitalised energy was so irrepressible that from the depths of the water-hole it pushed upward and broke on the surface in shimmering bubbles. Those who draw from such a living spring always speak of it reverently and as of something akin to the divine. The pilgrim prays there at break of day, the Buddhist erects a shrine in its vicinity, the Moslem goes to it for water of purification, and when I stood and looked into the moving depths I better understood the question asked of Christ, 'Where do you get living water?' and the answer He gave: 'The water I give becomes a spring, welling up to eternal life.'

It is water which marks the stage, and only where there is water are there human habitations. The people who live there may be terribly poor, but though poverty-stricken and sordid, their houses are homes and their hamlets are oases because water, which is an essential of life, is accessible to them. These men of the water-holes had another supreme need beyond that of bread and water, for man does not live by these alone, and though I could not bring to them life's normal amenities yet I was there to offer each one that living water for which his spirit craved.

I sat for long hours in my sand-chair by the Cresent Lake and reflected on the teaching of those desert experiences, the illusive mirage, the tormenting bitter water, the sweet water of the *karez* channel and the invigorating water of the living spring. Then slowly the lovely lake at my feet recaptured my attention, seeming to say, 'Now consider what lies before your eyes.' So I dismissed all thought of desert rigours and yielded myself to the charm of the moment.

The whole scene, from the brilliant glazed-tiled roofs, the light loggia, the golden sand, the silver trees, the fringe of green sedge, and the delicate hues of wheeling pigeons, was reflected in the still water as sharply as in a mirror. An acolyte came to the water's edge, stooped, filled a bucket with lake water and turned back toward the temple. The scene had an unreal quality which held me motionless as though a movement on my part might shatter the spell and disperse its beauty like a dream. Overhead the great dunes towered threateningly. 'Why,' I asked, 'why was this lake not long since buried by these encroaching sands? Why does its fragile beauty last when the whole configuration of the landscape is changed by obliterating sand-storms? Towns and villages have vanished in a wilderness of death and desiccation, yet this lake remains and no one has ever seen its water margin low. What is the secret of its permanence and of the unseen source from which it draws such plentiful supplies that drought has no effect on it?'

At that moment I saw one of my comrades walking over the crest of the hill, ploughing a deep furrow in the sands as she went. From the summit she slid down the face of the dune, and as she did so I heard the sands sing, then she walked to the guest-house and passed through the door, leaving the whole line of her path, from the top of the hill to the lip of the lake, profoundly disturbed. The sands which, before, had not shown one wrinkle were now furrowed with deep ridges, but, as I watched, I saw their surface slowly but surely smoothed out again till, gradually, every mark was obliterated. The ceaseless winds of God were at work and, as always, they blew off the lake and upward toward the crest of the hill. By some mystery of orientation the lake was so placed that every breath which stirred the encircling sand-mounds blew upward and lifted the drift away from the water. I picked up a handful of sand and threw it downward, but the breeze caught it and blew it back in my face. This, then, was the secret of this exquisite lake's permanence – its exposure to the upward-wafting winds of God, and its deep unfailing source of supply.

'Do you understand this picture of one who has attained what you seek and reached the goal of your desire?' something within me said. 'In the midst of threatening danger this lake lifts its face heavenward, reflecting as in a mirror the glory of the sky. It is not withdrawn from the terrible sand which constantly threatens to engulf it, its position is always perilous and it lives dangerously, but every time the sand threatens, the winds of God are there to protect it, and no harm touches it. This is why its peace, its purity and its serenity can never be destroyed. Surely the parable is clear – it is the pure in heart who see God.'

The sight of a red-robed lama walking in my direction called me back to the immediate, and I rose, greeting him, then sat down and talked with him, first of his long pilgrimage and later of the search for God which urged him to such an arduous undertaking. Walking back together toward the guest-house we met the guardian of the temple, who appeared strangely agitated. 'Look,' he said, 'did you ever see anything like that?' He pointed to a curious triple halo in the sky. The three rims of light spread a diffused radiance, and we all stood and watched the strange atmospheric effect. 'This is a terrible omen,' said the priest, 'a sign of awful happenings, and of trouble coming such as the world has never known. Alas, alas for this world!' Too profoundly disturbed to say more, the old man turned off to the temple shrine to burn incense and seek to pacify the anger of the gods.

Next morning the lama, carrying his little bundle, passed on his way toward Tibet. With my companions I walked once more round the lovely lake, gazing till every detail of its beauty was impressed on my memory. Then we said goodbye to the priest, walked to the foot of the great sand-hills, stood there for a moment and gave one last backward look, then waved a long farewell to the lovely lake, and rode away.

An aerial view of the Desert of Gobi on a midsummer day would show a burning arid waste of dunes interspersed with monotonous rolling expanses of gravel and crossed by occasional ridges of high mountains whose foothills dwindle to low rocky mounds. The whole plain is shadeless and exposed to scorching heat under a pitiless sun. All living creatures seek shelter from its fierce rays and the roads are deserted, for the reverberation of heat makes travel almost impossible.

By night it is quite otherwise, and as darkness falls the desert quickens into life. Scorching heat gives way to a sudden chill which rises from the ground and strikes the traveller with a cold impact which makes him lift his head to catch the warmer upper stratum of the air as a relief from that too palpable cold. Soon that layer too will be permeated by the chill, and he will wrap a sheepskin coat around him in an endeavour to keep warm.

At this hour the observer would see caravans emerge from all the oasis inns and move slowly in various directions. Long trains of two hundred camels, roped together in strings of twelve, stretch out in thin lines over the narrow tracks; caravans of large carts, each laden with a thousand pounds of merchandise, follow one another across the plain; these join up for safety and keep within hailing distance of each other. Pedestrians carrying their own baggage balanced over the shoulder from the two ends of a pole come from many places and look like swinging dots as they move briskly at first, but later settle down to the inevitable pace of Gobi travel.

Half-way through the night all these travellers are seen to halt. This is the moment when caravans moving in opposite directions meet and greet each other. Carters recognise friends from other towns, but there is no more talk between them than is necessary for the passing of needed warnings. Camel-drivers on their immensely long journeys are alert for all unusual sights or sounds, and often carry letters to be handed to those whom they may meet at some halting-place. Pedestrians lay down their loads, rest aching shoulders and drink from their water-bottles, squatting lightly on their heels for a while before they make the second half of the stage. All these men speak but little and there is no easy chat on a desert night journey, nor is loud conversation ever heard; desert talk is always spare, subdued and unhurried, for the spaces teach men to be sharers of their dignity, and to scorn noise and tattle as only suited to the vulgarity of towns. Moreover, in the still air voices carry dangerously well, and silence becomes a cautionary instinct.

The sand deadens the sound of wheels, and camels' soft padded feet move quietly between the dunes. The camp watch-dogs might give a sharp sound by day, but at night they follow at the camels' heels or leap on to the back of one beast and lie there until the halt is called, when they jump down to take on duty. The sonorous, monotonous camel-bell has no sharp clang, but only a deep dull boom, and the rhythmic dip of the camels' neck keeps it in perfect measure. This bell is such a part of desert quiet that it breaks silence without disturbing it. When the great carts draw up for the mid-stage halt, a heavy smell of opium often comes from the pipe of some smoker hidden behind the curtains who lies there listless while the drivers exchange their greeting and then move on again.

Not only humans but innumerable small animals and insects come from their hiding-places as soon as darkness falls. All through the hours of heat they have slept in the tunnelled world which they have burrowed for themselves a few feet underground, and of which the openings are on the sheltered side of many a tiny sand-mound, blown up round the foot of a tuft of camel-thorn or of a low bush of scrub. All through the night the little live things move ceaselessly, silently and invisibly over the sand, and only by chance does a traveller become aware of their presence; after sunrise, however, he sees the sand patterned with all kinds of beautiful markings left by small rodents, beetles, centipedes and other insects which scuttle back to their sleeping-quarters with the first ray of sunshine.

Near the oases an observer might see slinking forms of wolves prowling vigilantly lest a goat or a child should wander from the shelter of the houses, and when some tired beast lags behind the caravan the dark forms gather from all sides to snatch a share of the spoil. Other sinister forms sometimes crouch behind rocks or in gullies – evil men waiting for lonely pedestrians or for some cart which has ventured unattached over the desert waste. The robbers hide themselves at those points on the route where caravans going north must pass just after sunset and where others, travelling south, come in shortly before daylight, for during the grey, twilight hours they will be unnoticed among the elusive shadows.

In the dry desert air the sky becomes a beautiful background for the brilliant stars which hang clear, showing themselves as shining orbs and never creating the illusion of lights twinkling through holes in a curtain, as is the case in dull and murky climes. The Milky Way is not the whitish haze seen in Western skies, but like a phosphorescent shower of myriad spots of light. Night travellers are great star-gazers, and look out over an uninterrupted line of horizon to skies which are always cloudless. The clearness and watchfulness of each planet suggests a personal and friendly interest toward the wayfarer, and Venus has served as beacon to many a caravan crossing doubtful stages.

Of starlight in the desert, Lawrence of Arabia writes: 'The brilliant stars cast about us a false light, not illumination, but rather a transparency of air, lengthening slightly the shadow below each stone and making a diffused greyness of the ground.'* Desert men, accustomed all their lives to that most subtle of all light diffusions, walk freely, even on rough ground, with no other illuminant. The moon, also, is more self-revealing than in heavier atmospheres, and never pretends to be merely a silver sickle or a cradle swinging in the void. She shows her full-orbed sphere, hanging in space, with a varying portion of brilliance outlining her darkened luminosity. With the rising of the moon the desert takes on its most captivating appearance, and through the long hours while she travels from one side of the horizon to the other she has her own way with human imagination, softening all the austere outlines and investing the barest formations with subtle charm. She is a mistress of magic and with one touch can turn the wilderness into a dream world.

Over these vast plains old ruined towns, surrounded with more or less decrepit battlemented walls, are scattered. The caravan track enters an enclosure at the place where a city gate used to stand, and leaves it at a gap in the opposite wall where another gate once stood. Inside the enclosed space are ruined walls, and the remains of houses long since destroyed. No one can build them up and use them again, for water has withdrawn itself from these cities of the dead and the old well openings are choked to the brim with sand and eroded matter. The main streets are often quite distinguishable, and even crooked lanes are sometimes recognisable. Silent progress by moonlight through such an ancient ruin vividly stirs the imagination and suggests that these old ruins may well be the haunt, not only of wild beasts, as they certainly are, but also of the ghostly habitants.

Not least remarkable of the Gobi night effects is the dancing magnetic light, which bewilders the inexperienced with its suggestions of men and camps in a region which is wholly deserted. The light flickers on the horizon, appearing and disappearing suddenly and unaccountably; one moment it is there, but a second later it has vanished, and when the traveller decides that it must be an illusion it is back again and yet again. Should he throw off his coat, or a driver touch a mule with his whip, the flash comes quite close, and the garment or the mule's back is streaked with light, and anyone holding a piece of silk, or touching a fur coat, may feel an electric shock. The Mongol poetically speaks of all these magnetic lights as 'the Rosary of Heaven', because, through the long hours of darkness, the fires flash and shine like falling beads.

During silent stages when nothing is heard but the soft grind of wheels on loose sand, sound becomes subtly rhythmic and the rhythms resolve themselves into music, harmonising according to the perception of the listener. The muleteer probably hears nothing but a monotonous grating measure, while the more imaginative traveller listens to the rise and swell of mighty cadences, broad melodies and spacious harmonies.

With the rising sun the aerial observer could watch all the caravans reaching their respective destinations at the end of their night's journey. The camels kneel among the sands to have their loads removed, and wide-open doors of oasis inns wait to receive the tired wayfarers who, throughout the night, have covered another thirty-mile stage of the desert road. By divergent ways they come, meeting at the welcome *serai*, and disappear into the darkness and quiet of inn cells to pass the day in sleep.

* *The Seven Pillars of Wisdom*, by T. E. Lawrence.

Beryl Markham

(1902–1986)

Of the books written by three of the best-known women aviators, Amelia Earhart, Amy Johnson, and Beryl Markham, only Markham's book, *West with the Night*, remains in print. Books by Earhart, the first woman pilot to cross the Atlantic, and Johnson, the so-called darling of the skies, the first woman to fly solo from England to Australia, were solid adventure tales, but Markham's book, admired by Ernest Hemingway, was praised as a work of literature, as well.

Had the book, her first and only effort, not been published while Markham was living in Hollywood with her husband and collaborator, Raoul Schumacher, then nothing more would have been said. But, in a town eager for scandal, Markham's critics claimed that she could not have written such a fine book; Schumacher must have been its true author. After the Second World War, Markham, the first woman pilot to traverse the Atlantic from East to West, returned to Africa, where she trained racehorses – eight of them ending up winners of the prestigious Kenya Derby. Yet the mystery of who wrote the lyrical *West with the Night* remains: Beryl Markham herself lived into her eighties, a near-forgotten woman who drank too much, a recluse in an African home. Her companion in the following excerpt was the former husband of Isak Dinesen, Bror Blixen-Finecke.

from **West with the Night**

I suppose, if there were a part of the world in which mastodon still lived, somebody would design a new gun, and men, in their eternal impudence, would hunt mastodon as they now hunt elephant. Impudence seems to be the word. At least David and Goliath were of the same species, but, to an elephant, a man can only be a midge with a deathly sting.

It is absurd for a man to kill an elephant. It is not brutal, it is not heroic, and certainly it is not easy; it is just one of those preposterous things that men do like putting a dam across a great river, one tenth of whose volume could engulf the whole of mankind without disturbing the domestic life of a single catfish.

Elephant, beyond the fact that their size and conformation are aesthetically more suited to the treading of this earth than our angular infirmity, have an average intelligence comparable to our own. Of course they are less agile and physically less adaptable than ourselves – Nature having developed their bodies in one direction and their brains in another, while human beings, on the other hand, drew from Mr. Darwin's lottery of evolution both the winning ticket and the stub to match it. This, I suppose, is why we are so wonderful and can make movies and electric razors and wireless sets – and guns with which to shoot the elephant, the hare, clay pigeons, and each other.

The elephant is a rational animal. He thinks. Blix and I (also rational animals in our own right) have never quite agreed on the mental attributes of the elephant. I know Blix is not to be doubted because he has learned more about elephant than any other man I ever met, or even heard about, but he looks upon legend with a suspicious eye, and I do not.

There is a legend that elephant dispose of their dead in secret burial grounds and that none of these has ever been discovered. In support of this, there is only the fact that the body of an elephant, unless he had been trapped or shot in his tracks, has rarely been found. What happens to the old and diseased?

Not only natives, but many white settlers, have supported for years the legend (if it is legend) that elephant will carry their wounded and their sick hundreds of miles, if necessary, to keep them out of the hands of their enemies. And it is said that elephant never forget.

These are perhaps just stories born of imagination. Ivory was once almost as precious as gold, and wherever there is treasure, men mix it with mystery. But still, there is no mystery about the things you see yourself.

I think I am the first person ever to scout elephant by plane, and so it follows that the thousands of elephant I saw time and again from the air had never before been plagued by anything above their heads more ominous than tick-birds.

The reaction of a herd of elephant to my Avian was, in the initial instance, always the same – they left their feeding ground and tried to find cover, though often, before yielding, one or two of the bulls would prepare for battle and charge in the direction of the plane if it were low enough to be within their scope of vision. Once the futility of this was realized, the entire herd would be off into the deepest bush.

Checking again on the whereabouts of the same herd next day, I always found that a good deal of thinking had been going on amongst them during the night. On the basis of their reaction to my second intrusion, I judged that their thoughts had run somewhat like this: A: The thing that flew over us was no bird, since no bird would have to work so hard to stay in the air – and, anyway, we know all the birds. B: If it was no bird, it was very likely just another trick of those two-legged dwarfs against whom there ought to be a law. C: The two-legged dwarfs (both black and white) have, as long as our long memories go back, killed our bulls for their tusks. We know this because, in the case of the white dwarfs, at least, the tusks are the only part taken away.

The actions of the elephant, based upon this reasoning, were always sensible and practical. The second time they saw the Avian, they refused to hide; instead, the females, who bear only small valueless tusks, simply grouped themselves around their treasure-burdened bulls in such a way that no ivory could be seen from the air or from any other approach.

This can be maddening strategy to an elephant scout. I have spent the better part of an hour circling, criss-crossing, and diving low over some of the most inhospitable country in Africa in an effort to break such a stubborn huddle, sometimes successfully, sometimes not.

But the tactics vary. More than once I have come upon a large and solitary elephant standing with enticing disregard for safety, its massive bulk in clear view, but its head buried in thicket. This was, on the part of the elephant, no effort to simulate the nonsensical habit attributed to the ostrich. It was, on the contrary, a cleverly devised trap into which I fell, every way except physically, at least a dozen times. The beast always proved to be a large cow rather than a bull, and I always found that by the time I had arrived at this brilliant if tardy deduction, the rest of the herd had got another ten miles away, and the decoy, leering up at me out of a small, triumphant eye, would amble into the open, wave her trunk with devastating nonchalance, and disappear.

This order of intelligence in a lesser animal can obviously give rise to exaggeration – some of it persistent enough to be crystallised into legend. But you cannot discredit truth merely because legend has grown out of it. The sometimes almost godlike achievements of our own species in ages past toddle through history supported more often than not on the twin crutches of fable and human credulity.

As to the brutality of elephant-hunting, I cannot see that it is any more brutal than ninety per cent of all other human activities. I suppose there is nothing more tragic about the death of an elephant than there is about the death of a Hereford steer – certainly not in the eyes of the steer. The only difference is that the steer has neither the ability nor the chance to outwit the gentleman who wields the slaughter-house snickersnee, while the elephant has both of these to pit against the hunter.

Elephant hunters may be unconscionable brutes, but it would be an error to regard the elephant as an altogether pacific animal. The popular belief that only the so-called 'rogue' elephant is dangerous to men is quite wrong – so wrong that a considerable number of men who believed it have become one with the dust without even their just due of gradual disintegration. A normal bull elephant, aroused by the scent of man, will often attack at once – and his speed is as unbelievable as his mobility. His trunk and his feet are his weapons – at least in the distasteful business of exterminating a mere human; those resplendent sabres of ivory await resplendent foes.

Blix and I hardly came into this category at Kilamakoy –

certainly not after we had run down the big bull, or, as it happened, the big bull had run down us. I can say, at once with gratification still genuine, that we were not trampled within that most durable of all inches – the last inch of our lives. We got out all right, but there are times when I still dream.

On arriving from Makindu, I landed my plane in the shallow box of a runway scooped out of the bush, unplugged wads of cotton wool from my ears, and climbed from the cockpit.

The aristocratically descended visage of the Baron von Blixen Finecke greeted me (as it always did) with the most delightful of smiles caught, like a strip of sunlight, on a familiar patch of leather – well-kept leather, free of wrinkles, but brown and saddle-tough.

Beyond this concession to the fictional idea of what a White Hunter ought to look like, Blix's face yields not a whit. He has gay, light blue eyes rather than sombre, steel-grey ones; his cheeks are well rounded rather than flat as an axe; his lips are full and generous and not pinched tight in grim realization of what the Wilderness Can Do. He talks. He is never significantly silent.

He wore then what I always remember him as wearing, a khaki bush shirt of 'solano' material, slacks of the same stuff, and a pair of low-cut moccasins with soles – or at least vestiges of soles. There were four pockets in his bush shirt, but I don't think he knew it; he never carried anything unless he was actually hunting – and then it was just a rifle and ammunition. He never went around hung with knives, revolvers, binoculars, or even a watch. He could tell time by the sun, and if there were no sun, he could tell it, anyway. He wore over his closely cropped greying hair a terai hat, colourless and limp as a wilted frond.

He said, 'Hullo, Beryl', and pointed to a man at his side – so angular as to give the impression of being constructed entirely of barrel staves.

'This,' said Blix, with what could hardly be called Old-World courtesy, 'is Old Man Wicks.'

'At least,' said Old Man Wicks, 'I have seen the lady from the Skies.'

Writing it now, that remark seems a little like a line from the best play chosen from those offered by the graduating class of Eton, possibly in the late twenties, or like the remark of a man up to his ears in his favourite anodyne. But, as a matter of fact, Old Man Wicks, who managed a piece of no-man's-land belonging to the Manoni Sugar Company, near Masongaleni, had seen only one white man in sixteen months and, I gathered, hadn't seen a white woman in as many years. At least he had never seen an aeroplane and a white woman at the same time, nor can I be sure that he regarded the spectacle as much of a Godsend. Old Man Wicks, oddly enough, wasn't very old – he was barely forty – and it may have been that his monkish life was the first choice of whatever other lives he could have led. He looked old, but that might have been protective colouration. He was a gentle, kindly man helping Blix with the safari until Winston Guest arrived.

It was a modest enough safari. There were three large tents – Winston's, Blix's, and my own – and then there were several pup tents for the Native boys, gun-bearers, and trackers. Blix's boy Farah, Winston's boy, and of course my Arab Ruta (who was due via lorry from Nairobi) had pup tents to themselves. The others, as much out of choice as necessity, slept several in a tent. There was a hangar for the Avian, made out of a square of tarpaulin, and there was a baobab tree whose shade served as a veranda to everybody. The immediate country was endless and barren of hills.

Half an hour after I landed, Blix and I were up in the Avian, hoping, if possible, to spot a herd of elephant before Winston's arrival that night. If we could find a herd within two or three days' walking distance from the camp, it would be extraordinary luck – always provided that the herd contained a bull with respectable tusks.

It is not unusual for an elephant hunter to spend six months, or even a year, on the spoor of a single bull. Elephant go where men can't – or at least shouldn't.

Scouting by plane eliminates a good deal of the preliminary work, but when as upon occasion I did spot a herd not more than thirty or forty miles from camp, it still meant that those forty miles had to be walked, crawled, or wriggled by the hunters – and that by the time this body and nerve-racking manoeuvre had been achieved, the elephant had pushed on another twenty miles or so into the bush. A man, it ought to be remembered, has to take several steps to each stride of an elephant, and, moreover, the man is somewhat less than resistant to thicket, thorn trees, and heat. Also (particularly if he is white) he is vulnerable as a peeled egg to all things that sting – anopheles mosquitoes, scorpions, snakes, and tsetse flies. The essence of elephant-hunting is discomfort in such lavish proportions that only the wealthy can afford it.

Blix and I were fortunate on our very first expedition out of

Kilamakoy. The Wakamba scouts on our safari had reported a large herd of elephant containing several worth-while bulls, not more than twenty air miles from camp. We circled the district indicated, passed over the herd perhaps a dozen times, but finally spotted it.

A herd of elephant, as seen from a plane, has a quality of an hallucination. The proportions are wrong – they are like those of a child's drawing of a field mouse in which the whole landscape, complete with barns and windmills, is dwarfed beneath the whiskers of the mighty rodent who looks both able and willing to devour everything, including the thumb-tack that holds the work against the schoolroom wall.

Peering down from the cockpit at grazing elephant, you have the feeling that what you are beholding is wonderful, but not authentic. It is not only incongruous in the sense that animals simply are not as big as trees, but also in the sense that the twentieth century, tidy and svelte with stainless steel as it is, would not possibly permit such prehistoric monsters to wander in its garden. Even in Africa, the elephant is as anomalous as the Cro-Magnon Man might be shooting a round of golf at Saint Andrews in Scotland.

But, with all this, elephant are seldom conspicuous from the air. If they were smaller, they might be. Big as they are, and coloured as they are, they blend with everything until the moment they catch your eye.

They caught Blix's eye and he scribbled me a frantic note: 'Look! The big bull is enormous. Turn back. Doctor Turvy radios I should have some gin.'

Well, we had no radio – and certainly no gin in my plane. But just as certainly, we had Doctor Turvy.

Doctor Turvy was an ethereal citizen of an ethereal world. In the beginning, he existed only for Blix, but long before the end, he existed for everybody who worked with Blix or knew him well.

Although Doctor Turvy's prescriptions indicated that he put his trust in a wine list rather than a pharmacopoeia, he had two qualities of special excellence in a physician: his diagnosis was always arrived at in a split second – and he held the complete confidence of his patient. Beyond that, his adeptness at mental telepathy (in which Blix himself was pretty well grounded) eliminated the expensive practice of calling round to feel the pulse or take a temperature. Nobody ever saw Doctor Turvy – and that fact, Blix insisted, was bedside manner carried to its final degree of perfection.

I banked the Avian and turned toward camp.

Within three miles of our communal baobab tree, we saw four more elephant – three of them beautiful bulls. The thought passed through my head that the way to find a needle in a haystack is to sit down. Elephant are never within three miles of camp. It's hardly cricket that they should be. It doesn't make a hunter out of you to turn over on your canvas cot and realize that the thing you are hunting at such expense and physical tribulation is so contemptuous of your prowess as to be eating leaves right in front of your eyes.

But Blix is a practical man. As a White Hunter, his job was to produce the game desired and to point it out to his employer of the moment. Blix's work, and mine, was made much easier by finding the elephant so close. We could even land at the camp and then approach them on foot to judge more accurately their size, immediate intentions, and strategic disposition.

Doctor Turvy's prescription had to be filled, and taken, of course, but even so, we would have time to reconnoitre.

We landed on the miserly runway, which had a lot in common with an extemporaneous badminton court, and, within twenty minutes, proceeded on foot toward those magnificent bulls.

Makula was with us. Neither the safari nor this book, for that matter, could be complete without Makula. Though there are a good many Wakamba trackers available in East Africa, it has become almost traditional in late years to mention Makula in every book that touches upon elephant-hunting, and I would not break with tradition.

Makula is a man in the peculiar position of having gained fame without being aware of it. He can neither read nor write; his first language is Wakamba, his second a halting Swahili. He is a smallish ebon-tinted Native with an inordinately wise eye, a penchant for black magic, and the instincts of a beagle hound. I think he could track a honeybee through a bamboo forest.

No matter how elaborate the safari on which Makula is engaged as tracker, he goes about naked from the waist up, carrying a long bow and a quiver full of poisoned arrows. He has seen the work of the best rifles white men have yet produced, but when Makula's nostrils distend after either a good or a bad shot, it is not the smell of gunpowder that distends them; it is a kind of restrained contempt for that noisy and unwieldy piece of machinery with its devilish

'By the time I had crawled three feet, I am sure that somewhere over fifty distinct species of insect life were individually and severally represented in my clothes…'

tendency to knock the untutored huntsman flat on his buttocks every time he pulls the trigger.

Safaris come and safaris go, but Makula goes on forever. I suspect at times that he is one of the wisest men I have ever known – so wise that, realizing the scarcity of wisdom, he has never cast a scrap of it away, though I still remember a remark he made to an overzealous newcomer to his profession: 'White men pay for danger – we poor ones cannot afford it. Find your elephant, then vanish, so that you may live to find another.'

Makula always vanished. He went ahead in the bush with the silence of a shade, missing nothing, and the moment he had brought his hunters within sight of the elephant, he disappeared with the silence of a shade, missing everything.

Stalking just ahead of Blix through the tight bush, Makula signalled for a pause, shinned up a convenient tree without noise, and then came down again. He pointed to a chink in the thicket, took Blix firmly by the arm, and pushed him ahead. Then Makula disappeared. Blix led, and I followed.

The ability to move soundlessly through a wall of bush as tightly woven as Nature can weave it is not an art that can be acquired much after childhood. I cannot explain it, nor could Arab Maina who taught me ever explain it. It is not a matter of watching where you step; it is rather a matter of keeping your eyes on the place where you want to be, while every nerve becomes another eye, every muscle develops reflex action. You do not guide your body, you trust it to be silent.

We were silent. The elephant we advanced upon heard nothing – even when the enormous hindquarters of two bulls loomed before us like grey rocks wedded to the earth.

Blix stopped. He whispered with his fingers and I read the whisper. 'Watch the wind. Swing round them. I want to see their tusks.'

Swing, indeed! It took us slightly over an hour to negotiate a semi-circle of fifty yards. The bulls were big – with ivory enough – hundred-pounders at least, or better.

Nimrod was satisfied, wet with sweat, and on the verge, I sensed, of receiving a psychic message from Doctor Turvy. But this message was delayed in transit.

One bull raised his head, elevated his trunk, and moved to face us. His gargantuan ears began to spread as if to capture even the sound of our heartbeats. By chance, he had grazed over a spot we had lately left, and he had got our scent. It was all he needed.

I have rarely seen anything so calm as that bull elephant – or so casually determined upon destruction. It might be said that he shuffled to the kill. Being, like all elephant, almost blind, this one could not see us, but he was used to that. He would follow scent and sound until he *could* see us, which, I computed, would take about thirty seconds.

Blix wiggled his fingers earthward, and that meant, 'Drop and crawl.'

It is amazing what a lot of insect life goes on under your nose when you have got it an inch from the earth. I suppose it goes on in any case, but if you are proceeding on your stomach, dragging your body along by your fingernails, entomology presents itself very forcibly as a thoroughly justified science. The problem of classification alone must continue to be very discouraging.

By the time I had crawled three feet, I am sure that somewhere over fifty distinct species of insect life were individually and severally represented in my clothes, with Siafu ants conducting the congress.

Blix's feet were just ahead of my eyes – close enough so that I could contemplate the holes in his shoes, and wonder why he ever wore any at all, since he went through them almost in a matter of hours. I had ample time also to observe that he wore no socks. Practical, but not comme il faut. His legs moved through the underbrush like dead legs dragged by strings. There was no sound from the elephant.

I don't know how long we crawled like that, but the little shadows in the thicket were leaning toward the east when we stopped. Possibly we had gone a hundred yards. The insect bites had become just broad, burning patches.

We were breathing easier – or at least I was – when Blix's feet and legs went motionless. I could just see his head close against his shoulder, and watch him turn to peek upward into the bush. He gave no signal to continue. He only looked horribly embarrassed like a child caught stealing eggs.

But my own expression must have been a little more intense. The big bull was about ten feet away – and at that distance elephant are not blind.

Blix stood up and raised his rifle slowly, with an expression of ineffable sadness.

'That's for me,' I thought. 'He knows that even a shot in the brain won't stop that bull before we're both crushed like mangos.'

In an open place, it might have been possible to dodge to one side, but not here. I stood behind Blix with my hands on his waist according to his instructions. But I knew it wasn't any good. The body of the elephant was swaying. It was like watching a boulder, in whose path you were trapped, teeter on the edge of a cliff before plunging. The bull's ears were spread wide now, his trunk was up and extended toward us, and he began the elephant scream of anger which is so terrifying as to hold you silent where you stand, like fingers clamped upon your throat. It is a shrill scream, cold as winter wind.

It occurred to me that this was the instant to shoot.

Blix never moved. He held his rifle very steady and began to chant some of the most striking blasphemy I have ever heard. It was colourful, original, and delivered with finesse, but I felt that this was a badly chosen moment to test it on an elephant – and ungallant beyond belief if it was meant for me.

The elephant advanced, Blix unleashed more oaths (this time in Swedish), and I trembled. There was no rifle shot. A single biscuit tin, I judged, would do for both of us – cremation would be superfluous.

'I may have to shoot him,' Blix announced, and the remark struck me as an understatement of classic magnificence. Bullets would sink into that monstrous hide like pebbles into a pond.

Somehow you never think of an elephant as having a mouth, because you never see it when his trunk is down, so that when the elephant is quite close and his trunk is up, the dark red-and-black slit is by way of being an almost shocking revelation. I was looking into our elephant's mouth with a kind of idiotic curiosity when he screamed again – and thereby, I am convinced, saved both Blix and me from a fate no more tragic than simple death, but infinitely less tidy.

The scream of that elephant was a strategic blunder, and it did him out of a wonderful bit of fun. It was such an authentic scream, of such splendid resonance, that his cronies, still grazing in the bush, accepted it as legitimate warning, and left. We had known they were still there because the bowels of peacefully occupied elephant rumble continually like oncoming thunder – and we had heard thunder.

They left, and it seemed they tore the country from its roots in leaving. Everything went, bush, trees, sansivera, clods of dirt – and the monster who confronted us. He paused, listened, and swung round with the slow irresistibility of a bank-vault door. And then he was off in a typhoon of crumbled vegetation and crashing trees.

For a long time there wasn't any silence, but when there was, Blix lowered his rifle – which had acquired, for me, all the death-dealing qualities of a feather duster.

I was limp, irritable, and full of maledictions for the insect kind. Blix and I hacked our way back to camp without the exchange of a word, but when I fell into a canvas chair in front of the tents, I forswore the historic propriety of my sex to ask a rude question.

'I think you're the best hunter in Africa, Blickie, but there are times when your humour is gruesome. Why in hell didn't you shoot?'

Blix extracted a bug from Doctor Turvy's elixir of life and shrugged.

'Don't be silly. You know as well as I do why I didn't shoot. Those elephant are for Winston.'

'Of course I know – but what if that bull had charged?'

Farah the faithful produced another drink, and Blix produced a non sequitur. He stared upward into the leaves of the baobab tree and sighed like a poet in love.

'There's an old adage,' he said, 'translated from the ancient Coptic, that contains all the wisdom of the ages – "Life is life and fun is fun, but it's all so quiet when the goldfish die."'

Ella Maillart

(1903–)

THE AUTHOR OF SEVERAL TRAVEL BOOKS, ELLA MAILLART WAS ONE OF THE FIRST WRITERS TO CONSIDER THE INNER JOURNEY. SHE STROVE TO INTERWEAVE POLITICAL AND HISTORICAL DETAILS WITH THE PERSONAL AND THE EVERYDAY, TO CREATE A FORM OF TRAVEL WRITING THAT CUTS DEEPER INTO ISSUES NOT NORMALLY ASSOCIATED WITH THE GENRE. IN HER QUEST FOR PERSONAL DISCOVERY, SHE LIVED AMONG KIRGHIZ AND KAZAKH TRIBESMEN IN THE 1930S AND, IN *FORBIDDEN JOURNEY*, SHE RECOUNTS A TRIP ACROSS THE GOBI AND TAKLA MAKAN DESERTS TO THE HINDU KUSH. PART OF WHAT MOTIVATED THE TRIP FROM GENEVA TO KABUL TO PESHAWAR, PAKISTAN, DURING THE SECOND WORLD WAR RECOUNTED IN *THE CRUEL WAY* WAS HER WISH TO CONFRONT AND BETTER UNDERSTAND THE DARK SIDE OF HER FRIEND, CHRISTINA, WHO WAS SEEKING FREEDOM AND A PERSONAL CURE FOR HER SEVERE DRUG ADDICTION. MAILLART HAS CURTAILED HER TRAVELS IN THE LAST TWO DECADES, AND NOW LIVES IN GENEVA, SWITZERLAND.

from **The Cruel Way**

At dusk we slipped through the mat of dust that hung motionless above the road. Under our headlights, riders clothed in white seemed to be moving silently through smoke. Later we thought with excitement that we were overtaking majestically pacing elephants, their narrow and sloping hindquarters ending in a tiny tail. But they were only tall camels, their grey bulk made of two vertical sacks that built a massive ridge above their backs.

Akcha loomed splendidly out of the night, a pale angular citadel surrounded by low flat-roofed houses. Men were stretched on their stringed charpoys; a group of brightly painted buses rested their tired bones, their bonnets touching. Once more we had that direct physical feeling of being in a remote corner of the world.

It was four in the morning, we had drunk our tea and wanted to start, hoping to reach Mazar-i-Sharif before the heat of noon. Since the road was now easy, we dismissed the escort who so cramped our style. But our man began to shout and soon we had many stalwart Afghans around us. Wearing a stylish *khalat* with brown stripes, an 'old beard' who spoke excellent Russian tried to settle the controversy. He understood our point: we were giving a letter to our escort saying he was not to be blamed because we had left him behind. In such a heat, when the slightest pressure exasperated our skin, we could not long bear to be squeezed three in front, especially when the man's dirty socks forced us to live with a handkerchief to our noses. (I do not know if all this was translated, but the sympathy of the crowd was certainly not with our horrible policeman.)

Meanwhile, because we did not want to lose face, the precious morning hours drifted away. The escort would only let us go if the mayor of Akcha ordered him. The interpreter went to the mayor. At last he returned accompanied by a new escort and a tray of figs for us! Defeated and impatient to start, we took the new man on board.

He was very tall and did not know how to keep his knees steady; he was prognathous and did not know how to keep his mouth shut. He had to keep it open anyhow, to be sick from the motion of the car: it was a change from his predecessor's spitting of tobacco-juice. This was enough to spoil the quaint charm of travelling through what looked like a lunar country asphyxiated by too much dry heat. It was the nature of the soil and the lack of relief, no doubt, that were responsible for the deadly whiteness of the light. Moving with the wind, the car was unbearably hot.

The country was quite flat, sometimes furrowed by great irrigation channels which disturbed waters born high and far among the hills of central Afghanistan, in the cool lakes of the Band-i-Amir which we were to visit.

To give some respite to our policeman, we halted at a hut in the desert where an Uzbek tending his samovar sold us some thirst-quenching *chai sabz* or green tea. The shade cast by the hut was all that could be found. A decent Afghan was sleeping there on the beaten earth, and before we could prevent it he was kicked awake and sent away by our man. It filled us with anger.

And that on the morning when we were approaching the ruins of Balkh, Bactres, the Mother of Cities, known to have been twenty miles in circumference, but dead now in this plain of the Oxus which, in the sixteenth century B.C. so they say, witnessed the first Aryan migration on its way to India by way of Herat, Kandahar and the Bolan pass south of Quetta. Balkh, where the religion of Zoroaster was for the first time adopted by a king, Balkh, where according to Marco Polo, Alexander the Great married the daughter of Darius, the town whose satrap Bessus had killed that Darius while he was escaping through Khorassan.

In the second century B.C. Chang Kien was at the head of a Chinese mission sent to the Yue-chi of Sogdiana (which is the same as Bactria); his journey seems to mark the beginning of the silk trade across Asia. The Yue-chi were Indo-Scythians who had recently invaded the country, until then a great outpost of Hellenism. 'It is because these successors of Alexander the Great were so forceful and active that you are going to excavate Graeco-Buddhist remains,' I said to Christina.

The white Huns were the next to invade Bactria in the fifth century A.D. In spite of their ravages, the country was still Buddhistic in style when two centuries later Hsuan Tsang the pilgrim arrived from China on his way to India 'in search of wisdom' – Hsuan Tsang whose tracks I have crossed during three journeys to Central Asia and whose writings had so greatly helped me to appreciate what I saw. There were still, in Balkh, a hundred monasteries rich in relics of the Buddha when he arrived from Kunduz, the capital of the Western Turks who ruled over Afghan Turkestan or Tokharestan.

At Balkh, Hsuan Tsang admired 'a magnificent plateau': there must have been more water in the country then than there is nowadays. The change may be due to the fact, affirmed by geologists, that the crust of the earth is still rising in this part of the world.

A century later the priest of the celebrated fire-altar of Balkh was converted to Islam and his example was followed by the landowners. In 1221 Balkh was laid waste by Genghis Khan. At first, the town that had sheltered Muhammad of Khwarezm had simply been occupied. But when Genghis Khan heard that the son of Muhammad had raised an army of seventy thousand men in Southern Afghanistan, he destroyed the town, marched to Bamian and later defeated the young man by the river Indus.

Fifty years later Marco Polo arrived at Balkh which he calls a large and magnificent city. 'It was formerly more considerable but has sustained much injury from the Tartars who in their frequent attacks have partly demolished its buildings. It contained many palaces constructed of marble and spacious squares still visible, although in a ruinous state.'*

Timur in the fourteenth century was the next invader and his example was followed by the Uzbeks who conquered Herat in 1506. It was one of their descendants, Abdul Aziz, who fought Prince Aurangzeb of Delhi, then governor of Balkh. The Moghul prince was brave, dismounting at sunset to pray during the battle, and winning the admiration of both armies. 'To fight such a man is to court ruin' cried Abdul Aziz, and suspended battle. It was the last attempt of the Moghuls to retain these far-away provinces.

We had no hope of emulating Renan and his *Prière sur l'Acropole* by meditating over the ruins of Balkh, comparing Asia with Europe: dreaming about the future of Paris, London or Berlin: our escort would have annoyed us, standing near, watching our movements, ready to forbid the use of our cameras as he had already done before. Photophobia was the latest affliction of Afghan officialdom – by contagion, probably, from Persia which tried to nip in the bud pictures that show her not yet entirely modern.

But we planned to outdo our gaping man.

Reaching the dead, bleached mounds of clay that had once

* *Travels of Marco Polo.*

been the ramparts of Balkh, Christina walked towards them, arming her camera and followed by the escort shouting *Mafi! Mafi!* Meanwhile, my gaze was fixed on a tall monument with a shiny blue dome that stood a few hundred paces away at the entrance of the living town. Jumping back into the car, I drove to it as quickly as possible, leaving behind me a man on the verge of being split between us.

I had gained a few minutes during which I busied myself with my three cameras, taking coloured stills, black-and-white stills, and coloured 'movie'. The sun shone harshly on the lofty ribbed dome and on the arched portal to which it was yoked. The dazzle of glazed tiles brought an unexpected touch of liveliness in a world that had fainted in the whiteness of the midday glare. Most of these tiles were too pale to please me, but that Green Mosque which stands by the side of the shrine of Khwaja Abdul Nasr Parsar stood proudly in the square and I liked the thick spiral minarets that framed the great portal.

Khwaja is a name given to a sect of holy men who once acquired sovereign power over the Khans of Turkestan and whose tombs are found all over Central Asia. This name is perhaps derived from *khojagian*, a teacher. They belonged to the darvish order of the Naqshbandis and they developed the 'Power of the Will' through perfect concentration: 'It is impossible to conflict with an *arif* or "knowing person" possessed of the "Power of the Will", is written in their books. The "Tarikh-i-Rashidi" informs us that "they were workers of miracles and healers of the sick and in these capacities obtained a hold over the minds of the mass of the people."' The Naqshbandis (painters) were so called because their founder Naqshband 'drew incomparable pictures of the Divine Science and painted figures of the Eternal Invention which are not imperceptible.'*

As soon as Christina joined me, shadowed by the policeman, we speeded toward Mazar-i-Sharif. To silence the expostulations of our man, I began to read aloud from the first booklet I happened on – Mr. Ford's instructions to owners of his cars. But I soon stopped: it was too disquieting to read all we had done that we should not have done.

The deep pot-holes of the road were a menace to our springs; but we forgot them more or less, in the question: 'Is it possible for our time to produce such mystics as the Naqshbandis?' Born at Balkh, the most famous of them was Jalal-ud-din Rumi, founder of the darvish order of the Maulavis. Like his friend Shams-ud-Din of Tabriz known as the 'Moving Spirit of the Order, the Sultan of the Mendicants, the Mystery of God on Earth, the Perfect in word and deed,' he lived at the beginning of the thirteenth century, the century during which Genghis Khan brought one world to an end by destroying all its great capitals – Balkh, Merv, Nishapur, Rey. Perhaps if a world-war – the modern equivalent to a Mongol invasion – was to destroy our present world, mystics would rise once more, eager to deal with facts more important and less sickening than the madness of men.

We travelled with a bookshelf fixed above the back of our seat. The poor books were shaken madly during all these days, but we rejoiced to be able to lay our hand on the right volume at the right moment. Rubbing against each other were Marco Polo, Pelliot, Evans-Wentz, Vivekananda, Maritain, Jung, a life of Alexander the Great, Grousset, the *Zend-Avesta*. I picked *The Darvishes* by John P. Brown and H. A. Rose, and read aloud a passage about Jalal-ud-din Rumi. 'When on a roof with other youngsters, he was asked if it were possible to jump to the next house-top. He answers: "Woe to the human being who should try to do what cats and dogs do. If you feel yourself competent to do it, let us jump towards heaven", and then he sprang and was lost from their sight. The youths all cried out as he disappeared, but a moment later he returned, altered in complexion, changed in figure, and said that a legion of beings clothed in green had seized him and carried him in a circle upwards. "They showed me strange things of a celestial character and on your cries reaching us they lowered me down to the earth."'

Later whenever he became absorbed in fervid love for Allah, he would rise from his seat and turn round; and on more than one occasion he began to recede upwards from the material world. Only by means of music could he be prevented from disappearing from among his devoted companions.

Years afterwards I came to know of lines of his that might have been written for Christina:

Knowing will, memory, thoughtfulness
A hell, and life itself a snare,
To put away self-consciousness;
It is the soberest of men who bear
The blame of Drugs and Drunkenness.
– Jalal-un-din Rumi

* John Brown and H. A. Rose: *The Darvishes*.

Rose Macaulay
(1881–1958)

Rose Macaulay, the celebrated English author, wrote only one travel book, *Fabled Shore*, but few books have had a greater impact on the way people travel. Macaulay's description of her automobile tour from Port Bou to Cape Vincent along the coast of Spain in 1948 enticed thousands to follow her lead and see for themselves. The coast has never been the same. Macaulay wrote several novels, including *Abbots Verney*, which established her literary reputation in 1906, and *The Towers of Trebizond*, which is often mistaken for a firsthand travel account, as well as poems, essays, and literary criticism. Macaulay was named Dame Commander of the British Empire in 1958.

from The Fabled Shore

Before the civil war broke, Málaga was a favourite winter resort of sun-seeking foreigners (perhaps it is so now again). The dirty streets complained of by nineteenth-century travellers have become clean, the hotels are improved. Possibly this is partly due to the winter visits of Queen Victoria (Ena) and her mother Princess Beatrice of Battenberg, who stayed there every year. I dare say even the lower orders are improved too. In 1830 a Mr. Inglis was warned (or so he believed) by the British consul that he could only ascend unaccompanied to the Alcázaba and the Gibralfera, the Phoenician-Moorish forts on the hill above the town, at risk of his life; when he did so one evening he was persuaded that a lurking Malagueño, whose dark face he descried watching him from the shadows of the ruins, meant to rob and assassinate him; he only escaped this fate by fleeing hot-foot and breathless down a path to the city. No such dangers today attend the visitor to these now restored and tidied up forts, except the dangers attendant on a steep climb in the sun. If you brave this, you get a fine sweeping view of Málaga and its bay, the broad basin of its splendid harbour full of the ships of the world – cargo steamers, cruising steamers, Spanish battleships, white-sailed yachts, fleets of fishing boats – a lovely sight. Beyond it stretches the line of coast that curves south-west to the Straits, and it is true that you can faintly see Ceuta and the mountains of Africa.

Walking down the steep narrow streets of the old town that climbs above the long alameda and park and modern frontage that lie along the harbour front, one passes an occasional broken gesture from the Arab past – part of a house, a gateway, an arch. There is, too, the cathedral, though this is not particularly interesting. It is, as Ford observed, a pastiche, since it was begun (on the site of a mosque and of the Gothic church run up just after the conquest, of which only a portal of the Sagrario remains) in 1538, and not finished until late in the eighteenth century. It was a good deal damaged in 1936, but still has a fine showy commonplace Corinthian façade and towers. I did not see the inside, which has, says Baedeker, pictures by Alonso Cano, Ribera and others (but I dare say they were burnt) and some good sculpture. There are other churches in Málaga, and an archaeological museum, and a museum of fine arts, all shut. More interesting is the general lie and feeling of the town and port, this oldest Phoenician Mediterranean port of Spain, anciently so powerful and so opulent a fair for Tyre, for Carthage, for Rome, for the Moor, and now again for Spain. Málaga has its industrial quarter, its cotton mills, its sugar refineries, its factories, west of the Guadalmedina, and its port is full of ships carrying grapes, raisins, wine, sugar, cotton, and (one hopes) bananas, sweet potatoes and custard apples, out to sea.

For those who like parks (I do not) there is a handsome modern park along the sea front. For those who like nice crowded bathing beaches (I do not) there is a nice crowded bathing beach. I remembered how Mr. Joseph Townsend, visiting Málaga in 1786, had reported that all the young people bathed for hours by night in summer, and the female section of the sea, carefully segregated from the male, was defended from eager gentlemen by sentinels with loaded muskets. Deaths in such a cause were, no doubt, numerous among Malagueño señoritos. Strange things were in those days related to visiting Englishmen; Mr. Henry Swinburne, in 1775, was 'assured that it was hardly possible to breathe in summer'. This sounds like the kind of assurance made by those patriots who desire to defend their city from any suspicions of chilliness, and was probably made to Mr. Swinburne on a day when the cool *levante* was blowing from the sea, or the icy *terral* from the mountains. Málaga, when I was there, was not too hot, but breezy and pleasant.

But I felt no temptation to stay there: as Murray succinctly expressed it, 'one day will suffice', I went on in the evening to Torremolinos, about eight miles down the western side of Málaga bay. The mountains had withdrawn a little from the sea; the road ran a mile inland; the sunset burned on my right, over vines and canes and olive gardens. I came into Torremolinos, a pretty country place, with, close on the sea, the little Santa Clara hotel, white and tiled and rambling, with square arches and trellises and a white-walled garden dropping down by stages to the sea. One could bathe either from the beach below, or from the garden, where a steep, cobbled path twisted down the rocks to a little terrace, from which one dropped down into ten feet of green water heaving gently against a rocky wall. A round full moon rose corn-coloured behind a fringe of palms. Swimming out to sea, I saw the whole of the bay, and the Málaga lights twinkling in the middle of it, as if the wedge of cheese were being devoured by a thousand fireflies. Behind the bay the dark mountains reared, with here and there a light. It was an exquisite bathe. After it I dined on a terrace in the garden; near me three young Englishmen were enjoying themselves with two pretty Spanish girls they had picked up in Málaga; they knew no Spanish, the señoritas no English, but this made them all the merrier. They were the first English tourists I had seen since I entered Spain; they grew a little intoxicated, and they were also the first drunks I had seen in Spain. They were not very drunk, but one seldom sees Spaniards drunk at all.

I got up early next morning and went down the garden path again to bathe. There were blue shadows on the white garden walls, and cactuses and aloes above them, and golden cucumbers and pumpkins and palms. I dropped into the green water and swam out; Málaga across the bay was golden pale like a pearl; the little playa of Torremolinos had fishing boats and nets on it and tiny lapping waves. Near me was a boat with fishermen, who were hacking mussels off the rocks and singing. The incredible beauty of the place and hour, of the smooth opal morning sea, shadowing to deep jade beneath the rocks, of the spread of the great bay, of the climbing, winding garden above with the blue shadows on its white walls, the golden pumpkins, the grey-green spears of the aloes, the arcaded terrace and rambling jumble of low buildings, was like the returning memory of a dream long forgotten. Lumpy cathedrals, tiresome modern parks, smartly laid out avenidas and alamedas, tented and populated beaches, passed out of mind, washed away in this quiet sea whispering against shadowed rocks. I climbed the ladder to the platform, and went up the vine-trellised garden to my annexe.

I had to go again into Málaga, to cash a cheque and get my exhaust pipe mended at a garage. They sawed off its end, and told me there was nothing to pay. I gave them ten pesetas and some English cigarettes, and told them how kind they were; they said I was *muy simpatica*, and we parted in mutual esteem. I like most Spanish mechanics very much; they are both clever and obliging, and often witty too. For that matter, so are most British and French mechanics; but the Spanish (or is it only the Andalucian?) negligence about payment is attractive.

Going back again through Torremolinos, I picked up a stout and agreeable woman laden with bundles and baskets, who asked me if I could take her to Marbella, twenty-eight miles on, as she had missed the bus. I said yes by all means, if she was not in a hurry and would not mind my stopping to bathe somewhere on the way. She said that she would not mind at all, but strongly advised me to wait till we reached Marbella, which had the best beach in the world. She was a Marbella enthusiast; whenever I showed signs of admiring some sequestered cove or beach she assured me, with much fervour and gesticulation, that it was nothing to Marbella, which had the best beach in the world, and that when I saw Marbella I should never again want to bathe anywhere else. She had me in such a state of pleasant anticipation about Marbella that I sped quickly on. We talked agreeably all the way about her family, the coffee she was taking them, the beauty of her married daughter, the terrible price of food, why I had come to Spain, why I was alone, why Spanish women did not drive cars nor Spanish little girls ride donkeys in the streets like their brothers; that is to say, she did not really know why, only that it was 'costumbre española', and the other 'costumbre extranjera'. She was rather a delightful woman, handsome, stout, loquacious, beautifully mannered, comfortably off; either a peasant or a small Málaga bourgeoise; I liked her a great deal.

We got to Marbella, which had a large, hot, quiet beach with a river running into it. The house which my companion was visiting was down by the shore; she invited me into it for refreshment, but I refused. Instead I drove down a track to the sands, undressed in the car, and bathed. The beach and sea were pleasant enough, but, after all my anticipations, I was disappointed, and did not think Marbella all it had been cracked up to be. It was once important both as trading port and coast stronghold, and in the days when, as old engravings show, it was ringed about with towered Moorish walls, gradually falling to ruin, it must have been a very picturesque city, standing before the sea with the fruitful mountains behind it. It was then full of convents and churches, had a fine alameda of trees watered by fountains; and its port was full of ships being loaded with wines, figs and raisins. But 'the present inhabitants', wrote a traveller of the 1770s, 'bear the character of an uncivil, inhospitable people, many of them descendants of the Moors, who still seem to resent the ill treatment of their forefathers; hence the Spanish proverb "Marbella es bella, pero no entrar en ella."' The Marbellians seem in these days to have improved in civility, so perhaps they have now forgotten the ill treatment of their forefathers. The town is guarded by two forts, but in vain, for African barbarians crossed the sea in A.D. 170 and devastated it, with Málaga and the other towns on the Baetican shore, and the Moors took it quite easily in the eighth century, and the Catholic Monarchs, though with more difficulty, in the fifteenth. It was after that peopled with Christians. The Moriscos made some trouble there later, but were expelled, and after that, says the *Crónica*, the inhabitants of Marbella devoted themselves to art, industry and agriculture, leading lives happy and tranquil, rich in the abundant fruits of their soil and sea. Fishermen drew from the liquid element nets laden with the most savoury and delicious fish in Spain; the sardines in particular are of exquisite taste. In few ports does one enjoy such beautiful sea, and such a variety of admirable objects. Opposite one may observe the mountains of the Riff, on the right the Rock of Gibraltar. The countryside (the description continues) is covered with vines and olives, oranges, pomegranates, wine presses, farmhouses, orchards. In the Plaza de la Constitución is a magnificent stone fountain. There is much trade and manufacture, and iron mines in the hills, and Marbella flourishes greatly. Obviously a remarkable place. On first seeing it, Isabella the Catholic threw up her hands and exclaimed, 'Que mar tan bella!' like my companion of the road. But the mar, anyhow the Mediterranean mar, is always bella.

I drove three kilometres on, to the half-ruined hamlet of San Pedro Alcantara, where a steep stony road turned up into the mountains for Ronda, thirty-five miles away. For the first twenty miles this track was covered with loose flints; apparently it was being mended. It climbed up in steep zigzags above tremendous ravines; a great basin of pine-clad mountains opened out, range beyond range, on my left, brown and indigo and purple and softly mauve, stretching into hyacinth-blue distance. Over the ravine great birds flew with wide wings. On my right the rocky precipice rose sheer. They were silent mountains, and a silent track, till, as I rounded a sharp bend, three roadmenders hailed me, black-a-vised, unshaven, wanting a lift to 'dieciocho', the eighteenth-kilometre stone, ten miles on. They got in: I thought their weight would make it bad for the tyres over the sharp flints, but it proved all right. They were very kind roadmenders. One of them got out at a spring he knew of and filled my earthen pot with fresh water; they kept collecting things they had hidden behind bushes along the track. They left me at dieciocho, where a path to their village went down into the ravine. If ever in the future, one of them said, they could do anything to repay me for my kindness, I was to let them know at once. I said that I would; I hope that an opportunity may offer. Meanwhile, I went on through the mountains. The road became good for the last ten or fifteen miles before Ronda. The mountains presently levelled out into a spacious amphitheatre, in which Ronda stood high on a sheer rock.

Barbaric, emphatic, noble-looking, yet questionable city: a chasm yawns across its face and across its history. For before the Moors made it known to the mediaeval world, under the name of Ronda, its existence is dubious. There have even been those who have said that the Moors built it new, quarrying material for it out of the ruined site now called Ronda la Vieja, seven miles north. But the Moors seldom built new cities; they enlarged and Arabized the Visigothic, Roman and Iberian cities and villages that they found. The present site of the Moorish half of Ronda, magnificently poised on its tremendous gorge, in the heart of that mountainous and embattled country, where peace never was, where turbulent tribes for ever warred with one another and with whatever dominant powers ruled them, cannot have been neglected either by Iberians, Romans or Visigoths. Indeed, Ronda is full of Roman relics and fragments; and the mosque on which the chief Christian church was built by the Christian conquerors was itself built on an earlier Visigoth temple. Ronda must always have been a place of importance; but under what name is unknown. Research has, I understand, dismissed Arunda and Acinipo (once held to be Ronda's Roman ancestors) from that district of Spain. One cannot enter this trodden and obscure field of controversy. Enough that before me rose the Ronda of the Moors, the Ronda of twelve centuries of known and turbulent history, famed Ronda, the Mecca of American tourists and of many English, the Ronda of the Great Gorge. It had, said a fifteenth-century chronicler, at the time of the conquest a hundred mountain towns round it (mostly vanished long since), but Ronda was the queen of the *serranía*, and known as the strongest fort of Andalucia. Ronda, says a much later chronicler, is combated by the north wind, and also by those from east and west, by this last with so much strength that on various occasions it tears up by the roots even the most corpulent trees. Yet it is a healthy climate, the ailments in winter being mainly lung affections and constipation, in summer intermittent fevers produced by excess in eating fruit.

As I drove up into the town, a group of lads threw stones at my car; I had heard before that this was an ancient Rondeño custom. I knew of a crippled Englishman staying in Ronda who had had to renounce his walks about the town because his foreignness and his lameness drew stones and jeers. I got out at the magnificent one-span eighteenth-century bridge, the Puente Nuevo, and looked down into the gorge, which is certainly very singular and noticeable. It is, of course, the great point about Ronda: whether it improves the look of the town or not might be argued; it depends on whether one likes towns to be cleft in two by a gorge, or whether one prefers them all in one piece. Be that as it may, it is a remarkably fine gorge, very wide and very deep; a Salvator Rosa kind of gorge. It actually has some water running in it – most unusual in Spanish rivers in summer. No wonder that the romantics of the eighteenth and nineteenth centuries adored it. Indeed, it is a romantic thing to stand on a bridge and look across from an old Moorish town of the eighth century to an old Spanish one of the fifteenth. Both towns, or rather, both halves of the town, have charm. The fifteenth-century town, the Mercadillo, a good deal rebuilt in the seventeenth and eighteenth centuries, is, for the most part, regular, clean and white; many of the houses have beautiful balconies and *rejas*; there are among them some narrow Moorish streets and Moorish houses. There is a handsome eighteenth-century bull ring, and a generally admired alameda with a fine precipitous view. But the more interesting part of Ronda is, of course, the older town, the Ciudad, with its narrow, twisting Moorish streets, and white houses with walnut doors. From one of the oldest houses, the Casa del Rey Moro (prettily restored and charmingly bijou, with terrace and patio and gorge view) stone steps cut into the rock by Christian slaves lead down into the Tajo. I did not go all the way down; after about a hundred steps I returned to the street, and followed it down past the two older bridges, the Moorish Puente Viejo and the later Puente de San Miguel. I got on to a path that wound down into the gorge and to the flour mills; the view of the river, the great bridge, and the sheer precipices on either side of the gorge, with apparently decadent houses clinging precariously to their edges, was, in the gathering dusk, intimidating in the extreme.

It takes Baedeker (who does it very well) to describe how one steers a tortuous course about the maze of the Mercadillo and the Ciudad, the Tajo and the streets. It is, to say the truth, confusing, and I made little of it that evening. But the next morning I arrived, largely by chance, at the various things that should be seen – the Renaissance house of the Marqués de Salvatierra (or so I was informed, though it had 1798 above the family arms on its carved stone door); various Arab houses and arches, various pretty plazas with ochre churches and charming belfries. The best church was Santa Maria Mayor, a fascinating pastiche mosque (of which some remains) built on Visigothic (nothing to be seen), 1485 Gothic on the mosque, sixteenth- and seventeenth-century extension on to this, very rich spacious and plateresque, with fine jasper pillars. There are other churches; and there is the Alcázaba, begun by the Romans, continued by the Goths, and finished by the Moors, and rebuilt after the French blew it up in 1809; it was once the most impregnable fortress in Baetica. There was a strong and

'I left Ronda at noon, for the magnificent silence of the mountain road, where there moved only a few donkeys with loads and a few groups of roadmenders.'

active resistance movement to the French in Ronda; the Rondeños were adept at maquis methods, and the French did not enjoy their occupation of this town.

I should have liked, but had not time, to visit the ruins of Ronda la Vieja; they are said, however, to be now negligible. I should have liked too, given time, to explore the *serranía* for the sites of all the perished towns of the neighbourhood listed in the fifteenth century. And how many little Iberian-Roman-Moorish villages and walled towns are still extant in these mountains, seldom visited because too remote? Ronda is famous, because of its size and its eccentric gorge, so admirable, so picturesque, so serviceable for the throwing down of enemies and slain bulls. But the mountains and ravines of Andalucia are set with the crumbling walled villages where Moors and Christians settled, desiring to live their lives unmolested, and to molest, so far as might be, the lives of others.

I left Ronda at noon, for the magnificent silence of the mountain road, where there moved only a few donkeys with loads and a few groups of roadmenders; I passed my three friends of yesterday, who waved their hats and called greetings. And so down through the great wild blue-shadowed sierras to the Mediterranean road again, smooth, easy and civilized, rich with sugar canes, orange groves, bananas and tropical plants. All along it were white villages. At Estepona ships were building on the beach, and donkeys ambled along untended with huge loads of straw and chaff. Beyond Estepona there was a pleasant beach, with a cove between two spurs of rock, one of which jutted out to sea. I thought I would bathe from these rocks, but a *guardia civil* emerged from a hut on the road above and told me that this beach belonged to an English general at Gibraltar, who allowed no one to bathe there. People might only bathe from the other side of the further rocks. It seemed that the general owned about half a kilometre of beach. I asked if I might swim out from further down the shore and land on the rocks of the general; the guard said no, the general did not permit that one landed on his rocks. Does the general own the sea too? I asked. Yes, the sea also was the general's. For how far out? For two kilometres, replied the guard – further than I would wish to swim, and I agreed. Who, I asked him, is this general, and how much does he pay for all this beach, sea and rock? The guard did not know the general's name, but believed that he paid nothing at all. The guard was a pleasant man, and had a sense of humour. It seemed either that the cove was a gift to the English general from the Spanish nation, which, in view of Gibraltar, was generous; or that the general had, with true casual British imperialism, just annexed it, and engaged a guard to defend it. I felt my customary admiring pride in the exploits of my countrymen, and thought there should be a Union Jack flying over the beach. It was Sunday afternoon; some Spanish families came presently to bathe and picnic; we were all warned off the general's cove and had to bathe further down. But it was a pleasant bathe, in that warm and scintillating afternoon sea. It was, I reflected, one of my last Mediterranean bathes, for it was only about twenty-five miles to the Straits, the Pillars of Hercules, where the known world ended and the dark bottomless void of the misty Ocean began.

Mary McCarthy

(1912–1989)

Often considered America's first lady of letters, Mary McCarthy chose to analyze cities instead of characters or ideas in her two books about place, *Stones of Florence* and *Venice Observed*. Nothing escapes her eye (or pen). Like Barbara Grizzuti Harrison and Kate O'Brien, she writes of her chosen place in the convincing way of the ambiguous devotee, her satire biting in direct proportion to the affection she feels for her subject. Consider how she describes the disintegration of a sixteenth-century building: 'Finally the sidewalk in front of that crumbling building was closed off and a red lantern posted: beware of falling masonry.' McCarthy wrote throughout her long life and is best known for the novel *The Group* (1963) and her memoir, *Memories of a Catholic Girlhood* (1957), both of which stand as classics of American social history. She grew up in Minneapolis and died in New York City.

from Stones of Florence

Everyone complains of the noise; with the windows open, no one can sleep. The morning paper reports the protests of hotel-owners, who say that their rooms are empty: foreigners are leaving the city; something must be done; a law must be passed. And within the hotels, there is a continual shuffling of rooms. Number 13 moves to 22, and 22 moves to 33, and 33 to 13 or to Fiesole. In fact, all the rooms are noisy and all are hot, even if an electric fan is provided. The hotel-managers know this, but what can they do? To satisfy the client, they co-operate with polite alacrity in the make-believe of room-shuffling. If the client imagines that he will be cooler or quieter in another part of the hotel, why destroy his illusions? In truth, short of leaving Florence, there is nothing to be done until fall comes and the windows can be shut again. A law already exists forbidding the honking of horns within city limits, but it is impossible to drive in a city like Florence without using your horn to scatter the foot traffic.

As for the Vespas and the Lambrettas, which are the plague of the early hours of the morning, how can a law be framed that will keep their motors quiet? Readers of the morning newspaper write in with suggestions; a meeting is held in Palazzo Vecchio, where more suggestions are aired; merit badges to be distributed to noiseless drivers; state action against the manufacturers; a special police night squad, equipped with radios, empowered to arrest noisemakers of every description; an ordinance that would make a certain type of muffler mandatory, that would make it illegal to race a motor 'excessively', that would prohibit motor-scooters from entering the city centre. This last suggestion meets with immense approval; it is the only one Draconian enough to offer hope. But the motor-scooterists' organization at once enters a strong protest ('undemocratic', 'discriminatory', it calls the proposal), and the newspaper, which has been leading the anti-noise movement, hurriedly backs water, since Florence is a democratic society, and the scooterists are the *popolo minuto* – small clerks and artisans and factory workers. It would be wrong, the paper concedes, to penalize the many well-behaved scooterists for the sins of a few 'savages', and unfair, too, to consider only the city centre and the tourist trade; residents on the periphery should have the right to sleep also. The idea of the police squad with summary powers and wide discretion is once again brought forward, though the city's finances will hardly afford it. Meanwhile, the newspaper sees no recourse but to appeal to the *gentilezza* of the driving public.

This, however, is utopian: Italians are not civic-minded. 'What if *you* were waked up at four in the morning?' – this plea, so typically Anglo-Saxon, for the other fellow as an imagined self, elicits from an Italian the realistic answer: 'But I *am* up.' A young Italian, out early on a Vespa, does not project himself into the person of a young Italian office worker in bed, trying to sleep, still less into the person of a foreign tourist or a hotel-owner. As well ask the wasp, after which the Vespa is named, to think of itself as the creature it is about to sting. The *popolo minuto*, moreover, *likes* noise, as everyone knows. '*Non fa rumore*', objected a young Florentine workman, on being shown an English scooter. 'It doesn't make any noise.'*

All ideas advanced to deal with the Florentine noise problem, the Florentine traffic problem, are utopian, and nobody believes in them, just as nobody believed in Machiavelli's Prince, a utopian image of the ideally self-interested despot. They are dreams, to toy with: the dream of prohibiting *all* motor traffic in the city centre (on the pattern of Venice) and going back to the horse and the donkey; the dream that someone (perhaps the Rockefellers?) would like to build a subway system for the city. . . . Professor La Pira, Florence's Christian Democratic mayor, had a dream of solving the housing problem, another of the city's difficulties: he invited the homeless poor to move into the empty palaces and villas of the rich. This Christian fantasy collided with the laws of property, and the poor were turned out of the palaces. Another dream succeeded it, a dream in the modern idiom of a 'satellite' city that would arise southeast of Florence, in a forest of parasol pines, to house the city's workers, who would be conveyed back and forth to their jobs by special buses that would pick them up in the morning, bring them home for lunch, then back to work, and so on. This plan, which had something of science fiction about it, was blocked also; another set of dreamers – professors, architects, and art historians – rose in protest against the defacement of the Tuscan countryside, pointing to the impracticalities of the scheme, the burdening of the already overtaxed roads and bridges. A meeting was held, attended by other professors and city-planners from Rome and Venice; fiery speeches were made; pamphlets distributed; the preservers won. La Pira, under various pressures (he had also had a dream of eliminating stray cats from the city), had resigned as mayor meanwhile.

But the defeat of Sorgane, as the satellite city was to be called, is only an episode in the factional war being fought in the city, street by street, building by building, bridge by bridge, like the old wars of the Blacks and Whites, Guelphs and Ghibellines, Cerchi and Donati. It is an uncertain, fluctuating war, with idealists on both sides, which began in the nineteenth century, when a façade in the then-current taste was put on the Duomo, the centre of the city was modernized, and the old walls along the Arno were torn down. This first victory, of the forces of progress over old Florence, is commemorated by a triumphal arch in the present Piazza della Repubblica with an inscription to the effect that new order and beauty have been brought out of ancient squalor. Today the inscription makes Florentines smile, bitterly, for it is an example of unconscious irony: the present Piazza, with its neon signs advertising a specific against uric acid, is, as everyone agrees, the ugliest in Italy – a folly of nationalist grandeur committed at a time when Florence was, briefly, the capital of the new Italy. Those who oppose change have only to point to it, as an argument for their side, and because of it the preservers have won several victories. Nevertheless, the parasol pines of the hill of Sorgane may yet fall, like the trees in the last act of *The Cherry Orchard*, unless some other solution is found for the housing problem, for Florence is a modern, expanding city – that is partly why the selective tourist dislikes it.

A false idea of Florence grew up in the nineteenth century, thanks in great part to the Brownings and their readers – a tooled-leather idea of Florence as a dear bit of the old world. Old maids of both sexes – retired librarians, governesses, ladies with reduced incomes, gentlemen painters, gentlemen sculptors, gentlemen poets, anaemic amateurs and dabblers of every kind – 'fell in love' with Florence and settled down to make it home. Queen Victoria did water colours in the hills at Vincigliata; Florence Nightingale's parents named her after the city, where she was born in 1820 – a sugary statue of her stands holding a lamp in the first cloister of Santa Croce. Early in the present century, a retired colonel, G. F. Young of the Indian Service, who, it is said, was unable to read Italian, appointed himself defender of the Medicis and turned out a spluttering 'classic' that went through many editions, arguing that the Medicis had been misrepresented by democratic historians. (There is a story in Turgenev of a retired major who used to practice doctoring on the peasants. 'Has he studied medicine?' someone asks. 'No, he hasn't studied,' is

* Nevertheless, finally an ordinance was passed by the municipality, setting a curfew of 11 p.m. to 6 a.m. on the use of motor scooters in the city's centre.

the answer. 'He does it more from philanthropy.' This was evidently the case with Colonel Young.) Colonel Young was typical of the Anglo-American visitors who, as it were, expropriated Florence, occupying villas in Fiesole or Bellosguardo, studying Tuscan wild flowers, collecting ghost stories, collecting triptychs and diptychs, burying their dogs in the churchyard of the Protestant Episcopal church, knowing (for the most part) no Florentines but their servants. The Brownings, in Casa Guidi, opposite the Pitti Palace, revelled in Florentine history and hated the Austrian usurper, who lived across the street, but they did not mingle socially with the natives; they kept themselves to themselves. George Eliot spent fifteen days in a Swiss *pensione* on Via Tomabuoni, conscientiously working up the background for *Romola*, a sentimental pastiche of Florentine history that was a great success in its period and is the least read of her novels today. It smelled of libraries, Henry James complained, and the foreign colony's notion of Florence, like *Romola*, was bookish, synthetic, gushing, insular, genteel, and, above all, proprietary. This sickly love ('our Florence', 'my Florence') on the part of the foreign residents implied, like all such loves, a tyrannous resistance to change. The rest of the world might alter, but, in the jealous eyes of its foreign owners, Florence was supposed to stay exactly as it was when they found it – a dear bit of the Old World.

Florence can never have been that, at any time in its existence. It is not a shrine of the past, and it rebuffs all attempts to make it into one, just as it rebuffs tourists. Tourism, in a certain sense, is an accidental by-product of the city – at once profitable and a nuisance, adding to the noise and congestion, raising prices for the population. Florence is a working city, a market centre, a railway junction; it manufactures furniture (including antiques), shoes, gloves, handbags, textiles, fine underwear, nightgowns, and table linens, picture frames, luggage, chemicals, optical equipment, machinery, wrought iron, various novelties in straw. Much of this work is done in small shops on the Oltrarno, the Florentine Left Bank, or on the farms of the *contado*; there is not much big industry but there is a multitude of small crafts and trades. Every Friday is market day on the Piazza della Signoria, and the peasants come with pockets full of samples from the farms in the Valdarno and the Chianti: grain, oil, wine, seeds. The small hotels and cheap restaurants are full of commercial travellers, wine salesmen from Certaldo or Siena, textile representatives from Prato, dealers in marble from the Carrara mountains, where Michelangelo quarried. Everyone is on the move, buying, selling, delivering, and tourists get in the way of this diversified commerce. The Florentines, on the whole, would be happy to be rid of them. The shopkeepers on the Lungarno and on Ponte Vecchio, the owners of hotels and restaurants, the thieves, and the widows who run *pensiones* might regret their departure, but the tourist is seldom led to suspect this. There is no city in Italy that treats its tourists so summarily, that caters so little to their comfort.

There are no gay bars or smart outdoor cafés; there is very little night life, very little vice. The food in the restaurants is bad, for the most part, monotonous, and rather expensive. Many of the Florentine specialties – tripe, paunch, rabbit, and a mixture of the combs, livers, hearts, and testicles of roosters – do not appeal to the foreign palate. The wine can be good but is not so necessarily. The waiters are slapdash and hurried; like many Florentines, they give the impression of being preoccupied with something else, something more important – a knotty thought, a problem. At one of the 'typical' restaurants, recommended by the big hotels, the waiters, who are a family, treat the clients like interlopers, feigning not to notice their presence, bawling orders sarcastically to the kitchen, banging down the dishes, spitting on the floor. 'Take it or leave it' is the attitude of the *pensione*-keeper of the better sort when showing a room; the inferior *pensiones* have a practice of shanghaiing tourists. Runners from these establishments lie in wait on the road, just outside the city limits, for cars with foreign licence plates; they halt them, leap aboard, and order the driver to proceed to a certain address. Strangely enough, the tourists often comply, and report to the police only later, when they have been cheated in the *pensiones*. These shades of Dante's highwaymen are not the only ones who lie in wait for travellers. One of the best Florentine restaurants was closed by the police a few years ago – for cheating a tourist. Complaints of foreign tourists pour every day into the *questura* and are recorded in the morning newspaper; they have been robbed and victimized everywhere; their cars, parked on the Piazza della Signoria or along the Arno, have been rifled in broad daylight or spirited away. The northern races – Germans and Swedes – appear to be the chief prey, and the commonest complaint is of the theft of a camera. Other foreigners are the victims of accidents; one old American lady, the mother-in-law of an author, walking on Via

Guicciardini, had the distinction of being hit by two bicycles, from the front and rear simultaneously (she was thrown high into the air and suffered a broken arm); some British tourists were injured a few years ago by a piece falling off Palazzo Bartolini Salimbeni (1517–20) in Piazza Santa Trinita. Finally the sidewalk in front of that crumbling building was closed off and a red lantern posted: beware of falling masonry.* Recently, during the summer, a piece weighing 132 pounds fell off the cornice of the National Library; a bus-conductor, though, rather than a tourist or foreign student, just missed getting killed and, instead, had his picture in the paper.

All summer long, or as long as the tourist season lasts, the '*Cronaca di Firenze*' or city news of the *Nazione*, that excellent morning newspaper, is a daily chronicle of disaster to foreigners, mixed in with a few purely local thefts, frauds, automobile accidents, marital quarrels, and appeals for the preservation of monuments. The newspaper deplores the Florentine thieves, who are giving the city a bad name, like the noisemakers (*i selvaggi*). It seeks to promote in its readers a greater understanding of the foreigner, a greater sympathy with his eating habits, his manner of dress, and so on. Yet an undertone of irony, typically Florentine, accompanies this official effort; it is the foreigners with their cameras and wads of currency who appear to be the 'savages', and the thieves who are behaving naturally. A series of 'sympathetic' articles on tourism was illustrated with decidedly unsympathetic photographs, showing touristic groups masticating spaghetti, tourists entering the Uffizi naked to the waist.

On the street, the Florentines do not like to give directions; if you are lost, you had better ask a policeman. Unlike the Venetians, the Florentines will never volunteer to show a sight to a passing stranger. They do not care to exhibit their city; the monuments are there – let the foreigners find them. Nor is this a sign of indifference, but of a peculiar pride and dignity. Florentine sacristans can never be found to turn on the lights to illuminate a fresco or an altar painting; they do not seem to take an interest in the tip. Around the Masolino-Masaccio-Filippino Lippi frescoes in the Brancacci Chapel of the Carmine, small groups of tourists wait, uneasily whispering; they try to find the lights for themselves; they try looking for someone in the sacristy. Finally a passing priest flicks on the electricity and hurries off, his robes flying. The same thing happens with the Ghirlandaio frescoes in Santa Trinita. Far from hovering, as the normal sacristan does, in ambush, waiting to expound the paintings, the Florentine sacristan does not make himself manifest until just before closing time, at midday, when he becomes very active, shooing people out of the church with shrill whistles and threatening gestures of his broom. If there are postcards for sale in a church, there is usually nobody to sell them.

This lack of co-operative spirit, this absence, this preoccupation, comes, after a time, and if you are not in a hurry, to seem one of the blessings of Florence, to make it, even, a hallowed place. This is one of the few cities where it is possible to loiter, undisturbed, in the churches, looking at the works of art. After the din outside, the churches are extraordinarily peaceful, so that you walk about on tiptoe, fearful of breaking the silence, of distracting the few old women, dimly seen, from their prayers. You can pass an hour, two hours, in the great churches of Brunelleschi – Santo Spirito and San Lorenzo – and no one will speak to you or pay you any heed. Touristic parties with guides do not penetrate here; they go instead to the Medici Chapels, to see the Michelangelos. The smaller churches – Santa Trinita, Santa Felicita, Ognissanti, Santissima Annunziata, Santa Maria Maddelena dei Pazzi, San Giovannino dei Cavalieri – are rarely visited; neither is the Pazzi Chapel in the court of Santa Croce, and the wonderful Giottos, freshly restored, in the Bardi Chapel of Santa Croce, still surrounded by a shaky scaffold, are seen only by art critics, their families and friends. San Miniato, on its hill, is too far away for most tourists; it is the church that, as they say, they missed. And the big churches of the preaching orders, Santa Maria Novella and Santa Croce, and the still bigger Duomo, where Savonarola delivered sermons to audiences of ten thousand, swallow up touristic parties, leaving hardly a trace. The tourists then complain of feeling 'dwarfed' by this architecture. They find it 'cold', unwelcoming.

As for the museums, they are the worst-organized, the worst-hung in Italy – a scandal, as the Florentines say themselves, with a certain civic pride. The exception, the new museum that has been opened in the old Fort of the Belvedere, with pale walls, wide views, cool rooms, sparsely hung, immediately became a subject of controversy, as did the new rooms of the Uffizi, which were held to be too white and uncluttered.

* The palace has since been restored.

In the streets, the famous parti-coloured monuments in geometric designs – the Baptistery, Giotto's bell tower, the Duomo, the façade of Santa Maria Novella – are covered with grime and weather stains. The Duomo and the Bell Tower are finally getting a bath, but this is a tedious process that has been going on for years; by the time the Duomo's front is washed, the back will be dirty again. Meanwhile, the green, white, and pink marbles stand in scaffolding, while the traffic whizzes around them. The Badia, the old Benedictine abbey, where the Good Margrave, Ugo of Tuscany (Dante's '*gran barone*') lies buried and which has now been partly incorporated into the police station, is leaking so badly that on a rainy Sunday parishioners of the Badia church have had to hear mass with their umbrellas up; it was here that Dante used to see Beatrice at mass. Among the historic palaces that remain in private hands, many, like Palazzo Bartolini Salimbeni, are literally falling to pieces. The city has no money to undertake repairs; the Soprintendenza delle Belle Arti has no money; private owners say they have no money.

Historic Florence is an incubus on its present population. It is like a vast piece of family property whose upkeep is too much for the heirs, who nevertheless find themselves criticized by strangers for letting the old place go to rack and ruin. History, in Venice, has been transmuted into legend; in Rome, the Eternal City, history is an everlasting present, an orderly perspective of arches receding from popes to Caesars with the papacy guaranteeing permanence and framing the vista of the future – decay being but an aspect of time's grandeur. If St. Peter's were permitted to fall to pieces, it would still inspire awe, as the Forum does, while the dilapidation of Venetian palaces, reflected in lapping waters, is part of Venetian myth, celebrated already by Guardi and Belloto in the eighteenth century. Rome had Piranesi; Naples had Salvatore Rosa; but Florentine decay, in the Mercato Vecchio and the crooked byways of the Ghetto (now all destroyed and replaced by the Piazza della Repubblica), inspired only bad nineteenth-century water-colourists, whose work is preserved, not in art galleries, but in the topographical museum under the title of '*Firenze Come Era*' ('Florence as It Was'). History, for Florence, is neither a legend nor eternity, but a massive weight of rough building stone demanding continual repairs, pressing on the modern city like a debt, blocking progress.

This was a city of progress. Nothing could be more un-Florentine, indeed more anti-Florentine, than the protective custody exercised by its foreign residents, most of whom have abandoned the city today, offended by the Vespas, the automobile horns, the Communists, and the rise in the cost of living. Milanese businessmen are moving into their villas and installing new tiled bathrooms with coloured bathtubs and toilet seats, linoleum and plastics in the kitchen, television sets and bars. These Milanesi are not popular; they too are '*selvaggi*', like their Lombard predecessors who descended on Tuscany in the sixth century to brutalize and despoil it. Yet these periodic invasions belong to Florentine life, which is penetrated by the new and transforms it into something newer. Florence has always been a city of extremes, hot in the summer, cold in the winter, traditionally committed to advance, to modernism, yet containing backward elements narrow as its streets, cramped, stony, recalcitrant. It was the city where during the last war individual Fascists still held out fanatically after the city was taken by the Allies, and kept shooting as if for sport from the rooftops and loggias at citizens in the streets below. Throughout the Mussolini period, the Fascists in Florence had been the most violent and dangerous in Italy; at the same time, Florence had been the intellectual centre of anti-Fascism, and during the Resistance, the city as a whole 'redeemed itself' by a series of heroic exploits. The peasants of the *contado* showed a fantastic bravery in hiding enemies of the regime, and in the city many intellectuals and a few aristocrats risked their lives with great hardihood for the Resistance network. Florence, in short, was split, as it had always been, between the best and the worst. Even the Germans here were divided into two kinds. While the S.S. was torturing victims in a house on Via Bolognese (a nineteenth-century upper-middle-class 'residential' district), across the city, on the old Piazza Santo Spirito, near Brunelleschi's church, the German Institute was hiding anti-Nazis in its library of reference works on Florentine art and culture. The chief arm of the S.S. was a Florentine devil strangely named 'Carita', who acted as both informer and torturer; against the S.S., the chief defence was the German consul, who used his official position to save people who had been denounced. After the Liberation, the consul was given the freedom of the city, in recognition of the risky work he had done. Such divisions, such extremism, such contrasts are *Firenze Come Era* – a terrible city, in many ways, uncomfortable and dangerous to live in, a city of drama, argument, and struggle.

Margaret Mead

(1901–1978)

When Margaret Mead went back to the South Pacific forty years after her first visit there, she was not so much the world's most famous anthropologist but a philosopher queen of observers. For Mead the secret of understanding lies in learning how to wait. Speaking of this anthropologist's skill, she writes, 'But it is always an active waiting, a readiness in which all his senses are alert to whatever may happen, expected or unexpected, in the next five minutes – or in an hour, a week, a month from now.' Mead, whose studies of adolescent and sexual behaviour of peoples in the South Pacific established her as the best-known anthropologist of the twentieth century, was born in Philadelphia and died in New York City.

from **A Way of Seeing**

I am writing in the little house made of rough wood and sago-palm thatch that was built for me by the people of Peri village. The wind brings the sound of waves breaking on the reef, but my house, its back to the sea, looks out on the great square where the public life of the village takes place. At the opposite end of the square is the meeting-house, and ranged along the sides are the houses of eminent men. Everything is new and paint sparkles on the houses. The handsomest ones are built of corrugated iron; the others are built of traditional materials, with decorative patterns woven into the bamboo.

This is the fourth version of Peri that I have lived in over the last thirty-seven years. The first was the primitive village. When I first came to study the Manus, they were an almost landless sea people and all the houses of Peri were built on stilts in the shallow sea. When I returned twenty-five years later, in 1953, the Manus had moved ashore and the new Peri, located on a small strip of marshy land, was their first attempt to build a 'modern' village, designed in accordance with their notions of an American town. By 1964, when I came back on a third field trip, this village had degenerated into a kind of slum, noisy, dilapidated, cramped and overcrowded, because the people of a neighbouring village had moved in so that their children too could go to school. Now, a year later, an entirely new village has been built on a spacious tract of land bought with the people's own savings, and here Peri villagers, for so long accustomed only to sea and sand, are planting flowers and vegetables.

For two months everything went along quietly, but now the whole village is humming with activity. Last-minute preparations are in progress for a tremendous celebration at which Peri will entertain some two thousand members of the Paliau movement – all the people who, under the leadership of Paliau Moluat, have taken part in the strenuous and extraordinary effort to create a new way of life. It is the holiday season, and every day more of the adolescents who have been away at school and the young people who have become teachers in faraway parts of New Guinea are returning home to visit their families, see the new village and join in the festivities. Some families have built special rooms for the visitors. In one house there is a real room in which bed, chair and bench, all made by hand, are arranged to make a perfect setting for a schoolboy – the bed neatly made, pictures of the Beatles on the wall, schoolbooks on the table and a schoolbag hung in the window. In another house a few books piled on a suitcase in one corner of a barnlike room are all that signal the return of a school child. But whatever arrangements families have managed to make, the village is alive with delight in the visitors.

The children have come home from modern schools. But some of the young teachers have been working all alone in small bush schools among alien peoples only a few years removed from cannibalism and head-hunting. So the tales circulating in the village are extremely varied. There are descriptions of boarding-school life, stories of examinations and of prizes won in scholarship or sports. But there are also stories about the extraordinary customs of the people in the interior of New Guinea. Listening, I ask myself which is harder for the people of Peri to assimilate and understand – a savage way of life, which in many ways resembles that of their own great-grandfathers but which now has been so enthusiastically abandoned; or the new way of life the Manus have adopted, which belongs to the modern world of the planes that fly overhead and the daily news on the radio. Nowadays this may include news of the Manus themselves. Yesterday morning a newscaster announced: 'At the first meeting of the new council in Manus, Mr. Paliau Moluat, member of the House of Assembly, was elected president.'

I have come back to Peri on this, my fourth trip to Manus, to witness and record the end of an epoch. The new forms of local self-government, supported by an insistent and originally rebellious leadership, all are legalized. Paliau, the head of what the government once regarded as a subversive movement, now holds elective office and is immersed in work that will shape the future of the Territory of Papua New Guinea. On a small scale this handful of people living on the coast of an isolated archipelago have enacted the whole drama of moving from the narrow independence of a little warring tribe to participation in the development of an emerging nation.

During the last two months I have been aware of all the different stages of change, as they can be seen simultaneously. On weekdays I see men and women passing by, stripped bare to the waist and holding pandanus hoods over their heads to keep off the rain. On holidays some of the younger women dress in fashionable shifts, bright with splashed flower designs. The oldest men and women, people I have known since 1928, were born into a completely primitive world, ruled over by ghosts, dominated by the fear of disease and death and endlessly preoccupied by the grinding work entailed in meeting their obligations and making the exchanges of shell money and dogs' teeth for oil and turtles, grass skirts and pots. The middle-aged grew up in the period when warfare was ending; as young men they still practiced throwing and dodging the spears they would never use as weapons of war. The next-younger group, in whose childhood the first Christian mission came, lived through the Japanese occupation and reached manhood when the people of the whole south coast were uniting in a small, decisive social revolution. And the youngest group, adolescents and children, are growing up in a world of school and clinic talk. Before them lies the prospect of career choice and the establishment of a new university, the University of Papua New Guinea, in Port Moresby. These are the first-comers to a new epoch.

Yet, in spite of everything, the Manus have preserved their identity as a people and their integrity as individuals. The shy little boys I knew in the past have grown up into shy, quiet men. The boastfully brash still are brash. The alert-minded are keen and aware. It is as if the changes from savagery to civilization were new colours that had been laid on over the hard, clear outlines of their distinct personalities. At the same time, where once the Manus feared and plotted war, they now hear only echoes of distant battlefields in places of which formerly they were totally unaware. Where once they suffered hunger when storms kept the fishermen at home, they now can buy food for money in the village shops. Where once flight to live precariously among strangers was the outcome of a quarrel, now it is proud ambition that takes the Manus abroad.

One outcome of the chance that brought me to their village to do field work in 1928 is that their history has been chronicled. Unlike most simpler peoples of the world, the Manus can bridge past and present. Here in my house I hang up photographs of all the 'big-fellow men belong before', who would otherwise be no more than half-remembered names. Seen from the vantage point of the present, pictures taken ten years ago and thirty-seven years ago have a continuity that overcomes strangeness. Instead of being ashamed of the life that has been abandoned, young people can be proud of an ancestral mode of life that is being preserved for others to know about and is mentioned in speeches made by visitors from the United Nations. Then old pride and new pride merge and the old men, nodding agreement, say: 'After all, the Manus people started in Peri.'

Each day I go about the ordinary business of field work. I accept the presents of fresh fish and accede to small requests for tobacco, matches, a postage stamp or perhaps four thumbtacks. Whatever I am working at, I listen to the sounds of the village, ready to go quickly to the scene of wailing or shouting or some child's uncharacteristic cry. As I type notes I also watch the passers-by to catch the one person who can answer a question, such as: 'Is it really true that the same two women first married Talikat and then later married Ponowan?' Or word comes that two turtles, necessary for the coming feast, have been brought in, and I hurriedly take my camera out of its vacuum case and rush to record the event.

At the same time I think about field work itself. For an anthropologist's life is keyed to field work. Even at home, occupied with other activities, writing up field notes and preparing for the next field trip keeps your mind focused on this aspect of your life. In the past, actual field work has meant living with and studying a primitive people in some remote part of the world. The remoteness has been inevitable, for the peoples anthropologists have studied were primitive because they lived far from the centres of civilization – in the tropics or in the Arctic, in a mountain fastness or on an isolated atoll. Remoteness also has set the style of field work. Cut off from everything else, your attention is wholly concentrated on the lives of the people you are working with, and the effort draws on all your capacities, strength and experience. Now, as the most remote places become known, the conditions of field work are changing. But the need to see and respond as a whole does not change.

I am especially aware of the conditions of field work on this trip because for the first time since my original field trip to Samoa forty years ago I am working alone, without any collaborators in the same or a nearby village. This and the fact that I am using only one camera, a notebook and a pencil – instead of all the complex paraphernalia of the modern field team – throws me back to the very core of field work: one person, all alone, face-to-face with a whole community. Equipped principally with a way of looking at things, the fieldworker is expected somehow to seize on all the essentials of a strange way of life and to bring back a record that will make this comprehensible as a whole to others who very likely never will see this people in their living reality. The role of the fieldworker and the recognition that every people has a culture, the smallest part of which is significant and indicative of the whole, go together. Once the two were matched, our field work helped us to learn more about culture and to train a new generation of anthropologists to make better field studies.

Nevertheless, as I sit here with the light of my pressure lamp casting long shadows on the dark, quiet square, wondering what may happen in the next few hours, I also reflect that field work is one of the most extraordinary tasks we set for young people. Even today it means a special kind of solitude among a people whose every word and gesture is, initially, unexpected and perhaps unintelligible. But beyond this, the fieldworker is required to do consciously something that the young child, filled with boundless energy and curiosity, does without conscious purpose – that is, learn about a whole world. But whereas the child learns as part of growing up and becomes what he learns, the anthropologist must learn the culture without embodying it, in order to become its accurate chronicler.

Whether one learns to receive a gift in both hands or with the right hand only, to touch the gift to one's forehead or to refuse it three times before accepting it, the task is always a double one. One must learn to do something correctly and not to become absorbed in the doing. One must learn what makes people angry but one must not feel insulted oneself. One must live all day in a maze of relationships without being caught in the maze. And above all, one must wait for events to reveal much that must be learned. A storm, an earthquake, a fire, a famine – these are extraordinary conditions that sharply reveal certain aspects of a people's conceptions of life and the universe. But the daily and the recurrent events that subtly shape people's lives are the ones on which the anthropologist must concentrate without being able to foresee what he can learn from them or when any particular event may occur. Equipped as well as possible with his growing knowledge of names and relationships, his experience of expectations and probable outcomes, the fieldworker records, learns – and waits. But it is always an active waiting, a readiness in which all his senses are alert to whatever may happen, expected or unexpected, in the next five minutes – or in an hour, a week, a month from now. The anthropological fieldworker must take a whole community, with all its transmitted tradition, into his mind and, to the extent that he is a whole person, see it whole.

And then my mind turns back to Manus. What is happening here is a kind of paradigm of something that is happening all over the world: grandparents and parents settle for the parts they themselves can play and what must be left to the comprehension of the children. The Manus have taken a direction no one could have foreseen thirty-seven years ago. Yet in the midst of change they are recognizably themselves. Field work provides us with a record of the experiments mankind has made in creating and handing on tradition. Over time it also provides a record of what men can do and become.

M. F. K. Fisher

(1908–1992)

Some places remain the same no matter how much change occurs over time, and M. F. K. Fisher captures that quality in her depiction of Dijon. One of the most acclaimed writers about food in the English language, but truly a connoisseur of all the senses, Fisher was first drawn to Dijon as a student at the University of Dijon and never fell out of love with the place. 'I feel I could survive there now as easily as I did the first three years, in spite of the inevitable changes that the short time of some sixty years can make in a place even as old as Dijon was and is,' she wrote in *Long Ago in France*. Fisher wrote numerous books about food, including *Dubious Honors* and *How to Cook a Wolf*, and two memoirs. The man she refers to as Al was her first husband, Alfred Young Fisher, whom she married in 1929, when he was a student in Dijon. She was born Mary Frances Kennedy in Michigan and she died in California.

from Long Ago in France

When I first went to Dijon in 1929, the rue de la Liberté was the main street in the old part of town. It split the town like a spine so that all life flowed on either side of it, and the life of the whole city was centered there.

Every settlement is divided into two parts by a main street, or even a river or a pathway. In Paris, for instance, the Seine River divides Paris into a left bank and a right bank, just as the main street in any small American town separates it into the right part and the left part of town . . . culturally, socially, economically, physically, statistically, and in every other way.

In Dijon, which was a small city but one of the oldest and noblest in a very old country when I went there in 1929, the rue de la Liberté divided the town inevitably, although it may not now be the centre it once was.

Its narrowness did not adapt itself well to the increasing traffic, since it had existed since the Romans first built a fortified wall around a small camp. In medieval times it was crowded and not as crooked as many, and it was a thoroughfare long before automobiles, tramways, and buses tried to crowd its constant stream of travellers on to the narrow sidewalks. In 1929, though, it was still the main street of the town, and it cut like a sword through the thick conglomeration of small streets spreading out on either side of it.

After the railroads came to France and the PLM was finally completed connecting Paris and Marseille to the south, with Dijon the first main stop, the station was built at the edge of the walled town, and the street that led from it was called the boulevard de Sévigné. This wider street, lined with beautiful trees, was by far the most modern part of town, and it ended at the *Grand Place D'Arcy*, which continues now to be the centre of the town, with the Bureau of Tourism located in its public gardens.

Somewhere on the place d'Arcy was an Arc de Triomphe, and it seems odd that I do not remember anything about it now, but the small Arc is an important part of the decor, especially because it was reported to be the model of the Grand Arc de Triomphe in Paris. It was designed by François Rude, one of the great sculptors; and it forms a part of the solid reputation of architecture and sculpture which has always made Dijon the centre of Burgundian culture.

In 1929 the place d'Arcy served as a liaison between the old and the new parts of town, and contained the leading movie theatre as well as the Hôtel de la Cloche and several bright *café-brasseries*. It was the entrance to the true old town and the rue de la Liberté.

The largest movie theatre in town was the D'Arcy on the

place d'Arcy. It was the kind where they rang the bell fifteen minutes before the movie, to notify people that it was time to come along, and then rang the bell again for the *entracte*, and it seemed to be heard all over town. The people would wander out to the cafés nearby and then they would come back to see the second half of the show.

Al loved the movies. He hated to stay home, and he believed very sincerely that we went to improve our French; because, first, there were subtitles, and then later while we were there, there came the sound pictures, in about 1931. We saw all the early Pagnol, and the Jean Giono stories that Pagnol made. We saw everything that was going . . . German films, the UFA films . . . we knew all the French and all the Italian films, which had subtitles in French. It was fun, but I got really fed up with going every single night to the movies. But Al loved it.

There was another theatre in the back of the Grande Taverne restaurant, with the Hôtel Terminus above the two, on the top two stories of the same building. This theatre was more like a music hall, however, with tables and one act of vaudeville. It was the first place that had a movie with a soundtrack. I had already seen the Al Jolson movie called *The Jazz Singer* when I came back to this country in 1931 and recommended it to several people who found it very puzzling: The soundtrack was to *The Jazz Singer*, with Al Jolson singing 'Mammy', and the movie was called *The King of Jazz*, with Paul Whiteman and his full orchestra.

There was another smaller movie house way up on the place Grangier, and it showed rather offbeat movies, like all of Charlie Chaplin's, which I saw for the first time in years. We saw horror pictures there, and westerns.

On one side of the place d'Arcy, on the rue Victor Hugo facing the municipal gardens and the fountain, was the Hôtel de la Cloche, the Ritz of the town, and opposite it were the newspaper offices and two or three older hotels.

We stayed at the Cloche for a few days before moving to Madame Ollangnier's on the rue du Petit-Potet, mainly because it was the biggest and best-known place in town. We had known little then to appreciate its famous cellars, and had found the meals fairly dull in the big grim dining room. Later we learned that once a year, in November for the Foire Gastronomique, it recaptured for those days all its old glitter. Then it was full of gourmets from every corner of France, and famous chefs twirled saucepans in its kitchens, and wine buyers drank Chambertins and Cortons and Romanée-Contis by the *cave*-ful.

But for us it was not the place to be in 1929. My mother and sister Anne later stayed there for a few days when Mother came down from London with a bad knee the first summer we were there. She soon grew bored with it and moved to the Central, which was comparatively new and not really stylish in those days. And later Timmy, my second husband, and I stayed there at the Cloche with his mother, who loved its provincial elegance.

The boulevard de Sévigné and the rue Victor Hugo came to a point in front of the Hôtel de la Cloche where the gardens were, and then the place d'Arcy opened at its other end into the rue de la Liberté. The rue de la Liberté went past the Ducal Palace with its parade grounds in front, and ended naturally at the Church of Saint Michel.

It seemed very narrow always, especially the first long block that split off from the place d'Arcy, and it was in direct contrast to the wide boulevard de Sévigné which led directly from the station to it.

We smelled Dijon mustard, especially at one of the most important corners of the rue de la Liberté, where Grey-Poupon flaunted little pots of it. And I remember that long after I was there, my nephew Sean and his wife Anne and their two little boys were in France one year, and I had told Sean about the Grey-Poupon shop . . . a kind of showplace, with beautiful old faience jars in the windows and then copies of them that one could buy for mustard pots.

The two boys were fascinated, because they said the floor opened, and their clerk simply disappeared down into the basement right in the middle of the store. Of course, I was not surprised, but the boys were, and they waited, and finally the little man popped up again with a small *moutardièr*. I broke the bottom of it about three years ago, but I used it until then for mustard, and I still have its top, I believe, and the little wooden spoon with the blue ball on the end of it. It was darling, and they brought it clear from Dijon to me. I liked that. . . .

We smelled Dijon cassis in the autumn, and stained our mouths with its metallic purple. But all year and everywhere we smelled the Dijon gingerbread, that *pain d'épice* which came perhaps from Asia with a tired Crusader.

Its flat strange odour, honey, cow dung, clove, something unnameable but unmistakable, blew over all the town. Into the theatre sometimes would swim a little cloud of it, or quickly through a café grey with smoke. In churches it went for one triumphant minute far above the incenses.

At art school, where tiny Ovide Yencesse tried to convince the hungriest students that medal-making was a great career, and fed them secretly whether they agreed or not, altar smoke crept through from the cathedral on one side, and from the other the smell of *pain d'épice* baking in a little factory. It was a smell as thick as a flannel curtain.

We knew most of the shops, and although I can't remember eating much gingerbread when we first went there, later when my younger sister Norah lived nearby, I bought it often. It was called *pavé de santé*, and it was the plainest and the most delicious, and the cheapest cut. It was made in huge loaves about six feet square, six inches thick, and it was sold in square blocks of about a kilo each, or a half-kilo maybe, and wrapped up in paper marked Mulot et Petit Jean or any of the other good gingerbread places. The smells were heavenly.

Mulot et Petit Jean was the biggest and oldest supplier of gingerbread, and its main store always looked something like a pharmacy. The women who worked there all looked the same, with tight high-breasted bodies and handsome hands and feet, and they went lightly over the tiled floors, behind the high polished counters piled with pretty boxes and the towering cash desk with a little carved fence around its top. They were deft and remote, and yet protective. Now and then for Christmas or birthdays, I sent loaves of the plain kind of gingerbread and boxes of the sticky kind to America, and they advised against shipping a round cake covered with candied cherries, and advised for a smaller square one stuffed with apricot jam, and I smiled at them without their knowing why, nor caring.

The Grey-Poupon shop was on the corner of one of the streets that led off the rue de la Liberté down to the place Bossuet, where Mulot et Petit Jean was, and across from it was a wonderful store where workmen got their clothes. Al bought a suit there, I remember. It was a navy blue corduroy, a thick-waled corduroy. One time there was a masked students' ball given by the Mayor in the Ducal Palace, and we both bought harlequin costumes alike there. I skinned my hair back, and was perhaps a little masculine. Al was rather effeminate, I think. Anyway, we both wore makeup, and he, to me, was obviously a man and I was obviously a girl, and it was fun.

The shop also had smocks for various kinds of working people (they all had their own smocks, navy blue, or dark gray), and there were lots of butchers' aprons. Every kind of workman had his own quality and cut and colour of suit. I still have a smock that I bought there. It is grey and ugly, but I still have it hanging in my closet. I haven't worn it for years, but I keep it, for some reason. It would be a nice thing for a sculptor or cabinet worker . . . something to wipe gluey old hands on. . . .

There were people who belted out street songs in 1929–1930. There were usually two people: One would be a wounded veteran from the war – World War I, which was still very keen in their minds, of course – and then there would be a woman. The man would sit on a little stool usually, and the woman would go around and collect pennies and sell sheet music now and then. They would sing a song, and sometimes they'd sing two or three, but they would sell the sheet music to people for a penny. I always stopped and listened, but it seems odd that I don't remember ever paying for and getting a piece of sheet music.

The Ducal Palace was at the far end of the rue de la Liberté facing the place d'Armes, and it was a series of majestic buildings, which housed the mayor's offices as well as the museums. In its courtyard was the Ducal Kitchen, which was nothing but a great chimney rising from a space which formed the oven itself.

There were several other things in the courtyard, including the brooding statue of Claus Sluter, the first great sculptor of Burgundy, who did the Puits de Moïse, which is outside the town. The great tower of Phillipe Le Bon was toward the back of the high buildings and rose high above even the churches. The rue de la Liberté separated the Ducal Palace from the place d'Armes, which was its natural parade ground and always seemed the centre of town.

Down the rue de la Liberté from the Ducal Palace, there was the Opera House, the place de l'Opéra, and the small Café de l'Opéra. There was also a famous printshop, where they printed James Joyce, D. H. Lawrence, and other writers forbidden in America and England. There were strange typos in them, because all the proofreaders were, of course, Frenchmen speaking English. They finally did print Al's thesis and later Larry Powell's, because printing theses was their livelihood. Then there was the grain market, and on Wednesdays and Saturdays there would be lots of pigeons walking around, picking up seeds that the merchants had dropped from their pockets.

Behind the Ducal Palace ran the oldest marketing street in town. It was very narrow and crowded and dirty, and it was the most picturesque part of town, with gabled buildings showing the famous tiled roofs of Burgundy . . . green and yellow and black and red. And there was the beautiful small place François Rude and finally the *place* where people gathered to see the famous gargoyles and the great clock Jacquemart with its mechanized figures on the façade of the église Notre-Dame.

The other half of the ancient city was where the place d'Armes spread out in front of the Ducal Palace. Out from the half-circle of the *place* ran a dozen small streets which led into the older quarter of the city, part commercial and part beautiful town houses, which seemed to end for us anyway on the corner of the Chabot-Charny and the rue du Petit-Potet.

The buildings on the place d'Armes were all two stories tall and fairly uniform, and they included several small cafés and tea shops and two restaurants, the Prés aux Clercs and Racouchot's Three Pheasants. On the corner of one of the streets that went down from the *place* was Venot's, the main bookstore of the town. It was the only one known to me then, and it supplied all the university books.

Monsieur Venot was a town character and was supposed to be the stingiest and most disagreeable man in Dijon, if not in the whole of France. But I did not know this, and I assumed that it was all right to treat him as if he were a polite and even generous person. I never bought much from him but textbooks, because I had no extra money, but I often spent hours in his cluttered shop, looking at books and asking him things, and sniffing the fine papers there, and even sitting copying things from books he would suggest I use at his worktable, with his compliments and his ink and often his paper. In other words, he was polite and generous to me, and I liked him.

When I told that to Georges and Henriette Connes, many years after I had stopped being a student, and after old Monsieur Venot had died and left a lot of money to a host of people nobody ever knew he would spit upon, they laughed with a tolerant if amused astonishment; and of course I too know that by now I am much shyer than I was then, or perhaps only less ignorant, and that I would not dream of accepting so blandly an old miser's generosity and wisdom.

In Monsieur Venot's shop I learned to like French books better than any others. They bent to the hand and had to be cut, page by page. I liked that; having to work to earn the reward, cutting impatiently through the cheap paper of a 'train novel', the kind bought in railroad stations to be thrown away and then as often kept for many years, precious for one reason or another. I always liked the way the paper crumbled a little on to my lap or my blanket or my plate, along the edges of each page.

'...all year and everywhere we smelled the Dijon gingerbread, that *pain d'épice* which came perhaps from Asia with a tired Crusader.'

All the streets of this old quarter off the place d'Armes were narrow and crooked and teeming with life behind their shuttered windows, and from our rooms on the rue du Petit-Potet we could hear fourteen or more bells ringing from the many small churches and convents. Between our house and the place d'Armes there was the Palais du Justice, which always filled me with a feeling of horror for the crimes that had been tried there for so many centuries. It was a very old and noble building, though, with a great hall made all of wood. Some of the streets in this part of the city had names like the Street of the Good Little Children; and they became more familiar to me than any I would ever know. Later when we moved to rue Monge we were still in the older part of the town but down by the canals and the River Saône.

The town was to become more familiar to me than any other place I had ever lived in before, or since. And I feel I could survive there now as easily as I did the first three years, in spite of the inevitable changes that the short time of some sixty years can make in a place as old as Dijon was and is.

Dervla Murphy

(1931–)

Like her Victorian predecessors, Dervla Murphy had to suspend her travel plans because of family obligations. At fourteen she was confined to the family home to care for her mother and remained there for another fourteen years. But since then her life has been lived at a pace true to the title of her first book – *Full Tilt* – in which she recounts a bike tour of India and Europe. The Irish-born author has written twenty-one books, sixteen of them about travel. In *Muddling Through in Madagascar*, twenty years after her first travel book, she lives up to her reputation for both taking risks and enduring their sometimes unfortunate consequences – hepatitis and a cracked rib among them.

from Muddling Through in Madagascar

Manalalondo's shops – some quite large – were either closed or almost empty. In the market-place the few occupied stalls sold little more than rice, onions, eggs, rotten sardines and unidentifiable wizened objects – probably traditional 'cures' and *ombiasas*' charms. Here, as in other areas during the weeks ahead, we got the impression that the rural Malagasay have reverted to a subsistence economy. Families depend on their own and their neighbours' produce, often exchanged rather than bought, and the flow of imported foodstuffs and consumer goods, stocked in colonial and immediately post-colonial days, has dried up.

On the edge of the town we sought refreshment in a thatched 'café' so tiny that our heads touched the ceiling and we had to leave our rucksacks outside. The young couple crouching in the smoky interior, and their four children, looked wretchedly unhealthy and seemed half-afraid of us. Husband sat slumped in one corner, his eyes dull, holding a whimpering filthy baby. We shared his unsteady bench while wife cooked rice-buns on a grass-burning mud stove. Suddenly he was overcome by a paroxysm of coughing and the baby howled in sympathy; he handed it to a toddler and lay on the ground at our feet. In the firelight I could see sweat glistening on his forehead before he drew his *lamba** over his head.

Wife had ladled the rice-bun batter from a rusty tin at Rachel's feet and was cooking two dozen at a time in a patty-tin used as a frying-pan. The eldest child, a girl aged perhaps six, continuously stuffed twists of grass, taken from a stack outside the door, into the flames. An even smaller boy was boiling coffee on a minute wood-fire in another mud-stove. Every few moments wife deftly turned the buns with a special wooden implement, adding a drop of grease to each 'cup' at each turn. We admired the skill with which she overcame all the limitations of her kitchen; the twenty-four buns were uniformly brown and crisp when she slid them on to a wooden tray. But hot rice-buns are only marginally less revolting than cold rice-buns. And the coffee was not coffee, though coffee coloured. If you use grass as fuel, you must know which berries serve best as a coffee-substitute.

Not far beyond Manalalondo a young couple, shy but smiling, caught up with us. When we had convinced them that we were *not* going to Ambatolampy they invited us to follow them on a cross-country short-cut and the next two hours had an endurance-test flavour. Our guides were a handsome pair, small and light-skinned, with compact muscular graceful bodies. Whether going uphill or down their pace never varied and we enviously compared their loads with our own. Husband's was a zinc bucket containing a litre tin of kerosene and an earthenware jar of honey; wife's was a head-basket containing two dozen oranges, one packet of biscuits and a small bar of soap.

We crossed three high grassy ridges, separating broad

* A large cloak worn by natives of Madagascar.

valleys. On the more precipitous slopes the narrow path was treacherous, its outside edge blurred by bushy red grass; a misjudgement here would have meant falling hundreds of feet. On the valley floors mini-chasms were spanned by dicey little bridges of thin sticks supporting loose sods of earth. From a distance we saw an isolated hamlet, on a hillside far above, and hoped for a brief pause. But our friends pressed relentlessly on, calling cheerful greetings to the inhabitants as we passed between hedges of tall sword-cactus. We glimpsed a six-inch orange and green chameleon while scrambling up long steep slabs of smooth rock, hot to the touch beneath the noon sun. Soon after we met a two-foot brown and green snake and the young woman shrieked fearfully, though no Malagasy snake is dangerous. At the base of another rock-slab mountain Rachel and I admitted defeat and let our guides, who were so evidently in a hurry, go ahead without us. We collapsed under a bush, our arms glistening with crystallised salt. Even in midwinter, and even in the mountains, it is hot at noon around the Tropic of Capricorn.

Five minutes later our friends were back, looking worried. No words were needed to explain the situation. They smiled at us, gently, and when we gestured to them to keep going they sat down instead and insisted on our eating two of their precious oranges. Again the young man offered to carry my rucksack. When I shook my head he picked it up, testingly, and registered comic dismay. On the next stage our pace was greatly reduced.

The granite summit of that mountain overlooked a deep valley holding an ochre track, a green river, many paddy-fields and our friends' home. Beyond their village the track was a continuation of the motor-road we had followed out of Manalalondo, without then realising that it was meant to cater for the internal combustion engine. Had we not taken photographs, I would now doubt my recollection of this highway. Where it had been bisected by years of flood-damage, never repaired, the two-foot-wide central rut was four feet deep and accompanied by numerous relatively minor side-ruts. When it abruptly disappeared on a sloping ridge, amidst evergreen bushes and hummocks of brown grass, we circled the area in search of any kind of path – and then, incredibly, found smudged tyre marks between bushes and hummocks. An hour later, in the next populated valley, we were fascinated to see rafts of vegetation, some twenty yards by thirty, floating on a jade-green river – anchored with stones in midstream. These are artificial paddy-fields, created where there is an urgent need for extra land.

During the afternoon we swam in a tingling cold pool, between high grassy mountains, watched by a pair of ceaselessly circling buzzards. An hour later we were back in fertile country – too fertile, for the sun was declining and we could see no possible campsite amidst the paddy-fields. Snatches of song came from substantial houses above the track, groups of men were sitting around playing the Malagasy version of violins or guitars, children's laughter sounded loud in the windless evening air. Not everyone greeted us and some chatting neighbours fell silent as we approached. But their reaction was understandable; few *vazaha** pass that way.

At last we spotted a low scrub ridge; the sun set as we pushed upwards through dense bushes, seeking tent-space. Suddenly an enormous ancient tomb loomed out of the dusk. Obviously it was no longer in use; equally obviously it housed *razana*** of some consequence and *vazaha* camping in its vicinity might not be amiably regarded. We hastened on and five minutes later – it was then dark – reached a level site carpeted with some powerfully scented herb. But the *razana* were still too close for comfort; a zebu-cart on a nearby track prompted us to switch off our torches and (feeling more than slightly foolish) lie doggo by our half-erected tent. 'Better to be undignified than got at by some *ombiasa*,'† remarked Rachel as we stood up. For supper we enjoyed Nomad Soup, poured on to surplus breakfast-rice smuggled away in our plastic bag.

A new two-(wo)man tent for the Malagasy expedition had cost only £15 but was alleged to be waterproof. However, within an hour of the rain's beginning at 9:30 P.M. pools were accumulating all around us. It was heavy rain, and steady. Rachel slept until midnight, muttering and squirming miserably as the chilly lake deepened. After that neither of us slept. My companion expatiated on the folly of parsimony at great length and with bitter eloquence. I curled myself into a soggy shivering ball and listened humbly, making occasional penitent noises. Wistfully I remembered the good old days when Rachel uncritically accepted the vicissitudes of travelling with a not very practical Mamma.

Towards dawn the rain dwindled and soon there was silence,

* Foreigners.

** Ancestors.

† Witch doctor, sorcerer hostile to the European order.

‘Through binoculars I studied the apparently pathless southern mountain-wall. “There must be a way over,” I decided, “even though we can’t see it yet.”’

apart from nasty squelchy noises caused by our slightest movement. As I unzipped the entrance the herbal aroma, intensified by the rain, acted on us (or at least on me) like a strong stimulant. Crawling out, I saw that we were in a slight hollow on the ridge-top, which restricted our view of the immediately surrounding terrain and emphasised the immensity of the sky. I stared in wonder at the still starry purple-violet zenith – a tinge belonging to neither night nor day. The stars vanished as I gazed. To the east lay distant chunks of mountain darkly colourless below a magnolia glow. To the west drifted royal-blue banks of broken retreating rain-cloud. I held my breath, waiting. Then the sun was up, behind the chunky mountain, and purple-violet changed to powder-blue – magnolia to the palest green – royal-blue to gold and crimson.

That was, I think, the most magical dawn I have ever attended. But when I remarked to Rachel that one wet night was a small price to pay for such an experience she merely grunted and went on wringing out her flea-bag. Perhaps at fourteen one’s aesthetic sensibilities are still latent.

We set off at 6:15, our loads perceptibly heavier, sucking glucose tablets for breakfast. Pathlets on which we met nobody led us for four hours through pine-woods and eucalyptus plantations, around bare red hills, over grassy ridges and across a wide cultivated bowl-valley where the soil seemed poor and the few inhabitants were timid and illiterate. Their illiteracy emerged when we produced Samuel’s letter as a preliminary, we hoped, to acquiring food by purchase or barter. It did not work in this area, serving only to increase the local fear of tough-looking *vazaha*.

While we rested in a tamarind glade, lying on feathery green-gold grass, the sun undid the rain’s damage. Its power astonished us; within thirty minutes even our thick flea-bags were dry. Here I heated our last Nomad Soup for Rachel and refuelled myself with our last fistful of peanuts.

‘How are we getting out of this valley?’ asked Rachel as we repacked.

Through binoculars I studied the apparently pathless southern mountain-wall. ‘There must be a way over,’ I decided, ‘even though we can’t see it yet.’

‘Why must there?’ demanded Rachel. ‘Who in their right mind would ever walk over *that*?’

‘People have to go from here to Antsirabe,’ I pointed out in my parent-being-patient-with-silly-child voice.

‘I’ll bet we passed the Antsirabe track ages ago,’ said Rachel, ‘at the junction where you *would* take this dotty little path. Maybe you thought your day would be spoiled by meeting one vehicle if we took the right track.’

I ignored this deserved taunt and persisted, ‘I’m sure there’s a path – we’ll ask.’

‘Ask who?’ enquired Rachel, sweeping the deserted valley floor with her binoculars. ‘Even if we do meet someone we won’t be able to understand them.’

Luckily this prediction was wrong. At the next hamlet a group of laughing women retreated into their hovels as we approached, then cautiously peered out when they heard me rather desperately shouting – ‘Antsirabe?’

‘Ambatolampy!’ yelled the eldest woman, pointing to the north-east. (Behind me Rachel muttered a word that was not in her vocabulary before she went away to school; is it for this that we court destitution to pay school-fees?)

Again I shouted ‘Antsirabe?’ The women conferred, then summoned a youth from within. He reluctantly advanced a few yards, pointing to a steep bushy slope rising above the hamlet. ‘Antsirabe!’ he affirmed, repeating the word while gesturing towards a distant cleft in the mountain wall directly behind the steep slope. There was no mistaking his meaning; to get to Antsirabe we had to climb that escarpment.

We found no path until reaching the top. Evidently those who use this route (perhaps not many, as Rachel suggested) have their own favourite ways up and down. One would not have chosen to tackle such a gradient on an almost empty stomach after a sleepless night and we often rested, collapsing where there was some boulder or ledge on which to lean our loads. At each halt the view was more spectacular, encompassing all of Imerina – and much more besides.

From the top we could see miles of undulating golden savannah unbroken by bush or tree or boulder, with mountain summits peering over the distant edges to remind us that we were, by Malagasy standards, at a great height. The faint path divided occasionally and sometimes an even fainter branch path seemed to be going more directly south. But we were following a trail of 'ecological litter', as Rachel called it – white wads of sugar-cane fibre spat out by villagers returning from market. At the far side of the plateau, after two hours fast walking, we might well have gone astray but for these clues. Here pathlets proliferated bewilderingly amidst hills, glens, spurs and ridges, some thinly forested, some entangled in thorny scrub, a few supporting potato-patches.

In the deepest glen we filled our water-bottles and bathed our feet in a rapid sparkling mountain stream that might have been Irish. Before replacing her boots, Rachel wordlessly extended her feet towards me. I looked – and recoiled. Uncooked steaks is the obvious simile. None of our plasters would cover the affected areas.

'Why didn't you say something earlier?' I demanded, as though the whole thing were somehow her fault.

'Well,' said Rachel, 'you can't piggy-back me any more and we couldn't just sit starving on a mountain.'

I gave minimal medical aid while repenting my earlier bitchy thoughts about the feebleness of modern youth. You have to be tough to carry a load for twenty miles on flayed feet. Luckily we did not then know how many more miles lay ahead.

Beyond the glen, several isolated houses and tombs stood out against the sky on far-away ridges. Fat-tailed sheep, small and dark brown, nibbled unattended beside the path in the shade of ancient, tall, unfamiliar trees: a sad fragment of Madagascar's primary forest. Soon we had to cross a tricky, unexpected marsh and then came an anxious fifteen minutes; our fibre-trail disappeared, leaving us to the mercy of our compass on pathless green grassland – the only green pasture we saw in the Ankaratra. Here zebu were being tended by two small boys wrapped in *lambas* and holding sticks twice as long as themselves. They fled from us, abandoning their herd, and hid in bushes.

Sullen clouds filled the sky as we climbed to a broken plateau covered with brown scrub, like winter heather. Our spirits rose when we saw a café-shack in the distance – but it was deserted. Then, without warning, we were on a wide cart-track, deeply eroded yet unmistakably going somewhere of importance. It began (or ended) just like that, in the middle of nowhere, for no particular reason. 'This is the maddest country I've ever been in,' reflected Rachel, intending no pun.

Moments later we met three men returning, as we later realised, from Ambohibary market. One carried a new iron blade for his plough, another carried a can of kerosene, the third carried nothing but was wearing a pair of brand-new blue jeans. Rachel deduced optimistically, 'If they sell jeans it's a big town, with lots of food!'

Soon the track could be seen for miles ahead, dropping into a broad valley before climbing high on the flanks of a long, multi-spurred mountain. The whole wide expanse of countryside beneath us was thronged, as people turned off the main track to go to their hamlets in the fertile valleys to east and west. After walking in solitude for ten hours, this bustle of humanity seemed quite urban.

We developed a guessing-game: identifying various improbable head-burdens from a distance. An empty tar-barrel – a pair of new shoes – a wooden bench – a ten-foot roll of raffia matting – a tower of dried tobacco leaves – a Scotch whisky crate full of vociferous fluffy ducklings – a basket of long French loaves. (Our mouths watered as we caught a whiff of that fresh crustiness.) Only cocks and hens were not carried on heads but tucked under arms. We were moved by the number of poultry-owners who were talking soothingly to their burdens, sometimes stroking them gently with one finger. Even more moving was the fact that almost everyone stopped to shake hands with us and murmur a greeting. They were all chewing cane and soon our hands were as sticky as theirs. No one tried to question us about our identity or destination; those greetings were brief, gracious – and unforgettably heart-warming. Apart from the Tibetans, I have never travelled among a people as endearing as the Malagasy.

While ascending the multi-spurred mountain we met many descending zebu-carts, which frequently left the track because the ground on either side was less difficult to negotiate; they were covering no more than half-a-mile per hour. The introduction of the wheel to this region was perhaps a mistake. Why, since horses flourish around Tana, has equine transport never become popular in Imerina? A similar returning-from-market scene in Ethiopia's highlands would have contained many speedy horsemen and nimble pack-mules.

'No one tried to question us about our identity or destination; those greetings were brief, gracious – and unforgettably heart-warming.'

At 4:30 Rachel rejoiced to see Ambohibary in the centre of a wide flat paddy-plain far below. But mountain distances are deceptive and I had my doubts about reaching it before dark. Three linked wooded hills still stood between us and the plain and our progress was being slowed by all those pauses to exchange courtesies. Yet the traffic also helped; we took several short-cuts that would have seemed imprudent, or impossible, had we not seen people using them. On such severe slopes, tiny children were carried up or down. Otherwise they walked sturdily for miles, hand-in-hand with a parent or older sibling. It was an odd sensation, being the only people – among all those hundreds – going *towards* Ambohibary.

As the foot-traffic thinned the slower cart-traffic increased and our imaginations boggled wildly at the thought of zebu-carts crossing these mountains by night. The town still looked very far away when sunset came as we were descending the third hill. In the twilight we passed an elaborate tomb on the edge of a pine-wood; its porch-like façade offered shelter from the probable nocturnal downpour but Rachel declined to share accommodation with corpses. I did not argue, her feet being my only reason for proposing this risky intimacy with the local *razana*. Here we were briefly able to follow the glimmer of wheel-marks, where the earth had been compacted and polished. Then total darkness came. Not a star shone through the heavy clouds and as all our batteries had been victims of the tent-flood we were reduced to cart-speed by the deep ruts and high tufts of grass. The blackness of the plain puzzled us; even from a non-electrified town one expects some faint glow after dark.

Without warning we were in a hamlet, astray amidst houses and trees occupying various shelves on the hillside. As we stumbled between the dwellings, none showing a light, one door opened and the oil-wicks flickering within seemed brilliant. Three men emerged, laughing loudly, and we decided to show them Samuel's letter. Unfortunately they were drunk; not very, but too much so for us to communicate in sign-language in the dark – not a particularly feasible scheme, when you come to think of it, even had they been sober. My query – 'Ambohibary?' – loosed a torrent of Malagasy from all three simultaneously. Then an elderly man appeared at the open door, shouted, 'Route Nationale No.7!' and pointed downhill. This was not helpful; we already knew our way led downhill. As the door was closed, and firmly bolted, the trio surrounded us, exhaling fumes reminiscent of the cheapest grade of Russian petrol. Gripping our arms, they led us down a twisting path apparently criss-crossed by tree-roots, all the while continuing to address us animatedly in Malagasy. On level ground they triumphantly chorused, 'Route Nationale No.7!' Then they groped for our hands, regarding impenetrable darkness as no excuse for a breach of etiquette, and having completed their farewells left us to make what we could of Route Nationale No.7.

'This *can't* be a national highway!' said Rachel ten minutes later. Already she had tripped over three chunks of rock and I had turned an ankle in a cavernous pot-hole. We continued with linked arms, for mutual protection.

The clouds parted slightly at an opportune moment. We were only ten yards from a rubble-filled chasm that had to be climbed into and out of – an exercise for which meagre starlight provided unsatisfactory illumination. By this time we had covered at least twenty-eight miles and I suggested sleeping by the wayside. Rachel however was determined to make Ambohibary, and food, though she admitted to needing a rest. I pointed out what seemed a suitable boulder-seat but unhappily it proved to be a prickly-pear cactus. For some reason (unclear in retrospect) this provoked us both to uncontrollable mirth and we sat in the middle of the road and laughed until our ribs ached as much as our shoulders.

The cloud gap closed as we continued and instinctively one listens more keenly when unable to see; otherwise we might have ended up in the wide, fast irrigation channel that soon after crossed the road. It took time to find a bridge of wobbly planks in an adjacent field.

Fifteen minutes later we became aware of tall houses on both sides of the track – Ambohibary, we presumed. It was only 8:15, yet there was no sound, no light, no movement. A Merina proverb advises: 'Do not arrive in a village after dark for you will be greeted only by the dogs.' Here not even dogs were registering our presence; the place might have been abandoned a century ago. 'Let's keep going,' said Rachel, 'this is just a suburb.' As she spoke five men materialised nearby, their leader's flaming resin-torch swaying like the mast-light of a ship on a stormy sea. They were much drunker than our three guides. When I asked, 'Hotely?' the leader belched (more Russian petrol fumes) and the other began to giggle and sing. 'We'd better push off,' said Rachel impatiently, 'before they all feel they must shake hands.' But she was at the end of a tether that for hours had been stretched to breaking point. Although the spirit was still willing the flesh had to be supported by me as she hobbled the next few hundred yards – which took us back into open countryside. We had merely passed through a village.

'That's it,' I said. 'Here we sleep, come hell or high water – probably high water. Even if we could get to Ambowhatsit, it's too late to find food.'

Starlight revealed a roadside trader's stall: four crooked branches supporting a sheet of corrugated iron. Beneath it I cleared a space of loose stones and spread our flea-bags on the bumpy iron-hard ground. Less than five minutes later Rachel was asleep.

I was too hungry to sleep; the lack of food for sale en route had taken me unawares. I reproved myself for being so illogically inhibited by the peasants' refusal to *sell* food to travellers – I often enough condemn the transfer to other societies of the standards and principles of our own. On the previous evening we should have sought hospitality instead of camping; we could then have eaten our fill and started the day with substantial breakfasts. Again, at the foot of the escarpment we should have explained that we were very hungry; no Malagasy peasant would have to go without to feed us. Yet my inhibition was not entirely based on a reluctance to cadge. Another factor was the extent to which, in rural Madagascar, daily life has a fixed and formal pattern governed by *fady*. It is a friendly and generous but not a relaxed or spontaneous society. And the complexity of local inhibitions about *vazaha* reinforces the *vazaha*'s own inhibitions.

To outsiders the Malagasy submission to ancestral decrees can seem absurd – even neurotic – yet that afternoon we had been impressed by some of its effects. If an old man is heavily laden, any young man catching up with him insists on carrying his load for some distance, though they may be total strangers. And young people ask permission before overtaking their elders on the track. Is it a measure of the uncouthness of the modern West that we marvelled so to observe these courtesies?

At that point in my ruminations a dog approached, sniffed curiously around us, then took fright at the *vazaha* smells (as anyone might have done, that evening) and ran away yelping shrilly. Otherwise nothing moved until 4:50 A.M. when two men passed, chuckling and chatting. They did not notice us. It rained lightly for a few hours: harmless straight-down rain – we were only dampened around the edges. I might have slept eventually but for the decibels of a corpse-turning party obviously intended to summon ancestors from Outer Space. This ceremony began at 8:45 P.M. and was still going loud and strong when we left the area. Luckily Malagasy music is pleasing to the ear, if a trifle monotonous.

An overcast dawn showed Ambohibary scarcely a mile away. Most windows were still tightly shuttered as we hastened towards the town centre, through lanes piled with morning-after-market refuse. Malagasy litter is ninety per cent edible and scores of truculent ganders, pompous geese and bumptious goslings were on garbage-disposal duty. Never have I seen so many geese in one place; at that hour they seemed to own the town.

A few café-stalls were open in the market-square and we devoured so many rice-buns so quickly that the attractive young woman who was serving us called her mother to watch. As we ate, other stall-holders began to light their charcoal-stoves and display rice-buns – to be bought in bulk and taken home for breakfast, a habit perhaps picked up from the French.

A short-cut over a eucalyptus-planted hill took us to the real Route Nationale No.7 and we realised why Ambohibary's market is so important. A link road that once was tarred is still capable of taking truck traffic to Ambohibary from Route Nationale No.7, the Tana-Antsirabe highway. Our bizarre 'road' of the previous evening is a continuation of this link, going to Arivonimamo via Manalalondo. But it is not, as we had seen, conducive to a free flow of goods throughout the Ankaratra.

The junction is marked – and marred – by a pretentious

'A Merina proverb advises: "Do not arrive in a village after dark for you will be greeted only by the dogs."'

new 'bar'-stall of pale varnished wood, designed to attract passing motorists. Sadly, the beer bottles lining its shelves were all empty. Here we relished a second breakfast of slightly sweet crisp fritters, fresh from the pan, while a plump gentle dog sat hopefully at our feet – his girth proving that his hopes were often fulfilled – and minuscule ducklings splashed ecstatically in a nearby puddle. Opposite the bar a barely legible kilometre-stone said 'Antsirabe 33' and we decided to walk on but take the first available bus out of consideration for Rachel's feet.

During the next four hours withdrawal symptoms afflicted me: inevitable on exchanging mountain-tracks for a motor-road, however light the traffic. I could not agree with our Air Mad guidebook – 'The Tananarive–Antsirabe road is bituminized, and the trip very nice.' But that was sheer prejudice; by normal standards the trip *is* 'very nice,' as Route Nationale No.7 undulates through miles of mature pine-plantations or densely populated farmland. Our guidebook explains:

> From the economic point of view, it must be stated that Antsirabe is at the centre of a rich agricultural region which produces: rice, beans, sweet potatoes, corn (maize), taro, soja, potatoes: all vegetables grow wonderfully. The vineyards give 350,000 to 400,000 litres of wine. Let us mention that the harvest of wheat has begun. Also to be found is a very wide range of european and exotic flowers. For stock tanning let us mention: cattle, sheep, numerous pigs, also poultry and horses.

In the woods government foresters were manhandling trimmed trunks on to decrepit trucks. Private enterprise was also active. Youthful entrepreneurs had gathered small branches into neatly bound bundles for sale to passing city-dwellers. And larger branches were being loaded into motor-vans by Antsirabe fuel-merchants.

In the 'rich agricultural region' traditional Merina dwellings were interspersed with colonial bungalows or dainty two-storey residences half-smothered in flowering shrubs. Yet even along this motor-road there were symptoms of economic collapse: rows of recently abandoned wayside market-stalls (the local equivalent of a supermarket), and derelict petrol-pump stations, and two colonial restaurants now used as vegetable depots.

Light showers refreshed us during the early forenoon but by midday the sky had cleared, the heat was brutal and Rachel was limping very badly. We sat in a wooden glen, overlooking a narrow river in a wide river-bed, and waited for a bus. From afar we could see a ludicrously sophisticated skyscraper flour-mill, to cater for the 'harvest of wheat'; we later learned that it is having severe (though hardly surprising) problems to do with maintenance and fuelling.

During the morning three buses had passed us, all preposterously overloaded. The fourth was no less so but two men gave up their seats to the *vazaha*. Large baskets of vegetables and small children standing on laps restricted our view of the approach to Antsirabe. Most of our fellow-passengers were well-groomed, wearing clean, brightly coloured *lambas* over neat shirts and pants or blouses and skirts. Their appearance did not match the state of their conveyance; I have never travelled in a more beat-up vehicle. As there was no door remaining, and not much floor, the dust-intake from the 'bituminized' road was considerable and both conductor and driver wore scarves around their noses and mouths. The driver sat crouched and tense and frowning, using accelerator and brake equally violently. Every few hundred yards he swerved acrobatically to avoid either straying livestock or a mini-crater. Mere pot-holes he took as they came and each jolt jarred us breathless. At the end of the ten-mile journey Rachel mused, 'What are we going to feel like when we've covered a few thousand miles in Malagasy vehicles?'

Barbara Grizzuti Harrison

(1934–)

Barbara Grizzuti Harrison takes a place within a select group of sophisticated stylists – including Edith Wharton, Vita Sackville-West, and Mary Lee Settle – adeptly weaving personal vision – her thoughts and feelings – with anecdotes about history and place. Her book on the Jehovah's Witnesses (*Visions of Glory*), of which she was a member for eleven years, shares the same conviction, ease with personal, political, and historical material, and open-mindedness that are hallmarks of her journalism and travel prose. Although her opinions and feminist politics inform her work, they don't take it over. A child of Italian-Americans from Brooklyn, where she still lives, Harrison had long wanted to make the journey she writes about in *Italian Days*.

from **Italian Days**

San Gimignano: 'City of Fine Towers'

There are places one comes home to that one has never been to: San Gimignano.

An English spinster, almost deaf, attaches herself to me on the bus to San Gimignano. She tells me of her adventures and misadventures in Spain, Portugal, Italy – all having to do with trains nearly missed, roads not taken, the kindness of strangers. I am not feeling particularly generous or kindly, except toward the green hills and the fields of yellow flowers in which I wish to lose my thoughts. 'Rape, I think those flowers are,' she says, 'horrible name. I think they make oil of it.' I think it is saffron, perhaps crocus . . .

Butter-yellow flowers bloom from the medieval towers for which San Gimignano is famous. They are variously called wallflowers and violets (and said by townspeople to grow nowhere else on earth). The small and fragrant flowers sprang up on the coffin of St. Fina (among whose gifts was the ability to extinguish house fires) and on the town's towers on the day of her death. (On that day bells tolled; they were rung by angels.) St. Fina is sometimes called the Saint of the Wallflowers. (*Wallflower*, in addition to its botanical meaning, in colloquial Italian means, as it does in English, a 'girl who is not invited to dance' – *ragazza che fa da tappezzeria*.) She died when she was fifteen. She was loved for her goodness and beauty, she had butter-yellow hair, she once accepted an orange from a young man at a well, and she died on an oak plank in penance for what seems to have been an entirely blameless life. In paintings by Ghirlandaio in San Gimignano's cathedral, she is so slender and delicate, so attenuated, as to cause one pain.

Modest St. Fina, a silent slip of a girl, might seem an odd choice for veneration in a walled city of military architecture – proud ramparts and aggressive towers built by suspicious patrician families to hide treasures and to assert the will for power. (Alberti railed against towers, regarding them as antisocial; in the sixteenth century Cosimo de' Medici ordered a halt to the expansion of San Gimignano, forbidding the commune of Florence to allocate to it 'even the slightest amount for any need, be it sacred or profane.')

There is a wrinkle in time in San Gimignano. There is no such thing as a mellow or lovable skyscraper, but the towers of San Gimignano, glibly called the skyscrapers of Tuscany, seem to have been born old . . . or at least to have anticipated the day when gentle St. Fina would, like Rapunzel, who also lived in a tower and whose hair was also gold, seem the perfect anointing presence. One imagines her – one imagines both Rapunzel and St. Fina – at the top of a steep, narrow, spiralling stone stairway, breathing silently in a slender shaft of brief light from a narrow window . . . everything military has retreated from this fairy-tale place.

There are fourteen tall towers in San Gimignano; there were once seventy-two. They are surrounded, on the narrow city streets, by palazzi and modest houses, all higgledy-piggledy, with projecting Tuscan roofs. They stretch from earth to sky and are built on shifting soil; and they speak, as Georges Duby says, two languages: 'on the one hand the unreal space of courtly myth, the vertical flight of mystic ascension, the linear curve carrying composition in to the scrolls of poetic reverie. And on the other, a rigorous marquetry offering the view of a compact universe, profound and solid.' They have one peculiar property: Their stones remain the same colour – a grey-gold with a suggestion, a faint pentimento, of black – whether wet with rain or hot with sun. The little guidebook I bought in San Gimignano is quite lyrical and accurate about the walls and towers of San Gimignano, which embody, as its author says, the contradictions of the medieval mind, a mind 'reserved and hospitable, bold and fearful. Fearful of enemies, of strangers, of night-time, of treasons.' The walls kept enemies out; they also kept people in; they imparted, to those within, a 'sense of community, of common interests and ideals never denied'. San Gimignano is formidable in its beauty; every description of it I have ever read makes it sound both forbidding and delightful. Forbidding it once was, in the days of fratricidal warfare, when families threw collapsible wooden bridges from the window of one tower-fortress to that of another (the days when it traded with Egypt, Syria, and Tunisia and men vied for great wealth); now it is simply delightful. And sheltering. The walls cup and cradle (as, in Niccolò Gerini's painting of St. Fina, she cradles the walled city in her slender young arms). The towers exist not to keep enemies – the Other – out, but to house the soul warmly; one has a sense of great bodily integrity in these spaces; one feels safe. When St. Fina drove the Devil out of San Gimignano with a gesture of her long and lovely hand, she did it for us.

Because one yields, in San Gimignano, to the fancy that the world is created anew each day, that time does not, in the way we ordinarily understand it, exist, it is exactly right, and so lovely, to find in a deserted piazza a small thirteenth-century church dedicated to St. Augustine, whose reflections on the nature and measurement of time so profoundly informed his love of God (and anticipated the existentialists):

> But if the present were always present, and would not pass into the past, it would no longer be time, but eternity. Therefore, if the present, so as to be time, must be so constituted that it passes into the past, how can we say that it is, since the cause of its being is the fact that it will cease to be? Does it not follow that we can truly say that it is time, only because it tends towards non-being?. . . How, then, can . . . the past and the future be, when the past no longer is and the future as yet does not be?

On the chancel wall of the church are lively fifteenth-century frescoes by Benozzo Gozzoli of the life of the great theologian. I am surprised to see St. Monica plump, peasant-sturdy, and careworn; I always imagined that one who prayed unceasingly, as she did, for the salvation of her son, would find one's flesh melting in the process. (I think of a life of prayer as inimical to fat.) Of all the charming frescoes, the most charming is that of Augustine chatting with the infant Jesus about the Mystery of the Trinity (that which might be remote and austere Gozzoli rendered immediate and intimate); the Child attempts to empty the sea into a puddle – much as any child might at the seashore, with a pail, or a shell – the impossibility of which convinces Augustine that the Trinity cannot be comprehended by reason alone.

Everything You have made is beautiful, Augustine said to his God, but You are more beautiful than anything You have made. In the cloister of the Church of St. Augustine, that beauty is palpable; one feels one has entered the light and peace of God. The cloister is divided by box hedges into four quadrangular plots of land in which grow irises and tulips and palm trees and white and yellow dandelions and pink and blue wandering flowers. . . . How sweet, these enclosures within an enclosed opening: open/close, close/open; a cypress punctuates each of four corners. A loggia – pots of yellow flowers and geraniums – looks out over a central cistern; the scent of lilacs is pervasive, the lilacs swarm with bees. The fragrance of lilacs mingles with the fragrance of wood-smoke. I walk beneath a tree the leaves of which are the colour of China tea; a cobweb brushes across my forehead. A jet plane streaks across the fragrance of lilacs; an orange-and-black cat mews piteously in the garden.

(Were mazes an outgrowth and elaboration of these enclosures within enclosures? Why would anyone wish to complicate and convolute so simple, satisfying, and sweet a design?)

'San Gimignano is formidable in its beauty; every description of it I have ever read makes it sound both forbidding and delightful.'

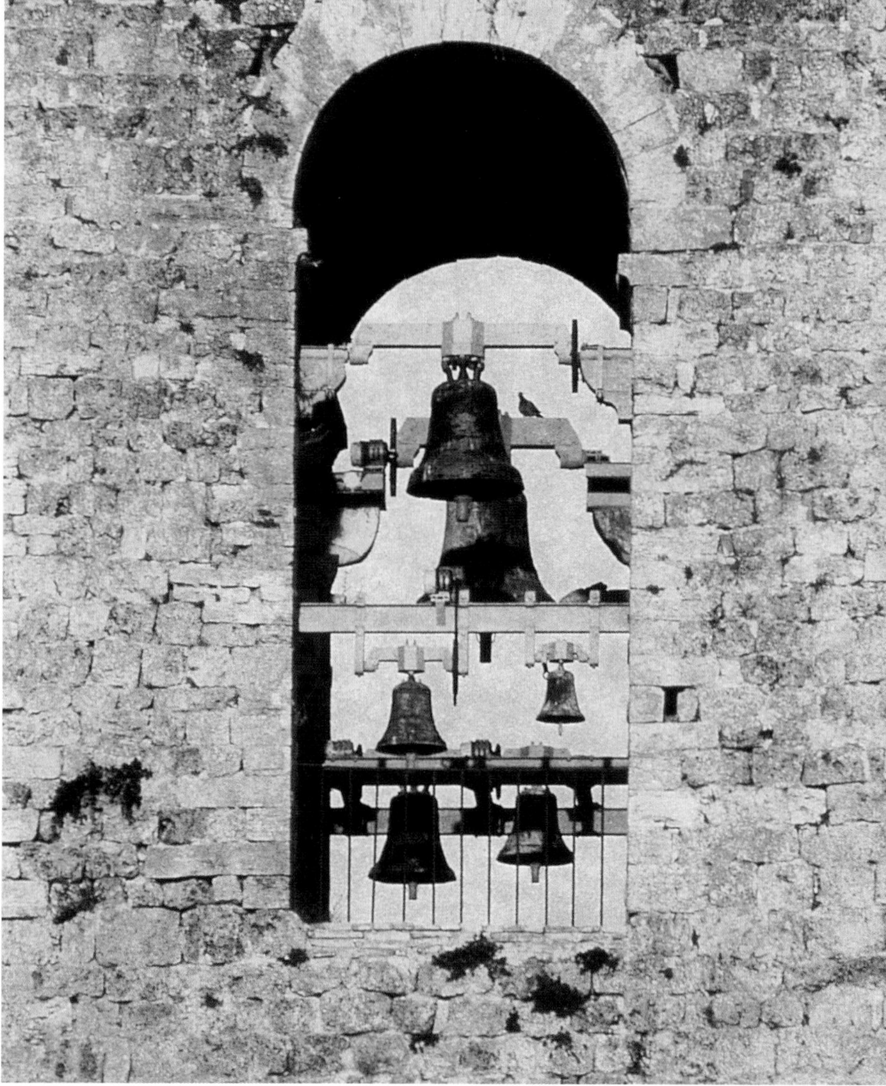

The sacristan plucks tenacious thorns from my coat. He is listening to a popular love song on his transistor radio in the sacristy. I light a candle and the sacristan extinguishes the flame. Even God has a *riposo* in Italy at lunch hour.

My hotel, once a palazzo, is in the Piazza della Cisterna, in the middle of which is a thirteenth-century cistern. From this piazza, through the battlemented archway, I can reach the square of the cathedral with its seven towers. I like the feel of the herringbone-patterned bricks under my thin sandals. I wander up and down steep hills, arched alleys, passing old men and women with canes. I never want to leave. My terraced hilltop room looks out over roofs and towers and blessed hills to the Val d'Elsa. I am beginning to believe the Annunciation did take place here. Art plagiarizes nature. I want to fly, as Cellini wanted to fly, 'on a pair of wings made of waxed linen'. And I want to stay here, rooted, forever. At dinner a baby boy crawls through the tunnelled legs of diners, to the cooing delight of waiters. A woman lights a cigarette, over which a British man and woman make a great disapproving fuss. 'There is no remedy for death,' the smoker says, coolly addressing the room at large. She says this in English and then in Italian.

After dinner, in a dim lounge, I watch *Two Women*, a movie with Sophia Loren. I am joined by the Italian woman who smokes. Out of an abundance of feeling I cry, not so much because this is the story of a rape, not because of the girl's loss of innocence and the mother's rage and grief, but because the injured girl is singing, her voice frail, a song my grandmother used to sing: '*Vieni, c'è una strada nel bosco* . . . I want you to know it, too . . . *c'è una strada nel cuore* . . . There's a road in my heart. . . .' The woman who smokes is crying, too. I am thinking of my daughter. When she leaves, the woman kisses

'To leave a walled city is to feel evicted, cast out – cast out of paradise; no matter that the countryside outside the walls is paradisiacal.'

the crown of my head. We have exchanged no words. Men have stood on the threshold and not come in. I never see her again.

I cross the piazza to sit in a brightly lit outdoor café. It is late. I am the only woman in the café. I fend off three approaches. I won't be denied the pleasure of seeing the light and shadows of the lovely square, the purple night sky. Inside, male voices are raised in a sentimental love song; they sing to the strings of a mandolin. Their singing is saccharine, their laughter is boisterous, and there are no women here. I wonder, with some little anger, what it would be like to be part of their sentimental, prideful, tough and tender world. I put on dark glasses. A little boy eating a gelato plays hide-and-seek, covering his eyes with sticky fingers (hide), waiting for me to smile (seek). A policeman strolls by apparently without purpose. I am an anomaly. I remove my glasses, thinking that if I can't see men's faces, they can't see mine.

What pleasure does it give men to sing of the beauty of women when there are no women in the café?

I find myself thinking of the handsome guide at the Davanzati who held the elevator for me.

The bed linen smells of lilacs. The air vibrates with the aftersound of bells.

In San Gimignano the birds sing all night long.

In the morning I drink my coffee from a mug bearing the words OLD TIME TEA.

In the Piazza della Cisterna there is a *sala di giochi* – video games. Is it possible that the children who grow up here – young men with studied, languid poses – think they are living in a hick town?

On the Via San Martino, away from the cathedral and the Cisterna, there is a café peopled entirely by old men. The café is part billiard parlor; newspapers are bought and read in common. I am accepted here in the morning light of day; I would not have been accepted here last night. I am served my morning coffee with old-fashioned gallantry by a man in a shiny black suit. With great difficulty he recites something he has been taught by an English-speaking cousin: '"We shall sit upon the ground and tell sad stories of the death of Kings." Is sad?' he asks.

To leave a walled city is to feel evicted, cast out – cast out of paradise; no matter that the countryside outside the walls is paradisiacal.

The bus, full of high-spirited schoolchildren, that stopped at Porta San Giovanni was the wrong bus, but the driver took me on anyway, avuncularly advised the children to be more calm in the presence of *la bella signora*, and deposited me at the right bus stop. We went by back roads, and I had the sensation, for the first time in Tuscany, not of passing but of being in the countryside, part of (not merely an observer of) a gorgeous (and calm) crazy quilt of silver-green olive trees and flowering peach and cherry trees; the yellow-and-red bus wound its way through the intricate sensual folds of hills dignified by cypress trees: 'And you, O God, saw all the things that you had made, and behold, "they were very good." For we also see them and behold, they are all very good.'*

The bus went slowly, like a swimmer who loves the water too much to race and challenge it, and the world unfolded like a child's picture book: gardeners turning over soil with gnarled, patient hands; bronzed youths of Etruscan beauty casually strolling by the roadside as if here were just anywhere and everywhere was beautiful; showers of wisteria framing old women shelling peas in doorways; lovers picnicking in a vineyard; laughing nuns pushing children on orange swings, their heavy habits flowing on magnolia-scented air: 'Your works praise you.'**

* Confessions of St. Augustine 13/28; 13/33.
** ibid.

Mary Lee Settle

(1918–)

Place is integral to the writing of Mary Lee Settle. When she began the work of fiction that would become the *Beulah Quintet*, she left New York to live in her home state of West Virginia, where the novels were set, so that they would be 'written not out of adolescent reaction but adult experience'. As in the writings of Freya Stark, Settle's travel writing evokes the hope and magic of a tale in *Arabian Nights*. In the following excerpt she trusts in her silent Turkish guide, as he mimes and ushers her through a house overlooking the ruins of an ancient city. Swiftly, effortlessly, she breaks barriers between East and West. Settle has written several novels and plays and won the National Book Award for fiction in 1978 for the novel, *Blood Tie*. She now lives in Norfolk, Virginia.

from Turkish Reflections

I thought that, instead of going by the main road, I would try to find and follow the path that Wood had discovered from the Artemision to the theater, if any trace of the sacred road still existed. I decided to search for it and, if I could find a trace, follow it around the mountain to the place where archaeologists think the Corresian Gate entered the city walls, although the gate itself has never been found.

So I, a foreign lady dressed in a large sun hat and sensible Reeboks, started one morning in the early sun, at the single standing column that is all that is left above ground of the hundreds of columns that were once the great temple. I set out on the main road until I saw that there was a dirt road, more direct, that ran at an angle through farm fields and up the mountainside.

I dodged invaders in tour buses and private cars on their busy ways, and in a few minutes I had found a path through country silence, headed toward the mountain that is on the north side of the ruins.

I walked past orchards and farmhouses. The little path grew faint beyond the last farmhouse. I began to climb the hill, watching the shadow of my hat on the ground. Nobody had climbed there for so long that weeds had grown high in the middle of it, but it was still marked if only by the slight dip in the otherwise weedy cover and tangled vines. I began to thrust my way through them.

In the middle of what had become a ghost path, I saw the bones and a little of the torn pelt of a large animal – a cow, a deer – eaten there by wild things, and I knew that I had found something of what that world was like when there was no civilized modern overlay. I told myself that whatever beast it was, wolf or wild dog, it was asleep. At least I hoped it was well-fed and asleep.

I went on climbing in the sun that was getting heavier, searching the ground and the undergrowth. At the crest of one of the lower foothills, I looked, and looked again, afraid of being fooled. There it was, a fragment of marble that had been exposed by years of weather, and beyond it, a long straight edge of white marble that glistened in the light.

I had played at being Wood and I had found it, the sacred road. I went all blithe and brave in the morning, a nice lady in a big hat. I parted weeds, and struggled through vines, and when I parted two small saplings I found that I had walked to what I first thought was a cliff. It was not.

Down below me, still far away from the ruins of the ancient city within its fence and with its guides and crowds, was the small marble atrium of a lost suburban house. Weeds grew in an empty shallow pool. On either side of marble steps, there were still two dolphins that had once been fountains that poured water from their mouths into the pool. I slid down the hill to the level of the floor, and I walked a short path of

ΙΡΟϹΚΡΑΤΗϹ
ΠΕΡΚΕΜΝΟϹΑΝΔΡΕΑϹ
ΟΙΑΜΙΝΩϹΗΛΥΚΟΥΡΓΟϹ
ΟΛΩΝ:ϹΤΗϹΑϹΤΕϹ
ΟΝΤΗϹΑϹΙΑϹΤΑ
ΜΑΤΑ·ΒΡΑΧΕΙΑΝ
ΗΝΤΩΝΠΟΝΩΝ
ΤΟ:

marble to its door, where the two truncated columns on either side still showed the grooves where, at night, they would have closed the house to marauders.

But one night the marauders had come to this house, and it had been so long abandoned that nothing of any world was left there but a Roman atrium, a little pool, two dolphins, a threshold, and silence in the sun.

I went on past it, up along the crest of the hill again. I slipped and slid and felt a fool, and at one point thought, if I break an ankle or my leg on this hill, I won't be found until I am a lady skeleton in a big hat, picked clean. I parted the underbrush and looked down upon another atrium, this one large and complete, with a fountain base in the centre, and roofless rooms beyond it. The wall looked about ten feet high, and I skirted the top of it, holding on to small trees for balance, to look for a way down.

I hadn't heard anything move, yet he stood there in front of me, smiling, quite silent, a large strong Turkish man, holding in his hand a small bunch of sweet wild thyme. He held it toward me, saying nothing, still smiling. There was something so gentle about him that I could not be afraid. I took the wild thyme, and I thanked him, in Turkish. He smiled again and touched his mouth and his ear. He was deaf and dumb. I still have the wild thyme, pressed and dried, kept like a Victorian lady's souvenir of the Holy land.

Dumb was the wrong word for him. There was no need for speech. He was an actor, an eloquent mime. I pointed to the atrium below and held my hands apart to show I didn't know how to get down into it. He took my arm, and carefully, slowly, led me down a steep pile of rubble.

He mimed the opening of a nonexistent door and ushered me through it. He showed me roofless room after roofless room as if he had discovered them. He dug and threw imaginary earth over his shoulder to show that it had been dug up.

I think that he had scared people before, and he was happy that there was someone who would let him show his house, for it was his house. Maybe he did sleep there. I don't know. I only know that he treated me as a guest in a ruin ten feet below the level of the ground, and that he took me from room to room where once there had been marble walls and now there was only stone, where he was host and owner for a little while.

He showed me a small pool, held out his hand the height of a small child, and then swam across the air. All the time he smiled. He took me to a larger pool and swam again. Then he grabbed my arm and led me through a dark corridor toward what I thought at first was a cave. It was not. He sat down in a niche in the corridor, and strained until his face was pink, to show me it was the toilet. Then he took me into the kitchen where there were two ovens. They were almost complete, except that the iron doors were gone. The arches of narrow Byzantine bricks were graceful over them, and the ovens were large as if there had been a large family there.

For the first one he rolled dough for bread, kneaded it in air, slapped it, and put it in the oven. Then he took it out, broke it, and shared it with me. I ate the air with him. The other was the main oven, and he picked vegetables from the floor of the cave kitchen, hit air to kill an animal, made a stew, and placed it in the stone and brick niche. We ate it and then we walked out into the sun of the larger atrium. Behind it, in the hill, he gestured that it had not yet been dug up, and then he pointed to a marble votive herma, whose head was missing, and knelt behind it, grinning, and set his own head there, to show me what it was. The grin was ancient, a satyr's grin.

We stood beyond his house on the edge of the hill, looking down on the buses and the crowd in the distance. Across and behind the noise and crowds, in a field, looking abandoned too, was the church of the Virgin Mary. The house where we stood had looked out over that and the harbour, and although it has not been found, I knew that it was near where the Corresian Gate had been.

When I gave my friend, my *arkadaş*, some money, he kissed my hand and held it to his forehead, and then, pleased with the sun and me, and the fact that someone had not run away from him who lived like Caliban in a ruin, he put his arms around me and kissed me on both cheeks. Then I went down the hill to Ephesus. When I looked back to wave he had disappeared.

What was the place? I've tried to find it in the books that tell what digging has been done at Ephesus, but this was outside the walls and not important enough to document, except for one obscure mention, that someone had dug there in 1926 and that there had been suburban mansions on the mountainside, and I already knew that. It exists across the tradition of a road, near a lost gate, near the stadium where Porphyrios the Mime was martyred as a Christian. Or maybe it was another Porphyrios; it was so long ago and there were so many martyrs.

Joan Didion

(1934–)

If Margaret Mead is the philosopher queen of observers, Joan Didion is the shaman, with a vision that projects the underlying meaning of things. In the following excerpt from her second collection of essays, *The White Album*, she says that Bogotá seems 'a mirage, a delusion on the high savannah, its gold and its emeralds unattainable, inaccessible, its isolation so splendid and unthinkable that the very existence of a city astonishes.' For the past twenty years, Didion has been one of the foremost chroniclers of the impact of American popular culture on foreign places, particularly Latin America. Didion says she is 'not so much interested in spontaneity. What concerns me is total control.' Didion has been criticized by feminists for being too tolerant of the condition of women and, indeed, says she does not believe in political solutions. 'I thought the answers, if there were answers, lay someplace in man's soul.' Among her nine volumes of fiction and nonfiction are *Salvador*, based on an extended visit to El Salvador in 1982, and several collections of essays – including *Slouching Towards Bethlehem* and *After Henry* – many of which first appeared in publications such as *Esquire*, *The New Yorker*, and *The New York Review of Books*. She lives in New York.

from **The White Album**

On the Colombian Coast it was hot, fevered, eleven degrees off the equator with evening trades that did not relieve but blew hot and dusty. The sky was white, the casino idle. I had never meant to leave the coast but after a week of it I began to think exclusively of Bogotá, floating on the Andes an hour away by air. In Bogotá it would be cool. In Bogotá one could get *The New York Times* only two days late and the *Miami Herald* only one day late and also emeralds, and bottled water. In Bogotá there would be fresh roses in the bathrooms at the Hotel Tequendama and hot water twenty-four hours a day and numbers to be dialled for chicken sandwiches from room service and Xerox *rápido* and long-distance operators who could get Los Angeles in ten minutes. In my room in Cartagena I would wake to the bleached coastal morning and find myself repeating certain words and phrases under my breath, an incantation: *Bogotá, Bocatá.* El Dorado. Emeralds. Hot water. Madeira consommé in cool dining rooms. *Santa Fé de Bogotá del Nuevo Reino de Granada de las Indias del Mar Océano.* The Avianca flight to Bogotá left Cartagena every morning at ten-forty, but such was the slowed motion of the coast that it took me another four days to get on it.

Maybe that is the one true way to see Bogotá, to have it float in the mind until the need for it is visceral, for the whole history of the place has been to seem a mirage, a delusion on the high savannah, its gold and its emeralds unattainable, inaccessible, its isolation so splendid and unthinkable that the very existence of a city astonishes. There on the very spine of the Andes gardeners espalier roses on embassy walls. Swarms of little girls in proper navy-blue school blazers line up to enter the faded tent of a tatty travelling circus: the elephant, the strong man, the tattooed man from Maracaibo. I arrived in Bogotá on a day in 1973 when the streets seemed bathed in mist and thin brilliant light and in the amplified pop voice of Nelson Ned, a Brazilian dwarf whose records played in every *disco* storefront. Outside the sixteenth-century Church of San Francisco, where the Spanish viceroys took office when the country was Nueva Granada and where Simón Bolívar assumed the presidency of the doomed republic called Gran Colombia, small children and old women hawked

Cuban cigars and cartons of American cigarettes and newspapers with the headline 'JACKIE Y ARI'. I lit a candle for my daughter and bought a paper to read about Jackie and Ari, how the princess *de los norteamericanos* ruled the king of the Greek sea by demanding of him pink champagne every night and *medialunas* every morning, a story a child might invent. Later, in the Gold Museum of the Banco de la República, I looked at the gold the Spaniards opened the Americas to get, the vision of El Dorado which was to animate a century and is believed to have begun here, outside Bogotá, at Lake Guatavita. 'Many golden offerings were cast into the lake', wrote the anthropologist Olivia Vlahos of the nights when the Chibcha Indians lit bonfires on the Andes and confirmed their rulers at Guatavita.

> Many more were heaped on a raft. . . . Then into the firelight stepped the ruler-to-be, his nakedness coated with a sticky resin. Onto the resin his priests applied gold dust and more gold dust until he gleamed like a golden statue. He stepped onto the raft, which was cut loose to drift into the middle of the lake. Suddenly he dived into the black water. When he emerged, the gold was gone, washed clean from his body. And he was king.

Until the Spaniards heard the story, and came to find El Dorado for themselves. 'One thing you must understand,' a young Colombian said to me at dinner that night. We were at Eduardo's out in the Chico district and the piano player was playing 'Love Is Blue' and we were drinking an indifferent bottle of Château Léoville-Poyferré which cost $20 American. 'Spain sent all its highest aristocracy to South America.' In fact I had heard variations on this hallucination before, on the coast: when Colombians spoke about the past I often had the sense of being in a place where history tended to sink, even as it happened, into the traceless solitude of autosuggestion. The princess was drinking pink champagne. High in the mountains the men were made of gold. Spain sent its highest aristocracy to South America. They were all stories a child might invent.

> Many years later, as he faced the firing squad, Colonel Aureliano Buendia was to remember that distant afternoon when his father took him to discover ice.
>
> – The opening line of *One Hundred Years of Solitude*, by the Colombian novelist Gabriel García Márquez.

At the big movie theatres in Bogotá in the spring of 1973 *The Professionals* was playing, and *It's A Mad Mad Mad Mad World*, two American pictures released in, respectively, 1967 and 1964. The English-language racks of paperback stands were packed with Edmund Wilson's *The Cold War and the Income Tax*, the 1964 Signet edition. This slight but definite dislocation of time fixed on the mind the awesome isolation of the place, as did dislocations of other kinds. On the fourth floor of the glossy new Bogotá Hilton one could lunch in an orchid-filled gallery that overlooked the indoor swimming pool, and also overlooked a shantytown of packing-crate and tin-can shacks where a small boy, his body hideously scarred and his face obscured by a knitted mask, played listlessly with a yo-yo. In the lobby of the Hotel Tequendama two Braniff stewardesses in turquoise-blue Pucci pantsuits flirted desultorily with a German waiting for the airport limousine; a third ignored the German and stood before a relief map on which buttons could be pressed to light up the major cities of Colombia, Santa Marta, on the coast; Barranquilla, Cartagena. Medellín, on the Central Cordillera. Cali, on the Cauca River, San Agustín on the Magdalena. Leticia, on the Amazon.

I watched her press the buttons one by one, transfixed by the vast darkness each tiny bulb illumined. The light for Bogotá blinked twice and went out. The girl in the Pucci pantsuit traced the Andes with her index finger. *Alto arrecife de Ia aurora humana*, the Chilean poet Pablo Neruda called the Andes. *High reef of the human dawn*. It cost the *conquistador* Gonzalo Jiménez de Quesada two years and the health of most of his men to reach Bogotá from the coast. It cost me $26.

'I knew they were your bags,' the man at the airport said, producing them triumphantly from a moraine of baggage and cartons and rubble from the construction that seemed all over Bogotá a chronic condition. 'They smelled American.' *Parece una turista norteamericana*, I read about myself in *El Espectador* a few mornings later. She resembles an American tourist. In fact I was aware of being an American in Colombia in a way I had not been in other places. I kept running into Americans, compatriots for whom the emotional centre of Bogotá was the massive concrete embassy on Carrera 10, members of a phantom colony called 'the American presence' which politesse prevented them from naming out loud. Several times I met a young American who ran an 'information' office, which he urged me to visit; he had extremely formal manners, appeared for the most desultory evening in black tie, and was, according to the Colombian I asked, CIA. I recall talking at a party to a USIS man who spoke in a low mellifluous voice of fevers he had known, fevers in Sierra Leone, fevers in Monrovia, fevers on the Colombian coast. Our host interrupted this litany, demanded to know why the ambassador had not come to the party. 'Little situation in Cali,' the USIS man said, and smiled professionally. He seemed very concerned that no breach of American manners be inferred, and so, absurdly, did I. We had nothing in common except the eagles on our passports, but those eagles made us, in some way I did not entirely understand, co-conspirators, two strangers heavy with responsibility for seeing that the eagle should not offend. We would prefer the sweet local Roman-Cola to the Coca-Cola the Colombians liked. We would think of Standard Oil as Esso Colombiano. We would not speak of fever except to one another. Later I met an American actor who had spent two weeks taking cold showers in Bogotá before he discovered that the hot and cold taps in the room assigned him were simply reversed: he had never asked, he said, because he did not want to be considered an arrogant *gringo*.

In *El Tiempo* that morning I had read that General Gustavo Rojas Pinilla, who took over Colombia in a military coup in 1953 and closed down the press before he was overthrown in 1957, was launching a new bid for power on a Peronist platform, and I had thought that perhaps people at the party would be talking about that, but they were not. Why had the American film industry not made films about the Vietnam War, was what the Colombian stringer for the Caribbean newspaper wanted to talk about. The young Colombian filmmakers looked at him incredulously. 'What would be the point,' one finally shrugged. 'They run that war on television.'

The filmmakers had lived in New York, spoke of Rip Torn, Norman Mailer, Ricky Leacock, Super 8. One had come to the party in a stovepipe preacher's hat; another in a violet macramé shawl to the knees. The girl with them, a famous beauty from the coast, wore a flamingo-pink sequinned midriff, and her pale red hair was fluffed around her head in an electric halo. She watched the *cumbia* dancers and fondled a baby ocelot and remained impassive both to the possibility of General Gustavo Rojas Pinilla's comeback and to the question of why the American film industry had not made films about the Vietnam War. Later, outside the gate, the filmmakers lit thick marijuana cigarettes in view of the uniformed *policía* and asked if I knew Paul Morrissey's and Andy Warhol's address in Rome. The girl from the coast cradled her ocelot against the wind.

Of the time I spent in Bogotá I remember mainly images, indelible but difficult to connect. I remember the walls on the second floor of the Museo Nacional, white and cool and lined with portraits of the presidents of Colombia, a great many presidents. I remember the emeralds in shop windows, lying casually in trays, all of them oddly pale at the centre, somehow watered, cold at the very heart where one expects the fire. I asked the price of one: 'Twenty-thousand American,' the woman said. She was reading a booklet called *Horóscopo: Sagitario* and did not look up. I remember walking across Plaza Bolívar, the great square from which all Colombian power emanates, at mid-afternoon when men in dark European suits stood talking on the steps of the Capitol and the mountains floated all around, their perspective made fluid by sun and shadow; I remember the way the mountains dwarfed a deserted Ferris wheel in the Parque Nacional in late afternoon.

In fact the mountains loom behind every image I remember, and perhaps are themselves the connection. Some afternoons I would drive out along their talus slopes through the Chico district, out Carrera 7 where the grounds of the great houses were immaculately clipped and the gates bore brass plaques with the names of European embassies and American foundations and Argentinian neurologists. I recall stopping in El Chico to make a telephone call one day, from a small shopping centre off Carrera 7; the shopping centre adjoined a church where a funeral mass had just taken place. The mourners were leaving the church, talking on the street, the women, most of them, in black pantsuits and violet-tinted glasses and pleated silk dresses and Givenchy coats that had not been bought in Bogotá. In El Chico it did not seem so far to Paris or New York, but there remained the mountains, and beyond the mountains that dense world described by Gabriel García Márquez as so recent that many things lacked names.

And even just a little farther, out where Carrera 7 became the Carretera Central del Norte, the rutted road that plunged through the mountains to Tunja and eventually to Caracas, it was in many ways a perpetual frontier, vertiginous in its extremes. Rickety buses hurtled dizzyingly down the centre of the road, swerving now and then to pick up a labourer, to avoid a pothole or a pack of children. Back from the road stretched large *haciendas*, their immense main houses barely visible in the folds of the slopes, their stone walls splashed occasionally with red paint, crude representations of the hammer and sickle and admonitions to vote *communista*. One day when I was out there a cloud burst, and because my rented car with 110,000 miles on it had no windshield wipers, I stopped by the side of the road. Rain streamed over the MESA ARIZONA WESTWOOD WARRIORS and GO TIDE decals on the car windows. Gullies formed on the road. Up in the high gravel quarries men worked on, picking with shovels at the Andes for twelve and a half pesos a load.

> Through another of our cities without a centre, as hideous
> as Los Angeles, and with as many cars
> per head, and past the 20-foot neon sign
> for Coppertone on a church, past the population
> earning $700 per capita
> in jerry skyscraper living-slabs, and on to the White House
> of El Presidente Leoni, his small men with 18-
> inch repeating pistols, firing 45 bullets a minute,
> the two armed guards petrified beside us, while we had
> champagne,
> and someone bugging the President: 'Where are the girls?'
> And the enclosed leader, quite a fellow, saying,
> 'I don't know where yours are, but I know where to find
> mine.' . . .
> This house, this pioneer democracy, built
> on foundations, not of rock, but blood as hard as rock.
>
> – Robert Lowell, 'Caracas'

There is one more image I remember, and it comes in two parts. First there was the mine. Tunnelled into a mountain in Zipaquirá, fifty kilometres north of *Bogotá*, is a salt mine. This single mine produces, each year, enough salt for all of South America, and has done so since before Europeans knew the continent existed: salt, not gold, was the economic basis of the Chibcha Empire, and Zipaquirá one of its capitals. The mine is vast, its air oppressive. I happened to be inside the mine because inside the mine there is, carved into the mountain 450 feet below the surface, a cathedral in which 10,000 people can hear mass at the same time. Fourteen massive stone pilasters support the vault. Recessed fluorescent tubes illuminate the Stations of the Cross, the dense air absorbing and dimming the light unsteadily. One could think of Chibcha sacrifices here, of the *conquistador* priests struggling to superimpose the European mass on the screams of the slaughtered children.

But one would be wrong. The building of this enigmatic excavation in the salt mountain was undertaken not by the Chibcha but by the Banco de la República, in 1954. In 1954 General Gustavo Rojas Pinilla and his colonels were running Colombia, and the country was wrenched by *La Violencia*, the fifteen years of anarchy that followed the assassination of Jorge Gaitán in Bogotá in 1948. In 1954 people were fleeing the terrorized countryside to squat in shacks in the comparative safety of Bogotá. In 1954 Colombia still had few public works projects, no transportation to speak of: Bogotá would not be connected by rail with the Caribbean until 1961. As I stood in the dim mountain reading the Banco de Ia República's dedicatory plaque, 1954 seemed to me an extraordinary year to have hit on the notion of building a cathedral of salt, but the Colombians to whom I mentioned it only shrugged.

The second part of the image. I had come up from the mine and was having lunch on the side of the salt mountain, in the chilly dining room of the Hostería del Libertador. There were heavy draperies that gave off a faint muskiness when touched. There were white brocade tablecloths, carefully darned. For every stalk of blanched asparagus served, there appeared another battery of silverplated flatware and platters and *vinaigrette* sauceboats, and also another battery of 'waiters': little boys, twelve or thirteen years old, dressed in tailcoats and white gloves and taught to serve as if this small inn on an Andean precipice were Vienna under the Hapsburgs.

I sat there for a long time. All around us the wind was sweeping the clouds off the Andes and across the savannah. Four hundred and fifty feet beneath us was the cathedral built of salt in the year 1954. *This house, this pioneer democracy, built on foundations, not of rock, but blood as hard as rock.* One of the little boys in white gloves picked up an empty wine bottle from a table, fitted it precisely into a wine holder, and marched toward the kitchen holding it stiffly before him, glancing covertly at the *mâitre d'hôtel* for approval. It seemed to me later that I had never before seen and would perhaps never again see the residuum of European custom so movingly and pointlessly observed.

Sarah Hobson

(1947–)

Dressed in men's clothing, Sarah Hobson sets off for Iran to see the forbidden shrine at Qum, a place barred to women. She accomplishes her goal travelling as 'John', complete with an elastic girdle around her chest and cropped hair. Iranian men she meets are suspicious of her and do not take her into their confidence. Rather, it is the Iranian wife Malake, in the excerpt that follows, who opens up to Hobson when she is told by her husband that 'John' is indeed female. Woman to woman, Malake quickly sheds formality; she is not alarmed or disgusted, but relieved, clearly relishing the opportunity to confide in the stranger. Hobson's witty narrative of her encounters with pilgrims of the Islamic faith was followed by a second book, about living with an Indian family. She now works on travel films and documentaries and lives in Yorkshire, England.

from **Through Persia in Disguise**

The south was to be a holiday, an exploration of the remote province of Fars, which gives its name to Persia and the language *farsi*, and whose history provides a galaxy of names in buildings and people: Persepolis, Cyrus, Alexander the Great, as well as Sassanians and Shirazi poets. My primary interest, however, was the Qashqai tribe who migrate across Fars each spring, and I hoped to study their designs. But it could be that I might not reach them, for they were bound in the mountains for the summer, and access was difficult without government passes.

I decided to take a bus to Shiraz, for I was told that not even champion motorbike riders used that stretch of road, so great was the risk of brigands.

The bus was leaving at seven in the morning, so I arrived early for my bike to be strapped to the roof. At half-past seven, the driver called:

'Come on, bring that motorbike here.'

I wheeled it over and stood helplessly wondering if I had to heave it up myself. The driver examined the petrol tank.

'But it's still full of petrol. It can't go like that. Empty it please.'

I turned Mephistopheles on his side, but only a trickle came out.

'Could you help?' I asked.

Cursing, the driver swung the bike over and I caught some of the flow in my petrol can. Then he yelled for a porter. An old man, his back bent permanently from the loads he had carried, came from behind the bus. Flinging a rope around it, he hoisted the bike on his back, and mounted the ladder at the side of the bus. Halfway up, he swayed with the weight, and I felt sure he was going to fall: I was ashamed I could do nothing to help. But he reached the top and tied it insecurely to the front.

The land we passed through was uncompromising in its bleakness and grandeur where the Zagros foothills swarmed to jagged peaks. Sunlight and paths prised themselves between outcrops of rock and then disappeared in the tiers of hills. The road sped through miles of scrubland and brown dust, passing small villages whose tea-houses competed for transient visitors. Towards evening, only silhouettes showed, defined against a whitening sky.

It was dark when we reached Shiraz: and as soon as my moped was unloaded, I went to find a hotel. I felt uneasy without the protection of daylight to reconnoitre and to assess the mood of the town: at night, people seemed hostile, the buildings withdrawn, so I could not deduce what type of quarter it was. By chance, I found a Travellers' Rest House with cold running water and a bed in the garden by a non-flowering rose-tree. An electric bulb in the corner was too dim to read by, so I stretched out on my bed. Suddenly the shutters of a room upstairs banged open. A man and a woman leaned out. She was unveiled, and her white shirt stretched over ample breasts. She looked down, her greasy hair flopping against her red mouth. I smiled. Then the man looked down, and pushing the woman back into the room, he closed the shutters firmly.

Half an hour later, she came into the garden with a transistor and a plate of biscuits.

'You American?' she asked in broken yet twanging English.

'No, English.'

'You have money?'

'Not much.'

'You good?' She placed the biscuits and wireless on the bed, touching my thigh as she did so. 'You how old?'

'Twenty-three.'

She seemed puzzled.

'I'm no good,' I said. '*Khajeh*, eunuch.'

Immediately she let her breasts drop from their thrusting position and turned to go into the house.

'You've left your wireless and biscuits,' I called.

She shrugged. 'Use them.' And she tightened her body again as a man came out to meet her.

I turned on the wireless. Iranian music coiled the air; a mellifluous voice listed the number of children at school; a rhetorical voice announced:

'Good evening. This is the British Overseas Broadcasting Corporation. We are now relaying the fourth and final part of a dramatised version of *Wuthering Heights*.'

A wind ensemble transported me to nineteenth-century Yorkshire. Catherine and Linton were elected by Earnshaw and a voice croaked:

'Aw were sur he'd sarve ye eht! He's a grand lad! He's gotten t'raight sperrit in him! *He* knaws – aye, he knaws, as weel as Aw do, who aud be t'maister yonder. – Ech, ech, ech! He mad ye skift properly! Ech, ech, ech!'

A man of about thirty-three came and sat on my bed. I looked up and he inclined his head.

'May God give you good health.'

I had to adjust myself quickly from the moors.

'To your kindness, I am well.'

'Do you understand?' he asked, pointing to the wireless. I nodded and we sat listening, the man moving his hand like a pendulum, his eyes closed. Some twenty minutes later the programme ended, and I turned off the knob.

'That was good,' I said.

'Yes, very good,' said the man, though he had not understood a word.

The following morning I saw little of Shiraz for I left for Persepolis early in order to avoid the midday sun. I had been riding for several hours, and was growing hot and stiff when I turned a corner in an avenue of trees to see an edifice like the Wailing Wall. This was Persepolis. Huge blocks of stone five feet square formed the base of a platform and above rose stark columns like factory chimneys. A pair of staircases indented one wall in the shape of a hexagon, and leaving Mephistopheles, I climbed one side. Four winged bulls, carved on to massive doorposts, guarded the top, their biceps swelling to a thick-set body. Their heads were human, surmounted by crowns, and each wore a beard like a nose-bag. I walked on through rectangular halls, past corinthian-type capitals and deeply fluted columns. Crenellated stairways led to different-levelled platforms – the King's apartments, the palace of audience, the Hall of a Hundred Columns. And blocks of hewn stone formed doorways whose lintels were carved in lines of stripes.

For this was pre-Islam, pre-Illahs and Allahs, a palace which was built in the early fifth century, B.C. It was classicism, not mysticism, and I found it impressive and straightforward, yet somehow more solid. Perhaps it was the lack of colour, for with so much stone, it presented a monotone of dull sandy brown.

Throughout, the activities of the court were depicted on the doorways and walls: the king swept by beneath an umbrella; the courtiers chatted, holding hands and lotus flowers; the Immortals lined up, an army whose number was always kept at 10,000, regardless of losses. On the staircases, representatives of the subject nations queued to pay obeisance at the New Year festival; they led rams, bullocks, dromedaries, and bore cloth, precious metals, tanned skins and vessels. There were Egyptians, Assyrians, Babylonians, Abyssinians, plus Indians, Armenians, Phoenicians. Some had cloaks which hung to their calves and some short rustic tunics; many wore hats, including the Sogdians who were redolent of Tolkien's hobbits in pointed funnel caps.

I trudged up and down the steps; but the overhead sun deadened the friezes by flattening their shadows, and by the end of the day I had only two queries. Why were no women shown, and what happened about sewage and water?

Of the harem only the foundations remain, but it surprised me that the queen was not depicted in the activities of the court. Sir Percy Sykes in his *History of Persia* comments with assurance on the position of Achaemenian women:

> Neither in the inscriptions nor in the sculptures does a woman appear . . . jealously guarded, [they] were not even allowed to receive their fathers or brothers. As this has apparently been the general rule in the East, the Persians were no worse off than their neighbours; but their decay as a great empire can be traced in no small degree to the intrigues of eunuchs and women in the *anderun*, as the harem is termed in Persia, where to do any work was degrading.

As for the water, I could trace no baths or pools on the site. But in the base of the platform a complex network of tunnels corresponds exactly with the walls of the palace above. They were used to protect the site during heavy winter rains, for the water was channelled through to them. On the platform itself, unmortared brick drains carried the rainwater off the roofs and along the floors before emptying into the underground network.

It is possible that the tunnels were also used for water supplies, for stone stairways lead down to them, serving both cleaners and carriers. And a cistern, about a hundred yards from the walls, and filled by the winter rains, probably contributed to the court's supply. In the south-east corner of the palace, a small water tank was used for immediate needs. In any case, the Achaemenian kings always took water with them from the river at Susa, when they moved from palace to palace. It was boiled and stored in silver flasks which were carried in wagons drawn by oxen.

The removal of sewage was less hygienic, for the drains of the garrison at Persepolis emptied into the street, and this was probably the case for most other buildings. It seems the Achaemenians paid little attention to their knowledge that flies carried disease from dirt.

Nowadays Persepolis is used for the Shiraz Festival, and the night I was there, a concert was attended by the Empress and élite. Dressed in jewels, bri-nylon, fur wraps, and cotton, the audience of several hundred streamed up the steps and along a tarpaulin carpet to the tiered benches, their way reddened by flames which surged from two cauldrons. The riff-raff, including myself, stood on the roadside, cheering and waving flags.

For the following year's festival, the British Council in Shiraz was organising an exhibition of Henry Moore sculpture. One of the teachers later told me of his visit to the cultural officer:

'I'm most grateful to you for giving me your time,' said the teacher.

'It is an honour,' replied the cultural officer.

'Well, to get to the point, I gather the Ministry in Tehran has agreed to help sponsor the Henry Moore exhibition for the festival.'

'Henry who?'

'Henry Moore, an English sculptor. I've brought some pictures of his work in this book by Thames & Hudson.'

'Aaah . . . Thames, yes, that great English river. But not as big as our Zayendeh Rud?'

'I don't know about that. Yes, I'm sure you're right. But about this Henry Moore exhibition.'

'More? More exhibitions? But we have no exhibitions.'

'But that's why I'm here. The Ministry in Tehran did say it was writing to you to say it was willing to help.'

'I have heard nothing.'

'Oh dear. But I assure you they're agreeable. You see, they have the exhibition in Tehran at the moment.'

'What exhibition? Who wants to show?'

'We do, I mean the British Council together with the Iranian Government . . . an exhibition by Henry Moore.'

'Henry who?' asked the cultural officer, and fingered the pages of the book with a beautifully manicured index finger.

The administrative success of the Achaemenians owed much to communications: roadways and staging posts filled the empire, including a 1500-mile highway from Susa to Sardis. It was covered in two weeks by mounted messenger, but when I returned to Shiraz, I could not match such speed, even with tarmac roads. And I was nearly defeated by the steepest hill, when I had to push Mephistopheles up. He was heavy and I kept stopping for breath and to wash out my mouth with water from my warm plastic bottle. The road was under construction and heavy machinery disturbed the earth into clouds of dust. I longed for a lorry to give me a lift, but the traffic was merciless in edging me into the bank and coating me with dirt. Finally I reached the top and free-wheeled down, gulping the fresh air. But I was disheartened, for if Mephistopheles could not manage this hill, he would certainly not take me into the mountains of the Qashqai tribe.

A few miles on, I saw a hut surrounded by pine trees, where some men were sitting languorously at a table scattered with empty glasses. I manoeuvred the bike between the trees, jumped over a channel of water and walked into the hut to see a man heaving lumps of meat out of a tall refrigerator. He turned, and his face dimpled with a smile.

'You want kebab?'

'Thank you, no, just tea.'

'You want yoghourt, or fruit?' He pointed to some grapes which were khaki in colour.

'Just tea, thank you.'

He put down the meat on the table and sighed.

'Always everyone asks just for tea. And what about this meat of mine, a prize sheep I killed especially for visitors like you?'

At that moment a child ran in, her face streaked with dirt and remnants of food. Reaching the table, she saw the meat and poked it with her fingers.

'Baba, is this the meat that man gave you for the paraffin?'

The man frowned at her.

'Well Mama says she knows the man had two sick sheep. Do you think this meat is sick too?'

The man ushered me out and told me to sit with the men. One of them pulled up a chair and with an oily rag wiped the crumb-scattered seat. Another offered me a cigarette, and asked:

'Have you come far on that?' And he jerked his thumb at Mephistopheles.

'Only from Persepolis.'

'Eeeh, you mean Takht-e-Jamshid?'

The palace is known as the throne of Jamshid, the legendary king whose spies, tradition says, used the subterranean tunnels. One of the tunnels led to a well so deep that an object thrown in would emerge in the sea three days later.

The man picked his wide nostrils with thumb and forefinger, then scratched the back of his neck. He was thickset, with short legs and heavy boots.

'I'm Mohammad,' he said and cracked each finger. 'This here is my friend, Hasan.'

Hasan's boniness showed through his clothes, and his cheekbones stuck out like knobs. Round his head was a strip of brown cloth, tied above his left ear. He saw me looking at it, so lifted the bandage. A three-inch gash ran across his forehead, its edges blackened with blood. I grimaced, shutting my eyes, and he burst into laughter.

'Holy prophets, this young man hates the sight of a wound.' And running his finger over the scab, he replaced the bandage.

'How on earth did you get it?' I asked.

'This Mohammad here. He was taking a corner and . . . yaaaah . . . he tried to send us to heaven.'

All the men laughed noisily, slapping their thighs, but Mohammad said indignantly:

'Curses on the devil, *you* can't get to Mecca. Why God made you a driver – He gave you no skill.'

'To Mecca indeed? I'd beat you any day. And I'd run this boy off his feet.' He looked at me mockingly.

'I'm afraid I don't know the way,' I said meekly.

'Oh I'll help you with that,' said Hasan, and looking at the sun, he pointed south-west. 'It's over there. Just keep going, and you'll soon arrive – maybe in six months on that bike?'

'And will you take me as a passenger?' scoffed Mohammad.

'No, I'm afraid you're too heavy.' And I added, casually, 'It only takes my wife.'

'Your wife?'

'Yes. And our child.'

Everyone looked at me with astonishment.

'But where are they?' asked Mohammad.

'I left them at home. I mean with this heat, what could I do with them?'

He nodded glumly. 'True, they'd only annoy you. But is she beautiful?'

'Like the moon. And she cooks like . . .' I closed my eyes and threw a kiss to the air.

'You have luck, my friend,' said Mohammad. 'But soon, at the rate I drive, *I'll* have enough money for the ripest fruit in Iran. Then I'll have fifteen children.'

An hour later, I emerged from the bare rust hills to see Shiraz laid out below me. A triumphal arch straddled the road in a complex of latticework and niches, and when I drove down, the town seemed spacious, light-hearted. The backdrop of mountains gave dimension, and destroyed the feeling of oppression, so frequent in desert towns where the sky is cut to a strip by high mud walls. Here, the houses were surrounded by cypress trees and large gardens; through open gateways I glimpsed balconies and flowers – not heavy, fleshy ones, but feathery, long-stemmed and many headed.

But as I explored the town, I felt, as I had done with Isfahan, that the reputation and image far exceeded the reality. Where were the roses and nightingales? True, there were cypress trees, but where was the wine, and the poetry of the place? Perhaps the wide tarmac roads, the hotel blocks, the huge new hospital, were now poetry to the Shirazis, but it was not my idea of Persian poetry.

So I paid my respects to the tombs of Hafiz and Sa'di,* two of Iran's most famous poets, both of whom came from Shiraz. The mausoleums sat in neat gardens, the buildings recently renovated for tourists and pilgrims. Kufic script screamed from coloured walls to convince those who could not read that the poet was illustrious. Men stood intoning the words from the walls, or reciting a passage by heart; women and children kissed the tomb, and ran their hands over the writing.

I sat on some steps in the garden of Hafiz' tomb and pulled out a book which contained some of his work.

When the wine sun fills the bowl of the East,
It brings to her cheeks a thousand anemones.
The wind breaks ringlets of hyacinth
Over the heads of the roses,
As among the meadows I inhale
The fragrance of her rich hair.
This does not express the night of separation,
For the fragments of her explanation
Would fill a hundred books.**

Now I was in Iran, I could understand this poetry more, the flamboyant addresses, the mystical undertones. For such imagery has been defended by a Persian Sufi author, so that wine may mean ecstatic experience with God; kisses, Godly rapture; beauty, the perfection of God. If this is so, then how magnificently Hafiz unites the sublime with the erotic without debasing either:

Her hair in disarray, lips laughing;
Drunk in the sweat of revelry
Singing of love, she came, flask in hand.

Dishevelled and her clothes rent
Last midnight by my bed she bent;
Her lips curved in regret.

I saw sorrow quarrel in her eyes
As her whispers spoke softly,
'Is our old love asleep?'

Given such a wine before dawn,
A lover is an infidel to love
If he does not drink.

Wine, the famous wine of Shiraz – I could not find it anywhere, and I thought how Jesus Christ would have laughed in Qum if he knew how the laws of Mohammad had thwarted me. Only before the invasion of Islam did a Chinese general remark on the Persians' love for wine, and their horses' love for lucerne. And so delighted was he that he took cuttings back to China.

Instead of wine I found lemon juice and syrup, in shops that replaced the normal *chai khane*. Each place I visited had a row of metal chairs, and every wall was lined with litre bottles of lemon juice. In one corner were crates of more bottles, where the proprietor, or his son, or his grandson, were sticking on the shop's label. Behind a partition were tumblers and syrups, murky yellow, vermilion, lime green.

Much of the lemon juice is produced in factories, but once I saw it made by hand. A brawny man, his legs wide apart clutching a small mesh-topped table, thundered down with a rolling pin on one small lemon to crush out its stomach; and as the juice dripped through the table, the deft hand of a boy snatched away the crumpled body and replaced it with a pregnant one.

There was a glut of fruit in Shiraz, and barrowfuls of melons lined the roads. The first pomegranates lay in piles beside seedless grapes; pears, apples, peaches and apricots grew mushy in the heat, to be picked over by stooping women. There was dried fruit, too – full-blown dates like horse-chestnut buds; figs, their shrivelled bodies threaded on string like a carved bead necklace; and other fruits, unidentifiable in their leathery non-shapes which were piled into sacks.

Fruit, white salted cheese, half a slab of unleavened bread, an oil rag, some cheap cigarettes, and my water-bottle, filled one side of my saddle-bag as I bumped south-east out of Shiraz one morning, heading for Firuzabad, the winter

*Sa'di died in 1292, Hafiz in 1390.

** Trs. R. M. Rehder. *Anthology of Islamic Literature* (ed. Kritzech), London 1967. First pub. Holt, Rinehart & Winston Inc., New York 1964.

headquarters of the Qashqai tribe. It was cool at that hour, six o'clock, and the jaded light of the street lamps was competing with the freshening sky. I had left my jersey in Tehran, forgetting that summer was turning to autumn, and I kept my arms together to ward off the wind. Small trucks and bicycles were already on the road, making their way to the orchards and outlying fields; and men were cutting corn, scything their way in rows down the yellow expanse. Much of the land was cultivated, but as I went further, the soil deteriorated and was strewn with rocks; the houses were fewer, the villages were scattered. It was the beginning of tribal country.

I came to a police road check, and they suggested I turn back. I continued, but the gradients grew until I was stopping frequently for rest. Then the road shrank to a dusty track and disappeared in contortions up the side of a mountain. I raced up the approach, kept the accelerator open, pedalled standing up, cursed my aching thighs, got off, pushed the bike, and finally sat down. I continued for an hour, with minimal progress, as the hill grew more aggressive, and the bike heavier. My body protested with cupfuls of sweat; my mouth worked the air like sandpaper. Red in the face from exertion, I dropped Mephistopheles on his side and slumped against a rock. With mortification I realised I would have to return to Shiraz. I sat for a few minutes and then, remounting the bike, I rattled back down the hill. I hardly noticed the oncoming lorry, which braked, spewed out its yelling occupants, ingurgitated five grinning men, one person sex unknown, one moped, and continued snorting on its way.

We jolted up, up through the mountains in a posse of dust and heat. Scrub bushes swam dizzily across the hillside, and an eagle circled against the ceiling of sky – only some tribesmen were needed to tomahawk their way through us. Or would this hurtling band of brigands take the opportunity first and remove my teeth for gold stoppings, gouge out my eyes to sell at market, strip me of my clothes and so find something else to use? I laughed manfully, slapped them on the back and breathed more freely as we tipped down towards the bottom of a shallow bowl where I hoped for the security of habitation. I was disappointed. There was no house nor human anywhere, only signs of the living in the cream area of stubble, crossed and recrossed by red dust tracks, where unaccompanied sheep made paths to nowhere. The unreality of the scene, focused by the encirclement of hills, was intense as the engine suddenly stopped. The men got out and beckoned me to follow.

'Oh Lord,' I thought, though with so many Muslims near me, He was unlikely to hear my prayer. 'Why should I get out?' I asked.

'Why, because we . . .' The explanation was lost in their gabble.

'No, thank you. I'm in a hurry to reach Firuzabad.' I tapped my watch.

They eyed it. 'How much is it?'

'It's very bad. Broken. I have very little.' I indicated my saddlebag. They saw my camera, a fat Nikkormat, bulging out of the top, and told me to come down.

'But I must reach Firuzabad this afternoon, soon, because . . .' My words were incoherent, for what reason does one have for arriving on time in a remote place where the hour is calculated by the sun and the stomach?

They told me again to get down, so I did. We stepped off the road and disappeared behind a large rock. Fear was hammering at my throat, and I felt like being sick. Then I noticed the men, rather than pulling out knives, were pulling down their trousers. They were going to urinate. But still I was in difficulty for I could not participate without revealing my sex. So, with a cry, I bent to the ground, picked up some pebbles and ran to the lorry, where I pretended to study them intently. The men's gaze followed my movements and then, shaking their heads, they turned idly back and completed their work.

My identity did not remain concealed once I reached Firuzabad, for the village supported a cumulation of gendarmes who made every unco-ordinated effort to check my passport, each time I left and returned to the village. Word soon spread that I was a girl and when I was in the streets, men cupped imaginary breasts and swayed their hips provocatively at me.

I reported at the gendarmerie for my documents to be examined. Within minutes, the place was crowded with officers comparing my physique with my passport photograph. A doctor was called, not as I expected to verify my sex but because he spoke English. He took me to his home, introducing me as a boy to his wife, and after lunch, he said:

'Sweet girl, shall we take our siesta in the next room? Don't be embarrassed, my wife suspects nothing. We can have beautiful hours together.'

I refused, and with a belch, he left the room to sleep by himself. His wife, Malake, brought tea, bowing as she gave it to me, and when I asked her to have some too, she sat on the carpet, tucking her feet under her short black skirt. She was plump, with full breasts and a protruding stomach which made her skirt wrinkle at her thighs; her black nylon shirt was unbuttoned at the neck. The room was hot so that her face glistened with perspiration and her oily skin looked sallow from lack of contact with fresh air; her eyes were small, the eyelashes coated with mascara; and the nose was flat, accentuating the darkness of her upper lip.

It was the first time I had been alone with a woman, indeed the first time I had dared to look in detail at one under fifty. But whether I was studying her as a boy or a girl I did not know, though I wondered if she made love well.

Malake picked up a box, opened it and handed it to me.

'Please, would you like a cigarette?'

'Thank you.' I took one and lit it. 'That was an excellent lunch you gave us. You cook very well.' I accepted quite easily her role as preparer of food.

She smiled. 'I'm glad. It's difficult to buy good food here, but we manage.'

'Do you like it here?'

She shrugged. 'It's remote. It's also difficult. Many of the women don't approve of me. They think I'm too free without the veil. And my husband doesn't let me mix with his friends, so really I see few people.'

She fetched a plate of sweets, placing them by me.

'Please, take some,' she said, and watched as I ate. 'You must eat more. You're thin. Don't you have a wife to cook for you?'

'Not yet,' I said. 'I like the freedom.'

'But my husband is free, even though he's got me. He's very clever, you know. He reads lots of books – he's making me learn English.'

She pulled from a shelf an illustrated textbook and read out slowly: '"Today it is raining, and I put on my mackintosh."' Then she gave me the book: 'My husband reads the hardest passages.'

I flicked through to see exercises on electricity and fox-hunting.

'Do you read?' she asked.

'Yes, a bit.'

'Philosophy? Medicine? You must be very clever. My husband says I'm very stupid. I know so little.'

She sat in silence, looking down at the carpet. Then I heard outside the beat of a drum and the noise of a crowd.

'What's happening?'

'I don't know.'

'Then let's go and see.'

We walked out of the house and crossed the street. A number of men had gathered in the dusty grounds of a school, to watch two men fighting and dancing in ritual. Armed with sticks, they tried to hit each other below the knee, making vibrant gestures to the noise of a drum and tin trumpet. Each time a hit was made, the vanquished left the field and another contestant took his place. After a few bouts, I was pushed into the circle of men and given a stick. My opponent was frightening, a tall, wiry man with muscular limbs and a supple body. But spurred on by the hand-clapping, and disregarding unsportingly the few rules I had noted, I managed to hit his thighs with a thwack. It was obvious he had let me do it, but the onlookers cheered enthusiastically, and making a deep bow, I walked off in glory with the doctor's wife on my arm. How easy, I thought, to have been a knight.

When we returned, the doctor was awake and Malake recounted my exploits. He laughed so uncontrollably that she questioned him.

'Why, you simpleton, this boy's a girl, and she's won in a game that only men play.'

Malake swung round to study me. 'Of course, that explains it.'

'Explains what?' I asked.

'Why you didn't move much during the fight. You were frightened of even lifting your arms. But come, sit down, and I'll make some tea.'

Later the doctor went to visit some patients. Malake moved herself closer to me and whispered confidentially, now that she knew I was a woman:

'You know, I've just had a miscarriage.'

'Oh, I'm sorry, it must have been terrible for you.'

'Yes, I was sad. I'm longing for children. It might bring my husband closer.' She brushed an invisible speck from her skirt. 'He's often away.'

'Can't you go with him?'

'Oh no, that's impossible, I must look after the house. Besides I don't know how much he wants me. Not even for children.'

'Don't worry, Malake,' I said, not knowing either. 'He probably just can't think of children yet. His work's preoccupying him, that's all.'

She smiled wryly. 'Well, I suppose you should know, Miss John.'

Mary Morris

(1947–)

In her three travel memoirs, *Nothing to Declare: Memoirs of a Woman Travelling Alone*, *Wall-to-Wall: From Beijing to Berlin by Rail*, and *Angels and Aliens* Mary Morris describes what she is thinking and finding – the 'inner journey' – as much as the details of the world around her. She feels compelled to relate these two kinds of experiences. When she realizes that she is going to have a child, Leningrad becomes more than just a city, it becomes a state of mind, and at the end of the selection from *Wall-to-Wall* she imagines a body within a body 'like those Russian dolls I carried with me as gifts.' Morris, the storyteller, travels to forge personal and social connections, not to acquire and catalogue experiences. In the best of her writing, she uncovers the mythopoetic and magical aspects of the land through which she is moving. Morris is also the author of five novels and three collections of short stories. She was born in Chicago and now lives in Brooklyn.

from **Wall-to-Wall**

It has been called the Venice of the North, the Second Paris, Babylon of the Snows, North Palmyra – the age-old romance with Asia Minor transformed into the frozen Russian North. To Peter the Great, it was his window on the West. It is a dreamer's dream, this city built on bones. It was of Leningrad that Pushkin wrote in his epic poem *The Bronze Horseman*, 'I love you, Peter's creation, I love your severe, graceful appearance, the transparent twilights and moonless gleam of your still night.' Yet it is also of Leningrad that Mandelstam, awaiting the security police who would take him to his exile and death, wrote in a poem named after the city he so loved, 'I returned to my city, familiar as tears . . . Petersburg! I have no wish to die . . . I still possess a list of addresses . . . I stay up all night, expecting dear guests.'

Like a once great but troubled starlet, Leningrad has led a tormented past. For its beauty it has paid a high price. Its light possesses a dark side. Tens of thousands died building this city under Peter's relentless command. A million and a half died trying to defend it during the nine hundred days of its siege in World War II. To the Romanovs it was the capital of the world, the seat of their absolute power. To Lenin it was a sweatshop, ready for agitation and revolution. To Stalin in his paranoia, because it was the birthplace of the 1917 Revolution he feared the city might rise up against him. He consolidated the seat of his power more firmly in Moscow. Some feel that when he knew the Nazis were planning an assault on Leningrad, he turned his back.

If it was Moscow's fate to confront Napoleon, it was Leningrad's to face Hitler. If it was Moscow's fate to burn, it was Leningrad's to starve. Neither city was conquered and both in their own way marked the defeat of the aggressor – in part because the opposing armies could not withstand the Russian winter. Yet Leningrad suffered almost beyond belief in World War II. The packing crates of the Hermitage Museum were used as coffins; children's sleds transported the sick, the dead. When the shellings ceased, the blockade was lifted, and the starvation of half its population over, the renovation began. Its power depleted, Leningrad became a living museum.

But for me, its potency remained. As the taxi hurtled along Nevsky Prospect en route to my hotel, I was immediately captured, taken in. Perhaps it was the shock of arriving at eleven o'clock at night and finding broad daylight, for it was White Nights – that time of year in the North when, because of the angle of the earth's axis, the sun never dips very far below the horizon. Perhaps it was the whirl of colours – the buildings of green and blue, pink and creamy white that darted by. Or the austerity of its imperial structures bathed in Northern light and reflected in the waters of the canals. Cold, expansive, indifferent. Leningrad, St. Petersburg, Petrograd, Sankt Piterburkh, or just Piter – Peter, as its denizens like to call it – casts a spell that won't go.

In this city of madmen and poets, its grip was visceral. I myself would not have trouble in the trade-off between beauty and bureaucracy, but Leningrad once had it all – the power, the glory, the exquisite looks. Now only the façade remains, though as splendid as any I'd ever seen; there was a poignancy about this city which perhaps reflected my own state of mind, a sadness I would be hard-pressed to name.

The lobby of my hotel was filled with the most beautiful women I have ever seen, dozens of them who seemed to have sprouted spontaneously out of the city itself. Women dressed in silk of shiny mint and pale gray, electric blue and soft violet. Women in shoulder pads and spiked heels with exotic tresses of spun flax or the darkest Mediterranean shade. Women who seemed to have materialized out of the pages of *Vogue*.

These were the women of Leningrad who emerged from their stale desk jobs or secretary pools every Friday night to service the Finnish men – often fat and jowly, with coarse ways and wads of money – who arrived like clockwork for the weekends. These modern-day Cinderellas transformed themselves into the beauties that they were. My hotel lobby appeared to be the ideal spot for this salient example of free enterprise which was taking place before my eyes.

I checked into the hotel, my room a quaint study of lace curtains and dark wood, a four-poster canopy bed tucked into an alcove. But I felt restless so I walked outside. I wanted to have a drink and be among people. There was a bar next door so I went in.

The bar was also filled with these same women who sat like mannequins, lips perfectly glossed, eyelashes thick as horse hair, curled to perfection, cheeks with just the right blush. They reminded me of actresses, when the call went out for a certain type, wearily awaiting their audition. Their dead eyes gazed at me as I entered their midst dressed in jeans, a bulky shirt. I thought about turning back, but it became a matter of pride. Instead I traversed the obstacle course set up by their legs which stretched across the room.

The reality of my pregnancy had not yet truly sunk in, so I ordered a drink. Vodka. After a few moments, a Finnish man sat down at my table and spoke to me in Russian. I glanced at my blue jeans, my bulky shirt. I felt the eyes in the room turn on me with icy stares. 'I'm American,' I said, wondering what had prompted him to select me out of all the possibilities in the room. 'Oh, I thought you looked different, but I could use a little company that's different. These women, they're all lonely. You know what they want more than anything else, they want to talk.'

'I can identify with that,' I said.

'What're you doing in this place?'

'I wanted a drink,' I said, 'I wanted to get out.'

'It can be taken wrong,' he muttered. He was stout with thinning yellow hair. He wore a wedding ring.

'Are you here on business?'

He laughed, 'Well, my wife thinks I am. A couple times a year I get over here, but,' his hand swept the vapid faces of women, 'it's getting a little tedious.' He was a rather jovial if crass man. 'But my wife, well, you know how it is. . . .'

Actually I didn't know and wanted to ask him more, but he took another line of discussion. 'Let me tell you something,' he spoke in a fatherly way. 'You've got to be careful here. Oh, no one will hurt you, it's not like that, but in this city people will buy anything. They'll buy your jeans,' he plucked at my leg. 'Your shirts, your jewelry, but mainly they want dollars, so be careful with your money. But you can trade anything you've got. Sunglasses, lipstick,' He slapped me on the leg, 'Anything.' I was enjoying his company and was sorry when he got up to leave, though clearly he did not just want to talk.

When he was gone, I looked around and saw that except for the bartender the room was filled with women. I was hungry to talk to a woman. I looked across for sympathetic eyes and found none. Just blank stares and suspicious looks. They must have been having a slow night, or business was generally bad. Whatever it was, they wanted to know what I was doing there, intruding upon their terrain. I sat nursing my vodka, staring into its cold glass.

At two in the morning I emerged from the bar into broad daylight. Knowing I would be unable to sleep and with a long, sunny night ahead, I decided to go for a walk. I wandered to the small square near my hotel across from the Russian Museum and found myself before the statue of Pushkin. This was his city and he was their poet, the father of Russian

'I walked until I stood on the cobbles of Palace Square before the astonishing Winter Palace. With hundreds of rooms, its blue-and-white façade shimmered like ice.'

literature. Descended from an Abyssinian prince named Hannibal, Pushkin was (and remains) Russia's most beloved writer. A free spirit, he lived intensely, gambled compulsively, and died in a duel with a man with whom his wife was probably in love, leaving generations of Russians to mourn. For two days after he was shot Pushkin lingered, his wounds turning gangrenous. After his death, the ordinary people of Russia filed past, dumbstruck at the premature death of their beloved poet.

As I sat beneath his statue, a disciple myself, the sun shone still bright and the wisteria were in bloom. I breathed in the nectar of lilacs. The air, fresh off the Gulf of Finland, was redolent with the smell of jasmine. Sweetness was everywhere. The park was not empty, nor were the streets as the citizens of Leningrad ambled as they would for two more weeks of White Nights, aimless and confused as a disoriented migrating herd.

With no map, I set off thinking I'd make a loop, then return along the wide boulevard of Nevsky Prospect in the direction of the river. But it was not long before I left the main street and was wandering down a side street lined with canals, across a footbridge crowned with gold-winged griffins, running my hands along the wrought iron, delicately webbed.

The buildings of imperial Russia loomed before me, painted in their shades of blue like robin's eggs, the pink of Norwegian salmon, the soft yellow of cut wheat, the white of fresh cream, all reflected in the brownish-green waters of the canals. I cut through other side streets, crossed other bridges, passing lime-green houses, others painted a muted red. Though I kept thinking I would turn back, I found I could not, for the colours and the night and the air kept me moving along.

I walked until I stood on the cobbles of Palace Square before the astonishing Winter Palace. With hundreds of rooms, its blue-and-white façade shimmered like ice. It was here on January 9, 1905, that Father Gapon led thousands of peaceful demonstrators to petition the Czar for help for their hardships and where they were met – men, women, children – with the gunfire of the imperial guards. Bloody Sunday, as the massacre came to be called, touched off the Revolution of 1905, and now in the middle of my first night in Leningrad

I stared into its vastness and imagined the slaughter that had occurred, the dark side of all this beauty slowly revealed.

Continuing on, I reached the Neva where I paused before its wide, turbulent, exquisitely blue surface, and the stately, palatial buildings that lined its banks. Frozen solid for six months of the year, the Neva now flowed into the Gulf of Finland with a force that astounded. Along its banks in this strange, late-night splendour, I admired the handiwork of the architects and landscape architects Peter had commissioned from abroad – Trezzini, LeBlond.

I hugged the banks. Small fishing boats floated by. A barge in no hurry meandered past. Two lovers in light jackets sat on an old boat ramp, kissing with abandon as the river lapped at their feet. Gulls hovered overhead, then dived at their feet for crumbs they tossed them. It was here on the shores of this river that Russian literature came to be. All Russian writers, the saying goes, 'came out of Gogol's "Over-coat".' In Gogol's story that coat was ripped off a poor civil servant on the streets of Petersburg at the beginning of the nineteenth century. But it was Pushkin who immortalized the city he loved in his epic 'The Bronze Horseman.' Like the American frontier to the pioneers, Leningrad to the Russians was their window on the West. Their place to imagine, to dream, and perceive other worlds.

Now I found myself standing before that statue from which the great Russian epic draws its name, with Peter astride his rearing horse, symbol of Russia itself, trampling a serpent representing the forces that tried to oppose his reforms. Peter, to cite Pushkin again, 'by whose fateful will the city was founded by the sea, stands here aloft at the very brink of a precipice having reared up Russia with his iron curb.' I read the inscription, 'To Peter the First from Catherine the Second 1782' and stood for a long time peering at the rising hooves of Peter's horse which I felt could easily trample me if it desired.

Then I turned back into the maze of winding side streets. I made my way along the murky canals, across arching bridges, down the narrow alleyways. I told myself I should go back to the hotel and sleep, but I was being sucked in, amazed at how easily I'd fallen into step with this city and its inhabitants. Like a Dostoyevskian hero, for this was his city as well, my emotions wound inside of me, a snail into itself, and I seemed to carry it all within, winding deeper and deeper, dragging it about.

I was like one obsessed, overcome, a fly in the radiant web. This was no linear, socially acceptably Tolstoyian world. There were no manners, no courtesies, no proprieties here. This seemed more like a city with a kind of perverse passion, a beautiful woman entrapped in vanity, the architectural equivalent of Narcissus: Leningrad staring at itself in its own canals, its beauty coming back to it over and over again.

I wandered its streets as one does through a museum, silently, with reverence. Or as you might after committing a crime, with stealth, yet feeling contemplative, planning your next move, your place to hide. I could imagine, as Pushkin had, the statue of Peter coming to life and stalking men along the ancient cobbles of this city. I walked as Raskolnikov might, plagued with guilt, or fearing you were about to meet your double – distracted, caught in your own thoughts. I saw how this could be a city to withstand a siege of nine hundred days, how it could withstand wars and progress and urban sprawl. It could just turn in on itself. It seemed I had walked into a Russian fairy tale and I could play any part – criminal, prostitute, destitute mother, coy mistress, woman alone – but not in some funky cardboard tourist attraction such as I'd done at the Ming tombs. This was all too real.

I have no idea how I came back to my hotel, but hours later I found myself there at about 6 A.M., the sun still in the place where it was when I left, but I was now exhausted, spent. The desk clerk gave me a perfunctory nod that was not without a sneer, for what was I doing out on those canals at this hour? A gloomy hooker, shoes off, slumped in a chair, did not move her legs as I made my way to the elevator and I had to step over her.

I crept into my room, bones aching, and pulled down the shade. The light from the day which would not end filtered in. Then I made my way through the velvet curtains that led to the small sleeping alcove. The bed was of dark wood, with a white lace canopy. Beside the bed was a small bedstand with a light, but I didn't even think to turn it on. Instead, I lay down for the first time on my narrow bed and pulled the canopy around it.

I lay in the small alcove, in the small room, and on that narrow bed enclosed in lace, I felt the small body contained within my own. We lay there together for the first time, one inside the other, inside the bed, inside the alcove, the room, like those Russian dolls I carried with me as gifts, each one smaller and smaller, tucked inside the other.

Christina Dodwell

(1951–)

An uncommonly zealous adventurer and battler of 'tick-bick fever' and rabid jackals, Christina Dodwell is a modern-day Mary Kingsley: despite the hardships she endures one can visualize a smile curving the corners of her mouth. The English travel writer was twenty-four years old in 1975 when she answered an advertisement in a magazine and set off with three others to cross Africa in a Landrover. That began a three-year African journey. Part of it she spent accompanied by Lesley, a New Zealand nurse, alongside whom she suffered relentless mosquito attacks; part of her adventure she faced alone. In addition to *Travels with Fortune* she has written four other travel books about journeys in such far-flung places as China and Papua New Guinea, and an intrepid traveller's guide called *The Explorer's Handbook*, which recounts 'tested exits from tight corners.' When not on the road she lives in West London.

from Travels with Fortune: An African Adventure

I woke up. It was 7 A.M., 4 August – the Great Day had arrived. Lesley and I drank beer with a huge breakfast, put our luggage in the car, filled the storage jar with fresh water, and went down to the dugout.

It certainly was a funny looking craft, but the patched holes hadn't leaked overnight and the inside was dry. The dugout was twenty-five feet (including the pointed ends) by one foot six inches. The sundeck at the stern, which hid the polystyrene buoyancy packing, was five feet long and raised several inches above the curved floor of the dugout. An old iron bar which was attached to the wood plank rudder extended from the point of the stern to the back of the sundeck. The tin trunk fitted neatly lengthwise in a less crooked part of the front end; we put the ropes and the anchor at the point of the prow and there was plenty of space in the middle for the water jar and our rucksacks. We didn't dare admit that we had no idea how to paddle.

All the American team came to see us off. A bottle of champagne and glasses appeared, and we used the dregs to christen the dugout *La Pirogue*, meaning dugout in French. Champagne finished, farewells said, we picked up our short spear-shaped paddles, hopped aboard, waved frantically, and we were off. Although it was the middle of the rainy season, the morning was sunny and the river was calm. Lesley, acting as lookout and chief paddler, was up front perched on the old tin trunk. I was perfectly happy to find myself at the back, and was therefore in charge of the tiller, navigation, and a paddle. I sat on the sundeck with my legs outstretched; the dugout was just wide enough to fit into comfortably, and it rode so low in the water that its rim was only eight inches above the surface of the river.

Bangui disappeared from sight. Now we were on our own and I felt an overwhelming sense of freedom. There was no going back, even if we wanted to we couldn't paddle upstream against the strong current. We had left the security of Bangui and were now out in the big African world of giant trees with roots gone crazy and pale trunks against the black depths of the rain forest.

At this point the river was about a mile wide, with occasional long islands covered in forest but sandy at the ends. We paddled slowly past a fishing village set in a large clearing where men were repairing their nets and women were pounding corn outside their thatched huts. Everyone shouted greetings in French and a man in a dugout paddled over to throw some fish to us. The fish landed on the sundeck. I had considerable difficulty in holding the squirming wet fish while keeping a smiling face. I put them down by my feet and they lay still.

Suddenly ten minutes later one leapt flapping onto my legs. I yelled and jumped, the dugout skewed sideways, hit a half-submerged tree, and Lesley fell off the tin trunk into the river. The dugout straightened up and sailed merrily on as I shouted, 'Stop, stop.' I pointed the front towards the river bank, but it went even faster downstream and no closer to the shore. I paddled desperately towards a bush which grew over the river, grabbed some branches and hung on grimly. They were full of red ants which ran down onto my hands and arms and bit me furiously. Lesley swam alongside, hauled herself aboard and I let go. We shot forwards and found ourselves hopelessly entangled in some reeds along the bank. It was going to be a long way to Brazzaville.

Keeping close to the shore was fraught with problems; the currents constantly pushed us around and we got caught in all the eddying pools with little power to choose our direction. We invariably ended up in the reeds. Many trees had fallen out across the water where the river had undermined the banks, and trying to dodge their sturdy far-reaching branches made me feel as though we were on an obstacle course.

By noon our muscles were aching and we were very hungry so we decided to stop and cook the fish. The shores were densely overgrown so we aimed for the sandy tip of an island. We paddled hard, but the river was stronger and we missed the island completely. Spurred on by our hunger we paddled more fiercely towards the next, but hit the shore at an angle and shipped a lot of water. While Lesley bailed it out I went to gather wood and started the fire. Two branches balanced on forked sticks made a good grill for roasting the fish. We ate a loaf of bread and four fish, which looked like perch, were very filling and tasty, but rather full of sand. Having eaten, we rested in the shade until a long black snake slid past us and into the river, swimming with its head above the water and a rat in its mouth. It was time to move on.

We spent the afternoon mid river, where the current was much stronger, though the only danger seemed to be from the clumps of water hyacinth which came spinning downstream. They wound themselves round the rudder making steering impossible. Legend said that the hyacinth was introduced at the source of the Congo by a Belgian missionary's wife who thought it was such a pretty flower. It was also the fastest spreading weed in the world, and could not be destroyed or used. It grew and multiplied on the surface of the water, with hairy roots, strange bulbous stems, attractive diamond-shaped leaves and delightful purple flowers. I picked some of the flowers and arranged them in my bailing can.

As clumps of hyacinth went past us, we had the impression we were going backwards. Lesley's clock had been soaked in one of the morning's accidents – it stopped working and we moved into a state of timelessness (I had sold my watch in Kano). When it was nearly sunset we found a parking space between overhanging trees alongside a low cliff of sand.

With blissful ignorance we set up camp, rigging our mosquito nets over the old tent poles in the central section of the dugout which was long enough for both of us to lie in comfortably. I lay down contentedly to listen to the night noises, but the only sound was a strange, loud humming, like mosquitoes. The noise was so loud that Lesley and I had to shout to make ourselves heard. I found some mosquitoes inside my net, and some more, so I assumed the net must be torn. I sat up and started looking for the tear, but couldn't find it. I looked again, but there were more and more mosquitoes inside. Then I realised what was happening, and I stared with fascination and horror.

The outside of the net was thickly coated in small mosquitoes, small enough to simply fold back their wings and crawl through the netting. Within five minutes I counted over three hundred mosquitoes in my net, and the number kept growing. They bit viciously and repeatedly, even stinging through a layer of cloth, so I threw on more coverings, until they couldn't bite that deep. I didn't dare move a muscle in case the padding slipped. It was a hot equatorial night and I became slimy with sweat. There was not a breath of wind and inside the dugout the air was still and close. Underneath all my coverings I felt claustrophobic. I wanted to scream and scream and scream. The high pitched howling of the mosquitoes made me feel twisted with loathing; my stomach felt knotted; and my fists were clenched tight. I pleaded with the night to end quickly while the sweat continued to pour off me until my bedding was soaked. I wrapped a towel around my head and face, leaving only a tiny slit for breathing. The mosquitoes crept through the crack aud stung my nose, lips, tongue and all round the inside of my mouth. In exhaustion I dozed off, but I woke up choking with my head under water. A torrential rainstorm. 'Lesley,' I yelled. She leapt up sleepily, overbalanced, fell in the river and was swirled away. The cliff

of sand beside our parking space became waterlogged and collapsed forwards onto the dugout, which started to sink. I sat down, put my head in my hands, and began to laugh.

Lesley somehow reappeared, and in the dark we bailed out the sand and water while the mosquitoes feasted on us. All our clothes, everything we had was wringing wet. The night seemed interminable. We huddled silently together wrapped in a sodden sleeping bag, shivering, constantly looking up to the sky for any sign that the night was ending, and praying that dawn would come soon.

The sky lightened, and the blood red sun rose slowly above the forest horizon. The horror of the night faded quickly in the beauty of the day. The howling mosquitoes had gone. We heard instead the cries of monkeys, the splash of pied kingfishers diving for fish, and the whirring wings of flocks of red and grey parrots flying overhead.

Our reverie was interrupted as a cross current flung the dugout head first into the reeds. We pushed through them to the bank, it was a good opportunity to stop, find dry firewood, make coffee, and rummage in the tin trunk for the nivaquine pills. Over the past month we had been taking one pill every day, but because there were so many mosquitoes we doubled the dose to two pills daily. At the bottom of the tin trunk we found a lovely surprise. It was a bottle of whisky which the Americans had hidden there and marked: 'For use on rainy days.' Next we re-erected the tent poles, strung a washing line from the front to the back of the dugout, and hung all our clothes and gear out to dry while we floated on down the middle of the river. We passed some local fishermen in a dugout. When they caught sight of us they stood up, their mouths hanging open and their eyes bulging. I suppose we must have made a strange picture: to them it would look like nothing on earth, to me we looked rather like a floating Chinese laundry.

Our day was heaven. It was peaceful drifting along in the gentle current, and every now and then when I had nothing better to do I would paddle lazily, listening to the riot of jungle noises, and watching clouds of large yellow and black butterflies against a sunny blue sky.

At dusk we moored *La Pirogue* to a fallen tree. It was another horrific night of mosquitoes and the darkness rang with their evil blood-frenzied song. This time I didn't use thick coverings, I climbed into my sleeping bag, but the sweat bath was just as bad and somehow the mosquitoes found a way inside the sleeping bag. I screamed a long anguished howl. Lesley didn't go to sleep; she sat up inside her mosquito net and used the torch to spot the mosquitoes, clapping her hands on five or six at a time and announcing the death toll in a monotonous voice all night long, while far away we could hear pounding drums of people celebrating in the forest. We opened the whisky bottle but took only a small drink, knowing that there would be many more nights when we would need it again.

As the sun rose we floated off downriver. Dawn in an iridescent world, hushed as the inner wall of a shell. Mist floating suspended in a never-ending sky, vulnerable as all beautiful things. The water was like glass; purple flowering hyacinth cast reflections as true as life; we drifted silently; it was not for us to disturb the tranquillity. The wide flat river went snaking through dense tangled mighty forest; trees tall and majestic, roped together with knotted vines, strung with white flowering creeper; branches hung shaggy with green trailing lichen, and enshrouded in cobweb; straight trees with pale luminous pinky-yellow bark, short squat trees with leaves like fans, or feathers; trees with leaves the size of umbrellas; gnarled old and crooked trees; immense trees 100 feet tall with roots like the fins of rocket ships; impenetrable dark undergrowth; monkeys fighting and thunder rumbling; parrots and hornbills flying overhead; hot and sultry sun; the smell of sweating earth in the forest, and the perfume of flowers hanging heavily in the air.

I caught sight of a movement on the water; it was a dugout going across the river to an island where there was a group of six small round huts. The dugout was paddled by a woman returning from her vegetable garden; she came over to look at us, steering close alongside. She sold us twenty maize cobs and a branch of plantain bananas for 50 CFA (11p), although what she really wanted in exchange was *La Pirogue*'s rudder.

I really enjoyed being helmsman and learning how to handle our dugout. There was a variety of factors which affected our course and every change in each small element altered our direction. I had to take into account the river currents, the breeze, what clothes were hanging up to dry, which side Lesley was paddling, and how strongly we were paddling. When we both paddled powerfully the dugout responded far more quickly to the rudder and was much easier to control. The kink in the middle of *La Pirogue* meant that it always looked as if it were moving crabwise. Navigation was no problem; we either aimed for the furthest river horizon between the islands, or else we chose a particularly beautiful water hyacinth and followed wherever it went.

We reached the junction of three countries, Central African Republic and Congo on our right, and Zaire on our left. It was about noon so we stopped on an island, made fire, roasted some corn and plantain, and finished off the fish from the previous day. We dug under the trees looking for worms to bait our fishing lines. Our tackle was rather primitive, just hooks tied onto nylon thread and wound round bits of wood, but then our fishing wasn't very skilful either. Generally I just dropped the hooks overboard and looped the lines through my toes.

Lesley fell asleep in the sand, she hadn't slept at all the previous night, and I went off to chase big colourful butterflies. A swarm of flies appeared which didn't bite but tried to crawl into my ears, eyes, nose and mouth. They had also besieged Lesley, so we jumped into the dugout and fled. One island that we paddled past produced an echo, and we started clapping, tapping and drumming on the sides of the dugout, the rhythm resounding back and forth punctuated by the screeches of the monkeys and the haunting song of the hornbills which sounded like the ringing of a crystal wine glass when you run a damp finger fast round its rim. Our melody ended with the hiss of rain which swept upriver, made the water bubble and drenched us. We tried to take shelter under the tarpaulin, but it was full of holes and totally porous.

As the day drew to a close I started thinking about the night ahead and I shuddered with fear. The dugout was too wet to sleep in, the river banks were sheer clay cliffs topped by thick forest, there was nowhere to stop, and we hadn't seen any villages or huts since early morning. We kept moving, hoping to find a stopping place; sunset became twilight, and the night arrived, but we still hadn't found anywhere, and then it was too dark to see. We knew that if we went along near to the shore the current would push us onto rocks and half-submerged trees, so we pulled further out into the river. In the dim moonlight and with the aid of our torch we could just make out the line of the cliffs; the torch batteries were failing, so we put in new batteries, but they didn't work. Obviously we weren't going to be able to spot a camping place. A couple of miles later Lesley called out that she had seen distant flickering light and our hopes soared: the flickers of light turned out to be moonlight glinting on waves, white waves; soon we could hear the roaring noise of fast-rushing water, though we couldn't see what was happening. Time stood still, and we kept moving.

The noise grew louder, and my eyes ached from straining to see in the darkness. The river became choppy, then it was churning and foaming, as we both paddled desperately; the dugout veered to the left and began to swing round; I pushed the tiller out against the current, a wave flooded in over my legs, the dugout responded, and we slid into calm water. Whatever it was back there, we had missed it. I was terrified.

It started to rain, and the miles stretched on. Then we heard voices, real voices, somewhere on the Congo shore ahead of us. We shouted to them, 'Help, help, please get us off this river,' and we kept yelling until we were hoarse. Lamps appeared, and we were guided to the bank by the light. We tied the dugout to a tree, staggered up the rough clay steps hewn in the cliff, and into a small clearing with a *campement* of three huts. Five people wearing grass skirts stood in the lamplight staring at us in astonishment. We shook hands with them all and when we smiled they beamed back at us with their old and wrinkled faces.

The language of the river tribes was Likouala. It was a harsh-sounding tongue but easy to understand from tones and expressions, and some of the words were derived from French. Many of the local fishing folk we had met spoke simple French, but here they only spoke Likouala.

'What are they?' one asked.

An old woman replied something to the effect of, 'I think they are girls.' Whatever it was she had said, the other disagreed and they took us to the fire to observe us more closely. We sat down by the fire. Since we couldn't converse with them in French we drew some pictures instead. They were delighted with the pictures and put them proudly in their huts. They gave us supper of highly peppered fish, which was so hot that I felt as though I was breathing flames. We slept on mats on the floor; more rain cooled the night, but the mosquitoes still tormented us.

A sore-throated rooster woke us at dawn. We thanked the people for their kindness and as we clambered into our dugout we found that they had put a pile of fish and cassava there as a present to us.

We drifted and paddled leisurely onwards, ran up against a submerged sandbank, climbed out and pushed, glided on, then hit another sandbank, climbed out and pushed again, but every inch only wedged the dugout tighter and higher on the sand. Soon it was stuck firm. The water was only a few inches deep. We pushed and pulled and dug away the sand from underneath, but got nowhere. A strong fisherman paddled up, gave our dugout a hearty shove, refloated it, and handed us another fish.

In a short time, we were out of the sandbanks and onto a fast straight stretch of river. We raced along feeling elated with the wind blowing through our hair as we sped the paddles in short rapid strokes through the water. We zigzagged among the clumps of hyacinth which floated spinning lazily in the swirling movement of the current. Then the surface of the river suddenly erupted and we shot head-on into the bank. The surface of the river could change abruptly; one moment the water would be flowing strongly but placidly, and the next instant it became a raging, bubbling mass of wide circles which spun with uplifted edges. I presumed that they must have been caused by the powerful underwater currents hitting rocks or shoals on the riverbed, and as the current veered to a specific angle, so the surface erupted in turmoil. The local people called them whirlpools. Many were permanent whirlpools, like the ones round every headland, some were small and weak, others were very large and very strong. Being caught in them produced a feeling similar to driving a car on ice; suddenly you were out of control, skidding and sliding weightlessly.

To begin with we were not very good at managing the dugout; we spent a lot of time hurtling downriver broadside or backwards, both shouting instructions to each other that neither could hear. We were growing expert at spreading out our soaked belongings to dry in the sun. The tarpaulin was constantly wet because it lay in the bottom of the dugout, and as soon as we dried it, something unfortunate would happen. Accidents such as once when Lesley was carrying the freshly dried tarpaulin down to *La Pirogue*, which had moved out slightly from the shore. Lesley took two paces in ankle deep water, and at the third step she fell up to her neck in the river. The tarpaulin was soaked again, and we laughed until we cried.

Nights were less horrifying after Lesley suggested that we try sleeping on the shore in the breeze and not too close to the water's edge. The first night we tried that we found a riverside glade on the Zaire bank and made camp there. Within half an hour three men arrived in a dugout, and one, who claimed he was a member of the militia, came ashore. He wanted to see our papers and examine our boat. We were rather anxious because we didn't have visas for Zaire, but we needn't have worried – he didn't know how to read. After looking intently at the pictures he turned to *La Pirogue*, started pulling all our gear out of the tin trunk and ordered us to tell him what it was for. We knew from experience that if we explained the items then every time he saw something he fancied he would demand it. So we offered him coffee and sat chatting with him instead. He was very pleasant and he left after dark. We dug the tent poles into the ground, draped our mosquito nets over them, and settled down to sleep. The mosquitoes invaded us but it was not as bad as before. Then it started to rain so we got up to pull the tarpaulin over the dugout. The rain was followed by the noise of monkeys fighting, squealing in anger and throwing nuts at each other which landed on us. Finally, there was peace and quiet, except for the eerie howling of a wildcat hunting nearby in the forest.

In the middle of the night the militia man returned. This time it was a social call – he had brought a huge smoked catfish to eat as a midnight feast. It was delicious, but the man showed no signs of going away. I had an inspiration. I started to scratch. I scratched my arms and legs and head as though I was thick with fleas; Lesley joined in. It had a potent psychological effect and after five minutes the militia man bade us goodnight.

Our second visit to Zaire was more fun. We stopped at a village to refill our giant water container which was almost empty and we found that the local water supply was of course the river. The river was a muddy brown colour from the rains which were falling here and to the north, but if the villagers could drink it then so could we. A huge crowd had gathered round us the moment we stepped ashore, the atmosphere was friendly, but they stared and stared. The bolder ones spoke to us in simple French and asked if they could touch our hair, exclaiming with wonder at its softness. Others peered curiously at the colour of our skin, assuming that the whiteness was due to a disease. Several people wanted to know if we were girls. Then they brought out two stools, sat us down, and stared at us for a long time. I was equally curious about them. Most of the people wore grass skirts, and I noticed some remarkable tribal brands, including many narrowly-spaced parallel lines which gave their faces a weird stripey look. At first I felt embarrassed about wanting to stare

'The surface of the river could change abruptly; one moment the water would be flowing strongly but placidly, and the next instant it became a raging, bubbling mass of wide circles...'

at Africans, I had always considered it impolite. But in Africa it is not rude to stare and by tradition a newcomer was usually expected to sit or squat while he was scrutinised for half an hour. When the people were satisfied having looked at his appearance, they would formally demand to know his tribe and destination.

'What tribe are you?' asked a big man standing at the front.

'English,' I answered.

'Where are you going?'

'To Brazzaville.'

A murmur ran through the crowd, and the big man who was obviously their chief observed (in all seriousness) that we would not reach Brazzaville before nightfall, so we had better stay the night in his village.

They were gregarious affable people; they wanted to know about the countries we came from and why we were paddling down the river. Lesley noticed a young girl with some infected sores on her arms and asked if she could help her. Our medical kit consisted only of aspirin, nivaquine and a tube of antibiotic cream, but Lesley couldn't bear to see untreated injuries or people in pain. The girl took us to her parents' hut where we boiled some water and someone brought a piece of cloth to tear into bandages. Then someone else came and requested Lesley to go and look at his sick father, and several people turned up who seemed to have malaria, so Lesley dispensed some nivaquine to them. Quinine was the only cure for malaria; I was surprised to learn that quinine trees did not grow in Africa. For white people malaria could be a killer, but it seemed that the Africans had adapted to some extent and only suffered from a mild form of it.

A tiny man whose chin only reached to the height of my waist asked in gestures for Lesley to come and attend to someone who had been wounded by an elephant. It was quite a long walk, inland from the river on a small path through the forest which was very overgrown with vines and creeper that wrapped itself round our necks and ankles. Every plant had thorns. Many of the trees had claws like large rose bushes which grew all over their trunks and branches. Other trees had spikes; the vines had thorns, the bushes had barbed prickles, the undergrowth was a tangle of brambles, briars and thistles. The little pygmy man slipped through the forest as though it was silk, but Lesley and I got lassoed, tripped up, and clawed by every plant we passed.

He took us to a pygmy village where huts were simple grass shelters in contrast to the mud and thatch of those of the river tribes. Pygmies seemed to live a hunter-gatherer style of existence, moving from place to place in search of a fresh supply of food. Six pygmies were standing beside one of the shelters, the tallest of them was about four feet high. They weren't dwarfs – but they looked like miniature people. They were wearing loin cloths and a couple had quivers of arrows slung over their shoulders, but all six of them vanished off among the trees when they saw us.

The man who had been hit by the elephant was lying in the shelter; he had a deep gash in one leg, but Lesley said it wasn't serious. He watched her every move as she cleaned and bandaged the wound, and when she finished he smiled and chanted a sing song speech. The forest was quiet. No one was going to return to the settlement while we were there, and since it was probably getting late we hurried back to the river village. The chief welcomed us back, and sat us on stools outside his hut. The crowd gathered to watch what we did. I felt like an animal on display and wished that I could perform tricks for them. My only trick was to fill and smoke my pipe, which startled them as effectively as if I had done a series of cartwheels.

During a supper of hot peppered fish and spinach, I asked the chief about the pygmy tribe. He told me they seldom came to the river (none of the pygmies were river people) and they never inter-married with other tribes. Other tribes considered the pygmies equivalent to animals. He added that we would see a few more of them in the morning because it was market day and they would bring dried antelope to trade in the village. Lesley and I shared a wooden bedstead in our hut; it wasn't sprung but the mattress was made of bundles of rushes and was very comfortable.

The morning market was a good time for us to stock up our food supplies which had dwindled to half a loaf of bread, jam and three maize cobs. It was not a busy market – it was more a village social gathering. We walked around chatting to people as we tried to decide what to buy. There was no need to buy anything because all the villagers came up to say thank you to Lesley for helping their sick families, and they gave us presents of plantain and sweet bananas, maize, smoked fish, cassava and pawpaw in such quantity that the centre section of the dugout was too full for us to move from front to back unless we balanced on all fours and clambered along the rim of the sides. We shook hands with everyone and just as we were casting off the little pygmy man came running down to give us a chunk of antelope. Then we set off and the people lined the bank to wave goodbye.

I enjoyed our stopovers in villages, but most of all I loved the free feeling of being alone with our dugout floating downriver, watching the day roll past, and threading our way at random among the islands. By now I had realised that I was wrong in assuming that tourists always paddled dugouts to Brazzaville. My original mistake was in thinking that there were other tourists, for as Lesley pointed out, Central African Republic was hardly an attractive resort. The astounded reactions of the fishing folk made it obvious that they had never seen white girls before and the nature of the river made it clear that this was not to be an easy jaunt. Lesley said she had known this all along.

'Then why didn't you tell me?' I asked.

'Because I didn't think you'd listen,' she replied.

Neither of us had any wish to change our mind, not that it would have made any difference if we had as we couldn't go back. The thought crossed my mind that this was certainly a good way to learn about taking responsibility for one's actions. We didn't regret our impulsive undertaking, not even at nights when we suffocated in sweat baths tortured by the mosquitoes, and when the ants tunnelled inside our mosquito nets, and when we were drenched by rainstorms, or during the day when we stopped on fly-infected islands, and when crocodiles plunged from the shores into the river where we had just been swimming.

The river was now a couple of miles wide, and every day it

provided us with a fresh challenge. It alternated from glassy calm to raging roughness in storms that whipped up out of the blue in a matter of seconds, and it took us to extremes of paradise, hell, exhilaration and fear.

With the heavy rainfall upstream the water level in the Oubangui and Congo basins rose, releasing acres of previously trapped hyacinth weed. Some of the hyacinth floated in single plants, each with its decorative purple flower; sometimes it came in clumps which were the size of small islands. Some days there was little hyacinth, while on other days such as this one the surface of the river was thickly coated in it. I deduced that the daily quantity of weed was equivalent to the amount of rainfall upriver; I smiled at its simple logic, then turned to stretch my arm down to the rudder and disentangle a clump of weed which had become wound around it. A gust of wind blew more hyacinth against one side of the dugout and I had no sooner freed the rudder than it became entangled again. The wind that had blown the weed against the dugout was still blowing and pushing both the weed and the dugout over into the main current, but we could do nothing to prevent it because the harder we pushed away from the build-up of weed the further we moved into the fast main channel. More weed jostled against the dugout and when a large clump bumped into the stern the dugout swung broadside. Everything happened very rapidly. The dugout was heavier and floated more slowly than the weed, so the weed quickly accumulated against the upriver side, pushing hard, trying to force its way underneath, and the dugout began to tip.

'It's going to roll us over,' screamed Lesley. We both threw our weight to counterbalance it and tore at the plants with our hands. We grabbed them to throw them aside but they slipped through our fingers in sludgy disintegration, and every moment more weed was massing up against us. It was moving so fast that the already tightly packed plants doubled up and wadges of hyacinth cascaded into the dugout. The dugout had become a barrage and was creating a backwash of water that roared underneath it from the free side, and it needed only one more push to flip it upside down. The danger girded us into a desperate balancing act on the upper rim of the dugout and with frantic efforts we bailed out the slimy plants. But we knew we didn't stand a chance of freeing the dugout from the wall of weed that mounted steadily higher over it. I glanced forwards and noticed that the river was swinging into a bend; the current swung wide round the curve digging the bend deeper into the forest; it had eroded under the banks and many of the giant trees had fallen out across the river. We smashed through the branches of the first. They ripped us to shreds but we didn't stop, our wall of weed pushed us through and on, sweeping us under the low-lying trunk of another tree which I hadn't seen. It knocked me flat and passed within an inch of my head. Then there was the grinding splintering of wood followed by oaths from Lesley. The dugout halted and I looked up to find that we were firmly stuck in the middle of a tree. The weed was left behind lodged against a strong branch in a monstrous bulwark of green foliage. The current was still forcing us on under low branches and in the pandemonium of swirling water and cracking wood we hacked our way forward, chopping at smaller branches with our paddles. In a last desperate effort we freed *La Pirogue*, drifted into a quiet cove, and came to a gentle stop on the sand.

Several sharp lessons were necessary before we learnt how to cope with the hyacinth. By paddling hard we could travel at the same speed as the hyacinth; we found we could keep control, and where shallow backwaters were choked with the weed, we cut down a sapling to use as a punt pole.

One afternoon as we floated lazily downriver, resting and sunbathing in the sweltering heat, I heard a noise that sounded like a series of grunts. There, sticking up above the water, was a pair of ears. Then a hippo surfaced, and a second one, a third, fourth. The dugout jolted abruptly and seemed to bounce backwards. Neither of us had noticed the hippo in our path and now we had forced ourselves on his attention. He turned, remarkably swiftly for such a bulky animal, opened his massive jaws, showed an amazing display of tusklike teeth, and went for us. We backpaddled frantically, steered hard right, and raced for the other side of the river. A storm broke overhead. We reached the shore, sheltered between the roots of a tree, and watched the hippos. The rain poured on and on, but we got tired of waiting, so we decided that if we ignored the weather it might give up and go away.

At sunset the sky cleared, and the river turned to molten gold. We made camp on a small sandbank with one tree, sat contemplating the beauty of the endless river horizons between the islands, and drank some more of the whisky. Lesley was so tipsy that when she went to fetch her mosquito net from the dugout she fell overboard.

We had spent exactly one week on the river.

Andrea Lee

(1953–)

When Andrea Lee's husband accepted a fellowship to study in Russia for ten months, she began a diary of the life she shared with him. A journalist and novelist, she set about writing a series of vignettes that offered an insider's look at Russians from the markets to the public baths to the nightclubs. Written before glasnost and perestroika, Lee's account of an Easter celebration intuits the decline of Communism and the resurrection of a new Russia. Born in Philadelphia, she now lives in Italy.

from Russian Journal

April 12
Easter

We've returned from our stay in Leningrad to a Moscow transformed by the approach of spring. The skies are a limpid blue filled with strands of cloud as thin and fine as thistledown, and the sidewalks around the university are swamps of mud and grit and the odd debris left at the tide line of receding winter. Last week, three days before Easter, I went to the peasant market near the Byelorussian train station and found it thronged with people shopping for the holiday, the day the State grudgingly permits to be celebrated but does its best to suppress. Instead of durable winter vegetables – big pale cabbages, waxed turnips, giant, mud-covered carrots – the counters were heaped with the fresh spring greens that were just beginning to make their frail way into the world: sorrel, dill, dandelion leaves. A *babushka*, perhaps the oldest in the world, with earth-coloured wrinkles closing in on themselves so that her tiny gleaming eyes were scarcely visible, and skinny fingers as yellow as beeswax, sold me a bunch of herbs, mumbling, 'Now, this will make you a fine Easter soup!' After her trembling fingers had counted out the kopecks in change, she crossed herself.

At outdoor booths in the sunny market courtyard, vendors were selling brightly painted Easter eggs; I bought several from a short man with cheerful blue eyes and frostbite marks on his cheeks. The eggs are all exuberantly painted with naïve scenes that suggest a religious and secular rejoicing at the fullness of new life awakening in the world: they show squat onion-domed Orthodox churches, ducklings in baskets, young suitors hurrying along with bouquets of flowers, bearded peasants clutching enormous sturgeons. All of the eggs bear the inscription XB, the Russian abbreviation for *Khristos Voskres* – Christ Is Risen. One of my most amusing eggs bears the XB inscription and, underneath it, the message: 'Happy Easter, dear Comrades!' Wishful thinking. Easter and comrades in fact don't mix at all. It was pleasant to walk out into the balmy afternoon with my net bag filled with green leaves and Easter eggs, but on the subway I began to notice the people staring at the colourful paint, and I started to feel that I was openly carrying contraband. Later I heard that the market had been raided, and the Easter eggs, absurdly enough, seized by the police.

'Easter,' Tom wrote recently in a letter home, 'like everything else here, is a deficit good.' To get into a Moscow church for the midnight Easter service, one often needs a printed invitation from the priest – something which, like every other deficit good, is easy enough for foreigners to obtain (there are, in fact, certain prominent churches to which foreigners are guided) but not easy for the average Russian. Russian friends told us that during the Easter service every church is surrounded by three rows of people: in the inner row stand policemen, checking tickets and intimidating the hesitant; in the second row, *druzhiniki* (volunteer police), wearing red arm bands, continue the intimidation; and the third row consists of hooligans and thugs ready to push around any churchgoer who happens to cross their path. Besides the physical barriers, distractions are arranged to discourage church attendance and bolster loyalty to the State.

As on the eves of Christmas and 'Old New Year,' the New Year of the Orthodox calendar, the Party schedules a special television program on the night before Easter, a program aimed at young people, usually featuring a popular rock group like Abba or Boney M. This year, ironically enough, the day before Easter was Lenin's birthday, and so there were even greater possibilities for distraction from the religious holiday. The city just awakening to springtime was festooned with red, and the day declared a nationwide Communist *subotnik*, a day on which everyone is expected to work for free for the good of the State.

All day on Saturday, in spite of the red flags and the frantic Radio Moscow harangues about the Great Leader, there was the feeling of a vast and growing secret in the city, a gathering power that had nothing to do with Lenin. On buses and on the sidewalks, shoppers carrying bags filled with preparations for Easter feasts turned their eyes away from one another. I went into the State bread store and found there a line for *kulich*, the special tall, puffy cakes that crown an Easter dinner; yet, in all the conversations I overheard in the line, there was no mention of the holiday. The sense of some great hidden emotion increased as twilight fell – a damp, purple twilight with some of the sting of winter still in the air. At about nine-thirty Tom and I took a taxi to a small nineteenth-century church near the Sportivnoye metro station; this was a church, we had learned, where you could get in without an invitation if you came early enough. The taxi driver gave us a strange look when we told him the address, but said nothing. When we got out of the taxi, we saw at the church entrance a milling crowd that, sure enough, turned out to be made up mainly of police, *druzhiniki*, and a number of loutish-looking young men. They saw that we were foreigners, and let us through without comment. Ahead of us, a group of three old Russian women was also allowed to pass. 'They know they can't keep the *babushki* away,' whispered Tom. But to one side of us, a pair of teenage girls, their heads wrapped in Orenburg shawls, were being harassed by an equally young *druzhinik*. 'What are you doing here, girls?' he said, cocking his cropped head to one side and grabbing one of them by the arm. 'This is no place for you! Where are your invitations?'

All this was going on practically in darkness on a narrow, badly paved street, where the only light came from a few bulbs at the church door. Though the crowd of officials and churchgoers was rather large, there was only a fraction of the noise normally made by a group that size. The policemen and *druzhiniki* seemed instinctively to lower their voices, as if they felt intimidated by an invisible presence. Before we stepped into the church, I turned around to watch a broad old woman with an imperious carriage roundly berating two policemen, who, momentarily abashed, were practically shuffling their feet with embarrassment. 'Why aren't you ashamed to be keeping people out of church?' she demanded in a voice that rang out above the silent crowd. 'This is very unattractive behaviour!' On the balcony of an apartment across the street, where a party seemed to be going on, two or three young couples stood leaning on the rail, observing the scene below, passing a bottle among them and giving an occasional catcall.

Inside, the little church was already massed with worshippers, who seemed to be made up of about three-quarters old women and a quarter young people; there were only a few people in their forties or fifties. The dim yellow lights lit up the metal covers of icons along the pillars and walls, and the room swirled with the suffocating odour of candle wax mixed with the smell of perspiring human flesh, too tightly packed. This was, in fact, a true Russian crowd, like many of those we'd learned to fight through in the metro, or in a line for food or tickets. After we had shoved our way to a place beside a wall, I felt someone tap me on the shoulder, and turned to find an old woman thrusting thirty kopecks into my hand. '*Peredaite, pozhaluista.* [Please pass this on to the next person],' she said. Every day, in the crushing crowds on Moscow buses, one is constantly tapped on the shoulder, handed a few kopecks that are on their way to the ticket machine, and told, '*Peredaite.*' These particular kopecks were for candles being sold at the entrance of the church, and the candles thus purchased were making their way up to the icons in the midst of a busy buzz of directions. 'Pass this candle to the Smolensk Icon.' . . . 'Where do you want me to send it?' . . . 'Pass it on to the Kazan Icon.' Fat women in kerchiefs squeezed past us, and I marvelled, as I do in every Russian crowd, at the seemingly indefinite capacity of human flesh to compress itself. Through the rippling crowd, I could see the thin brown candles burning, massed like strands of wheat in front of the icons. 'There was a fire here last Easter,' I heard a woman behind us say in a barely audible whisper.

'*Gospodi!* What happened?' came another woman's voice.

'An old woman fainted, and her kerchief caught on fire. But she wasn't hurt. We put it out, all of us.'

At that moment a church official – oddly enough, also wearing a red arm band – appeared at the front of the church to announce that no more people would be let through to the altar to kiss the Easter Icon. 'The passageway is closed!' he shouted. It was time for the service to begin.

The two hours we spent standing – before midnight brought the climax of the service – were a blur of candlelight, the steadily increasing heat of the airless chamber, and the voices of the crowd singing the hypnotic Old Church Slavonic phrases of the Easter service. Several times, exhausted and faint from lack of air, I felt my legs slowly giving way; each time I was buoyed up by the packed bodies around me. The first and most subtle miracle of Easter had already taken place: the crowd, which before the service had been very much like an assemblage in a marketplace, every mind intent on an individual and petty transaction, had at some point been transformed into a single body, as if the archaic words of adoration and rejoicing were a catalyst as potent as communion wine.

It had all happened as spontaneously and imperceptibly as the coming of spring itself. The priest, a man with a dwarfish body and a large head covered with greasy hair above his brocade robe, chanted in a high tremolo, and periodically turned upon the congregation a face whose rather heavy contours were illuminated by an expression of tender joy. The congregation replied to him in a single voice whose defining note was – as it almost always is in the Russian churches I've seen – the quavering treble of old women. I thought how different this serene yet passionate joining of spirits was from any other mass gathering I had seen in the Soviet Union. There was no feeling of compulsion, or of the carefully orchestrated hysteria that culminates in the violent cheers that seem almost torn out of the throats of the crowds gathered to celebrate Komsomol Day or the October Revolution.

Midnight approached. A quiver of activity ran through the crowd as people lit the candles they had saved for the climax of the service and hurriedly wrapped them in paper to protect their fingers. Then two churchmen somehow cleared the passageway through the congregation, and the priest advanced from the altar, surrounded by a procession of acolytes carrying icons, crosses, and candles. The congregation silently fell into line behind the procession, and soon we were outside, moving in a circle around the church. The cold night air roused me instantly from the dreamy stupor that had seized me; I looked with newly clarified vision at the moving line of candlelit figures stretching in front and back of me, and felt the keen surge of physical gladness and the sense of endless possibilities that one sometimes feels upon arising very early after a night of deep sleep.

As the procession passed the little square in front of the church, where the police and *druzhiniki* had been standing, I noticed that the hostile throng had inexplicably vanished, and that now a crowd of about fifty people – many of them young and middle-aged – stood facing the procession with candles of their own. Finally the priest stopped at the church door, and turned to call his message to the gathering: *'Khristos Voskres!'* – Christ is risen! The traditional reply came back in a glad shout from dozens of throats: *'Voistine Voskres!'* – He is truly risen! Back and forth, over and over again, went the exchange, while an expression of rapture transformed the faces of the young and old, and the deep yellow glow of candlelight lit up the square. The apartment balconies were thronged with spectators who stood silently looking down at the single mass public observance in Russia that has nothing to do with Communism.

Near the gate to the churchyard stood a group of worshippers who wanted to press forward and come inside. A deacon stood at the door and addressed them. '*Pravoslavnye*,' he called. 'You may come to the door, but only if you come calmly, without making any noise.' Tom and I looked at each other. We had never heard the word '*pravoslavnye*' uttered in this country, where the crowds of people are normally addressed as 'Comrades,' or 'Citizens.' *Pravoslavnye* means all orthodox Christians, all members of the flock. The group passed through the doorway, and for the first time this year I saw a crowd of Russians move without shoving: their faces, like all the faces around us, still wore the same look of rapturous rejoicing. *'Khristos Voskres!'* . . . *'Voistine Voskres!'* Candle wax was dripping on my hand, and I glanced off into the distance, where I could just make out the red stars gleaming on top of the Kremlin towers. I thought of a church I'd seen recently that had been transformed by the State into a storage facility for sinks, pipes, and toilet bowls; of the former monasteries that are now factories or institutions. It was smart of the officials, I thought, to try to stem this passionate tide of belief, for if they didn't, would there be as many voices to cheer in Red Square?

A little later the crowd began moving back through the doorway of the church to resume the service inside. It was now about one-thirty. We were expected at an Easter supper on the Sadovoye Kol'tso, so we slipped quietly into the square, leaving our candles, as the others had left them, stuck, burning, into the iron railing of the churchyard. As we walked away, I looked back once. Except for a for stragglers, the square and churchyard were almost totally deserted. Only the irregular ring of tiny flames remained as proof of the magical hour when all churches all over Moscow had been ringed with holy fire, and had regained, for the short span of the ceremony of rebirth, their ancient hold over Russian hearts.

We didn't see any taxis, so we walked for an hour along the boulevard toward the Sadovoye Kol'tso. The night had grown cold and still, a thick layer of clouds reflecting the grayish lights of the city. The trees and bushes we passed were still leafless, but looking closely, I could see the tips of twigs swollen with clustering buds; in this calmest hour of the night, a subtle odour of vegetation – more a phantom than an actual smell – floated lightly in the air. We were silent and elated, walking down the centre of the deserted street with a buoyancy to our stride as if we were half flying, infrequently passing other night-walkers who were also returning from Easter services. We crossed Herzen Street and entered a neighbourhood of beautiful old mansions, many of them embassies, the grey-uniformed Soviet guards looking out curiously at us from their tiny sentry boxes. We had turned down a side street when we heard shouts, and saw, on the corner across from us, a man and woman circling and aiming blows at each other, while two or three men stood looking on. From their features and language, they all seemed to be Tartars. The woman's long dark hair was spilling over her shoulders, and her slanted eyes and high cheekbones were clearly visible in the streetlight. She cried out again and again at the man, and in her voice there was something violent yet wailing and mournful that seemed to echo up and down the street. A child of about two stood crying unheeded a few yards away. The sight of this evil little drama gave me a chill; a *militsiya* car turned the corner and we hurriedly cut through a muddy alleyway. We emerged facing a tree-filled park immortalized in Bulgakov's *Master and Margarita* as being the site of the Devil's first appearance in Moscow; here, after encountering Lucifer in the shape of a dapper foreigner, a pompous journalist slips in a pool of sunflower-seed oil and is decapitated by a passing tram.

The first thing that happened when we arrived at Easter dinner at Lidia Borisovna's apartment is that Lidia herself, wearing a long skirt and a traditionally embroidered Russian blouse (these days, such blouses are almost impossible to obtain outside of the hard-currency stores), came up and gave us each a threefold Easter kiss, and standing back, announced quite dramatically: *'Khristos Voskres!'* Lidia is a dramatic soul, a tall, gaunt woman in her forties, with a Dutch-boy haircut and a clever, complaining, manipulative manner. She is one of the most important figures in the unofficial art world of Moscow, so flamboyant in her unorthodoxy that she probably has KGB connections; her apartment is always full of foreigners, artists, and paintings. Often she receives guests while reclining on a mattress, complaining of vague back pains and chain-smoking the cigarettes that have yellowed her beautiful hands.

'Voistine Voskres!' we told her dutifully, and hung up our coats. The brightly lit three-room apartment was crowded with guests; I recognized about half of them as the painters, poets, and musicians who haunt parties where foreigners are likely to appear. At the beginning of the year this had all seemed very exciting, but now the prospect of four hours of conversation about 'my art – stifled in this country' seemed unbearably wearisome. I was glancing about the room for Rima, who had promised to meet us here, when I felt a small heavy hand on my arm. It was Ludmilla, a very short, fat artist who wears dresses made of long swags of embroidered material, and whose round timorous eyes in a plump pink face make her look constantly like a child about to be smacked.

'Khristos Voskres!' she said in a plaintive voice. 'Why do you refuse to visit me? You must not like me. Next week I am giving a party, with lovely cakes. And I have some new creations.' Luda makes strange little quilts and collages from scraps of hides, furs, and feathers, she tries to sell them for dollars, but to my knowledge, no one has ever bought anything.

'I'm sorry,' I said. 'We have wanted to come and visit you for a long time. Perhaps we can do it soon.'

'Yes, come next week. I want to do your portrait. Come – I insist on it!' She spoke in the insinuating, nagging way in which some timid people try to exert their wills. Luda was a despised hanger-on in this artistic circle, and she knew it. I looked closely at her and realized that she was wearing a present I had given her as a joke back in the fall: a miniature Coca-Cola can hung on her necklace chain. I had chuckled about this silly present often enough, but now it seemed like a truly wicked thing to have done. I went on talking to her, and thought that my head would split with depression and fatigue. It was about three o'clock in the morning.

Two tables had been pushed together in the main room, covered with white cloths, and spread with a handsome array of *zakuski*: cold meats and cheeses, radishes and fresh coriander, cucumber and tomato sandwiches. In the middle lay two bowls of hard-boiled eggs that had been decorated with dyes, and between them lay the traditional Easter *kulich* and the sweetened raisin-filled farmer cheese that is traditionally served with it. I was approaching the table when a painter whom I vaguely knew, a balding man with purplish cheeks and a skewed eye, came up to me and tried in a vigorous whisper to convince me that I should try to smuggle a portfolio of his enormous canvases out to a dealer in New York.

'I'd get caught the same as anyone would,' I protested, trying to maneuver out of the corner where he had pulled me.

'Nonsense. You could slip them right in among your luggage. Americans always have a great deal of luggage. . . . You materialists!' he added, wagging his finger at me in playful admonishment. 'Tell me, my beauty,' he went on in the same low voice. 'When are we going to meet privately? Foreign women are always drawn to Russian men, with good reason! We're real men! Once I met a French woman who was a *lesbianka* – hated men. But I convinced her differently!' He began an interminable smutty story, and I glanced around the room, whose walls were covered every few weeks with an exhibition of works by a different artist. This time there was a really wonderful set of paintings, showing Breughelesque scenes of traditional life in a Russian peasant village. Lidia Borisovna had turned off the harsh overhead light and had lit candles on the table, and the figures in the paintings – short-legged, broad-faced peasants in the marketplace, in the bathhouse, by the frozen river – seemed to take on life in the moving light. It seemed to me that they bore more relationship to the Easter service we'd just attended than did the people in the room around me.

Chairs were drawn up to the tables, and we sat down to eat pieces of Easter cake; as we ate, we chose eggs and duelled with our neighbours in a tapping game to see which shell was the strongest. Tom sat discussing Paul Robeson with a short musician with a droll winged mustache, while I played the tapping game with a young man with big glistening dark eyes and perspiring hands. Apropos of nothing, he remarked to me, 'My grandfather, you know, spoke French.'

'Why was that?' I asked. 'Was he French?'

'No,' he said, picking up a piece of shattered eggshell with the end of his moist white finger, and then, leaning earnestly toward me: 'But he was, well, an officer . . . ah . . . in the Guards . . . before the Revolution, if you know what I mean . . .'

'Are you trying to hint that you have noble blood?' I asked sharply, and the frigid hauteur of my tone shocked me as much as it did the young man, who at once pretended that he had to reach for another Easter egg, and began talking briskly with the woman on his left. Far away, at the other end of the table, I heard someone say, 'I disagree. It's literary mitosis!'

Then came that strange hour in a sleepless night when everything seems distorted; lights are too bright; darkness, unfathomable; conversations seem to stretch out into infinity, and the barrier between dream and observation seems to have dissolved. The hour itself seemed to last only for a minute, and suddenly it was five o'clock, the candles were drowning in pools of wax on the chaotic table, and the big square windows at the end of the room were gleaming with a pale light. From the divan in the corner came a medley of snores, and I saw the skew-eyed painter sleeping among other supine figures. My annoyance at the idiocy of the party had suddenly evaporated, and as I looked at the few people left – Lidia, our hostess, and a beautiful red-haired writer sitting whispering to each other on one hard chair, their arms around each other's necks; the short musician and a large group of others still arguing about literature, their elbows among the eggshells and empty bottles at one end of the table – I found that their voices and faces had softened, that the advent of the dawn had given a measure of dignity and humility and happiness to their manner as the Easter service had to the crowd at the church. Some kind of passion – for company, for art, for a good time – had kept them vigilant tonight as it had other nights, and any vigil makes dawn seem a blessing. Our hostess stretched, ran her fingers through her thick hair, then rose and opened the curtains to a watery sky the bluish colour of skim milk. 'See, friends, it's the dawn of a holy day,' she said in her deep, clever voice. *'Khristos Voskres!'*

I repeated the answer with the others.

Helen Winternitz

(1951–)

An author of two books, American Helen Winternitz takes more than the typical journalist's interest in a good story. For *East Along the Equator*, a book about travelling 2,000 miles up the Congo, she learned Lingala. She learned Amharic in Ethiopia, and Swahili in Eastern Africa. For her second book, *Season of Stones*, she lived for two years in Nahalin, a small Palestinian village of shepherds and peasant farmers near Bethlehem on the West Bank, where she survived during the Intifada by speaking Arabic. Winternitz, with Timothy M. Phelps, is the author of *Capitol Games: Clarence Thomas, Anita Hill, and the Story of a Supreme Court Nomination*. She lives in Washington, D.C.

from Season of Stones

The weeks wore on, and little changed except that intermittent rains were falling, rains that soaked into the dirt and turned it dark. Occasionally the clouds parted and the sun warmed the earth. It was on just such a sunny day that I returned to the village from Jerusalem, carrying with me medicines and books for some of my friends. I tried driving in first from Kilo Sabatash but found the army had been hard at work refurbishing the roadblock, closing off the *shabab* detour permanently by bulldozing a wide pile of dirt up against the multi-ton rocks, the refrigerator shell and the upturned car chassis, which were already in place.

As I was turning back, I paused for a few minutes to watch a shepherd herding his long-haired goats in a rocky field below the new Neve Daniel houses. It was a warm afternoon made strangely moody by half-white, half-blue clouds lingering in the autumnal sky. The branches of the leafless fig trees stood out grey against the sky.

I had noticed soldiers everywhere on the way out. It was a Palestinian strike day, to protest the demolition of houses in the occupied territories. Because of the strike, most West Bankers were not working in Israel but were at home waiting for trouble to come along. Aware that more rocks were thrown on strike days, I did not take the next most obvious route back to the village. I avoided the villages of Husan and El Khader, where the Palestinians did not know me well, as they did in Nahalin, and drove around past the settlements to Nahalin's south. At Kfar Etzion, I was struck by the anomaly of an old white-bearded Palestinian wearing a white headcloth and riding a white donkey along the newly paved black road that runs between the kibbutz and the neighbouring religious settlement. I was aware of details that afternoon, or I thought I was.

At the turn into the valley by Abu al-Koroun, I met a woman I knew. I had a chat with her and admired the embroidery of her dress. All was auspicious. I continued down the road and looked for, but could not see, the flag on the minaret of the mosque. Was it down? I wondered. Had the lack of wind let it flop out of sight? But I did notice a smaller flag on a rough pole stuck in a rock wall perpendicular to the road about halfway down from Abu al-Koroun. Near the flag I came to a line of rocks across the road. I stopped and, without thinking, put the car in neutral and got out to move a few of the rocks so that I could go on to the village. I had my SEHAFI sign on the windshield and the red *kefiyeh** across the dashboard. I was thinking that I had nothing to worry about since most people in the village would recognize me. Besides books for Sena, I was bringing rheumatism medicine for Halima, the Najajra grandmother with whom I had worked in the olives. The books and medicines were on the passenger seat.

* A kerchief worn as headdress.

Without warning, rocks began hitting the car, the road and all around me. Hard. I was being ambushed. I twirled around and rushed for the car. More rocks came but they missed me somehow. I leapt into the driver's seat and reversed crazily down the narrow, windy road under a further hail of rocks. Coming out from behind a grove of olives on the right and from behind the boulders on the left were *mulethamin*, translated as 'wrapped ones', *shabab* with their faces covered in black-checkered *kefiyehs* so that only the slits of their eyes were showing. They chased me and stopped only when it was obvious I had outdistanced them.

Once out of range, I stopped. I was trembling, shocked by the attack and by the realization that these were Nahalinis, *shabab* from Nahalin, behind the *kefiyehs*. This was the village where I had spent so many days and nights, where I had tried again and again to prove that I was not an enemy, that my aim was to learn about the village, not to injure it. I couldn't tell who had ambushed me, and I didn't know why they had done it. I only knew that if I kept retreating now, these *mulethamin* would be convinced that I was frightened. And I was, but I couldn't show my fear, or I might not get back into the village. I also believed that my attackers would soften when they realized I was returning to Nahalin with no ill intent.

I rolled down the car window and waved the red *kefiyeh*. I shouted that I was a journalist. Some of the *mulethamin* walked toward me a little and then beckoned, making big welcoming motions with their arms, that I should come forward. I did, pulling back abreast of several of them. I said again that I was a journalist, and I motioned to the books and boxes of pills, saying I was bringing medicine to an old woman.

Someone grabbed my *kefiyeh*, and rocks came battering down on the car. The windshield was hit but it didn't break. The *mulethamin* were attacking from the olive trees, and I went again into a maniacal high-speed reverse until I was once more out of range. The masked Palestinians stood on the road and glared at me. I sat in the car, more frightened than I had been since I first set foot on the West Bank. I wasn't going to drive forward into the same trap again, but I also wasn't going to retreat. I was in a quandary.

Then, as if in answer to my dilemma, three villagers came walking up behind me from the direction of Abu al-Koroun. I didn't recognize the trio of men, but they knew me by sight, as many villagers did. They tried to calm me, telling me not to be afraid. I was still trembling; my left leg was shaking on the clutch pedal. Two of the villagers stayed with me in the car, and the other went and talked to the *mulethamin*. He returned with the *kefiyeh*, and all three got into the car. We drove to the ambush point, got out and moved the rocks, drove past the ambush point, got out and carefully replaced the stones. The *mulethamin* had blended into the landscape. I asked my newfound benefactors who my attackers were, but they didn't tell me.

'I told the *mulethamin*,' one benefactor said, 'that they made a mistake just now, that you are good. It is up to them whether they believe this. It won't help you to know their names.'

We made it into the village, and my benefactors went their own way. I headed for the house of Naim Najajra, the schoolteacher who was Ratiba's youngest brother and who had helped so merrily and briefly with the olive picking. The driveway to Naim's place was narrow and led to a courtyard protected by the houses of relatives. I pulled hastily into the driveway and brought the car to a screeching halt, startling Halima, who had been basking in the sun on a blanket in the courtyard. I told them what had happened, and Halima told me that the army had riled the village the day before. Soldiers had come upon the flag on the minaret and had ordered a young man to climb up and tear it down. They had fired tear gas through the whole village to keep the *shabab* indoors and then had sped away. The ambush I chanced upon could have been laid by rankled *shabab*. But whatever the reason, I was still upset.

Halima was upset, too. She brought out coffee. I had to drink two cups of the strong stuff before my hands ceased shaking. At first, I spilled from the cup. Halima then hefted herself inside and brought out a platter of leftover lunch, chicken and rice, and tried to get me to eat it. The village hospitality never ceased, but I could not eat anything. Naim came out from his house. Halima and he tried to coax me to go sit in his cloud-painted guest room, where I could feel safe. I refused.

Slowly I was becoming angry. The fear that had shaken me was transmuting into an anger that came from deep inside. The bunch of villagers who ambushed me could have killed me. The windshield could have shattered into glass-sharp shrapnel. A rock could have struck me in the face. Had they wanted to kill me? Were they just trying to scare me off? I didn't know.

'The fear that had shaken me was transmuting into an anger that came from deep inside. The bunch of villagers who ambushed me could have killed me.'

I had a taste of what Israelis felt when they travelled the West Bank. Transmitted along the arc of a rock being thrown, the Palestinians' anger was personal and deadly. There was nothing accidental about it. You were the target. But what made me even angrier and what hurt me was that I was not an Israeli settler. Although all the Palestinians in Nahalin might not be convinced, I had done nothing to harm them.

Hussein Najajra, an Arabic teacher and relative of Naim, came out into the courtyard, and I made a speech to him about the need of the American people to understand the Palestinians and that this stoning of my car was not helpful.

He agreed. 'Whichever people did this, they were stupid,' he said.

Halima again offered me food. 'It is a shame that they threw stones on you,' she said.

Sena arrived in the courtyard, having already heard what happened. She hugged me. 'Helen,' she said, 'this was unnecessary. This was not good. You should not stop coming to Nahalin.'

I gave Sena the books and Halima the medicine. By then, I had calmed down enough to think ahead. I was again flooded with fear. Naim's courtyard made a temporary sanctuary. I guessed there must be *mulethamin* in ambush on any route I would try to take out of the village, but I couldn't stay cowering in this courtyard in a village that was on edge.

A single stone was tossed at me as I backed out of the driveway and headed for the other side of the village, the neighbourhood where Hanan's and Hilmi's houses were and where I was well-known.

On the way, I saw another bunch of *mulethamin* milling around on the main road. Some were rolling tires toward the Valley of the Cow. My impulse was to yank the car around and head in the other direction, but that would only have taken me back to the place of the first ambush. I proceeded, and the anonymously wrapped figures let me pass. I could recognize none of them. As I was weaving down the road, avoiding the *mulethamin*, one stepped out in front of the car. As I stopped, he pulled his *kefiyeh* aside. It was one of Hanan's brothers, and he said it would be OK for me to drive out the other way if he came with me.

'It's Jebha on this side of the village. We like you,' he said.

I hoped he was telling the truth. One of their tires was already burning. The *mulethamin* had laid down a strip of nails across the road, which they directed me around. Just outside the village, in the high olive grove where the *shabab* had fought the army, *mulethamin* had gathered in coloured garb. Others stood in the open with rocks in their hands. One of the leaders ordered the *shabab* to come quickly, and they came, some carrying clubs. They surrounded the car, and for a moment I wondered whether this was another, more terrible trap. But nothing happened and I drove forward, out of the village. The *shabab* ran along both sides of my car to ensure that nobody on high made a mistake. I was not to be stoned by this faction of the Palestinians. Jebha approved of me and Fatah had not.

Rocks were the starkest of weapons. There was nothing to them; there was no elaboration; there was no apparatus between the thrower and the target. Rocks were direct, much more so than guns, which could be fired accurately and cleanly from a distance. Rocks were primitive, employed for millennia before mankind developed tools and weapons.

The *mulethamin* could have killed me with their rocks, and I wanted to know why they wanted to. I wanted to talk to them. I wanted them to explain to me the depths of their paranoia and anger, an ugly mix, I was sure. I wanted to understand.

The warm afternoon had passed, and the evening chill had been settling on Jerusalem, where I was holed up, shaken and writing notes about what had happened. I was wondering why, or how, the *mulethamin* had failed to kill me. They were close enough. Maybe they were momentarily unsure. Maybe I was lucky. Or maybe they just wanted to terrify me or warn me. I planned to see Fawzi and get an explanation.

The next day Fawzi came to see me.

'I am sorry,' he said. He said that I had been caught in a rending fissure between the village's Fatah and Jebha factions.

'I talked all last night to people with importance about what happened. I said that you were writing about the village and that this was a good thing. The world needs to understand that Palestinians live like human beings. They listened. We agreed to send representatives from each one, from Fatah and Jebha, to Jerusalem to ask questions about you. To find out if you are straight.'

Readily I agreed that the investigation should proceed, but I had plenty of doubts. I had no idea who would be judging my integrity. I assumed members of the underground leadership of the Intifada would be my arbiters, but I did not know them. Or if I did, I did not know their clandestine roles. I was jittery.

'The problem you had was not because of you,' Fawzi continued reassuringly. 'These people who attacked you thought you were against them because you were spending too much time with the Jebha.'

A lesson had been learned the hard way. From then on, I vowed to make friends with more Shakarnas, with anybody who might think I had been taking sides.

I had been blind to the obvious. I lost another layer of naïveté. Bucolic was no longer a word that occurred to me when I thought of Nahalin. Complex, yes. Difficult, yes. Hospitable, yes. But what was behind the smiles? Had one of the masked stone throwers previously invited me on to his guest porch and plied me with tea? How was I to know whom to trust?

I asked Fawzi if any of my attackers would speak to me.

'No,' he said flatly. Clearly this was not something that could be talked about within the village.

I asked whether I had ever been in any of their houses.

'Perhaps you have by chance,' he said, offering no clues to their identity.

Fawzi was perturbed not just by my account. He hated seeing the village fighting itself. 'We should put these things away. Now is not the time to be fighting inside the village. The fight is much larger than just our village. It is not a game that we should be playing now. We have to be more serious. The enemy is not you, and it is not the other Palestinians.'

Talk had been bouncing around Jerusalem that the different Palestinian factions were rubbing against each other on the West Bank as a whole, trying to gain ascendancy in the national and international arenas.

I was going to have to prove my neutrality on yet another level. I gathered once more proof of my writing and my identity. A few days later I was summoned by telephone to an office in East Jerusalem. Fawzi was not there. Two men whom I had never seen before were seated at a table. One was tall and thin with a sharp face. He did the talking. He started by asking me the details of the stoning. He paused and looked at me hard.

'Do you know who I am?' he asked.

'No,' I said.

'Tell me everything, because I will be hearing the other side. Others saw what happened in Nahalin. I will be hearing the truth. Any lies will finish you.'

I was telling the truth, but that did not stop me from squirming in my chair. I had no idea what my attackers might say, and it seemed that my questioner was from the Intifada's leadership. What would happen to me if lies about me went up through the Palestinian ranks?

After a few more questions about my motives for travelling on the West Bank, he ended the questioning abruptly. 'That is enough. Go now and do not remember what I look like. Do not tell anyone about me.'

I said that I wanted only one thing, which was to talk to some of those who had stoned me, disguised or not. I wanted to make them realize I was not the enemy.

'If you have told the truth, they will understand,' he said. 'Don't make the mistake of asking me too many questions.'

He rose as I did and walked stiffly toward the door, as if something in his legs caused him pain. He opened the door and closed it quickly behind me. I heard a lock click.

Back in my apartment I waited to find out whether I was doomed or saved. Four days after the meeting he telephoned.

'You have done excellently. Now don't worry. You will be safe everywhere you want to go around Bethlehem and the area. You have my word. I am the man from Fatah.'

He hung up. I took this cryptic message to mean that he represented Fatah and could guarantee that members of his group would not bother me. I suspected the ambushers had been among them.

Gwendolyn MacEwen

(1941–1987)

A wide-ranging and thoughtful writer, Gwendolyn MacEwen published one travel narrative, *Mermaids and Ikons: A Greek Summer*. In her storytelling and poetry she displays a commanding interest in history, politics, and magic. In Canada she is best known for her poetry; she won the Governor General's Award for poetry for *The Shadow-Maker* in 1969. At 20, her first poetry collection, *The Drunken Clock*, was published, and she wrote two novels and one story collection. She also published plays, a translation, and a children's book. The excerpt that follows, *The Holyland Buffet*, is from a collection of fact-based short stories entitled *Noman's Land*. All of the events in the selection are true and Kali is a woman whom MacEwen met while travelling through the Middle East. MacEwen was born and lived in Toronto.

from **Noman's Land**

The Holyland Buffet

'The most amazing thing I saw in all my travels,' Kali was saying, 'was that streetcar in Cairo.'

'I thought you never travelled,' said Ibrahim the Syrian, who was sitting across the table from her in a new vegetarian restaurant called Mythological Foods. 'When you get mad, you always swear that you're going to pack up and go to India. But you never go, so I assumed you never travel.'

'Ah, but I have, you know. I have been to two holy lands – Israel and Egypt. I have also been to Greece, which is not really a holy land. But to get back to that streetcar –'

'Tell me about Israel,' Ibrahim said. 'I want to comprehend the enemy.'

'On my first day there I took a walk alone along the beach at Jaffa, which means *The Beautiful*. Some boy about eleven or twelve came up and asked me the time – everybody there asks you the time, don't ask me why – and when I told him he attacked me and threw me to the ground and starting punching me all over. We punched and kicked for a while until he finally got bored and walked away. I never knew what it was all about, except that because I was wearing shorts I probably offended him.'

'Bloody aggressive Israelis,' Ibrahim said. 'That's all they know, how to punch and kick their way through the world.'

'The boy was a Palestinian Arab,' Kali said. 'He thought *I* was an Israeli.'

'Then the story is entirely different,' said Ibrahim. 'It needs re-examining.'

The mythological food arrived at their table and they dug in. Ibrahim showed her how to eat a dish of dark brown powder with an indescribable smell.

'This is *zaatar*,' he said. 'We've been eating it for centuries in the East. You dip the bread first in the olive oil to moisten it, then into the *zaatar* – so.' He popped a piece into her mouth. 'Jesus Christ ate this all the time,' he said. 'Him and his disciples. This is the bitter herbs they wrote about. Anyway, tell me more about Israel.'

'It's really the streetcar I want to talk about,' Kali said.

'Never mind the streetcar.'

'Well I was walking through this village called Lifta, outside Jerusalem, and I was wearing shorts again, so I looked like a *sabra* again, and a whole tribe of little Arab boys came screaming up the mountain path toward me and started pelting me with stones. Stoned outside of Jerusalem, can you imagine, in the twentieth century, and me a Kanadian. In the clinic they put something called a spider clamp into my head where the worst wound was, and covered it with bandages that looked like a turban. They said now I looked like an Arab, and told me not to do anything exciting for a few days. I tried not to do anything exciting, but the Israelis are hooked on speed – I mean anything that goes fast, the faster the better. So I had this wild motorcycle ride with a guy who thought he was doing me a favour by giving me a ride up to Tiberias, and every moment I thought I was going to die, which was of course the whole point, the thrill. Then I walked around Tiberias with the spider clamp rusting in my skull, holding my thoughts together as it were, keeping my head from flying apart in a hundred directions; then I brooded and felt biblical in a small hotel, and the next day another guy offered me a ride in his motor-boat in Lake Tiberias. I should have known better. He rode at top speed to the middle of the lake and informed me that now, two minutes either way, meant the difference between Israel and Jordan, life or death. Then he laughed and laughed like a madman and started going around in crazy wild circles. Can you imagine – this maniac in the middle of the Sea of Galilee and us going round and round and the laughter so loud they could probably hear it on both shores. . . .'

'Bloody insane Israelis,' said Ibrahim, and passed her a plate of ripe green figs.

'Well all the guys are on the make over there,' Kali said, 'and I was a female tourist travelling alone, so what could I expect? Come on, it would be the same in your country.'

Ibrahim addressed his full attention to the figs.

'Oh wait,' Kali remembered, 'I knew I forgot something, I forgot to tell you about the Holyland Buffet. . . .'

'What?'

'The Holyland Buffet. It was this crazy little place at the foot of the Mount of Loaves and Fishes. Nothing more than a little shack, really, with a counter in the front and a few shelves behind full of orange drinks and cigarettes and halvah bars. I must have been the first person the owner had seen for days, because –'

'Wait!' Ibrahim cried. 'Wait wait wait! I have a cousin in Jordan who has a place called the Holyland Buffet, just outside of Bethlehem!'

'Well this one was in Israel.'

'It's impossible that there are two!' Ibrahim cried, his face getting very red. 'It's just impossible!'

'Well, I didn't know if the guy who ran this one was Arab or Israeli. Anyway, as I was saying, I must have been the first person or maybe just the first woman he'd seen for days because he leaned over the counter after he served me my drink and clutched my wrists and pleaded *Come with me to Haifa! The lights, the cabarets, the people!* I said that I couldn't, and I didn't even know him. He said that didn't matter, we'd have a wonderful time anyway. *To Haifa, to Haifa together!* I wonder where he is today; what a beautiful man. . . .'

'There can't be two Holyland Buffets,' Ibrahim said, and proceeded not to listen to her as she went on.

'And then there was old Ephraim, the painter who lived in the old village of Safed in the mountains. He wanted to seduce me too, although he went on for hours about Eisenstein and Isadora Duncan and Stanislavsky and all the others he had known who were black-listed in the States. Now in Israel the tourist bureau warned tourists against having their portraits done by the infamous communist Ephraim, so he ended up with more business than anyone. . . .'

'Let's change the subject,' said Ibrahim, dejectedly sipping a Turkish coffee. 'What about Egypt?'

'At last we're getting to what I wanted to tell you in the first place. The streetcar –'

'Who cares about a streetcar? What happened in Egypt?'

'Well of course, it's even worse there for a woman to walk around alone. When I went every day to the museum in Cairo because there was so much to see, the guards thought I must have been playing some really sexy game with them; it was inconceivable that I would go alone to a museum every day – why? What was my *real* reason? I could not possibly have travelled half-way around the world to stare at statues and mummies of the dead lords of Egypt, the gold of Tutankhamen, the most exquisite sculpture imaginable. No, I was indeed a tart, a slut, a whore. So they kept plying me with sugary tea and cigarettes, and they smiled and joked among themselves, and when I didn't want more sugary tea they offered me *Misra-Cola* and more cigarettes and endless offers of escorted tours around Cairo. Within a few days I had acquired a reputation of being one of the loosest women in the city, a tramp, an easy lay; and of course each one of them boasted to the others of his conquest of this piece of garbage, this foreigner. I don't know how I got to actually see what I wanted to see in the museum, but somehow I did.'

'Would you like some *halvah*?' Ibrahim asked. 'It's the lovely kind with chocolate marbled all through it. Here, have some.' And he popped a piece into her mouth. 'Now, what else?'

'The pyramids,' Kali said. 'Not the pyramids themselves – what can one say? But the washrooms, the horrible little

washrooms that had no doors on the cubicles and no doors closed to the outside, and you had to pay the guard – a man – to go and pee, and you sat there in the shameless light of day staring at the Great Pyramid of Giza from the vantage point of a toilet seat, for Christ's sake. I remember it well; I have tried to forget.'

The waiter at Mythological Foods produced the bill for the meal, and Ibrahim frowned darkly as he checked it over.

'It's amazing and disgusting what they think they can charge for food that has been eaten since before Jesus Christ walked the earth, before Ulysses set sail from Ithaca, before there even was a Holy Land,' he said.

He paid, and they left. Outside the sky was a frail blue, the colour of Roman glass.

'But you come back from these travels, and it's wonderful,' Kali mused. 'You come back to Kanada, and the jet going from East to West interferes with the world's turning. You realize there are other times, arrested sunsets, moments that go on forever, cities whose walls trap time. . . .'

'That bill was too high,' Ibrahim muttered. 'We'd have gotten a better meal at the Holyland Buffet. The one my cousin owns. In Jordan.'

They waited for a streetcar; they were both going in the same direction.

'*Now* will you listen to my story, the one I was going to tell you in the first place?' Kali asked.

'All right, but make it fast.'

'Well there I was, standing in the middle of Cairo one afternoon, hot, mad, and completely disoriented, with people screaming all around me and donkeys braying and a chaos that exists nowhere else in the world – when what should I see?'

'I don't know. What did you see?'

'What should I see, coming toward me with the slowness and grace of a dream, its colours an unmistakable dark-red and yellow, the sign on its metal forehead a magic name recalling a distant, mythic land. . . .'

'What did you *see*?' Ibrahim's mood was black.

'A *King Street streetcar*.'

'A what?'

'A King Street streetcar. From Toronto, Kanada. The city gives old ones away to Egypt and I guess other places, when they're too worn out to use here. There it was, coming toward me, this great, fabulous beast. Try to imagine it, Ibrahim, try to imagine what I felt.'

But Ibrahim was too angry about the meal, about the bill, about the second Holyland Buffet which was in the country of the enemy, and about the coldness of the day in this country of his exile, to pay much attention to what she said.

Annie Dillard

(1945–)

The recipient of the Pulitzer Prize for general nonfiction in 1974 for *Pilgrim at Tinker Creek*, a book of recollections of a year spent alone in the country, Annie Dillard has travelled widely, gaining a reputation for going into areas well off the beaten track. In her writing, she excels at reflecting a sense of innocent wonder without abandoning the quality of 'active waiting' that anthropologist Margaret Mead calls the secret of understanding. In the following excerpt from a collection of short essays titled *Teaching a Stone to Talk: Expeditions and Encounters*, Dillard shows that women are not bound by their gender to react in ways expected of them. Born in Pittsburgh, she is the author of several volumes of nonfiction and a novel, *The Living*. She teaches poetry and creative writing at Western Washington State University.

from **Teaching a Stone to Talk**

The Deer at Providencia

There were four of us North Americans in the jungle, in the Ecuadorian jungle on the banks of the Napo River in the Amazon watershed. The other three North Americans were metropolitan men. We stayed in tents in one riverside village, and visited others. At the village called Providencia we saw a sight which moved us, and which shocked the men.

The first thing we saw when we climbed the riverbank to the village of Providencia was the deer. It was roped to a tree on the grass clearing near the thatch shelter where we would eat lunch.

The deer was small, about the size of a whitetail fawn, but apparently full-grown. It had a rope around its neck and three feet caught in the rope. Someone said that the dogs had caught it that morning and the villagers were going to cook and eat it that night.

This clearing lay at the edge of the little thatched-hut village. We could see the villagers going about their business, scattering feed corn for hens about their houses, and wandering down paths to the river to bathe. The village headman was our host; he stood beside us as we watched the deer struggle. Several village boys were interested in the deer; they formed part of the circle we made around it in the clearing. So also did four businessmen from Quito who were attempting to guide us around the jungle. Few of the very different people standing in this circle had a common language. We watched the deer, and no one said much.

The deer lay on its side at the rope's very end, so the rope lacked slack to let it rest its head in the dust. It was 'pretty', delicate of bone like all deer, and thin-skinned for the tropics. Its skin looked virtually hairless, in fact, and almost translucent, like a membrane. Its neck was no thicker than my wrist; it was rubbed open on the rope, and gashed. Trying to paw itself free of the rope, the deer had scratched its own neck with its hooves. The raw underside of its neck showed red stripes and some bruises bleeding inside the muscles. Now three of its feet were hooked in the rope under its jaw. It could not stand, of course, on one leg, so it could not move to slacken the rope and ease the pull on its throat and enable it to rest its head.

Repeatedly the deer paused, motionless, its eyes veiled, with only its rib cage in motion, and its breaths the only sound. Then, after I would think, 'It has given up; now it will die,' it would heave. The rope twanged; the tree leaves clattered; the deer's free foot beat the ground. We stepped back and held our breaths. It thrashed, kicking, but only one

leg moved; the other three legs tightened inside the rope's loops. Its hip jerked; its spine shook. Its eyes rolled; its tongue, thick with spittle, pushed in and out. Then it would rest again. We watched this for fifteen minutes.

Once three young native boys charged in, released its trapped legs, and jumped back to the circle of people. But instantly the deer scratched up its neck with its hooves and snared its forelegs in the rope again. It was easy to imagine a third and then a fourth leg soon stuck, like Brer Rabbit and the Tar Baby.

We watched the deer from the circle, and then we drifted on to lunch. Our palm-roofed shelter stood on a grassy promontory from which we could see the deer tied to the tree, pigs and hens walking under village houses, and black-and-white cattle standing in the river. There was even a breeze.

Lunch, which was the second and better lunch we had that day, was hot and fried. There was a big fish called *doncella*, a kind of catfish, dipped whole in corn flour and beaten egg, then deep fried. With our fingers we pulled soft fragments of it from its sides to our plates, and ate; it was delicate fish-flesh, fresh and mild. Someone found the roe, and I ate of that too – it was fat and stronger, like egg yolk, naturally enough, and warm.

There was also a stew of meat in shreds with rice and pale brown gravy. I had asked what kind of deer it was tied to the tree; Pepe had answered in Spanish, '*Gama*.' Now they told us this was *gama* too, stewed. I suspect the word means merely game or venison. At any rate, I heard that the village dogs had cornered another deer just yesterday, and it was this deer which we were now eating in full sight of the whole article. It was good. I was surprised at its tenderness. But it is a fact that high levels of lactic acid, which builds up in muscle tissues during exertion, tenderizes.

After the fish and meat we ate bananas fried in chunks and

served on a tray; they were sweet and full of flavour. I felt terrific. My shirt was wet and cool from swimming; I had had a night's sleep, two decent walks, three meals, and a swim – everything tasted good. From time to time each one of us, separately, would look beyond our shaded roof to the sunny spot where the deer was still convulsing in the dust. Our meal completed, we walked around the deer and back to the boats.

That night I learned that while we were watching the deer, the others were watching me.

We four North Americans grew close in the jungle in a way that was not the usual artificial intimacy of travellers. We liked each other. We stayed up all that night talking, murmuring, as though we rocked on hammocks slung above time. The others were from big cities: New York, Washington, Boston. They all said that I had no expression on my face when I was watching the deer – or at any rate, not the expression they expected.

They had looked to see how I, the only woman, and the youngest, was taking the sight of the deer's struggles. I looked detached, apparently, or hard, or calm, or focused, still. I don't know. I was thinking. I remember feeling very old and energetic. I could say like Thoreau that I have travelled widely in Roanoke, Virginia. I have thought a great deal about carnivorousness; I eat meat. These things are not issues; they are mysteries.

Gentlemen of the city, what surprises you? That there is suffering here, or that I know it?

We lay in the tent and talked. 'If it had been my wife,' one man said with special vigour, amazed, 'she wouldn't have cared *what* was going on; she would have dropped *everything* right at that moment and gone in the village from here to there to there, she would not have *stopped* until that animal was out of its suffering one way or another. She couldn't *bear* to see a creature in agony like that.'

I nodded.

Now I am home. When I wake I comb my hair before the mirror above my dresser. Every morning for the past two years I have seen in that mirror, beside my sleep-softened face, the blackened face of a burnt man. It is a wire-service photograph clipped from a newspaper and taped to my mirror. The caption reads: 'Alan McDonald in Miami hospital bed.' All you can see in the photograph is a smudged triangle of face from his eyelids to his lower lip; the rest is bandages. You cannot see the expression in his eyes; the bandages shade them.

The story, headed MAN BURNED FOR SECOND TIME, begins:

> 'Why does God hate me?' Alan McDonald asked from his hospital bed.
>
> 'When the gunpowder went off, I couldn't believe it,' he said. 'I just couldn't believe it. I said, "No, God couldn't do this to me again."'

He was in a burn ward in Miami, in serious condition. I do not even know if he lived. I wrote him a letter at the time, cringing.

He had been burned before, thirteen years previously, by flaming gasoline. For years he had been having his body restored and his face remade in dozens of operations. He had been a boy, and then a burnt boy. He had already been stunned by what could happen, by how life could veer.

Once I read that people who survive bad burns tend to go crazy; they have a very high suicide rate. Medicine cannot ease their pain; drugs just leak away, soaking the sheets, because there is no skin to hold them in. The people just lie there and weep. Later they kill themselves. They had not known, before they were burned, that the world included such suffering, that life could permit them personally such pain.

This time a bowl of gunpowder had exploded on McDonald.

> 'I didn't realize what had happened at first,' he recounted. 'And then I heard that sound from 13 years ago. I was burning. I rolled to put the fire out and I thought, "Oh God, not again."
>
> 'If my friend hadn't been there, I would have jumped into a canal with a rock around my neck.'

His wife concludes the piece, 'Man, it just isn't fair.'

I read the whole clipping again every morning. This is the Big Time here, every minute of it. Will someone please explain to Alan McDonald in his dignity, to the deer at Providencia in his dignity, what is going on? And mail me the carbon.

When we walked by the deer at Providencia for the last time, I said to Pepe, with a pitying glance at the deer, '*Pobrecito*' – 'poor little thing.' But I was trying out Spanish. I knew at the time it was a ridiculous thing to say.

Leila Philip

(1962–)

Leila Philip followed Mrs. Bridges's credo 'the sooner one falls into the ways of a country the better' in her poetic memoir of learning the potter's craft in Japan, *The Road Through Miyama*. In the excerpt that follows Philip spends a day off from her apprenticeship and learns how to harvest rice with the women of the village. Unlike many contemporary travel writers, who include a lot of self-reflection in their narrative, Philip, as a student of the culture, concentrates on accurately recording the customs of a people hidden from Western view. She lived in Miyama from 1983 to 1985 and graduated from Princeton University's Comparative Literature and East Asian Studies programs in 1986. A graduate of Columbia University's Masters Program in Creative Writing, she lives in New York City.

from The Road Through Miyama

I walk down the path to Nagata-san's white house on the corner. The October air smells musty and sweet, not unlike the fall scent of an orchard, but tinged with the sharp odour of distant fire and smoke. Through the tall stands of still bamboo a pale morning light filters down over spreading cinnamon leaf and scattered fern. A quick grey cat leaps across the narrow bamboo-lined pathway, a fish bone dangling from its jaws. Seven-thirty on a Sunday morning. Reiko is busy dyeing leatherwork in the yard, her wide brush leaving trails of scarlet, indigo, magenta, sunflower-yellow and brown. Just inside the glass doors to the living room–gallery Nagayoshi-san sits cross-legged before a pile of wooden boxes, signing each one with steady strokes of his cat-hair brush. Most Miyama households are still sleeping or lingering over breakfast; tourist buses won't start arriving until after nine. Miyama's tailless cats scratch through garbage heaps, compost piles, yards and kitchen doorways for scattered fish bones, their quick eyes bright, watchful. As I walk I scan the fern for broken teapots, chipped plates, old black vats – over three hundred years of pottery history flung into the forest. Pieces of twig and coin-sized potsherds crunch underfoot. My footsteps echo in the still green like the steady fall of hoofbeats on gravel.

Surrounded by a well-swept yard and a low hedge of tea, Nagata-san's house rises on the corner among thick poles of bamboo. Black vats, some of them chest-high, bulge with rainwater, wooden-handled plastic scoops, broken ends of tools, slim bamboo poles, a forgotten plastic sandal, extra gloves and lengths of rope. Others have become planters for stout miniature plum trees. One large kuromon vat leans against the house under a sheet of corrugated metal that covers a Toshiba air conditioner. Built five years ago, the modern stucco house stands on land once occupied by a small wood-firing kiln used by Nagata-san's husband, who died many years ago. In the back, the grey tile-roofed house connects with a low wooden shed that was once his workshop. Inside, waist-high black kame, crocks that once held glaze, still line the walls. But the potter's old kick wheel, split at the base and covered with mold, lies overturned in one corner.

When I arrive, Nagata-san is stepping down from the tiled entrance with a round bundle wrapped in a green-and-blue cloth, the size of a stuffed laundry bag. Concentrating on her load, she mumbles a rough complaining monologue – 'Bad weather!' – and shuffles over to a wooden wheelbarrow piled high with similar bundles wrapped in newspaper or faded pastel cloths of red, green and blue. Several pairs of brown chopsticks poke up amid coils of rope, and a clump of bright yellow bananas crowns the precarious load. Part of the payment for labouring in the fields is food; I wonder how many obāsan will help in Nagata-san's field today.

'Good morning, it's Leila,' I call across the hedge as loudly as I can without rousing Nagata-san's irritable neighbour, the obāsan with bulging black marble eyes. Nagata-san places the last bag on top with a thump and squints toward the lane. Her face relaxes, then opens into a thin smile.

'Good morning. Early, aren't you?'

'I've come to help with the rice harvest,' I say. 'Aren't you going to the fields today?'

'Oh yes, but it's hard work. You'd be of no use.'

'Look, I've borrowed boots for the rice paddy,' I answer quickly, holding up one leg to show off the blue rubber cloven-toe boots that fit tightly around the ankle and pull up over my lower calf, sealing in the bottoms of my baggy mompei. 'I have the day off.' At the sight of my crab-claw feet Nagata-san's narrow eyes become bright, the lines across her brow quiver, her head shakes. I realize she is laughing at my outfit. Above my mompei, the long sleeves of a black cotton shirt are tucked into white cotton gloves. Dressed for work in the rice fields, I've hidden my yellow hair under a maroon bandanna. Only a pale face and blue gaijin eyes show. I could almost pass for a younger Nagata-san. Her lopsided smile suddenly vanishes, the shaking stops, her whole face tarnishes like copper, twisting into a long frown.

'Come on, then, and be quick, we're already late. Here, carry these.' A long-sleeved shirt and a loose apron of sky-blue cover her front, while a white towel tied at the corners forms a loose tentlike sunshade for her head. Her mompei are the plaid design of small blue and white checks with flecks of yellow worn by older farming and pottery women. Like mine, her feet are bound in thin-soled tight-fitting boots that stay on even in the deep gluey mud of the rice fields.

'*Yōka!* Let's go,' she shouts, handing me a green thermos of hot water, a length of straw rope, extra pairs of white cotton gloves, and a short saw-edged sickle over the hedge. Grasping the handles of the wheelbarrow with both gloved hands, Nagata-san bends into the load, half shoving it out of the yard and down the lane. Up the path we stop at a laden persimmon tree to gather some of the soft orange fruit before heading on. Despite her crooked gait, her stride behind the heavy load is light and quick and I have to walk briskly to keep up.

By the moon-shaped mulberry fields at the corner we pass the low stone marker for Ta no kami, the guardian deity of the field, small blue-and-white cups of water or clear shōchū resting on its ledge. The front bears the grinning face of what looks like a hobo under a mushroom-shaped hood. From the back it is shaped to resemble a large phallus. Markers like these line the fields throughout Kagoshima, and in many places a stone or wood phallus is enshrined, adding to the region's reputation for feudal, patriarchal attitudes. While an urban women's movement slowly grows, Kagoshima staunchly preserves its conservative ways. In Miyama, although women work in the potteries, workshop owners are all men, and there are no recognized female 'master' craftsmen in the village. Reiko says that when she first moved to Miyama from Tokyo, older women scolded her for not hanging her husband's laundry on separate lines from her own 'impure' clothing.

We turn onto the main road to the coast. In the west slim rays of sun slice through the clouds, shining over the waves in streaks of shimmering gold. Across Miyama the sky is a sullen lead-gray.

'Bad weather,' grumbles Nagata-san in local slang. Though she can understand my standard Japanese, she speaks the rough, uneven Kagoshima ben. Young people don't learn the dialect, saying that they don't want to sound like hicks, but it is still the common speech of village elders. And although Kobe-born Reiko won't have it spoken in the house, in the workshop Nagayoshi-san talks on the phone to his mother and brother in nearby Sendai, to friends and even to me in the thick dialect. I speak it sometimes. I like the way the sounds roll off the tongue, rising and falling in lazy circles. '*Jiyashtonah*,' I answer, Kagoshima slang for 'I see,' and keep on walking. The rain is worrying. If the rice gets wet it may rot on the stalk. We must finish harvesting her three fields today.

Across from the Aiko food store, the small valley of terraced rice paddies spreads out in a mosaic of green and brown where harvested and unharvested fields meet. Nagata-san pushes the teetering wheelbarrow off the main road and down a narrow grass pathway twisting like a brown snake down the slope. Late-maturing fields still wave wet and green. But most paddies, drained of water and shaved of rice, extend in neat rows of brown stubble. Harvested rice, bound in broom-shaped bundles, hangs chest-high over long bamboo poles suspended by props at each end. Each harvested field is full of identical racks of drying rice, bridging the fields in straight lines.

Though most farmers in Miyama use machines to till, plant and thresh, Nagata-san avoids them. '*Kikai?* Machines? They're terrible,' she says. 'They tear up the mud, and lose the grain in harvest. No, by hand is much better!' One hundred

'...the small valley of terraced rice paddies spreads out in a mosaic of green and brown where harvested and unharvested fields meet.'

years ago swaybacked oxen lumbered through the thick mud during planting and harvest. But today the only bovines in Miyama are a herd of white-and-black Holsteins in the small dairy farm on the hill. Some Miyama farmers now use machinery to plant and thresh, but many small farmers like Nagata-san, who plants only three small fields, barter help with friends instead. During the summer she will work alone, weeding, managing the water, and spraying the fields for rice stalk borers, paddy-borers, plant hoppers and rice blight, which, if unattended, would smother the heads of grain in a deadly white film.

We head across the valley where two bent figures make steady progress across the field of waving yellow. Where they pass, the yellow-green rice falls. The rhythmic swishing of sickles cutting through straw grows louder as we approach. Even under the grey sky the arching blades glint silver. I recognize the pair as Takara-san and Nagai-san, the two old women who had helped in the June rice planting.

Ohayō. Ohayō. Ohayō.

We exchange morning greetings. Nagata-san motions for me to join the other women. Sickle in hand, I step down onto the firm mud of the drained paddy. The soil smells rank and sour, a combination of musty old hay and ripe sulfur – Nagata-san's source of fertilizer is her outhouse. I stand still for a minute, pretending to adjust my gloves while my stomach turns. Dark-eyed Takara-san, the youngest of the three and the most talkative, works toward where I stand. Her upturned face catches my gaze and she flashes a set of gold-filled teeth.

'Well, you're back. Didn't you go back to America to see your parents?' she says quickly. 'Did you see Brooke Shields? Did you bring me some Sunkist oranges?'

'Oh, I've been back two weeks now, but my family grows apples, not oranges. Where they live is about as cold as Sapporo.'

'I see,' answers Takara-san, still smiling. 'Well, I've never had an American apple.'

I quickly change the subject. I had been in the States for two weeks. Returning with *omiyage*, travel souvenirs, was a mandatory gesture. For Eri, who was interested in fashion and design, I had brought copies of *Vogue*. For Keisuke, studying photography in Tokyo, I had found a book on Ansel Adams. To my teacher I gave a thick art book about the Mimbres Indian pottery of the Southwest, and for Reiko I had purchased an entire deerhide. Half of my luggage had consisted of boxes of maple sugar candy, soaps, university pins, decals, T-shirts and stationery, New York City mementos, postcards of Niagara Falls and assorted towels and key rings. Even so, the presents ran out. 'Just don't tell anyone you ever left,' Reiko said firmly. But within days everyone in the village knew that the yellow-haired apprentice had gone on a trip.

I step out onto the rice paddy, following Takara-san and doing my best to imitate her swinging movements.

'That's not too bad. Not even young Japanese girls these days know how to harvest rice,' shouts Takara-san. 'Why don't you find a nice Japanese man and settle down here!' She laughs, glancing at me from the corner of her eye as she works. I grunt a noncommittal reply, too busy trying to manage the swinging sickle to converse.

'Yes, what about *omiai*?' a quiet voice pipes up on my right. 'It's about time for you to get married, anyway.' Working her way up next to me, Nagai-san is not going to miss out on the fun.

'Me, an okusan? *Muri gowandonah* – impossible,' I banter back. 'I can't make miso soup, and I'm hopeless at tea ceremony. And anyhow, I'm not looking for a husband – I'm too busy.'

Nagai-san giggles softly, her long face hidden by her wide sunbonnet. But Takara-san laughs so hard she misses a swing and her sickle gets stuck in the mud. Across the field Nagata-san, busy setting up props and cross poles to hang the rice, hears the laughter and turns with a dark face. 'Hurry up, and stop joking around,' she scolds. 'It's going to rain.'

The cutters progress in an even horizontal line across the field, felling several clumps of rice with each sweep of their curved blades. I fall into line with Takara-san, working toward her so that when we meet we finish a row and then move on. Underfoot, the rice paddy feels as slippery as a fresh cow pie. Beneath the dark mud lie streaks of clay and russet iron-rich sand dug for centuries by Miyama potters as the crucial ingredient in the deep black glaze for kuromon. Cutting the straw off evenly to leave a clean two-inch stub is a craft requiring skill, not power. I hack at a clump of rice in frustration. The straw bends like flax, scattering rice grains in the mud. I stoop to pick them up and Takara-san catches sight of me. She comes over and demonstrates how to hook a straw clump with the blade's sharp side and pull upward with a quick tug. A hearty ripping sound, and fallen straw lies flat and even behind her. I try again, and this time, my blade hooks neatly over the base, then cuts through the straw with a loud rip.

Soon three or four rows of straw lie behind us. Takara-san motions me to follow her to the head of the field.

'Well, that's not bad. But two people cutting are enough. Follow behind us now and tie the bundles,' she says.

I nod and follow. Already my arms ache from the constant swinging. Taking up a thick armful of scratchy straw, she binds it with three or four strands from the sides. She works quickly, placing a bundle between her knees and twisting the straw deftly despite her thick cotton work gloves.

As a child I loved to braid onion tops, bending and plaiting the rough stems until the whole pile of freshly pulled bulbs hung like a clump of ghostly grapes. This should be easy. I hold up my first effort to have a look: strands of straw stick out from the sides, the whole bundle threatens to collapse. Hung on a pole to dry, this clump would soon be blown across the village. I untie the loose ends, now limp and tangled as wet hair, and start again.

'Pretty bad, huh.'

'Watch again,' she says, and shows me how to tie the bundle tight, without knocking off grain or breaking the straw.

Imitating her quick movements, I hold the rough rice straw tightly between my own knees and reach around the outside for the straw binders. Tied together, they form a compact sheaf.

'I guess that will do. You're not bad – better than my daughter,' jokes Takara-san, pushing back her bonnet. 'She's hopeless – won't even come out here!'

'Why not?'

'Her job is studying!' answers Takara-san proudly. Like most children and young people in Miyama, Takara-san's teenage daughter doesn't help in the rice fields or even much at home. Overweight and suffering from acne, she looks as if a day in the sun would do her good. Like Western teenagers, she has a penchant for junk food, especially Coca-Cola and chocolate. The only time I have seen her outside is when she heads off in her blue knee-length uniform to the local high school in Ijuin. For the past month Takara-san has been working an extra night job in order to buy her a red motor scooter so that she won't have to ride the bus to school.

Around where we work many of the tambo lie fallow; the owners are too busy at jobs in Kagoshima City or nearby towns, or like American wheat farmers, they receive government subsidies not to plant. After one or two weeks of good weather, when the husks and straw are thoroughly dried, Nagata-san will send the rice to a thresher in the next town. Last week I'd seen Suzuki-san sit down in his formal garden before a manual wooden thresher. All morning clouds of dust and a loud clatter came over the hedge. By noon, when Nagayoshi-san and I went to have a look, straw was piled up in the yard next to a heap of ivory rice. Suzuki-san's khaki clothes were white with rice chaff and dust.

Rice straw has been used in Miyama for generations to thatch roofs, insulate walls, fill futons, make tatami and rope, and provide ash for pottery glaze. Inside the roaring kiln the ash melts, fusing with the clay and leaving a shiny silicate surface on the pottery. The first Korean potters in Miyama in the early seventeenth century knew to mix small amounts of wood ash with water and crushed iron-rich rock containing traces of feldspar to make the black glaze for kuromon. Later, potters began mixing wood ash, water and finely ground white clay from Kaseda to make a clear glaze for shiromon. Still later, the potters began to use rice straw ash, which opacifies the glaze and creates a distinct bluish-white finish.

Every fall Nagayoshi-san waits like a farmer for the rice to mature. When the rice is shorn, he returns to his mother's fields and burns great bonfires of straw. The fire rises up orange against the sky, reaching for oxygen to consume the piles of dry stalks. When all that is left is a cool black mound, he gathers it up in bags for the year's supply of glaze.

Isabella Bird

(1831–1904)

For a travel writer the road forever beckons. But journeys end. We break chronology here in order to close with a departure. When Isabella Bird said goodbye to the Rockies in *A Lady's Life in the Rocky Mountains*, she did so on such a bitterly cold day that moisture in the air turned into 'feathers and fern-leaves, the loveliest of creations'. As Bird takes one last look at her guide, Mountain Jim, and the peaks beyond, we feel her profound sense of loss. Yet it's the pull of the road ahead, and the promise of other endings like this, that feels stronger still.

from A Lady's Life in the Rocky Mountains

Cheyenne, Wyoming, December 12

The last evening came. I did not wish to realise it, as I looked at the snow-peaks glistening in the moonlight. No woman will be seen in the Park till next May. Young Lyman talked in a 'hifalutin' style, but with some truth in it, of the influence of a woman's presence, how 'low, mean, vulgar talk' had died out on my return, how they had 'all pulled themselves up', and how Mr. Kavan and Mr. Buchan had said they would like always to be as quiet and gentlemanly as when a lady was with them. 'By May,' he said, 'we shall be little better than brutes, in our manners at least.' I have seen a great deal of the roughest class of men both on sea and land during the last two years, and the more important I think the 'mission' of every quiet, refined, self-respecting woman – the more mistaken I think those who would forfeit it by noisy self-assertion, masculinity, or fastness. In all this wild West the influence of woman is second only in its benefits to the influence of religion, and where the last unhappily does not exist the first continually exerts its restraining power. The last morning came. I cleaned up my room and sat at the window watching the red and gold of one of the most glorious of winter sunrises, and the slow lighting-up of one peak after another. I have written that this scenery is not lovable, but I love it.

I left on Birdie at 11 o'clock, Evans riding with me as far as Mr. Nugent's. He was telling me so many things, that at the top of the hill I forgot to turn round and take a last look at my colossal, resplendent, lonely, sunlit den, but it was needless, for I carry it away with me. I should not have been able to leave if Mr. Nugent had not offered his services. His chivalry to women is so well known, that Evans said I could be safer and better cared for with no one. He added, 'His heart is good and kind, as kind a heart as ever beat. He's a great enemy of his own, but he's been living pretty quietly for the last four years.' At the door of his den I took leave of Birdie, who had been my faithful companion for more than 700 miles of travelling, and of Evans, who had been uniformly kind to me and just in all his dealings, even to paying to me at that moment the very last dollar he owes me. May God bless him and his! He was obliged to return before I could get off, and as he commended me to Mr. Nugent's care, the two men shook hands kindly.*

Rich spoils of beavers' skins were lying on the cabin floor, and the trapper took the finest, a mouse-coloured kitten beaver's skin, and presented it to me. I hired his beautiful Arab mare, whose springy step and long easy stride was a relief after Birdie's short sturdy gait. We had a very pleasant ride, and I seldom had to walk. We took neither of the trails, but cut right through the forest to a place where, through an opening in the foothills, the plains stretched to the horizon covered with snow, the surface of which, having melted and frozen,

* Some months later 'Mountain Jim' [Nugent] fell by Evans's hand, shot from Evans's doorstep while riding past his cabin. The story of the previous weeks is dark, sad, and evil. Of the five differing versions which have been written to me of the act itself and its immediate causes, it is best to give none. The tragedy is too painful to dwell upon. 'Jim' lived long enough to give his own statement, and to appeal to the judgment of God, but died in low delirium before the case reached a human tribunal.

'I never saw the mountain range look so beautiful – uplifted in every shade of transparent blue, till the sublimity of Long's Peak, and the lofty crest of Storm Peak, bore only unsullied snow against the sky.'

reflected as water would the pure blue of the sky, presenting a complete optical illusion. It required my knowledge of fact to assure me that I was not looking at the ocean. 'Jim' shortened the way by repeating a great deal of poetry, and by earnest, reasonable conversation, so that I was quite surprised when it grew dark. He told me that he never lay down to sleep without prayer – prayer chiefly that God would give him a happy death. He had previously promised that he would not hurry or scold, but 'fyking' had not been included in the arrangement, and when in the early darkness we reached the steep hill, at whose foot the rapid deep St. Vrain flows, he 'fyked' unreasonably about me, the mare, and the crossing generally, and seemed to think I could not get through, for the ice had been cut with an axe, and we could not see whether 'glaze' had formed since or no. I was to have slept at the house of a woman farther down the canyon, who never ceases talking, but Miller, the young man whose attractive house and admirable habits I have mentioned before, came out and said his house was 'now fixed for ladies', so we stayed there, and I was 'made as comfortable' as could be. His house is a model. He cleans everything as soon as it is used, so nothing is ever dirty, and his stove and cooking gear in their bright parts look like polished silver. It was amusing to hear the two men talk like two women about various ways of making bread and biscuits, one even writing out a recipe for the other. It was almost grievous that a solitary man should have the power of making a house so comfortable! They heated a stone for my feet, warmed a blanket for me to sleep in, and put logs enough on the fire to burn all night, for the mercury was eleven below zero. The stars were intensely bright, and a well-defined auroral arch, throwing off fantastic coruscations, lighted the whole northern sky. Yet I was only in the foothills, and Long's glorious Peak was not to be seen. Miller had all his things 'washed up' and his 'pots and pans' cleaned in ten minutes after supper, and then had the whole evening in which to smoke and enjoy himself – a poor woman would probably have been 'fussing round' till 10 o'clock about the same work. Besides Ring there was another gigantic dog craving for notice, and two large cats, which, the whole evening, were on their master's knee. Cold as the night was, the house was chinked, and the rooms felt quite warm. I even missed the free currents of air which I had been used to! This was my last evening in what may be called a mountainous region.

The next morning, as soon as the sun was well risen, we left for our journey of 30 miles, which had to be done nearly at a foot's pace, owing to one horse being encumbered with my luggage. I did not wish to realise that it was my last ride, and my last association with any of the men of the mountains whom I had learned to trust, and in some respects to admire. No more hunters' tales told while the pine knots crack and blaze; no more thrilling narratives of adventures with Indians and bears; and never again shall I hear that strange talk of Nature and her doings which is the speech of those who live with her and her alone. Already the dismalness of a level land comes over me. The canyon of the St. Vrain was in all its glory of colour, but we had a remarkably ugly crossing of that brilliant river, which was frozen all over, except an unpleasant gap of about two feet in the middle. Mr. Nugent had to drive the frightened horses through, while I, having crossed on some logs lower down, had to catch them on the other side as they plunged to shore trembling with fear. Then we emerged on the vast expanse of the glittering plains, and a sudden sweep of wind made the cold so intolerable that I had to go into a house to get warm. This was the last house we saw till we reached our destination that night. I never saw the mountain range look so beautiful – uplifted in every shade of transparent blue, till the sublimity of Long's Peak, and the lofty crest of Storm Peak, bore only unsullied snow against the sky. Peaks gleamed in living light; canyons lay in depths of purple shade; 100 miles away Pike's Peak rose a lump of blue, and over all, through that glorious afternoon, a veil of blue spiritualised without dimming the outlines of that most glorious range, making it look like the dreamed-of mountains of 'the land which is very far off', till at sunset it stood out sharp in glories of violet and opal, and the whole horizon up to a great height was suffused with the deep rose and pure orange of the afterglow. It seemed all dream-like as we passed through the sunlit solitude, on the right and the prairie waves lessening towards the far horizon, while on the left they broke in great snowy surges against the Rocky Mountains. All that day we neither saw man, beast, nor bird. 'Jim' was silent mostly. Like all true children of the mountains, he pined even when temporarily absent from them.

At sunset we reached a cluster of houses called Namaqua, where, to my dismay, I heard that there was to be a dance at the one little inn to which we were going at St. Louis. I pictured to myself no privacy, no peace, no sleep, drinking, low sounds, and worse than all, 'Jim' getting into a quarrel and using his pistols. He was uncomfortable about it for another reason. He said he had dreamt the night before that there was to be a dance, and that he had to shoot a man for making 'an unpleasant remark!' For the last three miles which we accomplished after sunset the cold was most severe, but nothing could exceed the beauty of the afterglow, and the strange look of the rolling plains of snow beneath it. When we got to the queer little place where they 'keep strangers' at St. Louis, they were very civil, and said that after supper we could have the kitchen to ourselves. I found a large, *prononcée*, competent, bustling widow, hugely stout, able to manage all men and everything else, and a very florid sister like herself, top-heavy with hair. There were besides two naughty children in the kitchen, who cried incessantly, and kept opening and shutting the door. There was no place to sit down but a wooden chair by the side of the kitchen stove, at which supper was being cooked for ten men. The bustle and clatter were indescribable, and the landlady asked innumerable questions, and seemed to fill the whole room. The only expedient for me for the night was to sleep on a shakedown in a very small room occupied by the two women and the children, and even this was not available till midnight, when the dance terminated; and there was no place in which to wash except a bowl in the kitchen. I sat by the stove till supper, wearying of the noise and bustle after the quiet of Estes Park. The landlady asked, with great eagerness, who the gentleman was who was with me, and said that the men outside were saying that they were sure that it was 'Rocky Mountain Jim', but she was sure it was not. When I told her that the men were right, she exclaimed, 'Do tell! I want to know! that quiet, kind gentleman!' and she said she used to frighten her children when they were naughty by telling them that 'he would get them, for he came down from the mountains every week, and took back a child with him to eat!' She was as proud of having him in her house as if he had been the President, and I gained a reflected importance! All the men in the settlement assembled in the front room, hoping he would go and smoke there, and when he remained in the kitchen they came round the window and into the doorway to look at him. The children got on his knee, and, to my great relief, he kept them good and quiet, and let them play with his curls, to the great delight of the two women, who never took their eyes off him. At last the bad-smelling supper was served, and ten silent men came in and gobbled it up, staring steadily at 'Jim' as they gobbled. Afterwards, there seemed no hope of quiet, so we went to the post-office, and while waiting for stamps were shown into the prettiest and most ladylike-looking room I have seen in the West, created by a pretty and refined-looking woman. She made an opportunity for asking me if it were true that the gentleman with me was 'Mountain Jim', and added that so very gentlemanly a person could not be guilty of the misdeeds attributed to him. When we returned, the kitchen was much quieter. It was cleared by eight, as the landlady promised; we had it to ourselves till twelve, and could scarcely hear the music. It was a most respectable dance, a fortnightly gathering got up by the neighbouring settlers, most of them young married people, and there was no drinking at all. I wrote to you for some time, while Mr. Nugent copied for himself the poems 'In the Glen' and the latter half of 'The River without a Bridge', which he recited with deep feeling. It was altogether very quiet and peaceful. He repeated to me several poems of great merit which he had composed, and told me much more about his life. I knew that no one else could or would speak to him as I could, and for the last time I urged upon him the necessity of a reformation in his life, beginning with the giving up of whisky, going so far as to tell him that I despised a man of his intellect for being a slave to such a vice. 'Too late! too late!' he always answered, 'for such a change.' Ay, *too late*. He shed tears quietly. 'It might have been once,' he said. Ay, *might* have been. He has excellent sense for every one but himself, and, as I have seen him with a single exception, a gentleness, propriety, and considerateness of manner surprising in any

'"Jim" was silent mostly. Like all true children of the mountains, he pined even when temporarily absent from them.'

man, but especially so in a man associating only with the rough men of the West. As I looked at him, I felt a pity such as I never before felt for a human being. My thought at the moment was, Will not our Father in heaven, 'who spared not His own Son, but delivered Him up for us all,' be far more pitiful? For the time a desire for self-respect, better aspirations, and even hope itself, entered his dark life; and he said, suddenly, that he had made up his mind to give up whisky and his reputation as a desperado. But it is 'too late'. A little before twelve the dance was over, and I got to the crowded little bedroom, which only allowed of one person standing in it at a time, to sleep soundly and dream of 'ninety-and-nine just persons who need no repentance'. The landlady was quite taken up with her 'distinguished guest'. 'That kind, quiet gentleman, Mountain Jim! Well, I never! he must be a very good man!'

Yesterday morning the mercury was 20° below zero. I think I never saw such a brilliant atmosphere. That curious phenomena called frost-fall was occurring, in which, whatever moisture may exist in the air, somehow aggregates into feathers and fern-leaves, the loveliest of creations, only seen in rarefied air and intense cold. One breath and they vanish. The air was filled with diamond sparks quite intangible. They seemed just glitter and no more. It was still and cloudless, and the shapes of violet mountains were softened by a veil of the tenderest blue. When the Greeley stage-waggon came up, Mr. Fodder, whom I met at Lower Canyon, was on it. He had expressed a great wish to go to Estes Park, and to hunt with 'Mountain Jim', if it would be safe to do the latter. He was now dressed in the extreme of English dandyism, and when I introduced them,* he put out a small hand cased in a perfectly-fitting lemon-coloured kid glove. As the trapper stood there in his grotesque rags and odds and ends of apparel, his gentlemanliness of deportment brought into relief the innate vulgarity of a rich *parvenu*. Mr. Fodder rattled so amusingly as we drove away that I never realised that my Rocky Mountain life was at an end, not even when I saw 'Mountain Jim', with his golden hair yellow in the sunshine, slowly leading the beautiful mare over the snowy plains back to Estes Park, equipped with the saddle on which I had ridden 800 miles!

A drive of several hours over the plains brought us to Greeley, and a few hours later, in the far blue distance, the Rocky Mountains, and all that they enclose, went down below the prairie sea.

* This was a truly unfortunate introduction. It was the first link in the chain of circumstances which brought about Mr. Nugent's untimely end, and it was at this person's instigation (when overcome by fear) that Evans fired the shot which proved fatal.

Acknowledgments

The editors are grateful to Katherine Wittemore, Glen Hartley, Joan Goodman, Michael Kowaleski, Justin Kaplan, Ihab Hassan, and John Theakstone for their contributions to the bibliography. Many other people helped expand the bibliography by providing us with names of women travellers. Others sent us their bibliographies outright. In some cases, rare old and fragile books were loaned; and photocopies of out-of-print books and manuscripts, as in the case of Willa Cather, were graciously sent.

We are grateful to each and every one who shared with us his or her lists, unknown or 'lost' favourite writer, or out-of-print book. We are especially grateful to Jenna Laslocky at Vintage, who responded so positively to our initial concept and whose knowledge and love of travel literature did so much to help shape this book.

The editors and publishers wish to thank the following for permission to use copyright material:

Mildred Cable and Francesca French, for an extract from *The Gobi Desert,* by permission of Hodder and Stoughton Ltd.

Emily Carr, for an extract from *Klee Wyck.* Copyright © 1941 by Emily Carr, by permission of Stoddart Publishing Co. Ltd.

Isak Dinesen (Karen Blixen), for an extract from *Out of Africa* (1937), by permission of the Rungstedlund Foundation.

Christina Dodwell, for an extract from *Travels with Fortune: An African Adventure,* W H Allen/Virgin Publishing (1979), by permission of the author.

Andrea Lee, for an extract from *Russian Journal.* Copyright © 1979, 1980, 1981 by Andrea Lee, by permission of Random House, Inc.

Robert Lowell, for an extract from his poem, 'Caracas' (included in an extract by Joan Didion, *The White Album*) from *Notebook* by Robert Lowell, by permission of Faber & Faber Ltd.

Dervla Murphy, for an extract from *Muddling Through in Madagascar* (1985), by permission of John Murray (Publishers) Ltd.

Mary Morris, for an extract from *Wall-to-Wall: From Beijing to Berlin by Rail.* Copyright © 1991 by Mary Morris, by permission of Doubleday, a division of Random House, Inc.

Edna O'Brien, for an extract from *Farewell Spain,* Virago (1987), by permission of David Higham Associates on behalf of the author.

Leila Philip, for an extract from *The Road Through Miyama.* Copyright © 1988 by Leila Philip, by permission of Random House, Inc.

Vita Sackville-West, for an extract from *Passenger to Teheran.* Copyright © 1926 Vita Sackville-West, by permission of Curtis Brown, Ltd, London, on behalf of the Estate of the author.

Mary Lee Settle, for an extract from *Turkish Reflections.* Copyright © 1991 by Mary Lee Settle, by permission of Simon & Schuster.

Freya Stark, for an extract from *A Winter in Arabia,* by permission of John Murray (Publishers) Ltd.

Every effort has been made to trace the copyright holders, but where this has not been possible or where any error has been made the publishers will be pleased to make the necessary arrangement at the first opportunity.

Picture credits

Pages 11, 85, 99 AKG London; page 169 Jan Baldwin; pages 40, 155, 213, 222 Barnaby's Picture Library; page 13 Lincolnshire County Council, Usher Gallery, Lincoln/The Bridgeman Art Library; page 17 The Bridgeman Art Library; pages 51, 240 Private Collection/The Bridgeman Art Library; page 89 Library of Congress, Washington/The Bridgeman Art Library; page 223 Jonathan Cape; page 15 Christies Images Ltd; pages 10t, 25, 45, 81, 120 Mary Evans Picture Library; pages 1, 18, 24, 44, 94, 193, 194, 228 Robert Harding; pages 9, 35, 92, 117, 151 Hulton Getty; pages 28, 56, 83, 84, 180, 183 Image Bank; pages 6b, 37, 90, 106, 109, 115, 130, 150, 172, 205, 209, 216, 238 Images Colour Library; page 7 Katz; page 203 Susan Jahoda; pages 2, 127 Photonica; pages 147, 157 Popperfoto; page 231 Powerstock; page 173 Gypsy P. Ray; pages 6t, 12, 16, 20, 33, 34, 38, 53, 62, 74, 76, 88, 105, 112, 123, 124, 140, 156, 162, 166, 186, 188, 202, 227, 233, 243 Tony Stone Images; pages 5, 66, 71 Superstock; pages 8, 10b, 141, 163, 195 Topham; pages 113, 131, 167 UPI/Corbis

Every effort has been made to trace the copyright holders but if any have been inadvertently overlooked the publishers will be pleased to make the necessary arrangements at the first opportunity.

'If we grow weary of waiting, we can go on a journey. We can be the stranger who comes to town.'

Mary Morris